MICROSOFT
SECRETS

MICROSOFT SECRETS

*How the World's Most Powerful
Software Company Creates Technology,
Shapes Markets, and Manages People*

Michael A. Cusumano
Richard W. Selby

HarperCollins*Publishers*

HarperCollins*Publishers*
77–85 Fulham Palace Road,
Hammersmith, London W6 8JB

Published by HarperCollins*Publishers* 1996
1 3 5 7 9 8 6 4 2

First published in the USA by
The Free Press 1995
A Division of Simon & Schuster Inc.

A catalogue record for this book is
available from the British Library

ISBN 0 00 255692 8

Set in Aster

Printed and bound in Great Britain by
Caledonian International
Book Manufacturing Ltd, Glasgow G64

Michael Cusumano would like to dedicate this book to the people of Microsoft. Their remarkable careers, openness, and cooperation made this study possible and fun.

Richard Selby would like to dedicate this book to his loving wife, Kimberly Ann Ofria Selby, whose support and spirit inspired him to make the book much more understandable, and to software entrepreneurs everywhere who are trying to bring their ideas to life and become billionaires in doing so.

CONTENTS

PREFACE

This study started in March 1993 as part of a project at MIT to compare the management of product development at PC software firms with that of older companies making software products for mainframes and minicomputers.[1] During this initial research, it became clear why Microsoft was able to remain on top in its industry while most contemporaries from its founding years in the 1970s disappeared: Microsoft has had remarkably effective ideas on how to compete and market products in a rapidly expanding and evolving industry. Microsoft people have also created an approach for product development and team management—we call it the *synch-and-stabilize* process—that superbly supports its culture and business strategy. This process has enabled the company to build an increasing variety of complex software products and features for the mass market and corporate customers.

In writing this book, we cannot overemphasize the unique opportunity we have had to probe broadly and freely inside Microsoft. We reviewed published articles and books to analyze the public record on the company's history, strategy, and range of activities and products. But most of the book is based on unusually candid interviews (all tape-recorded and transcribed into several thousand pages) as well as our analysis of several thousand pages of confidential internal documents and project data. We interviewed thirty-eight Microsoft employees in depth; typical sessions lasted two hours, and we interviewed many people twice. These formal interviews took place at Microsoft (either its headquarters

in Redmond, Washington, or its offices in nearby Bellevue) between March 1993 and September 1994. Telephone and e-mail
correspondence as well as additional meetings with Microsoft people to receive their feedback on the manuscript continued through
July 1995.

We spread our interviews across different categories of people
(Bill Gates and other top executives, middle managers, senior and
junior software developers, program managers, testers, product
managers, recruiters, and product support staff) and across different product areas (Word, Excel, Office, Mail, Windows NT, MS-
DOS, Windows 95, advanced consumer products, and research).
Among the highly sensitive documents we asked for and received
were key memos on the development process and written "postmortems" on major projects between 1987 and 1994. The postmortems were particularly valuable sources of quantitative data
on quality, scheduling, and project management as well as the evolution of Microsoft's practices for product specification, software
development, testing, and user education (documentation for
users). We also received samples of product specifications at different stages, as well as training materials for product design and
implementation, documentation on tools (special software programs used to write other software), test plans, customer problem
reports, and an internal employee survey.

We agreed with Microsoft to avoid specific discussions on features or schedules for unannounced products, and to let Microsoft
people review the manuscript before publication and suggest
changes. But we retained the right to publish whatever we felt was
appropriate about the strategies, processes, methodologies, or organizational structures used at Microsoft. For this reason, Microsoft exerted no editorial control over the content of this book
(except for suggestions on how we treated some sensitive issues
and confidential data), nor did we receive any financial support
from Microsoft (although we did use an office during our visits).
The result is a study about the company written by two outsiders
but told primarily through its own people and documents. We recognize that competitors or people openly critical of Microsoft
might want to put a somewhat different slant on the material that

we have analyzed. Nonetheless, we have tried our best to present an accurate picture of how this firm operates.

We have tried to summarize the "best practices" used in Microsoft. We acknowledge that there are variations across groups. Microsoft does not always manage small projects (like Macintosh versions of its products) or operating systems upgrades (like Windows 95) as well as it manages highly strategic applications that are major revenue generators (like the Windows versions of Excel, Word, and Office) or new technology platforms (like Windows NT). Nor do managers try to control projects engaged in first-time invention as closely as they do more mature products or products targeted for the mass market. We discuss why operating systems such as Windows NT and Windows 95 are particularly difficult to build, test, and deliver on a predictable schedule.

Why did Microsoft agree to reveal many of its innermost secrets? One reason is that Microsoft managers seem driven to critique themselves. They want to identify and spread knowledge about "best practices" in product development as well as in organization and management more generally. They were not afraid of being analyzed. To the contrary, this book seemed to them like another postmortem report, but with an added twist: We were an outside party attempting to be objective, and we reviewed key projects and the entire company over numerous years, not just one project.

The second reason why we think we received cooperation is that Microsoft has had a lot of pressure from customers to improve its ability to deliver reliable products in a predictable time frame. Though still far from perfect, company people are proud of the improvements they have made—especially in quality control—and want to communicate them to customers. They also felt confident that talking publicly was less a risk for them than a competitive advantage, even if Microsoft had to divulge some proprietary information.

Microsoft people have been deeply affected by increasing demands for higher reliability in their products, and they have realized that satisfying customer concerns now requires not only a better public image but also a better development process. As part of their shift to using PCs and workstations, many large firms build or buy "mission critical" software systems that today depend heavily on such Microsoft products as Windows, Office (including Word and Excel), and Windows NT. A famous internal memo from 1989 on "zero-defect code" pointed out that a defect or "bug" in a spreadsheet or word-processing program could cost a customer enormous sums of money. (This is a lesson that the Intel Corporation, with a calculation error in its Pentium microprocessor, now understands.) Indeed, PC hardware producers such as IBM, Compaq, and Dell, which bundle Microsoft software with their products, have been particularly critical of Microsoft on some occasions. These hardware producers, as well as applications developers and retail software stores, all gear up in the expectation of new products, especially operating systems. When Microsoft ships a product late or, worse, ships a "buggy" product that it has to recall, the result can be a technical, public relations, and financial disaster for an entire industry and user community.

Neither we nor Microsoft people claim that its problems are over and that no more Microsoft products will ever be late or have defects. No software producer can make these claims. PC software products are extraordinarily complex to build. They are also getting larger and more intricate every year, while PC software companies often put unrealistic pressure on themselves to deliver new products and replace existing products in short periods of time. Microsoft has made, and continues to make, laudable improvements in its process for product development and in its ability to organize and share what its people know as a company. Microsoft managers have also rethought conventional practices in software development and made critical departures that go beyond existing good practices in many other firms. Microsoft people often cited the desire to let people know about these advances in their responses to the question "Why let us write this book?"

> It's good for our corporate customers to know more about development because they do a lot of development. In aggregate, they have a lot more developers than the commercial software industry does. And so we want to remind them that we have some good ideas, and share those ideas with them. Maybe they'll buy more PCs. (Bill Gates, chairman and CEO)
>
> We have a philosophy that ideas and vision are important, but execu-

tion is the thing that distinguishes companies. By and large, we're [a] pretty open book. We tell a lot of people a lot of the things that we do. . . . In the ability to emulate and execute on our ideas, we think we've got an advantage in terms of the people and in terms of what we're doing. So there's not a proprietariness issue. And to some extent, it's probably ego driven. It's nice to have you guys write a book and tell us how good we are, or tell us where we're screwed up, and we can at least go work on that. . . . To some extent, you guys help us with spreading the word on our best practices. (Mike Maples, former senior executive vice president)

My philosophy is that I've seen groups here have to go through a transformation. They have to go through phases and those phases take time. . . . [Competitors] have to go through the same transformations and phases, and it will take them years in some cases. In that time, we've also gone through years, and we're advancing and improving at a quicker rate than they have been. So we're not worried about exposing things that compromise our competitiveness. . . . And if they try to duplicate us, we'll know the failings of that system we have in place today by the time they reach this point. (Dave Moore, director of development)

This is the first book that Bill's talked to anybody for, ever, that I know of. . . . My opinion is that no book in the world is going to be able to capture how we actually do it. . . . It's not going to be a manual. You're not going to be able to go out and hire all the same people. That's the whole craft-versus-engineering thing. Even in engineering, you can't build a bridge by reading a bunch of books, no matter how many books about building bridges you've read. (Steven Sinofsky, former technical assistant to Bill Gates and current group program manager, Office Product Unit)

We would like to make two additional comments to readers. First, we have targeted some of our discussions for people familiar with PC software products (Chapter 3) as well as software development (Chapters 4 and 5). Readers more interested in the overall picture of how Microsoft operates as a company might want to read these chapters selectively and focus on the broader themes behind Microsoft's approach to organizing, competing, and developing new products.

Second, on all the dimensions of division and group-level organization, people management, and software development management, there are differences among the various Microsoft product units. Statements that we make about the Excel group, for example, do not necessarily apply to the Windows 95 group. Differences are particularly large between the applications as opposed to the systems and languages divisions. Many differences reflect variations in the products these groups build or in the customers they serve; others stem from separate histories, preferences of managers, and additional factors that have little to do with technology and markets. We highlight key differences among the groups throughout this book. Nonetheless, compared to other companies, Microsoft groups are far more similar than they are dissimilar. What we try to describe, then, are strategies and "best practices" that most people within and outside the company would recognize.

INTRODUCTION

Practically every day, 140 million out of the 170 million people who use personal computers (PCs) turn on their machines and see the words "Starting MS-DOS" (or a similar message).[1] Seventy million people see another message—"Microsoft Windows"—as their computer screens fill up with graphical symbols called icons. About half of these 70 million people, as well as most of the 15 million users of Apple's Macintosh and PowerMac PCs, then start one of Microsoft's desktop applications by "clicking on" an icon. In the 1995 version of Windows, customers can click on another button and enter the information highway and the Microsoft Network. This is yet another new world where Microsoft competes with another portfolio of "on-line" products and services delivered over telephone and cable-TV wires.

This is *power*. Like other products of modern technology, such as the telephone, the automobile, and television, PCs are changing the way millions of people live, work, and think. They are useless, though, without software—the instructions that make computer hardware perform an almost infinite variety of tasks. Microsoft is by far the world's largest and richest company dedicated to PC software development, and thanks to an expanding stream of new products it continues to grow with astounding—many say alarming—speed.

This book provides a detailed portrait of how Microsoft organizes, competes, develops new products, and tries to learn and improve as an organization. We have focused on describing "best

1

practices" from the most successful groups within the company. Open access to Microsoft made it possible for us to write this story. Although we are not the first authors to study Bill Gates and Microsoft, which are in the news almost every day, most of the many articles, academic case studies, and popular books have focused on the history of the company and the personality of the founder.[2] What remains largely a mystery are Microsoft's crown jewels: the key concepts that it has used to create technology, shape the markets in which it competes, and manage the creative energies of thousands of highly skilled technical people.

MICROSOFT'S EVOLUTION

Current chairman and CEO Bill Gates (born in 1955), listed in 1995 as the richest person in the world with a net worth of about $13 billion, cofounded Microsoft in 1975 with Paul Allen (born in 1953), who retired from Microsoft in 1983, became another multi-billionaire, and is still a major shareholder and member of the board of directors. Microsoft's revenues surged from $16,000 in 1975, when the company consisted of one product and three people, to nearly $6 billion in 1995, when the company had some two hundred products and approximately 17,800 employees (Table 1). Microsoft controls between 80 and 85 percent of the most important market segment for PC software—operating systems, the programs that determine the basic functions of the computer. It produces 25 percent or more of all PC applications products (or "packaged software"), which run on top of the operating system. They enable users to perform specific tasks on a computer, such as writing a letter or calculating numbers on a spreadsheet grid.

MS-DOS (which stands for "Microsoft Disk Operating System") is probably Microsoft's best-known product. It has sold in the millions each year since 1981, when IBM—and then a host of other companies—adopted it as the operating system for their personal computers. Windows is probably Microsoft's second best-known product. This is a graphical or picture-based "user interface" and operating system that works with MS-DOS and makes the computer easier to use. Microsoft is also the largest independent software producer for Apple's Macintosh (and now PowerMac)

Table 1   *Microsoft Company Data, 1975–1995*

Year	Revenues ($1,000)	Growth Rate (%)	Employees (people)	Operating Profit (%)	R&D/ Revenues (%)
1975	16	—	3	na	na
1976	22	38	7	na	na
1977	382	636	9	na	na
1978	1,356	256	13	na	na
1979	2,390	663	28	na	na
1980	8,000	235	38	na	na
1981	16,000	100	130	na	na
1982	24,486	53	220	na	na
1983	50,065	104	476	na	na
1984	97,479	95	778	na	na
1985	140,417	44	1,001	na	na
1986	197,514	41	1,442	31	11
1987	345,890	75	2,258	37	11
1988	590,827	71	2,793	32	12
1989	803,530	36	4,037	30	14
1990	1,183,000	47	5,635	33	15
1991	1,843,000	56	8,226	35	13
1992	2,759,000	50	11,542	36	13
1993	3,753,000	36	14,430	35	13
1994	4,649,000	24	15,257	37	13
1995	5,937,000	28	17,800	36	14

Notes: "na" refers to "not available." Microsoft began publishing data on operating profits after going public in 1986. Years refer to July through June fiscal periods. The employee figure for 1995 is an estimate.

Source: Microsoft annual reports from 1986 to 1995; for prior years, Philip M. Rosenzweig, "Bill Gates and the Management of Microsoft" (Harvard Business School, Case #9-392-019, 10/9/92).

computers, and it makes the two top-selling Macintosh applications for the desktop: Word, a word-processing program, and Excel, a spreadsheet program. These products are the largest-selling Windows applications as well, with more than half of their sales coming through Microsoft's low-priced Office "suite" of applications. Microsoft has also entered or is planning to enter just about every market that relates to computers and information technology, from children's video games to corporate networking, interactive TV, and on-line network services. Due to its market share and broad product offerings, Microsoft probably has more influence than any other single firm over the evolution of technical standards for computer software and information-based industries in general. No manager in any industry related to computers or information technology, and no current or future user of a computer, can really avoid or afford to ignore what Microsoft does.

Microsoft has developed such power by moving from one software mass market and distribution channel to another. It started by selling programming languages and then operating systems primarily to computer equipment manufacturers, then moved to selling a variety of applications products directly to retail stores. Microsoft has done this first in the United States and then abroad (Table 2).

Many people, though, fear the power that Bill Gates and his company have accumulated. Microsoft has been so successful in its markets that the U.S. Federal Trade Commission, the U.S. Department of Justice, and the European Union all have launched probes of its pricing, marketing, and management practices. (The U.S. government also did this with IBM in the 1970s and AT&T in the 1950s.) Since signing an agreement in August 1994 with the U.S. Department of Justice, Microsoft has modified how it licenses and prices its operating systems. The agreement has slightly weakened Microsoft, but its basic practices and ability to influence markets and technology remain essentially intact.

According to Bill Gates, he realized when starting Microsoft—with remarkable insight for 1975—that the real money in the computer industry was in software. Gates's partner, Paul Allen, wanted to produce both hardware and software products; most companies in the computer industry, including IBM, DEC, and even such new entrants as Apple Computer (founded in 1976), also were focusing on hardware. Gates recalled his thinking in a recent interview: "I thought we should do only software. When you have the microprocessor doubling in power every two years, in a sense you can think of computer power as almost free. So you ask, why be in the business of making something that's almost free? What is the

Table 2   Microsoft Sales Breakdown, by Percentage of Dollar Sales, 1986–1995

Year	Product Type Breakdown			Geographic Breakdown		Channel Breakdown	
	Systems	Apps.	Other	U.S.	International	OEM	Retail
1986	53	37	10	32	68	46	54
1987	49	38	13	35	65	35	65
1988	47	40	13	32	68	31	69
1989	44	42	14	29	71	32	68
1990	39	48	13	30	70	26	74
1991	36	51	13	31	69	18	82
1992	40	49	11	34	66	17	83
1993	34	58	8	31	69	19	81
1994	33	63	4	34	66	25	75
1995	31	65	4	32	68	28	72

Notes: "Systems" includes language products. "Apps." refers to all types of applications. "Other" refers primarily to hardware (mainly Microsoft Mouse) and books by Microsoft Press. "Geographic Breakdown" refers only to retail sales. "U.S." includes Canada from 1994. "International" refers to retail sales outside the U.S. (and Canada). "OEM" refers to direct sales to all "original equipment manufacturers," which are computer hardware vendors. "Retail" refers to sales of separate software and other products through computer software stores and other retail outlets.

Source: Microsoft annual reports.

scarce resource? What is it that limits being able to get value out of that infinite computing power? Software."[3]

Other companies have since realized the value of software as well. As a result, Microsoft has had to be constantly concerned with competition as well as with introducing enough new features to get customers to buy updated versions of its products. It has also had to seek new markets and applications for its technologies and programming skills. Microsoft was late in recognizing the potential of some product concepts, such as corporate networking, home finance software, and "groupware" networking (pioneered by Novell, Intuit, and Lotus, respectively). It faces stiff competition as it enters such new arenas as information-highway products and services. Microsoft also has a long (and continuing) history of problems in quality control and on-time product delivery, although it has responded with many improvements in how teams develop and test products as well as analyze information from users.

As many as 90 percent of new firms fail within five years. Among those that survive, many do not adapt well to growth.[4] This is because new companies often cannot put into place the specialized skills and managerial systems needed to control a larger organization or compete successfully over long periods of time. Bill Gates and Microsoft have handled extremely rapid growth with great skill, and they are both worth careful scrutiny for this reason alone. At the same time, Microsoft retains much of the loosely structured, antibureaucratic, small-team culture that characterized the company in its early days. We believe that, unlike large older companies such as General Motors or IBM, Microsoft over time has actually been getting closer to—rather than farther away from—most of its customers. (Apple users of some Microsoft products might disagree strongly with this statement, since Microsoft tends to pay far more attention to the much larger Windows market.) One example of this is how Microsoft now incorporates customer feedback into product development throughout the development cycle, as we will explain later.

Many factors, though, affect the fate of a company. Although some very smart people at Microsoft have made some shrewd decisions over the past two decades, the company has also benefited from good fortune: It received the opportunity in 1981 to provide what quickly became the world's largest selling operating system (DOS) for the original IBM PC. And its competitors and partners have made large mistakes: For example, Apple might have become the dominant producer of operating systems had it licensed the Macintosh operating software to other computer hardware vendors in 1984 rather than 1994. And IBM, though it paid Microsoft to deliver DOS only for the IBM PC, failed to retain exclusive rights to this product. When firms such as Compaq learned (with Microsoft's help) how to make PC hardware compatible with IBM personal computers, Microsoft sold them millions of copies of DOS—renamed *MS*-DOS—at volume discounts. Personal computers quickly became a multibillion-dollar industry; Microsoft and Bill Gates, in turn, became the PC industry's first billionaires.

To our knowledge, no one foresaw exactly how fast and how big the PC market would grow. Bill Gates, however, clearly understood the enormous economic potential of PC software and the importance of IBM as the hardware vendor that would establish market standards. He saw the value of cultivating PC-compatible producers to extend the mass market well beyond IBM. He also realized the importance of replacing the original DOS technology with Windows and graphics-based computing, which Apple pioneered as a mass market product with the Macintosh. But this combination of an insightful CEO, a wonderful market opportunity, and the errors of Apple and IBM was no more than a fine recipe for a strong beginning: Microsoft has continued to grow in size and influence since the early 1980s because of how well it has built upon the MS-DOS foundation with Windows and a continuing stream of other new products.

WHAT THIS BOOK IS ABOUT

We do not claim that any one principle of competition, organization, management, or product development Microsoft has followed is the sole source of its success or unique among companies. Instead, there is a small set of complementary strategies—we discuss seven—that characterize how Microsoft competes and operates. Microsoft puts each of these basic strategies into practice through another small set of complementary principles; these define a style of leadership, organization, competition, and product development that is consistent with the company's PC-programmer culture and remarkably effective in producing software products for mass markets. Moreover, though, Microsoft is unique in the way it has brought together all the elements necessary to get to the top of an enormously important industry and then stay there. We think of Microsoft's "secrets" as these fundamental strategies and principles of implementation.

We must emphasize that the strategies and principles we identified represent our *interpretation* of how Microsoft works, based on a study of the company's history and current operations, extensive interviews with its personnel, and internal documents and project data going back to the mid-1980s. We did not go into this research with any particular strategies or principles in mind, nor did Microsoft people suggest any to us directly. In this book, we devote one full chapter to each strategy:

1. Organizing and managing the company: *Find smart people who know the technology and the business.*
2. Managing creative people and technical skills: *Organize small teams of overlapping functional specialists.*
3. Competing with products and standards: *Pioneer and orchestrate evolving mass markets.*
4. Defining products and development processes: *Focus creativity by evolving features and "fixing" resources.*
5. Developing and shipping products: *Do everything in parallel, with frequent synchronizations.*
6. Building a learning organization: *Improve through continuous self-critiquing, feedback, and sharing.*
7. *Attack the future!*

The first strategy—*find smart people who know the technology and the business*—deals with how to organize and manage the company. Microsoft's success story, beginning with the talents and insights of its founders, has continued at least in part because of the company's rigorous process for selecting and screening new managers and other employees. These people deeply understand software technology and how to translate this knowledge into a money-making business. If the CEO, senior management team, and key employees truly understand their technology and markets, seize opportunities as they arise, and make the future follow *their* vision, then they have a chance to dominate not one but many promising markets. They have a solid basis to create an organization centered around the right products and markets. They should be able to reorganize as needed, find more outstanding people to help run the company, and prepare for the future. We think this is an apt description of the role Bill Gates and other key people have played in the Microsoft organization.

The second strategy—*organize small teams of overlapping functional specialists*—deals with how to nurture creative people and technical skills. There is much talk in today's management literature about training people broadly and using them in "multifunctional" teams in order to promote both innovation and efficiency. For example, it is argued firms should make specialists in product design, manufacturing, marketing, and quality control work together in small groups, rather than in large bureaucratic departments that "hand off" work to each other in a sequential, compartmentalized way. But remember the airline called People Express? Pilots sometimes acted as stewards or carried baggage, accountants as reservations clerks, and vice versa. This low-cost but chaotic operation was fine in the beginning, but demand for services eventually got too large and complex to handle, and the airline folded after only a few years.[5]

Although Microsoft empowers people to learn and act broadly, managers realized in the 1980s that they need to cultivate basic functional skills to create the larger and more complex products demanded by more powerful computer hardware. As a result, they established distinct functional skills and responsibilities, but overlap them at the boundaries. This means that people work together in small multifunctional teams and formally share tasks. People in the specialties have enough independence from top management and from a centralized personnel department so that they can continually redefine the skill sets they need. They can also hire new people—and new skill sets—as they need them. They learn by doing and from more experienced people, without a lot of bureaucratic rules and regulations, or formal training programs, which can easily become outdated in a fast-moving industry. Like other companies who value their technical personnel as much as their managers, Microsoft has also created formal career paths and "ladder levels" to recognize and compensate people for achievements within their technical specialties.

The third strategy—*pioneer and orchestrate evolving mass markets*—deals with how to compete as a company by creating product portfolios and setting industry standards. Firms need not be inventors, but it is often useful to be first or early to market. Many managers also need to think about more than one set of customers because markets can easily become saturated, and then they will find their sales and growth rates collapsing. It is useful to target *mass* markets because these are where the money is; directing the evolution of such markets to your company's advantage is the best way to ensure that you end up with a good deal of the money!

Accordingly, Microsoft has either created or aggressively entered every major PC software mass market with products that are at least "good enough" initially to set de facto industry standards. To preempt the competition, Microsoft development teams then continuously improve products incrementally, replacing old products with more advanced versions. (It is much better to make your own products obsolete than allow a competitor to do it.) To support product development, another set of practices helps to maximize volume sales, which are necessary to establish and maintain products as industry standards. (This is also a good way to ensure long-term profits.) Microsoft uses other tactics to encourage sales of its new products as well as to influence the direction that markets and the industry overall take. More recently, it has been simplifying and packaging new products to expand their potential sales to hundreds of millions of novice home consumers.

The fourth strategy—*focus creativity by evolving features and "fixing" resources*—deals with defining the new products and development processes that facilitate the targeting of mass markets. While having creative people in a high-technology company is important, it is often more important to *direct* their creativity. Managers can do this by getting development personnel to think about features that large amounts of people will pay money for, and by putting pressure on projects by limiting their resources. Without such steps, software developers may never ship anything to market. This is a particular problem in fast-moving industries with short product life cycles, and when individuals or teams change interdependent components during a project or do not synchronize their work.

Microsoft gets around these difficulties by structuring projects in "milestones" or subprojects of prioritized features. It uses "vision statements" to guide teams but with no attempt to determine everything that they do in advance. This leaves people room to innovate or adapt to change or unforeseen competitive opportunities and threats. Particularly for applications products, development teams come up with features that map directly to activities that average customers perform, and then they design products and projects around these features. Managers also limit the number of people they allocate to any one project, and try to limit the time they spend (though this is not always possible).

The fifth strategy—*do everything in parallel, with frequent synchronizations*—adds some structure to the loosely organized Microsoft culture. Many managers talk about making their companies less bureaucratic, more innovative, and faster to react. But large-scale projects are simpler to schedule and manage if they proceed with clearly defined functional groups and sequential phases, and precise rules and controls. This approach, however, may excessively restrain innovation. Communication and coordination difficulties across the functions and phases may also result in the project taking more time and people to complete than projects that overlap tasks, make people share responsibilities, and delegate work to small, nimble teams. Microsoft's approach to product development allows many small teams considerable freedom to work in parallel yet still function as one large team in order to build large-scale products relatively quickly and cheaply. The teams also adhere to a few rigid rules that enforce a high degree of coordination and communication.

Microsoft developers are free to design the details of their features as they proceed. The development process, though, encourages them to synchronize their designs and resolve conflicts with other developers' components on a very frequent basis. For example, one of the few rules developers must follow is that, on whatever day they decide to check in their pieces of code, they must do so by a particular time, such as by 2:00 P.M. or 5:00 P.M. This allows the team to put available components together and create a new "build" of the evolving product by the end of the day or by the next morning, then start testing and debugging immediately. The term *build* refers to the act of putting together partially completed or finished pieces of a software product during the development process to see what functions work or what problems exist. (This rule is analogous to telling children that they can do whatever they want all day, but they must go to bed at nine o'clock.) Another rule is that, if a developer checks in code that "breaks" the build, he must fix the defect immediately. (This actually resembles Toyota's famous production system, where factory workers stop the manufacturing lines whenever they notice a defect in a car they are assembling.[6])

Product teams also test features as they build them from multiple perspectives, including bringing in customers from "off the street" to try prototypes. Nearly all Microsoft teams work at a single site, with common tools, so they can more easily debate design ideas and resolve problems face-to-face. Microsoft also uses a small set of quantitative measurements or metrics to guide decisions such as when to move forward in a project or when to ship a product to market. Particularly in the applications groups, this semi-structured process is highly effective; it results in a continual stream of new products and incrementally enhanced features, as well as totally new features for old products.

The sixth strategy—*improve through continuous self-critiquing, feedback, and sharing*—deals with building a learning organization. Companies filled with smart people can easily degenerate into a motley collection of arrogant and fiercely independent individuals and teams who do not share knowledge, learn from past mistakes, or listen to customers. Microsoft surely was such a company in the past, and many outside observers might say that parts of the company continue this tradition.[7] We believe that this is no longer true. Since the late 1980s, the company has been utilizing a variety of mechanisms to learn from past and ongoing projects, and from customers' experiences with Microsoft products. Teams are also trying harder to share knowledge in project management and quality control, as well as to build components that more than one project can utilize. Sharing and standardization save engineering and testing costs, make products more coherent to customers, and reduce the need for large customer support staffs.

The seventh strategy is really a concluding impression from our observations of everything Microsoft has done since 1975: *attack the future!* Microsoft has weaknesses, like any organization, and it faces many future challenges and strong competitors as it enters new markets. But it also has many strengths, such as the ability to create a seemingly endless array of new products and take advantage of an enormous base of existing products and customers. Microsoft people could easily have become complacent years ago. Instead, though, they have aggressively confronted internal problems, external challenges, and new market opportunities. They change direction when new opportunities arise. In fact, Bill Gates pushes the company forward as if all its current markets were about to dry up tomorrow, or at least in the next year or two. Whatever one's opinion of Microsoft and its products, one can admire Gates and his people for not waiting for the future to happen. Instead, they try to *make* it happen—their way. Microsoft does not always succeed, but it succeeds often enough.

SYNCH AND STABILIZE

We believe that a special contribution of this book is the unprecedented opportunity we have had to dissect Microsoft's organization and approach to product development. Since the mid-1980s, Microsoft has gradually been reorganizing the way it builds products in response to quality problems and delayed deliveries. Microsoft managers have found it necessary to organize larger teams in order to build today's PC software products; these now consist of hundreds of thousands and even millions of lines of computer code, and require hundreds of people to build and test over periods of one or more years. Microsoft's general philosophy has been to "scale up" a loosely structured small-team (some might say "hacker") style of product development so that *large teams can work like small teams*. These teams then focus on evolving features and whole products incrementally, with direct input from customers during the development process.

We have labeled Microsoft's style of product development the *synch-and-stabilize* approach. The essence is simple: continually *synchronize* what people are doing as individuals and as members of different teams, and periodically *stabilize* the product in increments—in other words, as the project proceeds, rather than once at the end. When team members build components that are interdependent but difficult to define accurately in the early stages of the development cycle, the team must find a way to structure and coordinate what the individual members do while allowing them enough flexibility to change the product's details in stages. This is useful to do as developers test the product with customers and refine their designs *during the development process*.

In software and other industries, there are now many companies that use prototyping as well as multiple cycles of concurrent design, build, and test activities.[8] In the software research community, authors have talked about "iterative enhancement," a "spiral model" for project management, and "concurrent development" since the mid-1970s.[9] Many firms have been slow to adopt these recommendations formally, such as for U.S. government contracting. Nonetheless, the basic idea is that user needs for many types of software are so difficult to understand that it is nearly impossible or unwise to try to design the system completely in advance, especially as hardware improvements and customer desires are constantly and quickly evolving. Instead, projects should "iterate" as well as concurrently manage as many design, build, and testing activities as possible while they move forward to complete a product. If possible, team members should also involve customers intimately in the development process.

This iterative as well as incremental and concurrent engineering style contrasts to a more sequential or "waterfall" approach to product development, which tries to simplify the process. In this approach, projects attempt to "freeze" a product specification, create a design, build components, and then bring these components together—primarily at the end of the project in one large integration and testing phase. This approach to software development was common in the 1970s and 1980s, and remains popular in many industries. It is gradually losing favor because companies usually build better products if they can change specifications and designs, get feedback from customers, and continually test components as the products are evolving. As a result, a growing number of companies in software and other industries now follow a process that overlaps activities and interacts more with customers. They also ship preliminary versions of their products, incrementally adding features or functionality over time in different product releases. Many companies also put pieces of their products together frequently (usually not daily, but often biweekly or monthly). This is useful to determine what works and what does not, without waiting until the end of the project—which may be several years in duration.

Of course, Microsoft resembles companies that do incremental or iterative development as well as concurrent engineering. It has also adapted practices introduced earlier by other companies, such as IBM, and "reinvented the wheel" on many occasions. We believe, however, that Microsoft is distinctive in the degree to which it has introduced a *structured* concurrent and incremental approach to software product development that works for small as well as large-scale products. Furthermore, we believe that Microsoft is a fascinating example of how culture and competitive strategy can drive product development and the innovation process. The Microsoft culture centers around fervently antibureaucratic PC programmers who do not like a lot of rules, structure, or planning. Its competitive strategy revolves around identifying mass markets, quickly introducing products that are "good enough" (rather than waiting until something is perfect), improving these products by incrementally evolving their features, and then selling multiple product versions and upgrades to customers around the world.

Critics may argue that Microsoft's key practices in product development—daily synchronizations through product builds, periodic milestone stabilizations, and continual testing—are no more than technical fixes for a "hacker" software organization that is now building huge software systems. We do not really disagree, but we also think that Microsoft has some good ideas on how to combine structure with flexibility in product development. The term *hacker* is not necessarily a bad word in the PC industry. It goes back to the early days of computer programming in the 1960s, when long-haired, unkempt technical wizards would sit down at a computer with no formal plans, designs, or processes.[10] This approach worked for small computer programs that one person or a small handful of people could write—for example, the first versions of DOS, Lotus 1-2-3, WordPerfect, Word, or Excel. It became unworkable as PC software programs grew into hundreds of thousands and then millions of lines of code.

Formal plans and processes existed first in the mainframe computer industry, where software systems had grown to this length even by the end of the 1960s.[11] Yet PC software companies have been unwilling to give up their traditions and cultures completely. Nor would it be wise for them to do so, given the rapid pace of change in PC hardware and software technologies, and the need for continual innovation.

No company has taken advantage of the exploding demand for PC software better than Microsoft. Similarly, we believe, no PC software company has done a better job of keeping some basic elements of the hacker culture while adding just enough structure to build today's and probably tomorrow's PC software products. It continues to be a challenge for Microsoft to make products reliable enough for companies to buy and simple enough for novice consumers to understand. To achieve these somewhat conflicting goals for a variety of markets, Microsoft still encourages some teams to experiment and make lots of changes without much up-front planning. Projects generally remain under control, however, because of how teams of programmers and testers frequently synchronize and periodically stabilize their changes.

As we discuss in this book, since the late 1980s, Microsoft has used variations of the synch-and-stabilize approach to build Publisher, Works, Excel, Word, Office, Windows NT, Windows 95, and other products. This process, though, does not guarantee on-time or bug-free products. Creating new, large-scale software products on a precisely predicted schedule and with no major defects are extremely difficult goals in the PC industry. Microsoft and other PC software companies also try to replace products quickly and usually announce overly ambitious deadlines, which contribute to their appearance of being chronically late. Nonetheless, without a somewhat structured approach, Microsoft would never be able to design, build, and ship the new products that it now offers and plans to offer in the future.

As Microsoft tackles new markets and its products become even larger, we believe the company will have to pay less attention to adding features incrementally and more attention to product architectures, basic design issues, and some more structured engineering practices, such as design and code reviews. For example, large-scale operating systems and particular types of applications (such as interactive video, or video on demand) have many tightly coupled functions. They also have an almost infinite number of potential user conditions or scenarios to test, based on what hardware and applications the customer is using. These new products can benefit from some incremental changes during the development process, but they also require more advance planning and product architectural design than Microsoft usually does in order to minimize problems in development, testing, and operation. Even so, the synch-and-stabilize process that we describe provides several benefits that serve Microsoft well in building any type of software product:

- It breaks down large products into manageable chunks—a few product features that small feature teams can create in a few months.
- It enables projects to proceed systematically even when team members cannot determine a complete and stable product design at the project's beginning.
- It allows large teams to work like small teams by dividing work into pieces, proceeding in parallel but synchronizing continuously, stabilizing in increments, and continuously finding and fixing problems.
- It facilitates competition based on customer feedback, product features, and short development times by providing a mechanism to incorporate customer inputs, set priorities, complete the most important parts first, and change or cut less important features.

In an interview for this book, Bill Gates highlighted the key advantages he saw in Microsoft's approach to product development:

Forcing these milestones, where you actually do the debugging and you get to a very stable point—not a point of perfection, but a very stable point—is super important for us. Then we know exactly where we are and we don't kid ourselves by just sort of throwing things in and then hoping. . . . [We used to] end up with those huge test periods at the end. It was just hopeless. What if there's a design mistake? What if it doesn't look like it's going to get done in time? Then you didn't have the ability to trade off features. . . . The last time you can do coding is way before product release, and then you're not getting the benefit of the latest ideas or what's going on in the marketplace. So the milestone approach is a major practice for us.

Before proceeding, we would like to make a general observation regarding the material in this book. Many of the strategies and principles we discuss support competition in the computer industry and software product development, because this is what Microsoft does. But we firmly believe that the ideas and examples revealed here provide useful lessons for firms and managers in many industries. What Microsoft does is especially suited to fast-paced markets with complex systems products, short life cycles, and competition based around evolving product features and technical standards. In particular, the work of any large team building many interdependent components that are continually changing requires a constant high level of communication and coordination, while still allowing designers, engineers, and marketing people the freedom to be creative. Achieving this balance is perhaps the central dilemma that managers of product development face in many different industries. Dave Maritz, a former tank commander in the Israeli army who headed the MS-DOS/Windows testing group, commented on how he and other Microsoft managers try to impose only enough direction and ironclad rules so that individuals and teams can work toward the common goal of getting a new product out the door:

In the military, when I was in tank warfare and I was actually fighting in tanks, there was nothing more soothing than people constantly hearing their commander's voice come across the airwaves. Somebody's in charge, even though all shit is breaking loose. . . . When you don't hear [the commander's voice] for more than fifteen minutes to half an hour, what's happened? Has he been shot? Has he gone out of control? Does he know what's going on? You worry. And this is what Microsoft is. These little offices, hidden away with the doors closed. And unless you have this constant voice of authority going across the e-mail the whole time, it doesn't work. Everything that I do here I learned in the military. . . . You can't do anything that's complex unless you have structure. . . . And what you have to do is make that structure as unseen as possible and build up this image for all these prima donnas to think that they can do what they like. Who cares if a guy walks around without shoes all day? Who cares if the guy has got his teddy bear in his office? I don't care. I just want to know . . . [if] somebody hasn't checked in his code by five o'clock. Then that guy knows that I am going to get into his office.

Chapter 1 begins with an examination of the role of Microsoft's leader, Bill Gates. We then analyze the characteristics of the organization, senior management team, and other people that make up the Microsoft Corporation.

1
Organizing and Managing the Company

Find "Smart" People Who Know the Technology and the Business

To organize and manage the company, Microsoft follows a strategy that we describe as find smart people who know the technology and the business. We break down our discussion of this strategy into four principles:

- Hire a CEO with a deep understanding of both the technology and the business.
- Organize flexibly around and across product markets and business functions.
- Hire the smartest managers you can find—people with a deep understanding of the technology and the business.
- Hire the smartest employees you can find—people with a deep understanding of the technology and the business.

These principles, in theory, are not unusual or unique to Microsoft. In practice, however, they have had a profound impact on both the firm and the industry. Few companies have chief execu-

21

tives who know their underlying technology *and* how to translate this knowledge into a multibillion-dollar business as well as Bill Gates. Many companies organize around product markets and business functions in ways similar to Microsoft, but many companies have difficulty simultaneously maintaining a strong product and market focus as well as a strong set of basic functional skills. For a company in a rapidly evolving and expanding industry, Microsoft has done an excellent job of organizing to match and sometimes lead the market. It has also acquired and nurtured the technical functions needed to build a huge and constantly expanding portfolio of products.

Many firms hire or promote people based solely on their managerial skills, not necessarily on how well they can combine their technical knowledge with an understanding of business and strategy. Microsoft puts knowledge of the technology and how to make money with this knowledge first in choosing managers. While this results in a shortage of middle managers with good people management skills, it has served Microsoft well in the highly technical world of developing computer software. At the same time, through new hires and acquisitions, Microsoft continually broadens its existing skill base such as by adding new groups for consumer software and information-highway products and services.

Microsoft is also particularly rigorous in how it screens people, especially software developers, hiring only 2 or 3 percent of all applicants. Moreover, as with managers, Microsoft looks specifically for people with a deep knowledge of the technology and a very clear sense of how to use this knowledge to ship products for the company.

In many respects, Microsoft's product unit managers operate like the Roman centurions of two thousand years ago. They are sufficiently competent that they do not need a lot of direction and can respond quickly to new opportunities and threats. Their organizations have most of the resources they need to operate independently; the centurions go off on their own and report back only occasionally. But they roam within certain limits, and the leader can rest assured that these centurions—and their troops—are fighting for the good of the whole organization. The record speaks for itself: Although not every customer is happy, Microsoft clearly has a leader, a top management team, and an army of employees who deeply understand both the technology and the business of PC software. They also know how to win.

PRINCIPLE   *Hire a CEO with a deep understanding of both the technology and the business.*

Much of a successful company's performance stems from the technical and business acumen, as well as the leadership and managerial abilities, of its chief executive officer. Bill Gates of Microsoft may be the shrewdest entrepreneur and the most underrated manager in American industry today. His talents appear both in a technical understanding of software and computers and in his ability to create and maintain an enormously profitable business. He acquired a reputation years ago as a cantankerous personality who often criticized (and even yelled at) his employees, but Gates has matured along with his company. He continues to guide the selection of new products and businesses, as well as the features that go into key products. Now, however, he relies heavily on several dozen senior executives and technical leaders, and has instituted formal and informal mechanisms to help him direct the Microsoft machinery.

Gates the Person: William Henry Gates was born in 1955 in Seattle, Washington, the middle child in a well-to-do family. (Neither parent was a technologist; his father was a lawyer, and his mother was a teacher.) By all accounts, Gates the child was similar to Gates the adult: His biographers describe him as a "high energy kid" who liked to rock back and forth in his chair, just as he did during our interview. A former teacher described him as "a nerd before the term was invented." His childhood interests included— but obviously did not end with—games such as Risk, where players compete for global domination.[1]

Gates's first exposure to computers came during 1968–1969, in his second year at the private Lakeside School. The school had a primitive teletype machine and access to a computer through a time-sharing hook-up. He learned the BASIC programming language and then teamed up with a tenth-grade electronics expert named Paul Allen to learn more about programming. When Gates was fourteen, he and Allen made money by writing and testing computer programs. The duo then established their first company, named Traf-O-Data, in 1972 and sold a small computer that recorded and analyzed motor vehicle traffic data.

In 1973 Gates enrolled at Harvard University. The following year, Allen, who had gone on to study computer science at the University of Washington, left college and took a job with Honeywell in the Boston area. It has often been described how Allen saw an issue of *Popular Electronics* in 1974 that advertised the new Altair microcomputer kit from MITS Computer, and how he and Gates wrote a version of BASIC using Harvard's computing facilities. Gates left college in 1975 to concentrate full-time on developing programming languages for the Altair (and then for other personal computers), relocating with Allen to Albuquerque, New Mexico, to be next to MITS Computer's office. They formed Microsoft during 1975 as a 60–40 partnership in favor of Gates, reflecting his larger role in developing Microsoft BASIC, the company's first product. (See Appendix 1 for an abbreviated chronology of Microsoft's history.)

Several characteristics stand out in stories about the young Gates. He was intelligent and ambitious, as were his friends. He was able to concentrate intensely on and master what interested him; most notably, computers and how to program them for practical purposes. Perhaps most important, Gates envisioned a world with computers not merely tracking traffic data but sitting on every desktop—and running his software. This was a great combination of skills and ambitions to have at the dawning of the PC era.

Observers from outside and Microsoft employees paint similar pictures of Gates. They describe him as a visionary with a maniacal drive to succeed, accumulate great power, and make money by taking advantage of his technical knowledge and understanding of industry dynamics. Microsoft the company emerges as an extension of Gates' unique personality and skills.

> Gates is a visionary. Very early in the history of the PC, he evolved a strikingly clear concept of where the industry was headed, and he has pursued that vision—despite many tactical setbacks—unwaveringly, relentlessly, and ruthlessly.[2]

This guy [Gates] is awesomely bright. But he's unique in a sense that he's the only really bright person I've ever met who was 100 percent bottom-line oriented—how do you make a buck? Not in a mercenary way. It's just like that's what's good in life, right? If you make money, clearly that's good. It's like he's this huge computing machine that knows how to make money. (Jim Conner, program manager, Office Product Unit)

He's a maniac. Bill knows more about the product than any of us. And you go into the meetings and you come out just sweating because, if there is any flaw, he will land on it immediately and pick it to bits. He is just unbelievable. (Dave Maritz, former test manager, Windows/MS-DOS)

IBM thought they had Gates by the balls. He's just a hacker, they thought. A harmless nerd. What they actually had by the balls was an organism which has been bred for the accumulation of great power and maximum profit, the child of a lawyer, who knew the language of contracts, and who just ripped those IBM guys apart.[3]

Gates the Manager: During an interview, we asked Gates to describe the main precepts behind how Microsoft has managed product development. His list impressed us and included elements we had already observed. Below are Gates's key principles for managing product development—which we will come back to later—with brief quotations from our interview to illustrate his points:

- *Smart people and small teams:* "We started using the very best practices, which was just hiring great people and having small teams. . . . The biggest advantage we have is that good developers like to work with good developers."
- *A development process that allows large teams to work like small teams:* "Then we had to have larger teams . . . and then we had to formalize a lot of things. We went into the whole approach of milestones and driving the zero defects at those milestones, and the way we did the project estimations. Those are all things that deal with the size of the project teams."
- *Product architectures that reduce interdependencies among teams*: "Good architecture can reduce the amount of interdependency within even a development group here."

- *Nearly all new product development done on one site:* "Our all being, with very minor exceptions, here on one site, so that whatever interdependencies exist you can go see that person face to face . . . [is] a major advantage."
- *People working on the same machines they build products for:* "Our development system and our target system are the same. Some people don't do it that way."
- *A single main development language:* "People can argue about which is the best development language, but we have one."
- *Large capital investments to support people:* "Our willingness to spend money to buy tools for people. Our giving people an office of their own."
- *Internal use of their own engineering tools:* "We have control over our tools because we use our own tools. . . . On balance, we have had a massive benefit by using our own tools."
- *More than one person who understands the product details:* "We don't have large bodies of code where just one person has looked at the code and everybody else goes, 'Oh my God, the prima donna is the only one who can change this code.'"
- *Managers who both create the product and make the technical decisions:* "We don't have non-technical management trying to make technical trade-offs."
- *Quick decision making on technical-versus-business trade-offs:* "[We have] an ability to get technical–business trade-offs made with high speed. If there's some question about it, either the business [product] unit manager will decide very quickly, or if somebody wants to send e-mail to me to get me involved in the decision, that'll happen very quickly."
- *An enormous feedback loop from customers:* "Most people don't get millions of people giving them feedback about their software products. . . . We have this whole group of over [two] thousand people in the U.S. alone that takes phone calls about our products and logs everything that's done. So we have a better feedback loop, including the market."
- *Deliberate efforts to learn from past projects:* "We do good postmortems after the projects and look at what were the source of the bugs, how could the design generate less bugs, [and] how could the tools generate less bugs?"

As Microsoft has grown, Gates has faced new problems. He has to study constantly to stay on top of a fast-moving company and industry, and to remain knowledgeable about Microsoft's expanding arsenal of products (as well as those of competitors). He has to decide every day what to control and what to delegate. To be sure, Gates has able help, although he and other Microsoft managers resist creating large staffs for anything. Gates has only one personal administrative assistant and one technical assistant, hired during the past few years. The technical assistant is generally a young program manager or software developer who holds the job for a year or two. The assistant reviews product ideas and specifications, takes notes in meetings, follows competitors and trade shows, and helps Gates keep track of different projects.

Microsoft executives have introduced fairly conventional management systems, but Gates remains closely involved. He presides over program reviews and planning sessions in April and October of every year that set the schedule for rolling out new products and establishing budgets. The October reviews center on three-year product plans; each division explains the products it is planning to deliver and any interdependencies with other products. After completing the October review, Microsoft's marketing staff (called product managers) create a sales forecast based on the divisions' product plans. Detailed budget planning then begins, and managers look at the sales versus budget estimates to determine how these compare with the profit objectives for the company. Based on this analysis, Gates and other top executives determine the employee head count they want for the fiscal year beginning in July. Gates not only takes an active role in all the significant review and planning sessions but gives direct advice to the key product units.

In general, Gates concentrates on defining strategic new products (or new versions of products) and keeping a check on development schedules, mainly through product status reports and electronic mail from project team members and managers. He receives short status reports from projects every month—these used to be biweekly—and actually reads them. He attends quarterly program reviews for many projects. He writes occasional strategic memos, perhaps four or five times a year. (One he was writing while we visited, his assistant told us, outlined "some of the big technical challenges we face and who's going to own particular solutions, and what solutions are the right ones from a strategic point of view.") Once or twice a year, he goes on "think weeks." During these times, he isolates himself and thinks about a particular problem: for example, how to improve customer support, how to get groups to cooperate more, or what a product should look like five years in the future. Gates also tries to "get the biggest bang for the buck" from the time he spends: "The products that comprise 80 percent of our revenue I choose to understand very, very deeply." This means that he spends most of his time following such key applications as Office and its Word and Excel components, as well as Windows. He also closely follows new high-growth areas, such as multimedia and on-line information services and products.

Project Status Reports: Each software product has a corresponding project status report. Project teams send these each month to Gates and other top executives as well as the managers of all related projects. They are a key mechanism for communicating between projects and top management. Gates usually responds to the relevant managers or developers directly by electronic mail, then uses the information he gathers for the formal program reviews. These reports also communicate target schedules, which project members set themselves. As Gates explained:

> I get all the status reports. Right now there might be a hundred active projects. . . . [The status reports] contain the schedule, including milestone dates, and any change in the spec, and any comments about "Hey, we can't hire enough people," or "Geez, if this OLE [Object Linking and Embedding] 2 Mac release isn't done, we're just going to have to totally slip." . . . They know [their report] goes up to all the people who manage all the other groups that they have dependencies with. So if they want to raise an issue, that's a great way to raise it. And if they don't raise it in the status report and then two months later they say something, that's a breakdown in communication. . . . The internal group is totally copied on those things, so it's sort of the consensus of the group.

The status reports are brief and have a standard format. Gates can read most of them quickly and still spot potential project delays or changes he does not want, although some projects and issues get more attention than others: "I read every one of those things. . . . It's not that hard to read a hundred status reports. . . . If it's an obscure mail gateway product, and if it hasn't slipped a whole bunch, then I just hit delete. The thing is very succinct. . . . It's like two screens full. . . . There's a line for each date, like milestone dates, spec-by dates, code complete dates . . . and then there's a column for the original date, the last date, and what they're reporting this time." Gates especially looks for schedule slips, cutting too many product features, or the need to change a specification:

> In any reporting period, there'll only be about ten to fifteen of them that catch my eye. . . . [because of comments like] "Several features were cut." Well, is there anything left? Give me a clue. Or "You know you just slipped the schedule." Not much of a comment; people really have to address size and speed requirements. Or when a competitor comes into the market with a new version, they have to really say in their status report are they choosing to stay with the spec as it is, or are they going to change the spec and go with the new schedule? It's a really major thing to get that straight. . . . The thing that jumps out right away is, are they changing the date this time? . . . And so, as you read the development commentary, the program management commentary, the testing commentary, marketing commentary, which are usually only about three or four sentences each, sometimes there's a lot going on. Then you know you have that context in mind. It's easy then just to shoot off a piece of mail and say, "Come on, I thought I asked to get drag-and-drop into this thing, and I don't see it in the status report." And "Don't we need this thing? Didn't we promise this thing to HP? And what about the RISC version? You don't mention that." . . . [But] I'm not the only sanity checkpoint on these things. There's quite a few other people.

Program Reviews: Microsoft holds program review meetings for each project every three months or so. These meetings, lasting about two hours, are usually attended by Gates as well as other senior executives. Project teams send one or two key people from each functional area: program management (the group responsible for writing down product specifications), software development (the people who write the computer code), software testing (the people who test the code), product management (the people in charge of product planning and marketing), and user education (the group that prepares product documentation). Gates told us that he focuses on the same types of issues he looks for in the status reports:

> You want to know is the project under control. That's fundamental. And you want to know if people are anticipating . . . major problems. If they're adding something that could potentially slow the product down, you say to them, "Prove to me it's not going to be ten times slower." . . . If something is taking longer to get done than they expected, was it because they just didn't understand the design? . . . You have to ask enough questions to really understand: Are we on top of what we're doing? And you have to listen for ideas that have come up during the project that might be worth changing the spec to accommodate. . . . Can [they] take something and push it to a higher level of generality? What's their relationship with all the other groups?
>
> . . . I believe in code sharing across the groups. I've imposed on them the necessity to get this thing from this group and that thing from that group, and those groups don't work for them. If they want to point out to me some dependency that is creating massive bugs or it's massively slow or they may never get that piece from that group in time, it's important to bring that out in the discussion. . . .
>
> If the marketplace environment has changed and we're asking them to change the spec, it's important they hear from me about that. There's [also] a need to set a tone in terms of telling them they're doing super well or not doing super well, once you have the data. Sometimes you have that before you go into a meeting, because the amount of e-mail that's generated about projects is rather massive.

Steven Sinofsky, Gates's technical assistant in 1993 and 1994 (and now group program manager for Office), downplayed the drama of the program reviews, claiming that senior executives usually know about problems beforehand and hold preliminary meetings with the projects: "It's just a chance to make sure they have their act together. And often they'll do them for Mike Maples or for Steve Ballmer previously or one of the senior VPs, and then they'll do them for Bill as well. It's not an ambush." But Gates does try to mix up his questions. He spends some time on obvious things and also probes more deeply: "I'll always surprise people with maybe half my questions, but about half the questions are fairly clear. I can remind people of which benchmarks really count. I can remind people of which system configurations really count." In some cases, he sends in some help:

> At my level, what do I really control? I have some very senior developers that I could shift over onto a project and have them help review the algorithms [mathematical or procedural recipes to accomplish particular tasks through computer code], review the code or just pitch in. So if a project really appears to be broken, then you want an independent review of the code. Very early in the company I'd say, "Hey, give me the source code. I'll take it home." I can't do that now. So I take somebody, a D14 or a D15 [the top technical ranks in the company] and say, "Go dig into this thing and let me know," or, "Help them out in terms of getting more personnel assigned." They're always going to have a recommendation in terms of what features ought to be cut . . . because they understand all the dependencies and how the pieces fit together.

Gates admitted, however, that he finds it difficult to cancel projects in trouble:

> We don't have that many we cancel, but sometimes things will shift in the marketplace and we'll cancel. That's a combined technical-business decision. The most famous one was the database we were doing. The first Windows database was inadequate. . . . You could say we started over. Some people would say we only rewrote 80 percent of the thing, but it was fairly radical. And Word for Windows was a classic; if you want to take a project that was late, that's our most famous late thing.

In reviewing specifications, Gates concentrates on a few key themes. He wants to know how "exciting" a new product is, as well as how it fits with other Microsoft products. Increasingly he also asks about quality, mainly defined in terms of bug levels. These three issues drive Gate's recommendation on whether a product is good enough to ship. Another rising concern is making sure that groups cooperate and share common components, and that products slated to work together or share code are coordinated and on schedule. Managing such interdependencies is no trivial matter for Microsoft's previously independent product groups, and it is likely to become a greater problem because many

Microsoft products may now come out every year (for example, Windows 95 and Office 95); delays beyond the control of any one project could force embarrassing changes in product names.

Gates prefers to set broad directions and then leave the product groups to solve these types of problems on their own. But he continues to astonish people with his ability to grasp the technical details of what the groups are doing. This has happened with products outside his personal area of expertise (like Windows NT), but more commonly with products he understands from personal experience (like BASIC, Word, and Excel). Mike Conte, formerly a product and program manager on Excel—and now with Office—recalled how the busy Gates took minutes to find a weakness in a new feature. The Excel team, which knew about the flaw but had not yet told Gates, had taken a month to find the problem:

> We did a thing called subminimal recalc[ulation] in Excel 3.0. Minimal recalc says you only recalculate dependencies; minimal recalc only recalcs the cells that were affected by the change you made, instead of recalcing the whole sheet. That was a big innovation for speed in recalc. For Excel 3.0, we did subminimal recalc, which said even in some cases you can skip the dependencies if the intermediate results haven't changed. . . . And so we're talking about this to Bill, and . . . [he] says, "What about this case, this case, and this case?" And Chris Peters, who was our development manager at the time, said, "Well, funny you mention those. After a month of thinking about this problem, those are the three cases we came up with. We were not optimal." So he's pretty good at following the technical stuff.

Preparing for an encounter with Gates can be intimidating even to seasoned employees and executives. Chris Peters, now vice president of the Office Product Unit, gave this advice to his colleagues in his now-famous 1990 video entitled "Shipping Software":

> You should keep Bill very informed about what you're doing and why; you should never hide anything from Bill, because he's so good at knowing everything. But you should be firm, and you should yell back. The only recommendation I can bring or give you guys is to bring your very, very, very best developers with you to the meeting so they can quote things off the top of their head and they can just bury him with facts. . . .

Don't ever be unprepared. But say no. Bill respects no. Bill understands shipping on time. I think the thing that we finally said is . . . it will be useful for Microsoft to know what it takes to ship a product on time, so please let us not do this feature. I think we ended up doing that feature actually, but that's why he's Bill Gates.

Control Over New Product Development: To the question of what are the first things he let go of versus those he has insisted on controlling, Gates responded as follows:

Well, [at] first, I wouldn't let anybody write any code. I went in and took every statement that anybody else had written in BASIC and rewrote it myself, just because I didn't like the way they coded. That product had a certain craftsmanship thing. I was very reluctant to let anybody get involved in it. But then we had products like FORTRAN and COBOL, where all I did was make sure that we were designing to the right spec and review the basic algorithms. . . . I have not delegated the general idea of products to develop. I don't come in and say, "Well, I didn't know there's a whole new product group here. Nobody told me about that." That is a good decision for a CEO of a software company to keep in his hands. That's about the only one that I really control nowadays.

A key role that Gates plays is to view the entire product portfolio of the company in light of the future directions he sees, including likely competitor moves. Then he makes the hard decisions: the technology-versus-business trade-offs. One example is how Gates, for five years, pushed for Excel and other groups to adopt Visual Basic as a common "macro language." (Macros are special commands that, at the user's discretion, combine many functions into one or two keystrokes. Using a standard macro language allows users to customize various Microsoft products all in the same manner.) Gates has also pushed groups to adopt Object Linking and Embedding (OLE) standards so that they can more easily share components.

Gates also works closely with key projects. He helps define current products as well as chart future directions. As Ed Fries, development manager for Word, recalled:

We interact with Bill a lot, especially in the early stages of a product when we're going over the spec and we're trying to decide what features we're going to put into the product. . . . Bill was here a few weeks ago and we walked him around and showed him all the stuff that we're doing in Word. He was on a "think week" last week, and during that week he probably sent ten pieces of mail to Chris [Peters] that said, "Oh, here's something I don't like about this version of Word. And here's something you should be thinking about in the future to make spelling better for all our products. Or Word and Help, and how can those things be combined into one type of thing." So Bill does a lot to define our future direction with the product, and he also does some quick criticism of where we are now. . . . He always represents where he thinks things are going to be five years from now. We're trying to balance going in that direction with meeting the needs the users have today that we think we're not meeting. So we try to come up with a compromise of making that happen. . . . That's always the conflict.

With the fiercely independent culture of Microsoft managers and developers, however, it is rare that Gates tries to mandate anything; according to Sinofsky, the "numbers of those things are so small that they all have a reputation of their own." Along with pushing groups to adopt Visual Basic and OLE, some key additions to products that Gates has demanded include an outlining feature in Excel, tables and drag-and-drop in Word, and custom controls in Visual Basic (called VBXs). Gates also once insisted that program managers and developers use Visual Basic for writing prototypes and special software programs; some groups successfully resisted when they found the language inappropriate for technical reasons. And executive vice president Steve Ballmer, with Gate's agreement, once mandated that Microsoft groups use a pre-ship version of Windows NT as their operating system, rather than Windows or OS/2. In addition, Gates told Microsoft's commercial tools group (which makes language compilers, among other things) to add features to support Microsoft's internal software developers, rather than just serve outside customers. Occasionally, Gates halts projects mired in delays and bugs, such as the Omega database product for Windows (which later evolved into Access). He has also consolidated projects working on multiple versions of the same type of function, such as text-processing code in Word, Excel, and Mail.

People argue with Gates and his suggestions fairly often; as Chris Peters observed, this is necessary to gain his respect. But people must have clear technical grounds and data to support their positions. Arguments based on personal or emotional reasons, or internal politics, have little impact on Gates or other key managers. Gates in particular seems to need a new intellectual "model"—a comprehensive argument that views the world differently—in order to change his mind. As Steven Sinofsky explained: "You can't repeat your argument over and over again if his model keeps refuting your argument. You need to find a new model that disproves his."

PRINCIPLE   *Organize flexibly around and across product markets and business functions.*

Bill Gates insisted to us that Microsoft's "dominant organizational theme is by products." We find this to be largely true, but Microsoft also pays a lot of attention to (albeit overlapping) technical or functional specialties. People in these jobs work in multifunctional teams organized by product, with some mechanisms to integrate across the product groups. Furthermore, in addition to divisions and product groups, Microsoft has two other organizational structures. One is formal, consisting of the management hierarchy. The second is informal; this consists of a loosely defined "brain trust" of executives and a network of technical people and managers who work on special assignments or projects, often at the suggestion of Bill Gates or other senior executives.

Organizational and Process Evolution: Microsoft adopted its current organizational structure and process for product development in stages and through trial and error. During the early 1980s, it created an End User Group to develop applications programs. This allowed the systems and applications groups to evolve independently. The company struggled, however, to improve functional expertise, especially in testing. It also had to overcome problems stemming from a lack of focus in the product groups, and relatively poor mechanisms for quality control and project management. As in many other companies, several turning points and key actors defined this evolution (Table 1.1).

The first turning point was a decision in 1984 to set up testing groups separate from development. This provided an independent check on the work of developers. The second, occurring about the same time, was when program management began to emerge as a function distinct from product management and software development. Third was a series of late and buggy products during the mid-1980s, which led to a growing consensus in the company that Microsoft had to become much more serious about quality control and project management. Microsoft groups now began documenting their experiences in projects through written postmortems, reflecting the belief that people could do a much better job at "learning from mistakes." Fourth was the arrival of Mike Maples in 1988 from IBM and his decision to create smaller business units; these added more focus to the operating groups and made them easier to manage.

The fifth key event was a 1989 retreat where top managers and developers grappled with how to reduce defects, and proposed solutions that helped Microsoft teams become more systematic in software development and quality control. One was the idea of breaking up a project into subprojects or milestones, which Publisher 1.0 did successfully in 1988. Another was to do daily builds of products, which several groups had done but without enforcing the goal of zero defects. These critical ideas would become the essence of the synch-and-stabilize process. Excel 3.0 (developed in 1989 and 1990) was the first Microsoft project that was large in size and a major revenue generator to use the new techniques, and it shipped only eleven days late.

A sixth key event was the 1992 establishment of the four-person Office of the President and the centralization of all product development responsibilities under Maples. These moves brought more structure to the operating systems groups, whose schedules remain difficult to predict. Seventh was a 1993 reorganization that centralized most product managers in marketing groups for the

Table 1.1   Key Events in Microsoft's Organizational Evolution

---

1984 Establishment of separate testing groups in each division.

Recall of Multiplan 1.06 spreadsheet for the Macintosh.

Establishment of technical specialties (functions) such as Program Management and Product Management, in addition to Testing.

1986 Beginning of postmortem documents to identify quality and project management problems as well as potential solutions.

1987 Recall of the Macintosh Word 3.0 word processor.

1988 Arrival of Mike Maples from IBM and the establishment of separate business units for each product group within the Systems and Applications Divisions.

Use of milestones in the Publisher 1.0 project.

1989 The May "retreat" and November "Zero-defects code" memo highlighting the importance of daily builds.

1990 Completion of the Excel 3.0 project (1989-1990) only 11 days late, using key elements of the synch-and-stabilize process (milestones and daily builds).

1992 Establishment of the collective Office of the President.

Centralization of Systems and Applications under the Worldwide Products Group, headed by Executive Vice President Mike Maples.

1993 Centralization of marketing teams (product managers) at the division level, except for product planners, and renaming of business units as product units.

Creation of the Office Product Unit, headed by Vice President Chris Peters.

1995 Creation of the Platforms Group, headed by Group Vice President Paul Maritz, and the Applications and Content Group, headed by Group Vice Presidents Nathan Myhrvold and Pete Higgins.

---

individual divisions, except for a few product planners who remained with the product development groups. Microsoft also renamed the business units "product units" to reflect this change, and it created the Office Product Unit. These changes have more clearly separated marketing from product planning and development, and they have facilitated sharing of common components across Microsoft's key applications products.

The split of Microsoft into systems and applications divisions came under former Microsoft president Jon Shirley, an MIT dropout and Tandy Corporation (Radio Shack) executive whom Gates recruited in 1983. Gates had assumed developers should report to developers, not general managers—and that all development should report to him, since he was the top developer in the company. Gates also tried to control other key areas such as marketing, an approach that quickly became obsolete as Microsoft grew beyond a handful of products. Shirley concluded that Gates had overstretched himself and that a reorganization was necessary. For example, Gates had a habit of pulling developers from one team and putting them on another, and making large changes in specifications with no prior warning or planning for such contingencies. Shirley felt the CEO should define products at a high level of abstraction and set strategic directions for the development organization, rather than be bogged down in the details of each project.[4] Gates agreed to the reorganization and to limit himself to overseeing applications, and he put Steve Ballmer in charge of systems. Gates gave this account of the changes:

> Before Mike Maples came in . . . all development worked for me, because there was this theory that developers should never have to work for somebody who couldn't write thousands of lines of code a day; it was just an insult to them. So all development management was purely developers, and at almost every step of the chain there was a developer who had written more code, basically. Then I broke it into systems and app[lication]s and I put Steve in charge [of systems]. Well, Steve is nontechnical. But he's fairly mathematical, and he has good personality. People trusted his ability when it came to a technical decision to turn to the right developers that, even though they weren't managers, were people that [everyone] had broad respect for. So we got by then.

Microsoft decided in 1984 to separate testing from development after bugs in different products prompted complaints from hardware manufacturers who bundled Microsoft's operating systems with their PCs. (Microsoft refers to these companies as original equipment manufacturers, or OEMs.) For example, the version of BASIC that Microsoft shipped with the IBM PC in 1981 gave the wrong answer when the user divided ".1" and other numbers by 10. After this incident, IBM insisted that Microsoft improve its processes for software development and quality control. Microsoft had other nonpublicized problems in the early 1980s as well, such as a bug in its FORTRAN product (a technical programming language) that corrupted data.[5] Individual customers also began complaining about quality problems in Microsoft's applications products, which they could buy in retail stores.

Senior managers finally saw the need to introduce better internal testing and quality control practices. There was resistance to this idea, since most programmers and even some senior managers (such as Ballmer) insisted that developers could test their own products, assisted on occasion by high school students, secretaries, and some outside contractors. Microsoft did make a special effort by hiring the Arthur Andersen consulting firm to test its new version of the Multiplan spreadsheet for the Macintosh before it shipped in January 1984. But an outside company usually cannot test a complex software product adequately. A serious data-destroying bug forced Microsoft to ship an update to Mac Multiplan's twenty thousand buyers at the cost of $10 each—$200,000 total.[6]

Microsoft managers concluded that they could not meet higher quality standards without setting up an independent testing group, following the lead of IBM and other companies with longer and more successful histories of software development. Dave Moore, Microsoft's director of development, recalled this realization: "We knew that we couldn't stand alone with development doing their own testing. We needed a separate group that would build the test, run the test, give some feedback to development. That was a turning point." Microsoft did not copy such IBM techniques as making large groups of people review all software items—from specifications documents to code and test plans—or requiring executives to "sign off" at the various development stages. These bureaucratic practices are common in software production for mainframe computers and defense applications, but they are still rare in the PC world. Nor did Microsoft start monitoring in detail how developers and testers spend their time, as IBM and a few other companies (including Japanese software factories) do. Instead, Microsoft people selected what seemed to be good techniques, such as a separate testing group and automated tests, and code reviews for new people or critical components. Then they promoted these not as IBM practices ("That's not the way to get it used in Microsoft," noted Moore) but as methods that worked.

But, Moore added, "We did it wrong." After Microsoft expanded the new testing groups between 1984 and 1986, developers "got lazy," thinking they could "throw code over the wall to testing." They forgot that developers find more of their own bugs than testers do, and that only developers can prevent errors from happening in the first place. Meanwhile, Microsoft shipped the next big disaster in company annals. Word 3.0 for the Macintosh, delivered in February 1987 after having been promised for July 1986, had approximately seven hundred bugs—several of which destroyed data or "crashed" the program. Microsoft had to ship a free upgrade to customers within two months of the original release, costing more than $1 million.[7]

By now, it had become apparent even to skeptics within the company that Microsoft was having enormous difficulties managing product development, and that groups would have to become more systematic to satisfy customers. Gates himself took over the applications division, but several key projects remained in chaos. None of the new applications for Windows, except for Excel, were progressing. A database program (dubbed the Omega project, which evolved into Access) and a project management application for Windows were in serious trouble.

The Opus project, later renamed Word for Windows, caused staffers to coin the now-famous phrase "infinite defects." This describes a situation where testers are finding bugs faster than developers can fix them, and each fix leads to yet another bug; under these conditions, predicting the schedule and eventual ship date becomes impossible. This sometimes occurred at Microsoft when summer interns wrote code and then went back to college without testing their work fully, and when developers moved from one feature or project to another, also without fully testing their work. During the "late and large" integration and testing periods that Microsoft used to attempt, developers had to return to old code whose details they had largely forgotten or whose authors had disappeared. In rewriting much of the code to fix the innumerable bugs, the developers tended to add as many new errors as they repaired.[8] Roger Sherman, Microsoft's director of testing, recalled this dark period in Microsoft's history:

> People got the message that they actually could screw up. . . . It's like driving a race car: They hit the wall, and now they know where the wall is. . . . [P]eople learned that they couldn't just throw code together, no matter how imaginative or how creative. They had to look at some things, external factors, and they had to have code that was testable and testing resources were not infinite. . . . They had to work on stable code. So from the negative experience of Omega and Opus, people learned something that pushed them into this milestone process. I think the lessons were probably learned better in Access than they were in Word. The bug databases were so large they couldn't keep them on a single server. There were so many active bugs that the test team really didn't have any work to do: "Why bother? Development has two years' worth of work backlog to catch up with us already." So they spent all their time automating and developing automation tools. Finally, somebody said these ship dates are totally unrealistic, the project is a mess, we're never going to be able to ship this on time. And that probably means that the whole definition of the product . . . is bogus as well. And so they had to go back and take small portions of the product and stabilize them. . . . They cut a lot of the product away and got back to a point where they had a stable code base and were able to proceed.

Rather than let more projects spin out of control, Gates decided to go outside the company for more management expertise. In July 1988, he brought in Mike Maples, who had been with IBM for 23 years and headed software strategy and business evaluation. He was also a central figure in the development of OS/2 and Presentation Manager, an early graphical interface product for the IBM PC.[9] Ironically, Microsoft people often criticized IBM for hiring too many programmers who were not very skilled developers (a practice they referred to disparagingly as "masses of asses programming"), and using a development process that was too sequential and compartmentalized.[10] Microsoft managers also believed that IBM required thousands of people to do what Microsoft could achieve with just a few hundred top-notch developers. But Maples seemed uniquely talented, and Gates wanted to see more processes in place to make sure Microsoft built and delivered its products and controlled their quality more effectively. A key 1989 memo summarizing discussions from the May retreat (which Dave Moore organized) galvanized the product groups to take corrective actions. The memo shown, titled "Zero-defects code" and written by Chris Mason, a development manager in the Word group, reflected the state of affairs and the new process Microsoft would adopt.

Over in the systems area, Microsoft was also having severe troubles with Windows. As Gates's biographers observed after Microsoft shipped the third version of Windows in 1990, the product was still far from perfect: "Once again, Microsoft's testers had not weeded out all the problems. There were problems installing the program on certain machines, troubles with networks, difficulties with the pointing device called a 'mouse,' data destruction with certain third-party disk management software—along with the usual collection of glitches and documentation errors. . . . The running gag in the industry was that Microsoft products were in beta test until version 3."[11]

Gates and many other Microsoft people had additional worries. Stock options had become a critical source of compensation in the company, and delayed products more than occasionally brought the price of Microsoft's stock crashing down. Delays and recalls also confused and frustrated customers, both on the OEM and retail sides. There was even a shareholder suit due to Microsoft's failure to ship Word—which then accounted for 20 percent of sales—that the company settled in 1990 for $1.5 million. (The suit charged that Microsoft managers concealed their knowledge of the delay.) As for the database project, it was supposedly three months from being finished when Mike Maples arrived in 1988; a year and a half later, he and Gates canceled it.[12]

These continuing problems in both the applications and systems

Microsoft Memo

To: Application developers and testers

From: Chris Mason

Date: 6/20/89

Subject: Zero-defects code

Cc: Mike Maples, Steve Ballmer, Applications Business Unit managers and
         department heads

On May 12th and 13th, the applications development managers held a retreat with some of their project leads, Mike Maples, and other representatives of Applications and Languages. My discussion group investigated techniques for writing code with no defects. This memo describes the conclusions which we reached. . . . *There are a lot of reasons why our products seem to get buggier and buggier. It's a fact that they're getting more complex, but we haven't changed our methods to respond to that complexity.* . . . The point of enumerating our problems is to realize that our current methods, not our people, cause their own failure. . . . Our scheduling methods and Microsoft's culture encourage doing the minimum work necessary on a feature. When it works well enough to demonstrate, we consider it done, everyone else considers it done, and the feature is checked off the schedule. The inevitable bugs months later are seen as unrelated. . . . When the schedule is jeopardized, we start cutting corners. . . . *The reason that complexity breeds bugs is that we don't understand how the pieces will work together.* This is true for new products as well as for changes to existing products. . . . I mean this literally: your goal should be to have a working, nearly-shippable product every day. . . . Since human beings themselves are not fully debugged yet, there will be bugs in your code no matter what you do. When this happens, you must evaluate the problem and resolve it immediately. . . . Coding is the major way we spend our time. Writing bugs means we're failing in our major activity. *Hundreds of thousands of individuals and companies rely on our products; bugs can cause a lot of lost time and money. We could conceivably put a company out of business with a bug in a spreadsheet, database, or word processor. We have to start taking this more seriously.* [italics added]

divisions created a receptive environment for Maples to suggest changes. In particular, he wanted smaller groups that worked in projects targeting specific leading competitors and products, such as WordPerfect, Lotus 1-2-3, and Harvard Graphics. He also wanted each of these groups to define and then refine their processes for software development, testing, and project management. After discussing the matter with Gates, Maples broke down the applications division into five business units: Office, Analysis

(Excel), Graphics (PowerPoint), Data Access, and Entry (Works). These now became independent profit centers—with self-contained resources for program management, development, testing, marketing (product management and product planning), and user education—very much patterned after the highly successful independent business unit that IBM used to launch its original PC in 1981. Maples, who got his introduction to Gates and Microsoft while working for this IBM unit, recalled his influence on Microsoft's reorganization:

> It was really funny. When I first came, I went to what we called resource planning meetings. The head of development, the head of marketing, the head of program management, and the head of test[ing] would be there, and they'd go over a project. Every week every project would move; some of them that were out eighteen months would move [their target date for completion] three days. And then they'd say, "Okay, we need more testers on this project," so we'd rip some testers off something and put them on another project. And then the next week we'd have another resource planning meeting and the one we took them off of was in trouble, so we'd move them. It was constant moving people around; people never owned projects. Then we built this whole idea of the business units. Conceptually, you lose the efficiency of moving people around. The testing group for Word stays the testing group for Word, even when there isn't anything to test. [But] it turns out that knowing what the continuity is in your resource pool allows you to plan. And that also did quite a bit in growing a lot of management people [by] giving people a lot broader responsibility. It brought a great deal of focus to customers, and sets of competitors. By and large, Microsoft is broadly organized that way now in terms of small business units.

Microsoft maintained this same basic organizational structure, with some refinements. In 1992, Gates moved Steve Ballmer from head of the systems division to head of the Sales and Support Group. He also created an expanded Worldwide Products Group, with Mike Maples overseeing product development for both applications and systems areas. This change gave Maples a chance to rein in the operating systems groups until he retired in 1995, at which time Microsoft once again separated responsibilities for applications and operating systems. In 1993, Microsoft also centralized marketing and created the Office Product Unit. In addition, Microsoft appointed directors for the key functional areas: development, testing, program management, and user education; since 1994, this staff group reports to an overall director of product development. The directors do not oversee projects or have well-defined responsibilities, although they help groups identify and share best practices. Gates reflected on the pluses and minuses of the new organization:

> It's a trade-off; all organizational things are a trade-off. It optimizes for the esprit de corps of the product: What are we trying to do with this product? What trade-offs do we need to make with this product? Did we ship a product, did it win the review? And so it breaks down the idea of specialization.
>
> There're two big drawbacks to the product organization: One is that, with any skill area, it's not as obvious that best practices—interviewing practices, new tools, new approaches—get shared as well. And if you take the extreme group, like a group that has one tester, how are they supposed to review that tester and tell him, "Hey, you didn't read the latest book on testing." And so we lay over a very small group of people that are supposed to make sure testing knows all the new things going on. But it's just a very small part. And second, it makes it hard to share code. But it's far, far better to do it that way. If we had tried over the last eight years not to use business units to do our stuff, this thing would break down.

A clear benefit of Microsoft's organization is that it provides the freedom for groups to operate as relatively small development centers totally dedicated to shipping products to particular markets. As Chris Peters explained:

> The business units, although we pretend that they're mini-companies, are really pure product development centers. . . . There is no sales or finance—all that stuff is removed from it. Everybody in a business unit has exactly the same . . . job description, and that is to ship products. Your job is not to write code, your job is not to test, your job is not to write specs. Your job is to ship products. . . . You're trying not to write code. If we could make all this money by not writing code, we'd do it.

Stimulated in particular by the 1989 retreat, Microsoft managers also now insist that developers and testers stay in their groups for more than one product cycle. They want developers to make more effort to "get it right the first time" and to "build in quality." Microsoft's strategy for doing this is to use the daily-build and multiple-milestone techniques—the essence of the synch-and-stabilize process we describe in Chapters 4 and 5.

Current Management Structure and Organization: Microsoft's current management hierarchy, below the board of directors, begins with the "communal" leadership first instituted in 1992: the Office of the President. After a July 1995 reorganization following the retirement of Mike Maples, this includes, in addition to Bill Gates as Microsoft's chairman and chief executive officer, five senior managers who direct Microsoft's four operating groups: Group vice presidents Nathan Myhrvold (formerly head of advanced technology) and Pete Higgins (formerly head of desktop applications) jointly preside over the new Applications and Content Group. Group vice president Paul Maritz (formerly responsible for product and technology strategy) heads the new Platforms Group. These two groups build Microsoft's products and conduct research and development. Executive vice president Steve Ballmer is in charge of the Sales and Support Group, while Robert Herbold is head of the Operations Group and also serves as chief operating officer. Reporting to these group executives are division vice presidents and general managers. Below them are product unit managers, followed by functional team managers and then team leads in the product groups.

As seen in Figure 1.1, the Applications and Content Group has four divisions: desktop applications, consumer on-line systems, and research. The Platforms Group also has four divisions: personal operating systems, business systems, developer and database systems, and advanced consumer systems. Most of these divisions contain their own marketing departments staffed by product planners and share a centralized usability lab (staffed by thirty to thirty-five people) to test features and product prototypes. The Sales and Support Group has separate divisions for worldwide OEM sales (primarily to AST, DEC, Dell, Compaq, Fujitsu, Gateway, IBM, NEC, Olivetti, Packard Bell, Toshiba, Unisys, and

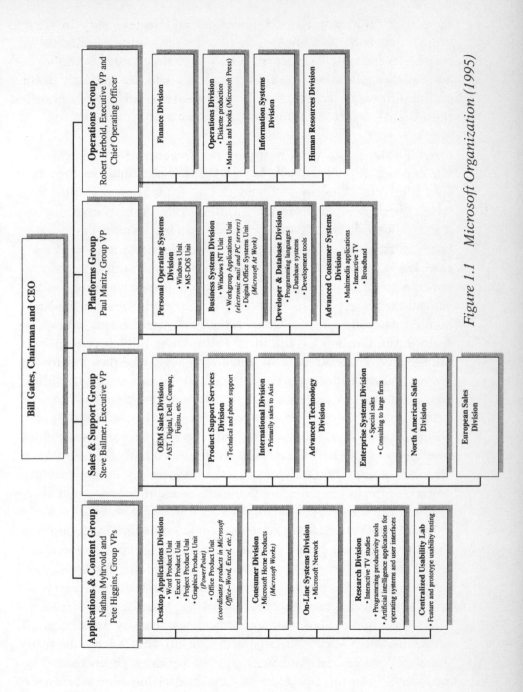

Figure 1.1 Microsoft Organization (1995)

47

Zenith), product support services (abbreviated as PSS), international operations (mainly Asia), advanced technology sales, strategic enterprise systems (special sales and consulting to large firms), North American sales, and European sales. The Operations Group includes finance, diskette production, manuals and book publishing (Microsoft Press), information systems, and human resource management.

Within the Platforms Group, the personal operating systems division produces Windows and MS-DOS. The business systems division produces Windows NT and Object Linking and Embedding (OLE), with a separate product unit for workgroup applications (electronic mail and PC server systems). The developer and database systems division builds programming languages such as Visual Basic, programming support tools, and database products such as Access and FoxPro. The advanced consumer systems division contains groups for interactive TV systems and broadband communications and multimedia technologies. Within the Applications and Content Group, the desktop applications division contains the Office product unit. This supervises the Word and Excel product units and works closely with the Graphics product unit (PowerPoint) to make sure that these three products function together properly in the Office applications suite. The division also builds Project, a popular project-management tool. The consumer division includes the "Microsoft Home" product groups, which build the Money home-finance product as well as multimedia applications for home entertainment and education, and a combination word processor, spreadsheet and database product for novices called Works. The on-line systems division develops and manages the new Microsoft Network. Research explores new product and programming technologies, and works closely with various product groups. (See Appendixes 2 and 3 for descriptions of Microsoft's main applications products and operating systems.)

The example of the desktop applications division in Figure 1.2 illustrates how Microsoft organizes the product units and functional specialties. Divisions contain more than one product unit. Each product unit generally has five functional teams run by a separate manager: program management, development, testing,

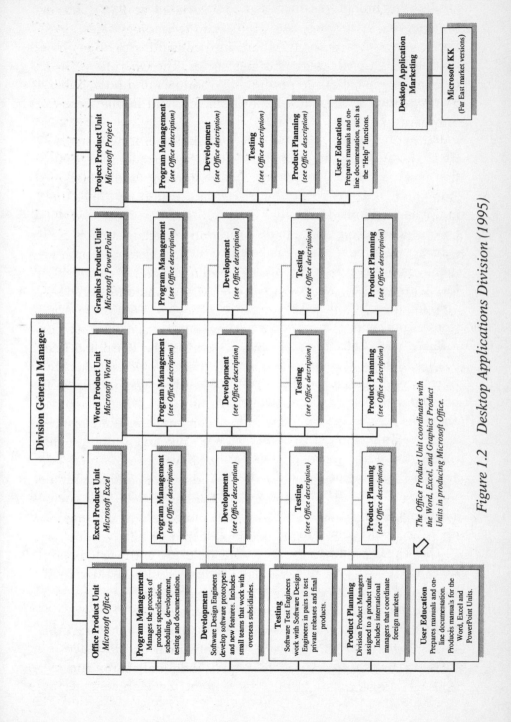

Division General Manager

Office Product Unit
Microsoft Office

Program Management
Manages the process of product specification, scheduling, development, testing and documentation.

Development
Software Design Engineers develop software prototypes and new features. Includes small teams that work with overseas subsidiaries.

Testing
Software Test Engineers work with Software Design Engineers in pairs to test private releases and final products.

Product Planning
Division Product Managers assigned to a product unit. Includes international managers that coordinate foreign markets.

User Education
Prepares manuals and on-line documentation. Produces manuals for the Word, Excel and PowerPoint Units.

⇨ *The Office Product Unit coordinates with the Word, Excel, and Graphics Product Units in producing Microsoft Office.*

Excel Product Unit
Microsoft Excel

Program Management
(see Office description)

Development
(see Office description)

Testing
(see Office description)

Product Planning
(see Office description)

Word Product Unit
Microsoft Word

Program Management
(see Office description)

Development
(see Office description)

Testing
(see Office description)

Product Planning
(see Office description)

Graphics Product Unit
Microsoft PowerPoint

Program Management
(see Office description)

Development
(see Office description)

Testing
(see Office description)

Product Planning
(see Office description)

Project Product Unit
Microsoft Project

Program Management
(see Office description)

Development
(see Office description)

Testing
(see Office description)

Product Planning
(see Office description)

User Education
Prepares manuals and on-line documentation, such as the "Help" functions.

Desktop Application Marketing

Microsoft KK
(Far East market versions)

Figure 1.2   Desktop Applications Division (1995)

product planning (product managers assigned to the product groups), and user education. Microsoft breaks down these teams into areas related to the products they build. For example, before the formation of the Office product unit, developers in the Excel unit had five small teams: recalc/functions, charting, printing/formatting, add-ins (special software programs, often imported from outside, such as for statistical analysis or spell-checking), and macros/conversions. Some product units combine their teams for user education, which prepare manuals and on-line documentation (such as "Help" functions). In the desktop applications division, the Office product unit's user education team prepares manuals for Word, Excel, and PowerPoint. Also, the development groups generally include small teams that work with overseas subsidiaries to prepare non-English product versions, and product management groups have international managers that coordinate foreign marketing. Microsoft K.K., a Japanese subsidiary that creates Japanese, Chinese, and Korean versions of desktop applications, reports directly to the division manager.

Table 1.2 breaks down Microsoft's seventeen thousand employees by functions. About thirty percent (5,100) work overseas in thirty-six foreign subsidiaries responsible for sales, product support, and some adaptation work into local languages. (Overseas accounts for nearly 70 percent of Microsoft's retail sales. See Table 2 in the Introduction.) Of the 13,300 employees in the United States, there are approximately 1,850 software developers, 1,850 software test engineers, and 400 program managers and product planners. Some 2,100 people work in customer support; 4,000 in sales, marketing, and consulting; 600 in user education; 2,200 in operations and administration; and 300 in research.

The bigger product units such as Office, Windows NT, and Windows each have between three and four hundred people, and several other product units have two hundred or more people. Groups building operating systems tend to have more developers and testers than applications groups; the latter need more people in product planning and program management, since their features are more directly visible and marketed to non-technical customers. Overall, these numbers represent enormous increases over the past decade. Groups such as Excel, Word, and MS-

Table 1.2   Approximate Breakdown of Microsoft Employees (1995)

Number	Area or Function
400	Program managers and product planners
1,850	Software design engineers
1,850	Software test engineers
2,100	Customer support engineers
4,000	Marketing, sales, and consulting services
600	User education
2,200	Operations and administration
300	Research
4,500	Overseas personnel (various functions, including 400 developers)
17,800	Total

Source: E-mail from Dave Moore, Director of Development, 7/18/95.

DOS/Windows had ten or fewer developers in the early 1980s and only a few dozen total employees. Other divisions have seen similar increases. The product support services staff has grown from a couple of dozen people in the early 1980s to a couple of thousand today, and it has become an invaluable source of feedback to the product development groups (see Chapter 6). Microsoft's highly effective sales and marketing force has also grown from a handful of people a decade ago to approximately three thousand. This number includes hundreds of consultants that help corporations install databases and network systems.

Sales and marketing (including advertising) are Microsoft's largest expenses, equal to about 30 percent of 1994 revenues. Operating costs (including product support) consumed about 15 percent of 1994 revenues, research and development (treated as a current expense) 13 percent, and general administrative costs 3 percent. This left Microsoft with about 37 percent of its revenues as profits before taxes (see Table 1, p.3). Rapid rises in R&D, sales and marketing, and product support expenses, however, have prompted Gates, Maples, and other senior managers to seek ways to reduce these costs—such as through more systematic engineering practices, better coordination among the product groups, and improved product quality and ease of use (to cut down on the need for customer support). Rising interdependencies among the product groups—as well as the growth in product size and complexity, and the need to always maintain compatibility with previous versions of a product—remain difficult problems to manage. At times, these problems have tarnished Microsoft's efforts to deliver reliable products on a more predictable schedule. As we discuss later, delays in shipping Office 4.0 and Windows 95 are typical of the difficulties Microsoft has been struggling to overcome.

Old Rivalries—Systems Versus Applications: The most significant aspect of the 1992 change in the top management structure is that it formally unified responsibility for the systems and applications divisions (as in the days when projects reported directly to Gates). This move placed both divisions under Mike Maples. It was important to bring these two divisions closer together because of their long-standing rivalries and growing strategic interdependence. Understanding in depth how Windows products work is essential to writing good applications; influencing the evolution of Windows and technologies such as OLE is equally important to writing good applications; and new systems products like Windows NT will never take hold in the marketplace if applications builders—led by Microsoft—do not write applications. The problem is that, historically, Microsoft's systems and applications divisions have never gotten along very well. Systems people (especially the group that has built Windows 3.1 and Windows 95) have also tended to be less organized and less systematic than their counterparts in applications, even though systems products are usually more difficult to build and test.

Maples succeeded in getting the applications groups to become more systematic and quality oriented, and he tried to do the same with the systems groups while these were under his direction until 1995. Managers such as Dave Cutler (who joined Microsoft from DEC) had similar values, but Maples did not succeed completely.

He acknowledged to us that his focus on customer problems and process was more suitable for applications than for systems software for two basic reasons. First, operating systems have to run on many different kinds of unique hardware. To test the various kinds of hardware requires "very long, extensive large-volume betas" (tests of preliminary product versions at customer sites) so that users can try many different combinations of machine and application configurations. Progress for this kind of testing is difficult to predict. Second, Maples observed that operating systems projects are generally much larger in terms of people, and they have components that interact with many different products. These make project management much more cumbersome: "One of the things that can make apps efficient is that they can have a small team, communicate well, and have fewer dependencies. Systems has lots more dependencies, bigger teams. It is a different process. I would say, not as a value judgment but as just kind of a fact, that the apps guys are more process driven . . . than the systems guys."

As a result, there is usually what some people have described as a greater level of chaos in the systems division, including the high-profile Windows 95 project. Windows NT is somewhat of an exception, as Maples noted: "In systems, we have very different processes. Dave Cutler in the NT group is very, very regimented. They have a workbook and write everything down. . . . a very strict, strong type of process, whereas in Windows and DOS it's much more of a gunslinger process. You know, 'Let's kind of start coding and see how it works out.'" But Maples believed that all the systems groups needed to show more concern with controlling defects and improving accuracy in predicting when they would finish.

Various managers with experience on both sides of the fence confirmed this view of systems as more problematic than applications, although this distinction is changing slowly. Chris Peters, who worked as a developer on MS-DOS 2.0 and Windows 1.0 (as well as on various versions of Excel and Word) before becoming vice president of Office, emphasized the lack of control in specifications and project management: "Systems, you'll find, is far less organized than the apps group. . . . I don't think they have proper specs. . . . They'll say, yes, we use milestones, but you'll say, 'How many milestones total in the project?' and they won't be able to tell you." Richard Barth, a senior product manager for Windows NT, agreed: "When I first came in 1990 there really was a pretty vast gulf between applications and systems in the way they were managed. In fact, from the systems side, we often looked at the applications side and thought of them as much better managed, that the development process was much more under control there."

One of the reasons for the different culture in the systems division has been the management style of Steve Ballmer. For years, he preferred a relatively unstructured environment, with no separate testing function and lots of freedom for program managers and developers to innovate and make changes in the product late in the development cycle. Dave Maritz, formerly head of testing for MS-DOS and Windows (and now retired from Microsoft), had this to say about Ballmer, his former boss: "He's very sharp, but it's very hard to work under Steve because he was so random. . . . He's not a structured type of guy. That's why he was moved out of controlling systems." Mike Conte, senior program manager in the Office group, suggested another reason for the different culture in systems:

I think that one of the shifts they're still making is away from an OEM-focus perspective to an end-user-focus perspective. . . . It's partly history and culture. Steve Ballmer was very much the leader of that division. He's not somebody who is structured or bureaucratic, and it just didn't evolve over there. Also, it's because they tend to be more technical. The developers tend to have more of a say. *And developers, without structure, are reasonably irrational: Left to their own devices, they will do things which may not make sense for marketing reasons or supportability or anything else.* So they haven't yet got straightened out. The applications division used to be kind of Wild West, too. Then Mike Maples had a real positive effect on rationalizing a lot of things. They haven't yet had that effect. This is an apps guy's perspective, so you've got to take it with a grain of salt. But he [Ballmer] can still rattle people's cages all over the company if he wants to. So he still has an effect over systems, and he has Bill's ear. . . . And Mike is . . . a very long-game player. He's not the type of guy to go up there and say, "Okay, scorch the earth. We're going to do it my way." He's much more subtle than that. I think his plan is to gradually change things over there.

Various Microsoft people echoed these sentiments and added to the picture of how systems differed from applications. There is even a geographical explanation: The applications groups are located in the more modern northern part of the Microsoft campus, with a road separating "the big fancy brown buildings and the southern suburbs down here," as Dave Maritz described the setting. (Despite the relatively greater affluence of the applications division, however, Gates maintains his office with the systems people.) The different technical natures of the products play a major role as well, but this too is changing as user interfaces and features become more important in operating systems. Chris Williams, the director of product development, expected systems people to come around slowly as they gain more experience:

> People in systems still feel that "we will sell no wine before its time," and so their approach to developing software is completely different. . . . I think you have to have lived through three or four project cycles, to have gone through the pain of a badly managed process several times. . . . And if you think about the people who are working in systems, their cycles are . . . twice as long as they are in apps. The guys who are coming off NT are the guys who are coming to me now going, "I cannot take this one more time!" And of the guys who are in Chicago [Windows 95], I'm convinced there will be a certain percentage who will come to me when that thing ships and go, "I cannot take this." . . . That's a fundamental difference. I also think the difference is that the people who are in charge of those projects are people who have succeeded. Windows 3.1 was arguably a fairly successful project, and these are people who have succeeded at creating software in the old-fashioned way. And it is not broken, as far as they're concerned, so why are you trying to fix it?

New Markets and Technologies: Microsoft does not only make operating systems and applications programs, even though these areas generate most of the company's current revenues and profits. The fastest-growing markets are new consumer products and on-line systems. These divisions have yet another culture, more concerned with mixing "leading-edge" science and technology with everyday consumer habits. Group vice president Nathan Myhrvold, who has been head of advanced technologies in Microsoft, described his three charters in a recent interview: (1) Help Bill Gates set technology strategy for the company, such as making decisions on what technologies to license, buy, or develop; (2) create products for the future; and (3) conduct research, focusing on areas of computer science that support Microsoft's product groups and Gates's vision for extending the personal computer.

In a broader sense, Myhrvold saw his role as preparing Microsoft for "paradigm shifts," such as that which seems to be occurring in digital information:

> A classic problem is that companies have one product that they do really well with, but they never move beyond that. What's distinguished Microsoft is that we're not afraid of making paradigm shifts, largely because our senior management is very technical. We understand the technology, which at the end of the day is really what drives the industry. You have to be very smart in business, but no amount of smarts will protect you from a technological revolution. It can overthrow you in a minute.[13]

The advanced consumer systems division, now part of the Platforms Group, has been particularly important. In cooperation with the research, broadband applications, and on-line systems areas, the advanced consumer systems division develops and markets multimedia products for the home and the information highway; these include interactive TV and the Microsoft Network. It also works on futuristic products. The division has a similar functional structure to other product units (i.e., people have assignments in program management, development, testing, and product planning). Job responsibilities are less distinct among the functions, however, to promote innovation and exploration of new ideas.[14]

Rick Rashid, a former Carnegie-Mellon professor of computer science, runs research, including interactive TV studies. His group has about two hundred and fifty scientists and an annual budget of at least $150 million. Its work targets new technologies five to ten years from commercialization but also includes projects with shorter-term potential. Researchers are studying programming productivity tools; applications of artificial intelligence to operating systems and user interfaces; computer-based decision making;

speech processing and understanding; supercomputer design; video-on-demand server technology; and different approaches to mixing video, audio, and text to create interactive TV, multimedia products, and pocket information systems (such as a "wallet PC"). Rashid explained that Gates feels Microsoft is now big enough to afford to have a research group and fund it lavishly. Gates and others also believe that Microsoft must generate more of its own technologies:

> Basically, Bill wants to see an organization that pushes specific areas of research. . . . We want those groups to be world-class and to be as good as or better—preferably better—than any of their competitors in their particular research arenas. Bill views this as a long-term commitment. It's something that Microsoft is able to do because it has reached a certain point in time and a certain size. It's also increasingly important because the company has to be able to develop its own ideas and its own technology to really prosper in the future. Besides, it never hurts having smart people around.

The research division has already contributed significantly to the new on-line service, new operating systems such as Windows 95 and Windows NT, and new user interfaces that provide "intelligent" assistance and make Windows easier to use for novice consumers. Myhrvold and Rashid are both confident that Microsoft will eventually produce whole new generations of technologies and products. They hope their research division will also outdo previous central labs at leading companies. Xerox's Palo Alto Research Center (PARC), for example, pioneered but did not successfully commercialize the personal computer and graphical user interface. IBM also has had difficulty commercializing computer technologies its researchers invented, such as reduced instruction-set computing (RISC).

Rashid explained why they are so confident: "The problem with Xerox PARC was not a problem with PARC. It wasn't that they were doing anything wrong; they were doing just exactly the right things. The problem was that they were working in a copier company. . . . And I think that's really the lesson that you get from all these things, that the research has impact in the areas that it's performed if the company is operating in those areas. Then it can take advantage of that research." Myhrvold added that unlike in these other companies, Microsoft ties its research directly to the heart of the company—to the CEO and to strategy: "Another problem with older labs is that they suffer from the ivory tower syndrome; they're completely separated from everyone else. I report directly to Bill Gates. Bill's very involved with our group's strategy, [and] I'm involved with the strategy we do elsewhere in the company."[15] (Gates has been reported to spend as much as a third of his time working with Myhrvold on futuristic product ideas.[16])

PRINCIPLE   *Hire the smartest managers you can find—people with a deep understanding of the technology and the business.*

The senior Microsoft managers we have already talked about (Bill Gates, Mike Maples, Steve Ballmer, Nathan Myhrvold, Paul Maritz, Pete Higgins, Chris Peters, Rick Rashid, and others) may have their weaknesses, but they are clearly very able in ways important to Microsoft. In fact, Gates and other managers frequently boast that they hire only smart people—managers, as well as developers, testers, and others. But what does being "smart" mean? To Bill Gates, this means being able to understand and probe complex things quickly and creatively, as he explained in a 1994 interview: "There's a certain sharpness, an ability to absorb new facts. To walk into a situation, have something explained to you and immediately say, 'Well, what about this?' To ask an insightful question. To absorb it in real time. A capability to remember. To relate to domains that may not seem connected at first. A certain creativity that allows people to be effective."[17] Gates himself exhibits these qualities and looks for them in potential Microsoft managers and employees.

As Microsoft has grown, Gates has personally interviewed hundreds of programmers, managers, and technical experts who complement and challenge his own skills and knowledge. From this group, he has cultivated a relatively small corps of senior people that serves as an informal brain trust to assist him in making decisions and overseeing critical projects or initiatives. Gates, though, has a tendency to promote programming experts into senior management at very young ages. Combined with very rapid growth, this has left Microsoft short of managers in the middle ranks who understand not merely the technology and the business but also the human side of management.

The Brain Trust: The core of Microsoft's brain trust consists of around a dozen people. They run the key product areas and new initiatives as well as constitute an informal oversight group to critique what everybody else is doing. There are also senior technical people working in the projects who are part of a broader network; although many of these people are Microsoft veterans from the founding years, a growing number have come from competitors or are experts in new technical domains that go far beyond the PC. Dave Moore, who does not consider himself a member of the inner circle ("I'm more modest than that"), described it as a group of people not listed anywhere but widely recognized for their exceptional knowledge and experience: "It's fairly informal. The one thing I would say that makes you part of the brain trust is your ladder level. Every developer has a ladder rating. . . . Each of the functional disciplines—development, testing, program management, user ed—they each are on their own ladder levels."

People associated with the Microsoft brain trust include the company's most senior executives as well as top developers and program managers.[18] Among the executive staff, there is executive vice president Steve Ballmer (age thirty-nine), a classmate of Gates at Harvard who studied management at Stanford for a year before joining Microsoft in 1980. He may not be the right person to manage the systems divisions today, but he goes where the challenges are—successfully taking over Windows development when this project was mired in delays during the mid-1980s, and recently taking over sales and customer support as these areas have become more critical. There is group vice president Nathan Myhrvold (age thirty-six), a Princeton University Ph.D. in physics who studied with Nobel Prize winner Stephen Hawking and joined Microsoft in 1986 when Gates acquired Myhrvold's software company. Myhrvold has been leading the way into corporate networks, multimedia, telecommunications, and on-line services.

Group vice president Pete Higgins (age thirty-seven) came to Microsoft in 1983 after obtaining a Stanford MBA. He formerly headed the desktop applications division and now, with Myhrvold, manages the new Applications and Content Group. Group vice president Paul Maritz (age forty), a Microsoft veteran since 1986, specializes in long-term product strategy and oversees the development of Microsoft's operating systems as well as other key consumer technologies. We should add to this group newcomer Robert Herbold (age fifty-three), a Ph.D. in computer science from Case-Western Reserve University who worked in Procter & Gamble for twenty-six years, most recently as a senior vice president in charge of management systems, market research and advertising, and technology acquisitions. He joined Microsoft in 1994 and brings a deep expertise in consumer marketing, important to Gates because consumer products are Microsoft's fastest growing area.

Several other senior executives fall into the brain trust category. Senior vice president Brad Silverberg (age forty-one), manager of the personal operating systems division, came to Microsoft in 1990 from Borland, and headed the Windows 3.1 and Windows 95 projects. Roger Heinen (age forty-three), senior vice president in charge of the developer and database systems division, entered Microsoft in 1993 after heading Macintosh software development at Apple and working at Digital Equipment Corporation before that. James Allchin (age forty-three), vice president and head of the business systems division, leads the Cairo (Windows NT 4.0) project. He came to Microsoft in 1991 from Banyan Systems. Senior vice president Craig Mundie (age forty-six), responsible for advanced consumer systems, joined Microsoft in 1992 after managing a super-computer company, Alliant Computer Systems. Jonathan Lazarus (age forty-four), vice president of strategic relations, is a marketing specialist who joined Microsoft in 1986. Vice president Chris Peters (age thirty-six) heads the Office product unit, which has generated nearly half of Microsoft's sales and profits.

Vice president Rick Rashid (age forty-three), head of research, joined Microsoft in 1991 after being a well-known professor of computer science at Carnegie-Mellon University. Rashid is the chief architect of Mach, a UNIX-based operating system that served as one of the models for Windows NT. Darryl Rubin (age forty-one), vice president for software strategy, is an expert in network technologies and a Microsoft employee since 1986. Although his influence has diminished as new people have come on board, another member of this select group has been Charles Simonyi (age forty-eight), a Stanford Ph.D. in computer science who designed graphical applications for Xerox PARC, including the famous Bravo word processor. He left Xerox for Microsoft in 1981, and for much of the next decade directed Microsoft's entry into applications, beginning with Multiplan, Word, and Excel.

Some members of this group are clearly on a faster track than others. Silverberg had this to say about one youthful colleague: "Chris Peters is the guy who understands the development process the best, who has had the most success, who has the development process most people in the company want to emulate. He's the guy we think we can learn the most from." Like other top managers in Microsoft, Peters has a solid technical background, but he also has broader than usual experiences in the company, having worked in systems, applications, and general management. He has both bachelor's and master's degrees in electrical engineering from the University of Washington, where he specialized in software engineering. After coming to Microsoft in 1981, he worked as a programmer on MS-DOS 2.0, the Microsoft Mouse 1.0, PC Word 1.0, and Windows 1.0. For five years, he was the development manager for Excel. After the successful shipment of Excel 3.0 just eleven days late (as a result of using the new development process), Peters became general manager of the Word product unit—a business that generated several hundred millions dollars in revenues for Microsoft. In 1993 Peters received the title of vice president when he took charge of the new Office product unit, now the key to Microsoft's applications strategy for desktop PCs.

Another essential member of the brain trust has been Mike Maples (age fifty-three), who served as executive vice president between 1988 and 1995. He is now an advisor to the company on such matters as mergers and recruiting. Maples is important because he gently but steadily nudged Microsoft further down the path of greater structure and less chaos in product development. He was not a developer, but he had the background to be one, with a college degree in electrical engineering from the University of Oklahoma as well as an MBA. He also seemed to know how to manage creative technical people who do not like a lot of managers above them. Maples left IBM because of the potential he saw in Microsoft as well as his disappointment with IBM. Within Microsoft, he tried to help Bill Gates avoid the pitfalls of large, bureaucratic organizations by emphasizing four general precepts that worked well in IBM. Maples recalled that the first was to introduce in Microsoft a full set of personnel management practices, covering hiring, training, compensation, and career paths:

> One of several things that IBM did really well, and that I think we continually improve on, is personnel management and management practices— the whole idea of having a level of consistency in terms of the way you measure, monitor, and reward people. Nobody likes to be "formula-ized" into a review system or a management system or an increase system. But . . . what ends up happening is [people] playing favorites and trying to keep everything in their heads. We were a size where that was starting to break down; it had probably started to break down a lot worse than we had even recognized at the time. So [we started] the whole idea of moving people between groups, and of having some guidelines and a philosophy of how people progress in pay and a definition of levels. Dave [Moore] has spent a lot of time working on what it means to be a D10 developer and an 11, and what it takes to get promoted, and how . . . we ingrain that in everybody's mindset so that when we move people across projects there are not huge disparities in pay, in expectations, or whatever.

A second precept, which remains a Microsoft weakness, was to nurture middle managers: "The other thing we spent more time on was management development—retreats, managers' meetings. A lot of time they're a waste of time, but everybody gets together and talks, and you have that opportunity to talk about common problems." A third was to continue cultivating functional expertise, such as in development and testing, but to make sure people move around and receive broad experiences. Maples wanted to avoid the narrow mindsets and departmental rivalries and turf battles that have plagued IBM and many other large organizations:

> The other thing that has happened is that people are much broader now,

and it's not the developers against the testers. Anytime you have a functional organization you always have these boundaries, and there gets to be quite a lot of animosity. In fact, it gets to be so bad that some people can never cross them; they have to change jobs or leave. I think we have a lot less of "the testers are bums and the developers are good," or "the developers are bums and the marketing guys are good." Each team is much more cohesive. We still do have a system that is slightly biased toward developers in terms of levels and pay, and prestige. You walk a little taller if you're a Microsoft developer than if you are anything else in Microsoft. And I guess that's the way it ought to be; that's our culture. We're a technically driven company, and most of the senior people in Microsoft are technically grown people.

Maples in particular tried to avoid the type of culture that prevailed at IBM, where there were many internal conflicts, and groups would hide "bad news" from management or the quality assurance people. Bill Gates does not like to hear bad news either, and some Microsoft managers have been reluctant to admit errors or slips in schedules, but Gates can be even nastier in meetings when he discovers problems that no one told him about. Maples liked frequent, frank communications aimed at constructive mutual criticism and learning how to do things better. Despite his more confrontational style, Gates has similar values: He wants openness, especially if there are serious problems in a product under development. He wants people to think about what is good for Microsoft, and not just for their own project or their own careers. And neither Gates nor Maples liked to see people repeat the same mistakes. Maples compared the atmosphere in IBM to what he has seen in Microsoft:

[At IBM] there were quality assurance people, not nearly as many people as we have here, and it was much more of an audit function. The development organization did some testing, and then there were the quality assurance guys, who were always telling them that they're screwed up. We don't have the kind of adversarial roles that IBM had. IBM had a conflict management system on purpose: If you let people represent their specific interest, then you'll get all the facts on the table and make better decisions. To some extent, that's certainly a valid management idea. We don't do that; we try to get better consensus and have people think broadly what's good for the whole. When I was in development at IBM, you just learned how to hide stuff from them. . . . And you'd go to the very last minute before you'd bring bad news. . . . You'd end up with some really bad tragedies. Things just go against you, or you don't have the experience to bear the risk right. And then all of a sudden the project that everybody thought was going great just totally bombs. We're much more "all cards up," very flat communication. I'll get an e-mail from one of the Word developers that'll say this thing is going screwy down here or whatever, and that's not thought of as being anti-Microsoft to communicate.

Maples's fourth precept was that a software company should define a *process* for product development: "If you're in IBM, you realize there is value and there are problems with process. The idea of having a process is important. The idea of having one that works for the particular organization or the particular unit is important." Maples recalled that, following the 1989 retreat, he and other senior people decided "each team could define their own process, as long as they know what it is and they follow it." He wanted to see evidence of a repeatable development process, but would not try to define standards for all of Microsoft to follow. Key people in each of the business units then went off and tried to write down how they could best develop and test software. Over about a year and a half, a consensus started to emerge: "People still feel they have some degree of freedom in terms of how they run their projects. But I'd say that there are really a couple of basic ways that we do things, and these have permeated throughout the organization—a few basic principles, and that's pretty much what has driven it." Maples listed his common principles; as with Gates's list, we include them in our later discussions:

1. Let people do their own schedules.
2. Build in buffer time for the unforeseen delays that always occur.
3. Assume change will happen, so don't waste time trying to write a complete specification up front.
4. Manage by milestones, starting with the most difficult things first.
5. Focus on customer problems, not technologies or processes.
6. Move people around, to mix the good and the bad.

Technically Competent Managers: Gates and other early executives in the company have made a special effort to populate Microsoft with technically competent managers, especially but not exclusively in the development organization. Rick Rashid, when still a neutral observer and accustomed to dealing with bright computer science students at Carnegie-Mellon University, recalled being struck by the senior people he met: "One of the things that I was very impressed with when I first visited Microsoft was the level of expertise and competence that you find basically all the way through the management hierarchy. It's just not that common in the computer industry to find strongly technical people in key management positions throughout the company." Dave Thompson, who had bachelor's and master's degrees from Cornell University and worked in DEC and Concord Communications for thirteen years before joining Microsoft in 1990 to head the Window NT network design group, echoed this sentiment: "I believe that one of the strengths of Microsoft is the fact that its managers are very technical, even at the most senior levels. . . . I believe that managers should be as technical as possible. Leads—that is, first-level line managers—absolutely should write code, should be able to fix problems in the stuff that their people develop."

It is common practice for managers in all the functions to continue doing their functional jobs after becoming senior managers. Even development managers of large groups such as Word and Windows NT still spend one-third to one-half of their time writing code. The rationale is that managers need to remain directly involved in the technology in order to make the right decisions and solve problems that occur in their groups. Lou Perazzoli, software engineering manager on the Windows NT 3.0 project, spends about half his time coding. He makes managers under him do the same:

I have these rules in my group that I try to follow. Number one is everybody who works for me actually has code responsibilities, so nobody just manages people. . . . I find that people who manage people lose sight of what the goal is and they don't appreciate the problems and issues . . . and they don't act on them quickly enough. Yet when you have code that you are doing, you tend to act on issues in a much more timely fashion, and you tend to be more concerned about how things are going. . . . I probably spend 50 percent of my time looking at problems and writing code.

Managers in the applications area, such as Chris Peters (speaking when he was the general manager of the Word unit), have similar values:

> At Microsoft . . . the functional managers still spend a great deal of their time doing whatever they do. In other words, the development manager of a group of 60 developers will still spend a fair amount of his time programming. . . . In larger organizations . . . they keep pushing down the level where people are actually doing the work. Pretty soon you get a development manager who decides that he's way too important to program, and pretty soon the feature team leads all decide that they're way too important to program. Pretty soon, the programmers are way too busy to program. . . . I have 270-some people working for me, and I'm the first layer in the organization that actually doesn't have to do any work, although I did write one feature in the new version.

Weaknesses in Middle Management: One consequence of promoting successful technical people into the management ranks, and encouraging them to continue working in their technical areas, is that managers may not spend enough time being or becoming good managers of other people. A common disdain for formal training and promotion systems, and for staffs and written procedures—all of which can support the management process—has not helped the situation in Microsoft. The key problem, in Dave Maritz's view, is Microsoft's habit of choosing managers for their technical ability, not for their managerial ability:

> Management at this firm sucks. . . . I had promotions when I didn't know I had a promotion; I suddenly saw a salary increase, and it happened. There have been times when I haven't even had a review because my manager has been scared of me. There is a problem at Microsoft at the middle management level. . . . Salary increments and bonuses and the one-on-one process is lacking, in my opinion. The managers are picked because of their technical ability, because they've all worked up through the ranks after being hired in as developers. And the best developers become the [top] managers.

Maritz agreed with others in the company that technical managers need to have superb technical skills, otherwise Microsoft people will not respect them. But he also argued that managers need to be more than just excellent programmers—they should exhibit qualities of leadership and charisma, which Maritz said he encountered too infrequently among Microsoft's middle management corps:

> To be a manager or a leader—in essence, a manager *is* a leader—you have to have one of two essential things; if you've got both, then you are just set for life. One is you have to be technically as competent if not better than your peers or the people you're going to manage. Two [is] charisma, and generally the managers at Microsoft are not the charisma types. I regard myself as a charisma type, not a technical type; I am unusual at Microsoft in that respect. At the first line level of management, you'll see a lot of non-charisma types. . . . those that bump up to the second level will be the ones that have both the charisma and the technical abilities. . . . and so it goes, higher and higher up the levels. When you get to about the third and fourth line up, you generally have people who can manage people well, in addition to managing the technical concepts well.

Maples admitted that he learned about this problem shortly after he joined the company, and he maintained that he (with Dave Moore and others) worked hard to improve the situation. But Microsoft grew so quickly that Gates and Maples had to put very young people in positions of great responsibility, and Microsoft's senior executives continue to promote people with technical backgrounds and successful records in technical achievement. Richard Barth acknowledged that finding suitable middle managers is "the biggest challenge" in the company:

> No question that we do not have a good set of middle managers. The Chris Peters of the organization *are* great managers, and that's another one of Mike's agendas—to create more managers. . . . But our biggest challenge is finding the appropriate set of middle managers. . . . They don't just happen. . . . One of the things we have discovered over the last couple of years is that you've got to value and cultivate management skills. . . . The culture of Microsoft has been if you yell loud and push hard, you were a manager. And again, just in the last year, I've seen that

change. . . . In the past, if you were somebody who could really get things done, you were a manager. That's no longer enough.

PRINCIPLE   *Hire the smartest employees you can find—people with a deep understanding of the technology and the business.*

As we discuss in the next chapter, to find people with good technical abilities and a desire to make money using those abilities to build and sell software, Microsoft has instituted a hiring process that rigorously screens candidates. In particular, recruiters look for people who fit into each functional specialty and who can work together well in small teams. Managers generally try to find young people who can adapt to Microsoft ways. They also look for people with the ability to act and learn on their own as well as make good decisions quickly, without a lot of formal training and written rules or guidelines. But there are both positives and negatives to bringing together so many bright and independent-minded people.

The Benefits of Smart People: Below the product groups and functional managers, Microsoft has approximately 5,000 software developers and test engineers. In a field where the best software programmers may write ten to twenty times more code in the same time as the least productive members of the same team, attracting talented people is a great advantage. It means that the apparent resources available to managers with a high percentage of talented people are far greater than simply the number of bodies they command. (We can think of a contrast to many companies building software systems in the United States, Europe, and Japan, who do not screen software developers so rigorously. Many companies also hire people of various backgrounds and minimal experience with computers, then train them in-house to write software. It is difficult for these people to perform well and be "smart" in a complex technology when they have such limited experience and training.[19])

In fact, every Microsoft manager that we talked to about this subject emphasized the value of having a highly selective pool of people. Mike Maples noted that "the quality of the people is an unmeasurable benefit. Not everybody has the luxury we have of getting MIT's best and Stanford's best." Rick Rashid agreed: "There are more good smart software developers here than I've seen any-place else in the world, concentrated in one place." So did Dave Thompson: "The . . . big difference between us and other compa-nies is the people that we hire. Our whole system is predicated on the fact that our people are very fast and smart. . . . It makes you feel like you have a much larger set of resources to work with. You feel like you have flexibility when you have people that can fix things in hours instead of days." As Bill Gates boasted:

> We benefit from having the smartest people actually get involved not just in the design and ideas but actually the code itself. They know the code extremely well, and large areas of the code. It's good to have one person who can think through any kind of design change, particularly when you're late in the process and you're trying to be very careful. They can review anything that goes on. They've got a very strong model in their head for what . . . side effects that change might have. . . . We have the benefit that people don't like to have bad developers around. It's just enough of a drag on them that they'll find a way to convince people it's a bad match to be in here if you're not a really top-notch developer.

In addition to providing an abundance of sheer technical skills, smart people can make even a large company seem relatively non-bureaucratic and flexible—more like a small company. Chris Peters held this view, emphasizing the value of people who can work and solve problems on their own: "This is not a company where there's a bunch of stupid people running around, and then some manager writes down a bunch of stuff in order to control stupid people. It's a company where there's a lot of smart people running around all trying to do the right thing. . . . I've seen stupid companies where they just hire bodies and attempt to make up for their hiring of lots of bodies by putting in lots of rules. I guess it may partly fix the problem, but the root cause of the problem was not lack of rules. It was hiring people that needed lots of rules to do their job."

Given the type of people that Microsoft screens for, it is not sur-prising that the company culture emphasizes technical compe-tence and shipping products rather than adhering to rules and regulations, respecting formal titles, or cultivating skills in political infighting. Dave Moore commented on this: "Titles aren't important in the company. What's always been important is shipping products—how many products have you shipped?" Brad Silverberg added that authority and responsibility tend to move toward those people who demonstrate the most competence: "Another key point about Microsoft development is that the balance of power within each group is more a reflection of the individuals and the strengths and capabilities of those individuals than any cookie-cutter approach. . . . We're flexible. If I hired a development manager who was a super, super great product guy, who knew how to make features, balance of power can go over there. I'm certainly not religious about it. I just adapt to the strengths of the people I have."

If a conflict emerges between individuals or groups, such as over which components to share, Gates often steps in as the final arbiter. John Fine, formerly a director of program management and currently group program manager for Excel, offered this view of Microsoft's culture and the role of Bill Gates:

> Things get done around here in many ways, from the most informal ear whisperings to the most formal orders. . . . Rules don't count. . . . Politics does not reign supreme here. So it is certainly not unthinkable for, say, the business unit manager of one piece of software to talk to the business unit manager of another piece and say, "You know, maybe our software should be inside of your software," or something like that. That is not a political gaffe; it's just another tactic in order to get the job done of benefiting the industry the most, therefore making the most money. But because those decisions are very costly in opportunity and have such a huge potential for negative effects if they're wrong, of course, they'll end up with Bill. In that way, the traditional management tree is used.

The Negatives of Smart People: The negative side of hiring people who do not want or need rules to work is that these people often have to learn by painful trial and error. It was our impression, for example, that Microsoft developers and testers (with some exceptions) were not so well read in the software-engineering literature and often reinvented the wheel, belatedly discovering good practices for software development other companies had recognized as important years ago. (These include doing more careful design reviews and code inspections as well as paying more attention to architecture and designs, sharing components, and having better quantitative metrics and historical data for project management.)

It is also difficult for senior managers—including Bill Gates—to tell these "smart" people what to do. They do not always like to cooperate and compromise, or share what they create and learn. As we discuss in Chapter 6, Microsoft has made some progress on this dimension, but there is much more that the company can do. Mike Maples gave one example of the problems he saw when he first joined Microsoft:

> There weren't many people who had experience in project management; things were just done loosely. The Microsoft people and the Microsoft culture was such that you had very smart people. They don't want to be told what to do, but they're willing to be allowed to discover what to do—and so you figure out the approach to let people discover what's a better way. "You've got to have this process, and this is the way you're going to do it," and so forth, would never work. But facilitating people sitting down and talking about it and working it out [does]. . . . That's a reasonable, good modern management style, if you've got capable people. You don't want too much of an authoritarian management. . . . I think we have a unique process that works better here than it would in most [companies]. . . . But it is tailored to the fact that we have very, very smart people who are very, very motivated.

As Microsoft has grown, it has introduced a number of policies to prevent groups from having to continually reinvent solutions to the same problems, but these generally remain as guidelines or principles rather than rigid rules. Brad Silverberg commented on this transition within the company: "Back in the early days you didn't really need rules, but the practices have adapted to fit the new needs. But I think the culture is very strong, firmly entrenched—decentralization, keeping things as flexible as possible but not too flexible. There are some rigid points, but each group adapts to the rules a little differently. . . . Dave Moore or Mike Maples doesn't come to me and say, 'You are going to run your development organization this way.' It wouldn't work." In the next chapter we discuss how Microsoft defines job categories, as well as how it organizes and cultivates creative technical specialists.

2

Managing Creative People and Technical Skills

Organize Small Teams of Overlapping Functional Specialists

To manage creative people and technical skills, Microsoft follows a strategy that we describe as *organize small teams of overlapping functional specialists*. We break down our discussion of this strategy into four principles:

- Establish functional specialties, but work in small teams and overlap responsibilities.
- Let functional experts define and hire for their technical specialties.
- Educate new hires through learning by doing and mentoring.
- Create career paths and "ladder levels" to retain and reward technical people.

Establishing functional specialties or career paths and separate promotion ladders for technical people are not unusual policies, though they are especially useful for companies where technology

73

is central to their business. Microsoft, however, seems to be unusual in the degree to which it *empowers* people in these specialties to define their jobs, hire new people, and train new hires. It also appears to us that Microsoft has relatively little formal orientation and education for a company with so many employees and products. This is both a strength (job categories are flexible, and people are independent minded) and a weakness (people have to learn by trial and error, "reinventing the wheel" in many cases).

Why these principles exist also has much to do with Microsoft's particular history and culture. In its early years, Microsoft consisted primarily of software developers who created and tested new products; made all the hiring, marketing, and contract decisions; and answered telephone calls from customers. As its products and lines of business grew in number and sophistication, the company added thousands of people. The risk and cost of designing the wrong products or delivering them late and with serious errors persuaded Microsoft managers to identify and institutionalize key functional disciplines. To avoid overcompartmentalization of these functions, however, technical specialists have overlapping responsibilities and work in small multifunctional teams.

Program management and software development, as well as testing, are the main technical specialties within the product units. In particular, Microsoft looks for budding "superprogrammers" with no dislike of the commercial aspects of the PC software business. They may not be the most innovative programmers in the industry, or be especially knowledgeable about other company practices in software engineering. But they are highly creative in generating new features and products that people buy, and these skills translate into huge revenues and profits for the company. As a result, Microsoft's programmers appear to rank among the most productive and cost-efficient in the industry.[1]

Within the product units, program managers, developers, and testers work side by side in small "feature teams." These typically consist of one program manager (who generally works on more than one feature) and three to eight developers (one of whom acts as a team leader or "lead"). There is also a parallel feature testing team whose members are paired with the developers (see Figure 2.1). User education specialists work as part of the product teams,

Figure 2.1   Microsoft Project and Feature Team Organization

Note: **Bold** type indicates project leaders.

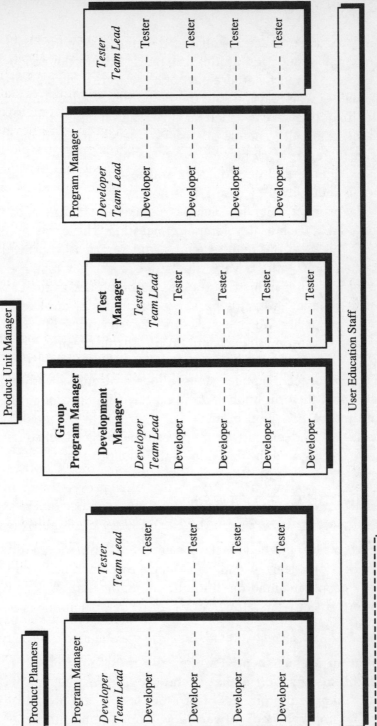

and product managers staff the division marketing departments and small groups for product planning within the product units. Customer support staff are part of a separate division, but product specialists work closely with the individual product units. Some of the functional areas (such as program management) have remained difficult to define precisely. Others (such as program management and development, program management and product management, and development and testing) cannot be separated too distinctly, and Microsoft does not try.

The product units have senior managers in charge of each functional area, such as development or testing. These functional managers work on the feature teams and report to the head of the product unit, who is very much like a project manager as described in other industries such as automobiles. In the case of the Office product unit, this person coordinates several related projects—primarily Word, Excel, and PowerPoint.[2] Microsoft managers delegate many decisions to the feature teams. Nonetheless, the product unit manager and the senior functional managers make major technical decisions, allocate resources within the constraints of the unit budget, and resolve conflicts among the different groups. They also meet as a group with senior product managers and executives to determine project schedules, milestone targets, and the decision to ship the product.

PRINCIPLE   *Establish functional specialties, but work in small teams and overlap responsibilities.*

Microsoft has created tracks for each basic functional area, but it makes people learn broadly and share responsibilities, and it organizes people in small multifunctional teams that work as part of a larger project team. How it does so in each discipline is described below.

Program Management: Perhaps the most difficult job to define and fill in Microsoft is that of the program manager. This person must manage the process of product specification, and serve as a crucial link between software development and marketing (product management). A company orientation presentation written by a program manager named Bruce Ryan described himself and his colleagues as "technical undergrads who drive fast cars and live in their offices." He also cautioned that "the program manager is a leader, facilitator, and coordinator, but is *not* the boss." Ryan goes on to list the key areas of responsibility for program managers, as follows:

- the product's vision
- the written product specification
- the product schedule
- the product development process
- all implementation trade-offs
- coordination of the product development groups[3]

The origins of the program manager function in Microsoft date back to the mid-1980s. At that time, it had become clear to senior managers that they had to wrest some control over product development from "superprogrammers." It was also apparent that managing the design process differed from developing software. Jeff Raikes, now a senior vice president responsible for marketing who moved from Apple to Microsoft in 1981, recalled in a 1990 case study the difficulties that superprogrammers created in Microsoft: "There are a lot of problems with relying on individual superstars: (1) they are in very short supply; (2) someone has to maintain and update the software they've written (which often doesn't interest them) and often other people have difficulty understanding their code; (3) sometimes they don't understand what the market wants; and finally if you try to put several of them on the same project you get real problems with design decision—'too many cooks spoil the broth.'"[4]

Jabe Blumenthal, who joined Microsoft in 1982 to work under Raikes, helped developers define the vision for the Multiplan spreadsheets and get it to market. In so doing, he served as a role model for what became the job of the program manager: "In early 1984, we began to work on a spreadsheet for the Mac. I got involved and became a sort of service organization for the development group. I helped document the specifications, do the manual reviews, and decide what bug fixes were important and what could be postponed to a later release. While I didn't make the design decisions, I made sure that they got made. The process worked out really well, so they decided to call it something and institutionalize it."[5]

Bill Gates supported the decision to formalize the program management function, even though it represented a significant change in how he liked to work. In the early years, he often rewrote nearly every line of code in every product that Microsoft shipped, as well as oversaw product marketing. As discussed in Chapter 1, though, by the mid-1980s it had become impossible for Gates to oversee everything. He agreed to create formal job categories, such as product managers to handle marketing issues and then program managers to work in between marketing and development. But Gates did not want program management to become too distinct from development or marketing. He wanted program managers to work side by side with developers in small teams as Jabe Blumenthal had done, both sharing and distinguishing their roles. Without this overlapping and close cooperation, Gates believed, separating the functions would have failed:

> We didn't have program management, and developers didn't like making up those big documents and sitting in long marketing meetings. And so there ended up being a new skills set, which is a very leveraged skill set, that is able to capture all that stuff. . . . Other people do have program management now, a little bit differently than we do, but I think the whole industry's found that's an important approach. . . . Program management and development every day are working together. . . . That's the closest relationship in the whole thing—closer than development to testing, closer than marketing to anybody. You could put program management and development under one common manager. In fact, sometimes, if you get the right personalities, we get groups and we do that. But if your program management and development aren't working well together, then forget it. Basically, you're not going to get anywhere.

Today, in the initial stages of a new project, program managers work closely with product planners to make sure that each new product has a distinctive "vision." Together they write up a vision statement that incorporates inputs from developers, customer support, and other sources, including senior managers such as Gates. Program managers then write up a product specification, which begins in outline form and describes the different features in the product. This document evolves as program managers and developers discuss the details of feature ideas and build prototypes. Each program manager generally oversees the development of more than one feature, and thus works as part of more than one feature team.

In many companies, it is common to have separate groups of software designers (sometimes called systems analysts or requirements engineers) who write down a functional design for other people (usually called programmers, implementers, or coders) to build. The designers then usually start on a new product, limiting their involvement in projects to just this first phase. Microsoft people insisted to us many times that program managers are not designers in this sense. In contrast, Microsoft program managers remain involved throughout a project, because their specifications evolve along with the product. Program managers may spend a lot of time in the beginning of a project to define features common to multiple products, resolve product architectural issues, and sketch out user interfaces (screens or menus that users see on the computer), and they frequently come up with ideas for new features. But they do all these things with the help of developers, who also generate many feature ideas (especially in the systems division).

What program managers do, then, is write down the specification rather than create the design. They also work with the feature teams and help manage the project. Chris Peters, vice president of Office, summed it up: "The program manager is responsible for writing down the specification. He's not responsible for all ideas. It's important that it get written down, that one person run that." Gates agreed with this description, emphasizing that developers are really in control of the ultimate design:

> We can argue about who comes up with the good features, because in some groups it's development, in some groups it's program management. But . . . there's no "design," in the sense of how that code works, that's ever done in program management. And development is still . . . in the strong position, let's face it. If they have an idea, they get to write the code; they can say this one's super easy, and everything else is super hard. So to the degree that development wants to do design, we love to

have them do design. And there are some groups like in Windows or NT or in the C compiler—most of systems, basically—where development is doing the design and program management is documenting it. . . . Then, when you get over to applications, it is far more balanced in terms of who's doing the design. The healthiest application, because it's always set a model for so many things, is Excel. There, probably 60 percent of the ideas come from program management, but 40 percent come from development. Take a guy like Jon De Vaan or some of those feature leads. Those guys area really proud of their features. It's not even easy to say on any particular feature, 'Okay, program management put in the idea for it, development said okay we can do this, then they showed it to program management," That's got to be super interactive. Believe that development feels like they own those features and that they care incredibly about those features.

Managing the process of specifying and designing the product means that program managers oversee critical activities throughout the project, but have little formal authority over the different groups on whom they must rely to get things done. In addition to the vision statement and specification, for example, program managers take charge of making trade-off decisions, such as which features to include and which to exclude. They often rely on a Microsoft technique called *activity-based planning* (see Chapter 4) to understand what customers really want to do with a product and determine whether a particular feature accomplishes those tasks efficiently. Also, as part of the design and decision-making process regarding features, program managers build prototypes and oversee the testing of preliminary versions of features or interfaces with novice users in Microsoft's usability lab (see Chapters 5 and 6).

Program managers are responsible for preparing a preliminary development schedule, based again on inputs from development, testing, product management, and user education. They keep track of progress on the schedule and make sure that developers test features in the usability lab and document them for external users as well as for internal maintenance and testing. They negotiate project milestones with other members of the team, and they work with testing and development managers to determine when coding of features within a milestone is complete, as well as when a product is ready to ship. Program managers also take the lead in coordinating with other groups through formal meetings, daily e-mail messages, and meetings in the hallways or over lunch. This coordination work, which has gained importance in recent years, includes standardizing interfaces among different products or pieces of code that must work together and synchronizing schedules among different groups that share features and code or are trying to ship their products together. (This occurs in the case of Excel, Word, PowerPoint, Access, and Mail—as well as OLE and Visual Basic for Applications—within the Office suite of programs.)

In their role as leaders and facilitators (rather than bosses), program managers try to make sure that communication occurs across the functional areas and throughout the development cycle. Developers, product managers, testers, and customer support engineers, as well as senior executives—beginning with Bill Gates— all have inputs into decisions about a new product: which features to keep, or when to move on to the next milestone or to ship. Once people agree on the goals, then, to quote from Microsoft's documents, "program management's responsibility is to deliver."[6] John Fine, formerly director of program management and now with the Excel group, described the key jobs of program managers:

> If program managers didn't exist at Microsoft, I'll tell you what would be different to me, and it's two things. First, program managers make sure the features that get shipped in the product are features that users will actually open their wallets for. . . . It's extremely easy to create a piece of software which is wonderful in all respects except that the features it has happen not to be features any large group of consumers are interested in. . . . So you could call causing that to happen "design management," maybe, depending on the definition of *design*.
>
> The second thing they do is make sure the product . . . actually hits the market at the optimal time with the optimal content. And it is traditionally well known that it's very easy for products to slip [or] . . . also to ship with too little stability or too much stability. . . . Information about the content of the product is not communicated perfectly between the different team members that are building the software and the documentation, and testing the software. The larger the project . . . [and] the larger the product, the lower the percentage goes. The implication, if that problem

isn't solved, is a product will come out [with] internal inconsistencies. The documentation will say something different than the actual functionality of the product. . . . The functionality of the product will be inconsistent between two different features. . . . The solution is that the program manager . . . has to somehow cause communication to occur.

The close connection of program managers to the market, as well as to developers, also creates problems. While they usually help impose more discipline over the development process, program managers sometimes have trouble making the trade-off decisions. One standard quip in Microsoft is that if developers are struggling between two different approaches to implementing a feature, the program manager is likely to suggest they do both. Program managers also tend to create overly long lists of features, which then become the focus of fierce debates as product managers, developers, and executives try to narrow down the options. As Gates noted, developers continue to have a special influence over this selection process, since they must evaluate the technical feasibility of implementing the features. Nor do all program managers have expertise in software design, yet they contribute to decisions that affect the high-level structure (or lack of structure) in Microsoft products, especially applications. Program managers in some groups also tend to become very technical and more concerned with the views of developers than of average users. This occurs most often with operating systems and language products. As Mike Conte, senior program manager for Office, observed: "In a lot of groups . . . it has evolved too much into being a very different, very technical ivory-tower position that doesn't have a lot in common with marketing. That's not a good thing for program management or for the product."

Development: We quoted Mike Maples in Chapter 1 as saying that developers—officially called "software design engineers"—walk a little taller than anybody else in Microsoft. In our visits, we observed this to be the case. Program managers generally focus on the vision for the overall product and what types of features make up this vision. Developers, in contrast, define the vision and create the details of individual product features. Steven Sinofsky, group program manager for Office, described succinctly what developers do: "They write the code, they implement the features, they know the code base. Their job is to ship products by writing code."

We noted earlier that Microsoft developers generally do not receive detailed specifications from program managers and then simply write code. Handing off detailed specs is a style of development once common in large-scale software producers like IBM. Charles Simonyi also tried to introduce this approach to Microsoft in the early 1980s.[7] It did not take root; developers usually evolve specs with program managers, then create the details of their own features. Nevertheless, a small number of senior developers and program managers on each project do take charge of the product architecture, and developer leads (first-line managers) provide guidance to their teams. Developers also share responsibilities with testers to make sure the features work. Microsoft literature described the broad and overlapping responsibilities of developers as follows:[8]

- determine the vision for new features
- design the features
- allocate project resources
- build the features
- test the features
- prepare the product for shipping

Suggestions for features come from developers, program managers, and other sources. Developers, however, need to clarify what each feature accomplishes and help program managers decide which features to include or cut from a new product. Developers thus need to evaluate each feature and how people might use it. Designing features consists mainly of figuring out what algorithms (computer instructions) might implement the desired tasks. This also involves considering the compatibility of a feature with other features and product versions, and whether it is possible to borrow code from other Microsoft products (an increasingly important concern).

Allocating project resources requires developers to estimate how long they think it will take to code each feature. Individual developers make these estimates in consultation with team leads and their development manager, relying on their judgments as well as records from past projects. Another step is to work with the program managers to determine the actual feature set for the new product, based on available time, personnel resources, and market demands. The development manager then consults with developers and program managers to assign specific features to individual developers and feature teams.

Building features consists of coding and reviewing code with other developers as well as with program managers. Microsoft literature cautions developers to look out for problems such as taking up too much memory, or writing code that is dependent on particular hardware processors. Developers also receive instructions on "zero-defect programming"—the synch-and-stabilize process that relies on daily product builds, milestone stabilizations, and daily testing as well as debugging (see Chapters 4 and 5).

Testing code is the responsibility of developers and testers, who work together in pairs. Developers test their own features, running automated tests on their code very frequently (usually every day). Developers also provide what Microsoft calls "private releases" of their features to their tester "buddies," before checking in their work to the "official build." Private releases give testers a chance to find bugs and developers a chance to fix them prior to disseminating the code to other members of the project and other internal users. In addition, developers put their code through the usability lab to get additional feedback from ordinary customers on their features as they develop them.

The final task of the developer is to prepare the product for shipping. This requires the discipline to refrain from making any more major changes to the code (such as by adding features); developers must also get the bug count as close to zero as possible and keep it there for a set period of time.[9]

Testing code frequently with testers and the usability lab, as well as with beta versions at customer sites, is a critical part of the developers' job. This is because developers have a tendency to stray from customer concerns with the usefulness of features as well as with the size and speed of a program. (Microsoft products have not usually been well received on these dimensions, particularly in their first versions). Senior vice president Brad Silverberg, a computer science graduate from Brown University with a master's degree from the University of Toronto, had been a beta tester of Windows 3.0 while working at Borland. He joined Microsoft in 1990 to head the Windows/MS-DOS group. Silverberg noted that one of his missions in Microsoft as the executive responsible for the Windows 95 project has been to get his developers to think more about customers:

> I've been very active in trying to create this connection between the end user and the developer so that you get into his mind what the end users' needs are. . . . With the next version of Windows . . . the next major milestone is the size and performance milestone. The next three months are just going to be spent on taking what we have and making it smaller and faster. I don't think that performance and size are something that you can just add at the end and say, "OK, we've added all the functions, let's tune it." I think you need to, at every point, not get too far from what your end goal is, because you can't take an elephant and put it on a diet and get a mouse.

Testing: Software companies from the mainframe and minicomputer industries rely on developers to test their own code but also have separate groups of specially trained people who perform final tests on completed software products. In many PC software companies, however, testing has remained an ad hoc activity. It is primarily up to developers to test their own products, sometimes with help from outside contractors. Microsoft used to treat testing in this manner. Since the late 1980s, however, and after 1991 in particular, Dave Moore and other managers have actively tried to make software testing into an accepted professional discipline within the company, separate from but comparable to development.

They have not succeeded completely; developers still "walk taller." But Microsoft's training literature points out three reasons now accepted in the company why testing should exist as a separate discipline: (1) Developers do not produce perfect code, and program managers do not produce perfect specifications; (2) it is necessary to have someone detached from the spec and the code provide an unbiased perspective on their quality; and (3) it is much less expensive and easier for developers—as well as much better for product reliability and customer satisfaction—to find and fix bugs as early as possible in the development process, when pieces of code are less intertwined. To be most effective, Microsoft literature recommends that testers examine products from six perspectives:[10]

- *User perspective:* Replicate how ordinary customers will use a feature and determine if the feature should make sense to them.
- *International perspective:* Make sure that formats and languages are correct for different languages and national areas.
- *Hardware:* Evaluate if the product is compatible with different hardware platforms and equipment configurations—such as Compaq versus IBM versus Gateway machines, as well as Apple—or with particular printers and other peripherals.
- *Software:* Evaluate if the product is compatible with other software. For example, Word should be able to read and convert WordPerfect files, as well as provide special help to WordPerfect users by feature. Systems products like Windows and NT must also work with non-Microsoft applications.
- *Specification compliance:* Check if the product complies with the original product concept and specifications "as envisioned by program management."
- *Product stability:* Check for product stability on two levels. One consists of "measurable metrics" (the bug-find rate versus bug severity, and other measures that we will discuss later). The second is qualitative, defined as "the gut feel for 'are we ready'" to ship the product.

Microsoft began hiring testers—officially called "software test engineers"—in 1984, when the company first set up separate testing groups. The few testers prior to this time reported to development management and did not have their own functional structure or track levels. Not until 1986 did Microsoft set up a position as director of testing for applications and hire someone to fill it. But Dave Moore later took over the job in a part-time role, adding to his title as director of development. Microsoft did not appoint a full-time director of testing until Roger Sherman took on this job in 1993. (As we pointed out in Chapter 1, the functional directors do not in practice supervise managers of development, testing, and the other functions. They primarily identify good practices for their specialties, promote these in the company, and perform occasional audits of the product units. We discuss their role further in Chapter 6.)

Most of Microsoft's testers, and nearly all the developers, are located at the Redmond, Washington, headquarters. There are also two small foreign testing sites: Ireland handles Microsoft products written in specific European languages, and Japan (called "the Far East" in Microsoft documents) handles Japanese, Korean, and Chinese versions. Overall, Microsoft has approximately one tester for every developer; this means there are about 1,850 testers in the company (see Table 1.2) out of a total development staff of about 4,100 people (including program managers and product planners). (In contrast, Japanese and U.S. producers of large-scale software systems usually put no more than 10 to 15 percent of their project staff in testing, and usually far less.[11] Microsoft's numbers are comparable, however, to Lotus.[12]) Microsoft could probably reduce these numbers if program managers and developers spent more time doing architectural planning and detailed design work before developers started writing features, or by making developers review more of their own designs and code. Such steps, however, would reduce the amount of flexibility that Microsoft projects currently have to let their features or components evolve incrementally. A large number of testers is also a type of insurance: They are relatively inexpensive compared to the cost of recalling and replacing products because of major bugs.

Microsoft thus assigns testers to work side by side with developers and in parallel feature teams from the early stages of a project. At the same time, testers report to test leads, who manage a group of testers working on part of a product. The test leads report to the test manager of the product unit, and the test manager reports to the manager of the product business unit—*not* to the manager of development.

Preparing for a new testing effort requires several activities. One is a general review of the previous project's postmortem report, as well as reports from other testing groups. These reports provide ideas on what types of problems to look for and how to find them. Microsoft managers also encourage testers to talk with product support personnel and customers, and to review media evaluations to determine what industry critics like and dislike. After this preliminary work, testers start devising special tools or code routines to help them test. Another activity is research: studying competitors' products as well as new features to see what Microsoft should be doing. The next step is to develop a testing strategy by identifying high-risk areas (including dependencies on other groups) that might delay an on-time simultaneous shipment of the U.S. and foreign versions of the product. Microsoft's training materials use Excel as a case study for how to conduct good testing preparations, including using test plans or "scripts"—lists of commands or functions to exercise in the testing process—for each feature. Other testers and managers can review them for completeness. Testers also develop automated "test suites" for themselves and developers. These sets of tests are faster and more complete than manual tests, and they eliminate the tedium of running the same series of commands or functions over and over. Finally, testers spend time doing what Microsoft groups variously call "unstructured testing," "scenario testing," "ad hoc testing," "gorilla testing," and "free-form Fridays." Here they go beyond the planned test scripts and use products in different ways in order to cause features to fail, if possible.

Testers have a major responsibility to test the private releases of the developers. Their efforts here provide quick feedback on bugs during the development process, both in terms of errors or problems in the design from a user's perspective, as well as coding lapses or mistakes. (According to Jeanne Sheldon, test manager for Word, about 80 percent of Microsoft's in-process errors simply consist of "missing lines of code.") Testers report bugs found in the private releases to the developers by e-mail. Only after this process of private release testing is complete do testers issue a public test release to other people. Testers also track bugs found in the test release and characterize them by feature area and severity. Meanwhile, developers create a testing release document (TRD), which identifies features that are done and ready to test; it also points out particular areas of concern or details of the code to help the testers focus their efforts.

Other Specialties: Microsoft has three more well-defined functions that also overlap with the other specialties. *Product managers* are marketing specialists; some work in product planning as part of the product units, although since late 1993 Microsoft has centralized most of them in division marketing groups. *Customer support engineers* provide technical assistance to users and analyze customer feedback; they work in the product support services (PSS) division, which reports to Steve Ballmer. *User education staff* prepare manuals and help documentation; they work in the product units as part of the product teams.

Product planners in the product units work intimately with program managers to define new ideas for products or product features and to write up the marketing specification (that is, the vision statement). In addition to outlining features, this document covers issues such as product packaging, pricing, and positioning in the marketplace relative to other products, and it requires an analysis of competitors and market trends. (Product managers in the division marketing departments also do some of this analysis.) Apart from these activities, product managers identify new product areas, provide some ideas for new products and features, and eventually prepare for the marketing and sale of new products by a separate sales force. Microsoft training literature, which described product managers as "MBAs" and "snappy dressers [who] . . . own their own homes," listed five key areas of responsibility:[13]

- oversee a "business"
- recognize and pursue market opportunities
- aggressively represent the customer in the product development process
- take responsibility for the trade-off between functionality and ship date
- take responsibility for the marketing and sales process

Customer support engineers answer customer questions, primarily on telephones but also via the mail and electronic means. They conduct extensive analyses of data on Microsoft customers and competitors. They also provide invaluable input to the product development and testing groups by highlighting problems to look for and helping the product groups set priorities. By answering customer questions, the PSS division provides assistance that most customers now consider an essential part of the product they are buying. Worldwide, Microsoft receives at least twenty thousand phone calls per day, in addition to hundreds of thousands of daily electronic inquiries (such as on an automated *FastTips* service). For dealing with customers, Microsoft literature described the key responsibilities of the customer support engineers:[14]

- handle customer calls by questioning customers to understand the problem and identify solutions
- research the problem and share all possible solutions with the customer
- code the call for the support database
- submit a bug report or documentation error report, if the problem is not a user error
- summarize the problem in an article for the Knowledge Base tool, if it is a user error

PSS prepares a widely read weekly report, called *Off-line Plus*, which details problem reports and helps set the agenda for testing, bug fixing, and next-version product development. In addition, people from this specialty work closely with program managers, developers, and testers, as well as the usability lab and user education staff. They provide input from the perspective of user support on new products and features while they are being developed. (See Chapter 6 for a fuller discussion of the role of PSS.)

In addition to writing up manuals and other documentation, user education groups work with marketing to provide input on product packaging and labeling, as well as product internationalization. They have followed the lead of the other specialties and formalized many of their procedures, and even characterize their processes in terms borrowed from software development. They refer to their "product development cycle" and "build," as well as quality assurance procedures that include "testing" the documentation as it is developed and fixing "bugs" in the materials. User education groups also hire a variety of specialists, such as professional writers, graphic designers, technical editors, copy editors, documentation assistants, indexers, and a production team that manages the printing process.[15]

PRINCIPLE   *Let functional experts define and hire for their technical specialties.*

In the 1980s, Microsoft created functional specialties (such as program management and testing) that did not have traditions of their own within the company and did not map directly to university curriculums. Accordingly, it seemed logical to managers to allow the initial members of these and other technical specialties (such as software development, customer support, and user education) to define their job characteristics, as well as take charge of hiring thousands of new people. Microsoft has continued this practice ever since.

The Recruiting and Screening Process: The average age in Microsoft is about thirty, although most people are considerably younger, especially programmers in the applications groups. Half of all employees come directly from college, and most Microsoft managers seem to prefer it this way. They especially want young people they can more easily socialize into "the Microsoft way."[16]

Microsoft has tried to retain a personal approach in hiring, as in the early days of the company, when Bill Gates, Paul Allen, Charles Simonyi, or another very senior technical person would interview every candidate. Microsoft recruits program managers, software developers, test engineers, product mangers, customer support engineers, and user education staff in a similar manner, following the practices established initially for hiring developers. Microsoft sends out recruiters to forty or fifty U.S. universities every year; they go to the best schools but also look carefully at local colleges and universities (particularly for customer support engineers and testers), as well as at schools in foreign countries. Recruiters from a centralized human resources department organize the visits, handle paperwork, and participate in initial interviews run by experienced employees from the technical functions and product groups. Promising candidates then come back to Microsoft headquarters for additional interviews. Recruiters, therefore, do not hire; they *manage* the hiring process, which reached huge proportions during the late 1980s and early 1990s (see Table 1 in the Introduction). Dave Thompson, a development manager in the

Windows NT group, described their role and Microsoft's approach to hiring developers:

> In the campus case, there's an extra level of interview, because somebody goes out and does a prescreening. After that, the process is basically the same for full-time experienced and non[experienced], with finer points of variation. They'll talk to probably four to six interviewers during the day, and then the end of the day is the person who makes the hiring decision—the "as appropriate," as they're called here. The interview process is very dynamic. The recruiters are one of the key elements of the process; they help manage the process. They make it as painless and effortless for development managers as possible. In a small company, I used to invest tons of time in hiring people. The only time I invest now is the time that only I could apply—the evaluation of feedback, the interviewing of the candidate, and making a decision. . . .
>
> When you try to grow fast, you've got to have an efficient process to interview people. . . . The good [recruiters] have an uncanny sense for some of the important characteristics. . . . They know what kind of person is more likely to make a good Microsoft person. Any company that has HR people do the hiring is doomed.

The Microsoft headquarters interviews are entirely with people from the functional areas in the product groups: Developers do all the interviews for developers, testers all the interviews for testers, and so on. The discussions aim at determining how smart a person is in an abstract sense—not simply how much people know about coding or testing, or a particular specialty like marketing. (Gates has been quoted as looking for four essential qualities in new hires: ambition, IQ, technical expertise, and business judgment, with IQ most important.[17]) Famous general questions from Microsoft interviews include being asked to estimate the volume of water flowing down the Mississippi River and the number of gas stations in the United States; the answer does not matter as much as the approach a person takes to analyze the problem.

Relatively few recruits make it through the screenings. Of the developers interviewed at their universities, Microsoft typically asks only 10 to 15 percent back for additional interviews, and then hires only 10 to 15 percent of the final group. In total, Microsoft hires between 2 and 3 percent of the people it interviews. Rick

Rashid, Microsoft's vice president for research, lauded the screening process: "It's a lot like going through oral exams. The interview process here is pretty stringent. I'm not sure that it screens for any given personality type, but it certainly screens for raw skill and talent, and ability to think on your feet."

Once hired, a new person encounters a continual series of confrontations and challenges. These may come from Gates himself at the annual newcomers' party, or even in one of Microsoft's cavernous corridors. (Each of the company's roughly two dozen multistory buildings has X-form wings and various angles to maximize the number of individual offices with windows and views of the picturesque landscaping and nearby mountains and forests. As a result, only smart people can successfully find their way through the hallways.) And only people willing to work long hours—fourteen-hour days and working weekends are common—survive. Furthermore, like the Japanese, Microsoft people take short vacations, if at all. Dave Moore described a typical day: "The Microsoft way: Wake up, go to work, do some work. 'Oh, I'm hungry.' Go down and eat some breakfast. Do some work. 'Oh, I'm hungry.' Eat some lunch. Work until you drop. Drive home. Sleep."

To test the resolve of employees further, Microsoft pays relatively low salaries. Gates used to balk at paying high wages and even refused, initially, to compensate secretaries and other people for overtime. He eventually settled on a policy of no overtime compensation but started giving annual bonuses, and then stock options, beginning in 1982. Total compensation in the 1990s has been generous because Microsoft's stock price continues to rise. Compensation now includes a biannual bonus of up to 15 percent, stock options, and payroll deductions for stock purchases. (An employee can exercise 25 percent of the stock options after working for Microsoft for only eighteen months, and another 12.5 percent every six months thereafter, anytime within ten years, with new options granted every two years. Employees can also put up to 10 percent of their salaries into stock purchases at 85 percent of market value.[18])

Burnout and Turnover: There is, of course, a negative side to how Microsoft manages people. One result of the rigorous schedule is burnout. People work such long hours for such a long time, and often on one particular product, that they grow weary and leave. Richard Barth attributed some of this to Microsoft's "conscious policy to hire about half the number of people we think we need. That cultivates this ownership process. It minimizes bureaucracy. . . . On the other hand, we tend to select people who would burn themselves out anyway. . . . We hire [Type] A people, because they like working their asses off." Dave Maritz, the former MS-DOS/Windows test manager, complained about the paucity of managers skilled enough to keep people from overworking and "peaking" too early on a project. Burnout particularly affects developers, who often grossly underestimate how long it takes to build their code. It also affects testers, who have to work with developers in pairs and often spend whole nights testing their code. Maritz himself was a burnout victim and retired soon after shipping MS-DOS 6.0 in 1993:

> For example, with the testing of making the compression data for DOS 6.0, it was all done at night. We'd tell people to leave the offices at five, and we'd go in and make an image of their disks, back up their files, and then run the compressor. When they came in the morning, a developer in the Windows group, or in the Win Word [Word for Windows] group, or Excel group, would have his disks compressed. Or they had actually been debugged and the image dumped back if we couldn't do it—all at night. It was constant night activity. And every weekend. If you do that too soon, people don't want to work here. . . .
>
> What I'm saying is, you never get laid back at Microsoft. You always have this tension: Am I doing enough, and have I done everything? And it's stressful. I know that I'm not going to die at Microsoft. Another year or two years, and I'm out of here. I don't want to see software again in my life! I've had it with this place. I will . . . sit in a canoe, fish, and catch salmon for the rest of my life.

Dave Moore estimated that as many as 10 percent of new hires leave each year, and that this rate continues during an employee's first five years in the company. After five years of experience, however, he claims that almost no one leaves permanently. (Some people take leaves of absence to rest and do other things for a year or so; Doug Klunder, for example, once picked lettuce in California.)

Moore further asserts that this turnover rate has held steady since the late 1980s, and that turnover in development groups is only about 3 percent annually. He maintains that most of the turnover company-wide comes from product support as well as from manufacturing, where the work is very routine and they hire a lot of high school kids "to stuff boxes twenty-four hours a day." Microsoft does encourage people to leave if they do not perform up to standards; various sources reported that the company in 1993 and 1994 let go the bottom 5 percent of its work force, based on managers' perceptions of who was productive and who was not. (Moore insisted, however, that these broad cuts did not apply to developers.)

The type of people who emerge from this rigorous process of recruiting, screening, and burnout are talented, ambitious, and willing to work long hours for long-term financial benefits. They are, in short, very much like Bill Gates and other senior people who helped found the company. As Jim Conner, a program manager for Office, observed:

> That's one of the things I respect about Microsoft. They're outstanding at hiring workaholics. . . . I think a lot of that has to do with our interview process. And they're really, really good at motivating people. My own perception, speaking to some degree about myself, I suppose, is that we're really good at finding people who are trying to hit that final home run. . . . And man, they give you a lot of at bats here. So they're very happy to load you up to death. And people accept that challenge. So one person is not enough, but somehow the work almost always does get done. You get weird cases where people literally move into their offices. I used to have problems when I was a test manager; I would have to order people to go home because they were exhausted. They'd work for three or four days straight. . . . They were just compulsive about it. And I think that's how Microsoft makes the strategy work.

Program Managers: Program managers have the broadest and most ill-defined set of responsibilities. They have to work most closely with people from other functional specialties, particularly development and product management. There is no particular university degree that qualifies someone for a program manager's job; consequently, what to look for in new hires has always been frustrating, as Gates himself observed: "Program management is weird, because where do you recruit program managers? What's the background for a program manager?"

Experienced program managers know what *not* to look for. They do not seek people with coding or marketing backgrounds. Rather, they prefer people with an interest in how companies design products in general and software in particular. There is some overlapping with the pool of people who become product managers, and Microsoft actively encourages talented people who do not work out as program managers to try their hand at product management. But product management is a relatively easy specialty to recruit for, as Mike Conte commented: "It is harder to find program manager candidates. . . . There's very little official background that you can have for designing today's commercial applications, whereas there's an awful lot that you can learn in school about marketing these applications." John Fine described the qualities he looked for:

> Hiring the right kind of person is absolutely essential, and the magic of the right kind of person for a program manager is two things. One is someone who is completely passionate about producing their software baby. They just have to be one of those people who feels ownership painfully. You've got to have that because, when all else fails, someone who spends every waking moment worrying about everything about a product is always going to produce a better product than someone who feels they can let go of responsibility.
>
> The second thing you need is someone who can view the process of creating a product from start to finish kind of like a chessboard . . . [They] always know to walk around the problem from every side they can think of and make other people help them walk around the problem from other sides, rather than focusing on their ten favorite dimensions of the problem and not even thinking that there are other dimensions.

Microsoft has struggled to find program managers but looks mainly to universities, which supply about 80 percent of the new recruits. According to Christine Wittress, product manager for systems line marketing, another source is transfers from other Microsoft specializations, such as product management, testing, and development. Most new program managers have technical undergraduate degrees and some have master's degrees. A few have studied liberal arts in college, and occasionally there is an MBA, although this degree is far more common among product managers. The only program managers we observed with formal training related to their jobs worked in visual standardization of user interfaces for groups such as Office, research, and the consumer division. They often have degrees in psychology or industrial design—backgrounds important for exploring new types of interfaces that are simpler to use.

Whatever their formal education, all program manager candidates have to demonstrate an ability to understand basic technical issues, even if they are not skilled programmers. Conte estimated that in the applications area, "about half of all program managers could do a decent job writing an app[lication] in Visual Basic. . . . It's generally not as much a measure of technical aptitude whether someone is a developer or a program manager. There are program managers who have all the aptitude necessary to be a developer. But it's a preference of what problems they like to solve." In the systems area, program managers are clearly more technical, because they help design features that often consist of application programming interfaces that developers use when writing code.

Program managers thus tend to have backgrounds that combine a strong interest in design issues with some knowledge of or familiarity with computer programming. John Fine, for example, was an anthropology major at Reed College in Portland, Oregon. He had taken many computer science courses in college and got a job as a programmer in a small company building development tools for the C language. He joined Microsoft in 1986 as a program manager for programming tools. Then he became a program manager for Quick Basic and eventually for the highly successful Visual Basic product; he also served a term as director of program management. (This involved organizing and giving talks, training new program managers, helping out where needed, and thinking about which group to join next.)

Mike Conte combined an understanding of the technology with an interest in business, and followed a career path similar to Jabe Blumenthal. He had a bachelor's degree in information systems and management from the Stern School of Business at New York

University. He worked for a small applications company and then as a freelance consultant before joining Microsoft in 1989. Conte began in the Excel marketing group, servicing large corporate accounts. As an extension of this job, he created a position within the marketing group for new product planning, doing high-level design work for new versions of Excel. After two years, he switched his title to program manager. He also became one of the team leads on Excel 4.0, and then a senior program manager for Excel 5.0, before joining the new Office group in 1993.

Another senior program manager, Jim Conner from the Office group, has had more academic leanings. He obtained a Ph.D. in psychology from the University of California at San Diego, where he studied learning behavior and neurobiology. He spent time as a postdoctoral fellow at Berkeley and the University of Michigan. He left a research career at the University of Washington to start his own software consulting and development company in 1983. Conner joined Microsoft in 1989, first as a contract tester and then as a test manager for network systems products. Then he became a program manager in the Interoperability Design Group, working on interface standardization as well as the definition of common features in Word, Excel, PowerPoint, and other applications. This group became part of the Office product unit in 1993 (see Chapter 6).

Developers: It is much clearer to Microsoft people what kind of skills they want in a developer and how to identify those skills. Developers look for people who are expert programmers in C, a highly portable language, and conversant with the lower-level assembler language, which is useful to make programs run more quickly and use less memory. They also want people who can demonstrate general logical capabilities and work accurately under pressure. At Microsoft, developers seem to believe that someone who performs well in a hiring interview is more likely to write solid code under a tight deadline with millions of users waiting for the product (whose defects will surely get publicized in the computer press and may go on to national or international infamy). They want people who are not simply interested in programming for the sake of programming, but who seek personal challenges and enjoy shipping products into the marketplace—making money for themselves and the company. Microsoft managers also prefer to hire computer science graduates directly from college and then get them involved in Microsoft projects as quickly as possible.

Because developers play such an important role in this company, writing the lines of code that *are* Microsoft products, their recruiting process is particularly rigorous. It has consumed onerous amounts of time during the major hiring years; according to Mikes Maples, during the late 1980s and early 1990s, Microsoft developers spent about 15 percent of their time recruiting other developers. Management now tries to limit individual developers to no more than two one-hour interviews per week. Overall, the average candidate sees one developer in the university campus interview, at least three developers for interviews at Microsoft, and then has lunch with another developer or two. Thus a minimum of four to five developers see each finalist candidate. If a group is still undecided, it invites the candidate back for more interviews. If more than one group shows an interest, the candidate may return for yet another full day with the other group.

Microsoft also requires each interviewer to prepare a written evaluation of the candidates. Since many people (including senior managers) read these reports, the interviewers usually feel a strong peer pressure to do a thorough interview and write a detailed commentary on each new candidate. Dave Thompson discussed this as he explained how the NT group recruited developers:

> Developers are the only people qualified to interview developers. . . . We structure the interviews where at least one major component of the interviews is coding questions. . . . The interview process is pretty well structured. Everybody supplies feedback to everybody, so there's a lot of efficient exchange of information. The fact that your feedback is read by everybody kind of sets the style and the quality of the feedback, which drives the quality of the interview. If you get to the end of the interview and you write a piece of feedback that doesn't say anything, doesn't have any data in it, you're embarrassed, right? And embarrassment drives the world, right? So you make sure you do a good interview the next time.

Testers: Microsoft has had trouble finding software test engineers. It is clear that testers of applications need to understand how average people use software products; in contrast, testers of systems products need to understand how developers use features and how applications programs and peripherals such as printers interact with the operating system. Testers of both types of software also have to like to "break things." They have to want software products to fail, not work—the opposite job of program managers and developers. This is not necessarily a common set of skills and predilections.

Dave Moore stated it simply: "It's been tough for us to find people who want to be career testers." The dilemma begins with the fact that Microsoft will not hire people who really want to do programming and think they can start in testing to "get in the door." It is complicated by the fact that a knowledge of programming is useful and even essential for some testing, such as for operating systems and languages.

Marc Olson, test manager for Excel, has precisely the type of background and mentality Microsoft managers look for in testers. A native of Tacoma, Washington, who was born in 1965, Olson grew up with computers and took several courses on programming and other technical subjects as a physics major at the University of Puget Sound. After graduation, he worked at IBM for seven years in semiconductor materials development. After growing tired of being trapped in a junior research position because he did not have a graduate degree, he returned to the Washington area to look for a new job. Olson described how he came to join Microsoft in 1989: "I had an interview at my alma mater for software test engineers. They were interviewing, of all things, bachelors of science majors in physics. At that time it was difficult to find an entry level job with that degree. . . . So I jumped at the chance, did some research on what the company was all about, and what testing was all about. . . . [I learned] that you had people whose responsibility it was to break software at the high level and understand how things work and make sure they work correctly."

Olson quickly became one of the top applications testers in the company, although he still finds it difficult to specify precisely the qualities that make for a good tester. In the interviewing process, he looks for people who think differently from developers—people who do not take for granted that a feature works and search for non-obvious contexts in which a feature might fail, such as a "multifeature scenario" (testing one feature in combination with another):

> It's often harder to define what's going to make a good tester during the interview process than for a job where it's very clear-cut if you can code. Being able to test requires not only having the skill or the ability to learn new software and grasp what the idea is without any documentation, but also have the aptitude for it. So we look for people who are eternal skeptics. They don't take anything for granted. Just because the developers say this works, they don't say, "Oh, okay. Great." They try it. . . . They push that to the limit. . . . I have to be smarter in a different way than the developer about how the feature should work. . . . You have to be able to understand what a spreadsheet does and how a customer is going to want to use it, and map a million people's use of a spreadsheet onto six months of focused testing by one or two people. That's the real challenge of testing—capturing all those scenarios.

An undergraduate background in science, such as Olson has, is common among testers. So is his lack of experience in testing software for another company. Microsoft managers prefer to hire testers directly out of college, or at least people with no experience in testing. Inexperienced but smart people are more likely to learn Microsoft's style of testing quickly as well as be satisfied with Microsoft's low salaries and high job expectations.

Some testers did have experience before joining Microsoft. For example, Jeanne Sheldon, test manager in the Word group, majored in history and physical science at San Jose State and received a master's degree in the history of science at the University of Wisconsin. She worked in sales for a computer systems company and then spent five years in testing and quality assurance for a Microsoft rival, Software Publishing, Inc., which produces Harvard Graphics. Sheldon joined Microsoft in 1990 and rose quickly through the ranks.

Testers sometimes come from other functional groups within Microsoft. Olson estimated that about 15 percent of the fifty or so testers in the Excel group during 1993 came from customer support, and they brought a deep appreciation for problems that average users encounter. Moshe Dunie, who served as both the test manager and program director for Windows NT 3.0, had earlier been a program manager. Managers do not, however, encourage developers to switch to testing—particularly in the applications division, because programmers often make assumptions about how their code works that good testers should not accept. Olson emphasized this point: "We want people who want to be testers. We don't want people who want to be developers. Developers have a very structured approach to writing code, and they make assumptions and they write code based on those assumptions. We don't want anybody who wants to make assumptions and just live on that as enough. We want people who question the assumptions and come up with things that go beyond that."

In contrast, however, many testers in the systems groups have backgrounds similar to the developers. Furthermore, they occasionally move from testing to development, and vice versa (though this is rare for truly talented developers). This mixture of people makes sense, since users do not interact very directly with operating systems; rather, the key users of the features in operating systems are developers writing applications for those systems. It is the same with computer languages and software development tools. Dave Maritz, for example, had college degrees both in ecology (from a university in South Africa) and computer science (from Technion University in Israel). He also worked as a tank commander and as an assembler programmer for airborne control systems in the Israeli military before joining Microsoft in 1987 as the development manager for OS/2. Maritz worked as head of the graphics engine team before taking a job as the test manager for MS-DOS/Windows.

Moshe Dunie had development experience, though not with Microsoft; he studied electrical engineering at Technion University in Israel and worked in software development for military applications. He joined Microsoft in 1988 as a program manager for OS/2, then became the OS/2 test manager. Dunie hired some fifty testers before taking over as the test manager for Windows NT, for which he hired more testers. He generally tried to recruit developers as testers, although Dunie admitted having a hard time: "We had to do some selling because, in many people's minds, software testing . . . didn't fit with what a competent software engineer viewed as a challenging role. . . . [But] they went through an interview process that was the same interview process . . . [and] screening criteria that any developer hired into the OS/2 project had to go through." Dave Maritz also had difficulties hiring people as testers and convincing them to be satisfied with this career:

> People get very tired testing. . . . We haven't had a sufficient career path amongst the testers. And also we've had a very bad way of hiring, in my opinion. Dave Moore and various other guys will say differently, but we go out and we hire what we call STEs [software test engineers] from colleges. These are young guys who've gone out and made a conscious decision in life to take a CS [computer science] degree. They want to write code; we bring the guys in here, and they just run tests. This is the sort of guy that gets pissed off . . . [but] that is the only candidate that will pass our acceptance criterion. The acceptance criterion is you come in for an interview and you have to ask the guy a coding question. If I get a guy off the street—an excellent guy that I can put in a lab and work him for three months testing applications and learning connectivity and how Novell works—and ask him to insert an integer in a linked list of C integers, he doesn't know. He's never going to be hired here, because he can't pass the hiring questions.

To make up for the shortage of testers, as well as to handle periods when testing demands are at a peak (such as when a beta version of a product is just finished), Microsoft continues to hire part-time or contract testers. These people generally are not knowledgeable about programming, and they tend to work long hours for low pay. Some, like Jim Conner, know a lot about programming and become regular employees and managers.

Other Specialties: Microsoft does not require product managers to have coding expertise, although many have backgrounds in engineering, and some have studied computer science. Typically they are familiar with using computer software in a variety of settings. Increasingly they have advanced degrees in business (such as an MBA) and some formal knowledge of marketing techniques. Mike Conte, for example, had degrees in management and information systems, as well as experience in sales and consulting, before joining the Excel group as a product manager. Richard Barth had an undergraduate degree in electrical engineering from the U.S. Naval Academy, worked for ten years in Air Force R&D program management, and then completed a master's degree in management at MIT before joining the NT group as a product manager in 1990. Sanjay Parthasarathy, group product manager in the business development group within the advanced consumer technology division, had an undergraduate background in computer science as well as an MIT master's degree in management. Christine Wittress, in contrast, majored in political science and psychology at the University of Puget Sound, moved from recruiting to product management in the Excel group, then moved into systems product marketing.

Customer support engineers have a wide variety of backgrounds as well. In recruiting people for this specialty, rather than technical degrees, PSS managers look for characteristics such as whether the candidate seems empathetic, likes to solve other people's problems and teach, and has good analytical problem-solving and communication skills.[19] Trish May, a former director of PSS marketing, adds that Microsoft also does some rudimentary psychological profiling and testing, especially of new hires headed toward management positions. Some customer support engineers have programming backgrounds, but their primary job is to assist individuals who range from novice users of MS-DOS and Windows to sophisticated users of highly technical products like language compilers or network communications systems. Mark Seidenverg, for example, had a degree in digital electronics and worked in computer hardware repair before joining Microsoft in 1984. He headed a group that supported Excel for the Macintosh, and then moved into Windows support, before taking on the position as product development consultant to the Excel group based in PSS.

PRINCIPLE   *Educate new hires through learning by doing and mentoring.*

The problem of how to educate and guide new people that join Microsoft, particularly in such hard-to-define functions as program management, has grown along with the diversity and sophistication of the company's products. In the early days, people communicated knowledge about product designs by word of mouth or by reading code and trying products themselves. New people watched more experienced people, and everyone learned through trial and error. For the most part, Microsoft continues to operate in this way. Rather than investing heavily in training programs, formal rules and procedures, or even detailed product documentation, Microsoft tries to hire people who can learn on their own on the job. It then relies on experienced people to educate and guide new people: Team leads, experts in certain areas, and formally appointed mentors take on the burden of teaching in addition to doing their own work.

This approach has its pluses and minuses. The pluses are that people feel empowered to learn and make decisions on their own, and their roles in the company are flexible and can become as broad as they can handle. But there are several negatives: It is difficult for new people to learn about Microsoft's complex products and sometimes vague job responsibilities. New people often interrupt the work of experienced people to ask questions. With Microsoft's rapid growth and shortages of experienced middle managers and team leads, new people often have to learn by trial and error or from mentors with no more than a couple years of experience. And mistakes can be costly—in terms of money and industry reputation—in the world of mass-market software.

Program Managers: Microsoft has found it difficult not only to hire but also to train people to become program managers. Mike Conte described his experience of finding out what a program manager does as "partly learning it and partly inventing it." This was especially true in the early years of the company. Even ten years after Jabe Blumenthal acted as the first program manager, though, Microsoft has yet to establish detailed guidelines for the job. Conte admitted this: "In general, at Microsoft and program management in particular at Microsoft, there isn't a very official orientation path. There isn't a very official training program. There isn't anything that necessarily says, as a guideline, all program managers have to write specs this way or have to do prototypes this way, or even have to do their scheduling this way."

Program managers can now receive formal orientation, including an optional three-week training program. In addition, Microsoft holds occasional "blue tray" lunches where program managers give talks on their experiences. John Fine, for example, once talked about what makes a good specification, and this discussion was circulated on videotape. Overall, however, Microsoft managers believe that learning by doing, mentoring, and choosing the right people to begin with are far better ways to create program managers than trying to educate them in a classroom. Fine, speaking when he was the director of program management, emphasized this point: "So assume you hire the right kind of person. Then, so far, I have seen 90 percent of the training process that is effective be from mentoring, meaning a new program manager has to work for a more experienced program manager who himself is a great, successful program manager. And the efforts that have gone over the years at training via other mechanisms account for the other 10 [percent]." Similar to developers and testers, Fine noted that program managers also learn by moving from relatively simple to more complex tasks:

When you first come in, you're given one feature area that hopefully can be stated in one sentence, or else the goal of what you're supposed to get done is not clear enough for you as a beginner: one feature area to be responsible for. That means make sure when the product ships that [your] feature area is okay in all dimensions—it didn't cause the product to slip, it has the appropriate level of stability . . . [and] functionality. . . . You typically do that for a while—six months, a year, whatever, with pretty close monitoring. . . . Then, after a proven success there, typically the same kind of work will occur, maybe for a bigger feature set, but [with] less close management. After some time goes by, the next step is you get to the point where you can own a small project or a major component of a large project. If you're on a very small project, you might end up being the only program manager on it. I think that is the kind of fifth gear for program managers. That's a career, right there . . . what I call "Ninja program management." This is, no matter how hard a project that gets dumped on you, from the first glimmer to out the door, to make it happen. . . . There are a couple of directions from there, of course. Like any other company, you can aspire to management. And a different track is you can start thinking more and more about more cross-product strategic issues. When you get that far, just like in any other company, your functional area almost becomes meaningless, and you do what needs to be done at the company.

Developers: The experience level as well as the need for specific training and orientation for new developers varies by group, product, and feature assignment. In areas such as Excel and Word, or even Windows and MS-DOS, most developers have only two or three years of experience. In Windows NT, however, the core designers have a dozen years or more of experience in operating system development with major organizations such as DEC. Most other NT developers have four years of experience, some coming from outside Microsoft and some from within (such as from OS/2 or languages). In all groups, it has been difficult to bring in new developers because Microsoft's main products are now so large and complicated in terms of the number of their components and potential interactions. Ed Fries, development manager for word, majored in computer science at the New Mexico Institute of Mining and Technology and worked in Excel before moving to Word in 1992. He explained his approach to dealing with newcomers:

> New people are a challenge. . . . It's very hard. They're coming in the middle of a huge complicated program. Fortunately, they don't need to know everything about the program to start and do some work. But they learn some painful lessons. They learn . . . they have to worry about [things] that [weren't] obvious. . . . Like they think that they're just going to put in a little feature somewhere. But they have to understand there is a macro language, and that macro language . . . affects how they do their feature. If they don't do it right, they'll break the macro language, or any other mode in the product. . . . Their feature might work in one mode but not in another, or it might work but not in print preview or it won't print. There're so many different interacting things.

Perhaps because developers are writing code that leaves little leeway on a computer—it either works well or does not—Microsoft has a longer history of formal orientation and training for this specialty. Microsoft offers several multiple-day workshops for new developers that deal with the development process, products, tools, and other topics. Still, Microsoft people continue to debate the usefulness of these courses, and managers have not made them mandatory. Dave Moore in particular stated that he prefers to have new people jump right into work, without even "watching some dumb video for a half hour about how Microsoft got started. They probably know that stuff already. And that's a morale killer; the first moment that they're here on campus has to be an exciting moment that will carry forward for their whole career. So projects are anxious to get those guys on the team, right now, their first day."

During their first few days, new hires meet with managers or other senior people from the various specialties. They receive a brief introduction to the development cycle at orientation, but learn the details of the development process as they work on a project. Development managers assign the new hires immediately to an individual task or to work with a feature team. They may also introduce the new people to more senior developers willing to serve as mentors, which in many groups is a formal assignment for one to nine months. "The mentor is the person that really does the lifelong training," Moore observed. New hires also start coding relatively easy features that take one week or so and have few interactions with other features. Senior people (the feature team lead, an area expert, or a person's mentor) then review the new people's code fairly carefully.

In some groups, new developers receive a document describing the internal structure of the product. For example, Word, Excel, and Windows NT have primers referred to respectively as "Word Internals," "Excel Internals," and "Newcomer.doc." These quickly become outdated and are not as detailed as newcomers would like, nor is it possible to explain all the intricacies of how computer code works in large systems through a written document. Hence new people still have to rely on mentors, as well as learn about products by reading code and doing actual coding and debugging themselves. Jon De Vaan, formerly with Excel and now development manager for Office, joined Microsoft in 1984 after studying mathematics and computer science at Oregon State University. He described the "Excel Internals" document and Microsoft's "oral tradition":

Excel Internals . . . explains the philosophy of a few of the basic things in Excel, like the cell table formulas, memory allocation, a little bit about the layer [a special interface with the operating system that allows Microsoft to use the same Excel core on both Windows and Macintosh platforms; see Chapter 5]. It's very sparse. We don't necessarily rely on that for people to learn things. I'd say we have a strong oral tradition, and the idea is that the mentor teaches people or people learn it themselves by reading code. . . . Over the course of a project, it goes from mostly truthful to less truthful, and then we have to fix it up. We don't fix it up as we go along on a project. We will give it some attention between projects.

De Vaan emphasized that the document, while not perfect, is still very useful because Excel is now a million lines of difficult code that is very stressful for new people to learn. This problem of learning the system on your own has become especially critical (and painful), since about half of the developers who work on Excel have been in Microsoft less than two or three years, and there is only one technical lead for the entire project. And maintaining the document is another time-consuming activity that De Vaan and other people in Microsoft dislike and tend to put off. As a result, they keep the document short and update it only in between versions of the product:

We're having some stress on this right now in the group. It [Excel] is hard to learn. You come in and a million-plus lines of code—how do you get your feet on the ground? . . . We always think that the way to make that easier is to have more things written down. But . . . now you don't only maintain your source code, but you maintain all the things that you have written down. And as I said, the mentor relationship has worked very well for us in the past. That may be kind of broken on Excel 5.0. Maybe we really do need to write more stuff down. But the flip side is all the new people are getting work done, [even though] there's a fairly high level of frustration for them.

The Excel group has played a special role within Microsoft as the technical leader in software process and feature standardization, and as a de facto training ground for talented developers and managers. Like John Fine in program management, De Vaan felt that new people learn best by doing: "What we like to do is just give people assignments, or people take assignments, depending upon their seniority level, and rely on people being smart enough to figure it out. . . . A lot of people get hung up in, 'Well, we can't have that person work on this. They don't have any experience.' And here, I think we say, 'Well, you don't have any experience, but we think you can learn it.'" De Vaan recalled for us his first job in Microsoft, when someone asked him to write the copy protection software for Mac Excel 1.0. This experience forced him to learn, at a very deep technical level, how Macintosh disc drives work, in terms of both hardware and software. De Vaan also realized that allowing people to learn on their own results in occasional mistakes, and that good managers must expect this:

> People have license to make mistakes, at first. You can learn a lot by doing it and seeing how it's wrong and fixing it up. That's also one of the key ways how I learned how stuff worked. . . . When someone's working even on a new assignment and maybe someone else was the expert in that area, before they check in code, they'll have the best expert review their code and tell them, "This was done right," or "This is a better way to do this thing." . . . The idea is that everyone is going to learn by doing . . . and mentors will answer questions. . . . But then when they think they're done with the code, they'll get a code review to get tips.

Of course, not all newcomers have a sanguine first experience. New developers in the smaller product groups, which receive far less attention from top management, can get lost in the shuffle. David Whitney, a 1990 MIT computer science graduate who worked on Microsoft Mail, related his experience: "They gave me sporadic tasks. They had an ongoing project that they handed off to the new hire every time: 'Here, work on this, we need some features.' And then once that got old, I got into some low-level stuff in the application framework, dealing with the memory manager, and debugging it, things like that."

Microsoft used to offer developers more orientation and training. During the 1980s Doug Klunder, then one of Microsoft's most talented programmers (he recently left the company), ran a "boot camp" for new developers. The camp lasted from a few weeks to a

few months, depending on the skills of the developer; it was referred to as "Klunder College" by its proponents and as "Klunder-
garden" by its critics. Newcomers learned, among other things, a
unique coding convention invented by Charles Simonyi and used at
Microsoft called "Hungarian." (See Chapter 5 for a discussion of
this.) Developers also had to pass other hurdles before managers
allowed them to join projects. Microsoft people frequently debated
the usefulness of having this long orientation for developers. In
fact, PC software companies tend not to have extensive newcomer
training, and most try to hire skilled programmers. (This contrasts
with producers of software for mainframes and minicomputers,
who typically have training programs of two or three months to a
year.) After ending Klunder College several years ago when Klunder got tired of running it, Microsoft switched to sending developers right into projects and providing them only with mentors and a
few short optional courses to upgrade their skills.

The mentor system is not perfect either. It depends on experienced people to teach inexperienced people, mostly by example
and word of mouth. This is fine, except that Microsoft has a shortage of experienced people at the same time that its products are
becoming more varied and complicated. This was the case with
Excel 5.0, which, for a variety of reasons, shipped in early 1994
several months behind schedule. (Previous Excel projects had
been only a matter of days or weeks late.) De Vaan admitted to this
problem and mentioned another—that Microsoft did not schedule
in time for experienced people to mentor: "This last summer we
probably didn't have enough mentors with enough experience to
do a good job. Also, we estimated very aggressively. So, towards
this part of the project, people are working hard to get their work
done. And when it's time to go do this stuff for someone else,
there's a pretty strong conflict there, which we'll probably address
next time by giving people some time every week to spend on mentoring tasks." Neither are there enough experienced people to
serve as effective team leads—the "mentors to the mentors." These
problems are lessening as Microsoft reduces new hiring and limits
new people to 50 percent or so of the developers in any one group;
Microsoft is also adding more formal training. As Gates remarked,

though, Microsoft people still prefer to rely primarily on mentoring to educate new people, and they do not think their current approach causes serious problems:

> The mentoring system? Actually, that's not that broken. . . . We used to have very formal training things that people . . . weren't super enthusiastic about. Either they were somebody who was never going to learn, in which case it was just three more weeks before we figured out it was a mismatch, or else they're some superstar guy who's laughing all the way. There are certain things, certain algorithmic techniques and things. But give the guy a copy of *Programming Pearls* [a basic text on how to write computer code], make sure he's read through the thing and understands everything in there. Show him a piece of code. Ask him some questions about it. So we are very formal about it now. We have a bunch of courses that we make available and that people are taking at a pretty good rate. But you get onto a project and learn from more senior people, and that seems to work very well for us.

Testing: There are specific strategies, techniques, and tools (such as the automated test suites and the bug database) that make testing more effective. Testers can learn these things in workshops and seminars, which Microsoft offers to all testers as basic training before they join the product groups. Other knowledge about specific products or how to use particular tools or techniques most effectively require mentoring and on-the-job experience.

Beyond the initial training, the product units each have their own approaches to teaching new testers about their products and testing support tools, although there is considerable commonality across the various product areas. The major groups have documents outlining testing concepts and sample test plans as well as checklists to help testers determine when they are finished testing (see Chapter 5). The Excel group even has an electronic help file that collects information useful to Excel testers. But there is no substitute for creating a structured, systematic approach to testing. Marc Olson noted this when he described how difficult it is to check all the different scenarios in which people use software programs: "The way you get good coverage or make sure you don't screw up is that you do have structure. You have some systematic ways of going through and verifying that a feature works. You have a list of things that you always try. And you grow that list, and you make sure that you don't lose subtle things in every feature. You train your development team to understand those up front as much as possible. They should take that into account when they write the code, not when you find a bug, so it comes to you and it works."

As in the other specialties, testers learn as part of a feature testing team of three to eight or nine people; this includes a mix of experienced and relatively new people. The testers also pair up with individual developers. Testers still report to test leads (heads of the testing teams) and to the test manager in the group. The testers also have mentors, although Microsoft does not rely on testing mentors for training as heavily as it does on the developer mentors.

Testers who do not know how to write code usually learn this skill after entering Microsoft by taking a course in BASIC or a more advanced language. Programming is becoming increasingly important for testers in all the groups. Any product with a macro language, including Excel and Word, needs tests that require writing code; indeed, more and more applications products are incorporating macro languages so that users can customize the products. (A macro is a series of commands that a user can group together into one simplified command or key stroke to perform a series of tasks in one step.) In the systems areas, many tests consist of code written to exercise different application programming interfaces (APIs), so coding there is essential. But even in the applications groups, testers are increasingly writing test cases using automated test-case generators and macro languages that require an elementary knowledge of BASIC or Microsoft's graphical version of this language, Visual Basic.

Other Specialties: Training in product management and user education is primarily informal, with new people learning by doing and from mentors. New hires also rely heavily on examples from past projects—previously done marketing reports and plans that were successful, or examples of good documentation. College courses in marketing for product managers and in a variety of subjects for user education staff (such as English writing and editing, graphic design, and book publishing) also prove useful.

Microsoft provides more formal training to customer support engineers. This training has become linked with company efforts during the past several years to improve its image and ability with regard to helping customers use—rather than simply buy—Microsoft products. Customer support engineers do not need the professional education that developers require (such as for computer programming), but they need a broad knowledge of how Microsoft products work, and eventually they need to specialize in particular products.

New customer support engineers receive three to four weeks of training, beginning with MS-DOS and Windows, the basic systems products, before specializing. They also receive general training in communications skills, including how to handle customers. To learn by doing, new PSS employees usually start with Windows support, then move into applications. At the time of this transition, they receive an additional two weeks or so of training on a particular application product. Also, as part of their orientation, they listen in on phone calls, work with mentors (there is about one mentor for every eight technicians), and answer letters from customers before they staff the telephones.[20] There is also continuous training after orientation of about twenty hours per employee per year.[21]

The senior PSS people, who train the telephone technicians, work closely with the development organization to understand new features as they evolve. Similarly, managers of the database tool known as the Knowledge Base (which support personnel use to help them answer questions) work closely with the development and user education organizations. Mark Seidenverg, the PSS product development liaison with the Excel unit, explained how training and input to product development worked in his division:

"Worldwide training will train new hires and do upgrade training. In our group, in Excel specifically, our trainers are part of the whole development communications cycle. They're part of our documentation review and spec review, so they're very involved with the product from the vision right through to when they're actually training people on it. Same with our Knowledge Base writers who provide a lot of the key information to the engineers. So they'll be coming through the product cycle. They understand why the product works the way it works, why decisions were made, and then they do the training.

PRINCIPLE *Create career paths and "ladder levels" to retain and reward technical people.*

After Microsoft created technical specialties within the product groups and hired people into these disciplines, a new problem arose. This is typical of many companies: how to keep people in the technical tracks and product groups in order to take advantage of the expertise they accumulate, as well as the tools, techniques, and training in which the company invests. As noted earlier, Microsoft tends to promote skilled developers into general management positions (such as head of a product unit), and middle managers continue to write code or test programs. But career management issues arise whenever developers, testers, or program managers simply want to stay within their discipline and rise to the top of that specialty without taking on managerial responsibilities.

Microsoft did something that is unusual for a firm that despises bureaucracy but relatively common among high-technology companies: It established formal career tracks within the technical domains (such as within testing or development) as well as within general management (in the product groups and at the corporate level). The technical career paths are essential to retain skilled people and afford them recognition and compensation comparable to what general managers receive. Maples acknowledged this: "We're very conscious of the dual career concept, where a guy who doesn't want to be a manager can progress in his career and get promoted just as well as a guy who does want to be a lead or a manager."

The typical career path within a functional specialty is to move from being a new hire to being a mentor, team lead, and then manager of the functional area for an entire product unit (such as the group program manager, development manager, or test manager for Excel). Above these managers are special positions that cut across product units. These include the directors for the functional areas, or positions in the Office product unit, which oversees the

Excel and Word product groups and builds common features used in the different Office applications.

Microsoft has also tried to achieve some comparability across the functional disciplines as well as to introduce incentives for people to rise within the functions. It has done this by establishing "ladder levels" for each specialty, represented by formal numerical rankings (starting from 9 or 10 for college graduates and going to 13, 14, or 15, depending on the area). These levels reflect experience in the company as well as performance and raw skill. Promotions require a formal review by senior management, and they are tied directly to compensation. Dave Moore recalled that Microsoft set up the ladder system during 1983 and 1984 to assist managers in recruiting developers and to offer "a scheme for normalizing salaries based on skill level." As Microsoft formalized other disciplines, each area created a parallel ladder system similar to what existed for developers.

For Microsoft employees, the most immediate impact of the levels is on their compensation. In general, Gates believes in relatively low base salaries for everyone—executives included—but high incentive compensation in the form of bonuses and stock options. Executives and senior employees also receive base salaries that are not too far above average salaries in the company (as in most Japanese firms). Gates took only $275,000 in salary and $180,000 as a bonus in 1994, although he also owns 25 percent of Microsoft's stock. Other senior executives received about the same or less. Steve Ballmer (who owns 5 percent of Microsoft and is the company's third billionaire, behind Gates and Paul Allen, who still owns 10 percent as a board member) received a 1994 salary of $240,000 and a bonus of $190,000. Mike Maples had a $240,000 salary and a $250,000 bonus.[22] New developer hires out of college with a graduate degree (Level 10) get around $35,000 in straight salary; with a master's degree, they receive approximately $45,000. Very senior or truly outstanding developers or research scientists for whom Gates has competed may make twice this amount or more, excluding bonuses. Program managers and product managers receive almost as much as developers. Testers have to settle for a bit less: around $30,000 to start, but as high as $80,000 or so for senior people. Approximately three thousand out of Microsoft's 17,800 employees are also millionaires due to the stocks they own—probably the highest percentage of millionaires for a company this size.

Even when rising quickly through the technical or managerial hierarchy, talented people grow tired of particular jobs. At the same time, product groups and functions benefit from having people enter with different perspectives. Accordingly, Microsoft managers encourage some mobility across the product groups, and they do not prevent qualified people from moving to different specializations. People usually move, however, only after accumulating several years of experience in a particular area. Microsoft's larger products, like Office, Word, Excel, Windows, and NT, take years to learn, and it is not advisable to move around too often.

For people interested in switching, there is a pecking order among the product groups, although this changes over time. People also consider some products within each group to be more desirable to work on than others. In applications, this seems based on how much the group contributes to Microsoft's sales and profits; in systems and languages, the criteria appear to revolve more around technical challenges and reputation. For example, Windows NT and OLE have been far more attractive products to work on than MS-DOS, which has been a huge revenue generator, and Visual C++ and Visual Basic are more challenging than less popular languages. Other parts of the company—such as multimedia, interactive TV, or on-line video and network services—attract people because they are new technologies in rapidly growing, nascent markets. In the applications division, Excel has historically been the most prominent group to work in, although it has also been the most demanding. With Office now the main application product, this is the new "place to be" for applications developers.

Program Managers: Program managers have the same potential career paths as the other specializations. Their positions range from mentor and team lead to group program manager; there is also the staff position of director of program management. (This has been a temporary or part-time position, however, that not a lot of people want. Program management remains a sophisticated but ill-defined function, with few tools, techniques, and concepts that a functional director can promote.) New hires in this discipline tend to have an undergraduate college degree and to start at Level 10. The program manager with the highest rank in 1994 was a Level 14. The challenge of assignments also varies considerably by the importance of the product.

Program managers have broad responsibilities. They oversee much of the coordination with other groups, although developers also coordinate at the level of features and shared components. Initially in Microsoft, this coordination primarily took the form of standardizing visual interfaces (for example, how menus and screens appear to the user) and functional commands (such as making sure that the way to save a document is the same in both Word and Excel). Until recent standardization efforts, interfaces as well as commands and tool bars differed widely among products that people commonly use together. More recently, the coordination efforts have focused on developing common features and shared components. Some senior program managers with development backgrounds work on this type of architectural standardization in both applications products (such as Office) and in systems products (such as Windows 95 and Windows NT).

Developers: Determining the ladder levels for developers (referred to as the SDE, or software design engineer, levels) seems to be a slightly more formal process than for the other specialties. This is probably because levels for developers set the promotion criteria and pay standards for all the technical specialties. Development managers review personnel annually and assign levels. The director of development, Dave Moore, also checks to make sure promotions are consistent across the company. Microsoft has no standard timetable for promotions, although managers seem aware of average advancement periods.

A new developer hired from college at Level 10 will normally spend six to eighteen months before moving up a notch. Someone with a master's degree might enter at Level 10 and rise quickly, or enter at Level 11. The movement from Level 10 to 11 is rather easy—a "no-brainer," according to Dave Moore: "Level 11 is typically someone who can run on their own, and basically write production code without a lot of supervision." Developers on average stay at Level 11 for two and a half years. Some stay at this level for many years, though, because the promotion reviews become much more intensive: "Typically," Moore continued, "moving from Level 11 to 12, I'll ask a few questions, and moving from 12 to 13, I'll ask a lot of questions. Moving from Level 13 to 14 typically requires that the manager describe the contributions that the person is doing in the division to myself and Mike Maples. Levels 14 and 15 are only done with Bill's approval." Moore, a Level 14 developer, elaborated on the promotion criteria and expectations:

> When you show that you are a solid developer, writing zero-defect code, and can do anything, basically, on a project, then you go to Level 12. Level 12s usually have significant impact on the project. As you start to do things that have impact across a business unit, then you may move to Level 13. As you have more impact across a division, you can go to Level 14. As you have more impact across the company, you have a Level 15. Generally, the folks who are considered part of the "brain trust" are software design engineers Level 14 or 15. And there are very few 15s in the company. Nathan [Myhrvold] is a 15—he also has the title of VP. Charles [Simonyi] is a 15. There're only five or six of these folks at level 15. Bill is not even on the scale. He's the CEO.

Moore estimated that 50 to 60 percent of all developers are Levels 10 and 11; 20 percent, Level 12s; 15 percent or so, Level 13s; and the remaining 5 to 8 percent, Level 14s and 15s. These numbers reflect Microsoft's rapid growth; for the past five or six years, half of the developers have had only one or two years of experience. While managers do not formally use ladder levels to estimate the capabilities of a team, they often assign their highest-level people to develop particularly critical features. Managers will argue that they "need a Level 12" or "need a 13" for an especially difficult part of a project. Feature team leads are generally Level 12 people, or very experienced Level 11s, and development managers Level 13s and 14s. Levels 14 and 15 people often work on the more difficult architectural issues in one or more products.

A developer might become a mentor within a year or two, then move up to team lead within a few years. A truly exceptional developer interested in management can then become a development manager of a group or even head of an entire business unit, like

Chris Peters. With growth in the number of developers slowing, however, such opportunities for promotion into the top development spot or into higher levels of management have become far fewer. Mark Walker, a developer in the Word group trained in computer science at Brigham Young University, reflected on these changes:

> The feel of the company has changed quite a bit in just the three years since I've started. The opportunities are different. We're still doing quite a bit of interesting things and probably more now than then; it's just we're not growing like we were in terms of employment. I've seen the group that I work in go from seven people to forty, and it's soon going to be sixty. But that kind of growth is at its end. . . . Now the whole structure changes. Before, you'd . . . move upward as the company grows, and there're always lots of opportunities. Now it seems to be going the direction of more traditional organizations, where you move up when somebody else leaves, and you wait for attrition and that kind of thing. Upward mobility in my current path really stops at the lead position.

The work is particularly challenging for senior developers, because Microsoft expects them to manage people and write code at the same time. The development manager of a product group is probably the toughest position. This person is almost always an expert in how a product works and how features interact; people expect him or her to help other members of the group, as well as to spend as much time writing code as possible. Because feature team leads are also experts in certain areas of the product, they must help their team as well as program full-time. As Ed Fries, drawing on his experience in the Excel and Word groups, commented: "We have one person identified as the technical lead. This tends to be the person who really has the biggest understanding of how the product in general works. . . . The team lead is [also] a very demanding position. For one thing, they're still expected to program all the time, and then they're managing and they're acting as a dispatcher and question-answerer. And so it means that they have to be good at programming and able to do this other stuff too."

Team leads have such full loads on the assumption that, because of their greater knowledge and experience, they can do as much work as other team members in less time. Fries explained the logic:

We'd like to believe that the team lead can do . . . at least as much as the members of his team and his other stuff. In other words, I've got some solid good programmer on my team. If I'm really qualified to be the lead, I should be able to do as much in a week as he can do. But I really do it in three days . . . and spend the other two doing my other duties. . . . You hear this sometimes in computer science, about how a good programmer is ten times better than a bad programmer. I don't know if our range is that extreme. But that's the idea, that they're so good at what they do that they can do that and . . . have time to do other things. And generally, that's how they got the job. They were not only doing their features but they were looking into other areas, and . . . learning about other parts of the product. . . . We're always looking for people like that.

Aside from moving up in the technical or managerial hierarchy, another option for developers is to seek new challenges in other groups within Microsoft. This occurs fairly often, especially within the divisions. As Chris Peters observed: "If you're a very good developer, you could work on any project in the company. If you're a very bad developer, it's very difficult to change groups. . . . But the fact is that most people don't change, because they start developing a certain expertise in these million-line programs."

There remains some disagreement within Microsoft over how much movement across the different product groups is useful for individuals and the company as a whole. The benefit of staying with a product for a long period of time is that the developer gets to understand a large part of a complex product very deeply. The disadvantage is that people get tired—and even burn out—if they stay in one job too long. Practices also tend to become parochial and not shared among the groups. Pushed somewhat by Mike Maples, there has been increasing movement of people, particularly from the Excel group to areas such as Word and Project. The consensus seems to be that developers should work on a product for at least two development cycles, or about three years, before they consider moving. Jon De Vaan offered his view on how much people should move:

Another thing that we like to do between versions of the project is give a fair number of people a chance to move around. The idea is that people get to learn more of the product and we have stronger programmers be-

cause they see more firsthand how other people have attacked problems. . . . Companywide we also have some percentage of people which
move between projects. . . . We don't encourage everybody to move
around all the time, because there is a leverage to having someone work
on the same thing two times in a row. We haven't had to assign guidelines, because people basically do what they want. It has worked out for
us in the past that we don't have twenty people trying to do this one
thing, if it's only a one-person job. So there hasn't been a need to formalize that. . . . I would say if someone's been working on the same thing for
three years, that's probably long enough.

Another way to distinguish individuals and different specializations is by compensation. Developers are the highest-paid group
within Microsoft; some talented developers with extensive experience in other companies (such as those that joined the original
Windows NT group) can occasionally negotiate salaries above the
average for their ladder level, although this is rare. This disparity
has the potential of exacerbating tensions within Microsoft regarding the "prima donna" position of the developers. Nonetheless,
people from other functions seem to recognize that developers
must have a special role in a software company. Richard Barth,
speaking as a senior product manager in the Windows NT group,
took this perspective:

> There is tongue-in-cheek resentment of developers from the rest of us, al-
> most jealousy. Daryl Havens is one of our lead developers from Windows
> NT. Daryl has nine Porsches; I wish I could afford nine Porsches. But do
> I resent Daryl? Hell, no. He earned them. He's damn good. If it were my
> check, I'd sign it, too. And so one of the nice things is that it's pretty clear
> that in the long run, over a year or two, you get paid what you're worth
> here. If for some reason we brought in Daryl and we were paying him
> nine Porsches' worth and he wasn't panning out, Daryl wouldn't be here
> very long. . . . [But] there is this undercurrent [that] developers are defi-
> nitely the chosen people around here. . . . The single negative is . . . a cer-
> tain amount of feeling that developers are prima donnas. That's just sort
> of the nature of the business.

Testing: As Microsoft managers gradually recognized the importance of turning out products that are more reliable and easy to

use, they have paid more attention to keeping good people within the testing career track. This makes great economic sense because testing involves considerable investment in tools and training, and personal experience with particular products and features is invaluable for effective testing. Marc Olson spoke about this issue:

> One of the keys, I think, to Microsoft's success and the quality of its products, the secrets to its development practices, is that testing is a valid and separate career path. It's not a dumping ground for developers who can't make it. It's not a starting point for people who want to be programmers, necessarily. We really strive to make it independent . . . in that we want people to want to be in testing. We want to attract people that are interested in doing that kind of work. And we want to retain them so that we can invest in training in methods that will carry from project to project. I think we have been very successful in doing that and in growing our organization and improving our process along the way.

Tester levels ranged from 9 to 13; no tester has yet received the same status or compensation as the most senior developers (or program managers). Dave Moore explained why: "If I have a tester who shows me that they're Level 14 material, I'll open up Level 14. . . . I'll go to Level 15 if I have to, although I haven't seen that yet." While Olson is not top-ranked, he has moved up unusually fast: "I'm a Level 12, actually. But when you figure at most levels it's about two or three years at each level, I have gone from a 9 to a 12 in half that time. In that sense there's a limited career path, but I feel like I have an opportunity to learn . . . and . . . grow in my understanding of how to do this better and improve our process."

It is important to be familiar with a particular product. Thus Microsoft managers prefer that testers, like developers, stay in the same group for several years. At the least, they prefer that testers remain within a common area, like desktop applications, systems, or the consumer division. Also, because of the experience testers accumulate, managers do not encourage people to migrate to other functions, such as to development or program management. Moore took the most extreme position against testers changing jobs: "They spend their life in testing. If they're hired in as testers, they stay as testers." Moore admitted, however, that Microsoft testers have existed only since 1984 and in large numbers only since 1991; the company has not yet established clear norms for career paths and mobility. Like Jon De Vaan, he preferred that people spend at least a few years in one job.

Of course, testers can also move upward. The usual career path is to move to testing team lead and then to test manager of a major product. Another step is the staff position of director of testing, although most testers would probably prefer to work as test manager in a key product unit. At least some testers also believe they can join other product groups and disciplines, even though movement might be rare. Olson described these frustrations:

> I think there is a limit to how long you can stay on this job and keep your sanity. . . . People move into program management. People move into programming occasionally from testing. . . . It's more limited by what level do you want to be involved technically and what level do you want to be involved in managing people, or whether you want to be involved in just doing the work.
>
> Within my group, I have six teams of people. Each team is headed up by a test lead who has management responsibilities for the people on their teams. There is growth within my organization for people to do only testing. We have people who have been doing only testing for four years, and they enjoy it. They don't want to manage people. They want to be technical. . . . Then they switch products because they want a taste of something new, and that is certainly an option. . . . It doesn't happen a lot. . . .
>
> The next step for me is whether I want to stay in technical management or move into general management. There really is not much above where I am now. In testing, I'm at the top. . . . I can get another promotion in terms of pay scale, but my title is going to be the same—the test manager for Excel.

As in program management or development, some jobs in testing clearly require less skill than others. In this sense, testing systems products is probably at the top of the testing hierarchy and often requires considerable programming knowledge. Testing simple features for low-volume consumer products is probably at the lowest end of the skill requirements, and within each product group, some features are far more challenging than others. All testing is important, however, because users are likely to complain and call up Microsoft (costing the company about $12 a call) for even the simplest problem. As Olson explained:

> There's also a certain percentage of features that aren't as glamorous, or the work is more drudgery [and] . . . doesn't require the technical understanding. Like testing the help file, for example. . . . You look at a word and then you push on the button, and if . . . the topic comes up, then it did the right thing. It doesn't take a lot of brain power to be able to do that. But it takes somebody who has a commitment to understanding how the help file works and understands the importance of making it work right, and we have to do that work. That person probably isn't suitable for testing the programming environment in Excel, but they fill a niche in the work that we have to do. . . . But that person may not have the same skill set as somebody who is testing something else. It's very difficult to value those two both equally important positions by comparing them against each other. You have to look at the work they're doing, where it fits into the group, are they working hard, and are they getting stuff done. So the performance evaluations are individual more than groupwide, as much as we can make them.

Firing testers is rare, compared to the 10 percent or so of new employees that quit the company each year. Olson recalled only four testers (out of fifty or so in his group) who left because of poor work performance during the past few years. Because of their investments in these people, managers prefer to provide more assistance and training to struggling testers, rather than firing them. Nonetheless, Olson acknowledged that the ceiling on the career path for testers has caused people to leave. A more serious problem for Olson is how to motivate people who choose to stay in testing as a career: "The challenge is more for people who have been in the group for two or three years. How do I continue to challenge them? How do I get them to grow?"

An increasingly common approach to motivating testers is to send them to professional software engineering conferences that focus on software quality or testing. Microsoft also sponsors in-house seminars and workshops, some of which bring in developers to talk about their specialties and the functionality of their code. These measures, as well as the 1993 appointment of Roger Sherman as a full-time director of testing, have reinforced the image of testing as a professional technical discipline. They have also provided a way for Microsoft people to get more exposure to testing concepts, tools, and practices being used elsewhere in the industry and in the company. Dave Maritz welcomed these developments: "The budget is for ten people a year to go to . . . testing seminars around the country. And I think it's just great, because . . . I'm not the world expert in testing."

Other Specialties: Microsoft's other major functional specialties— product management, customer support, and user education— have career paths, formal ladder levels, and compensation schemes that resemble those for developers and the other functions. As we noted earlier, there is also some mobility out of these specialties, particularly from product management into program management, and from customer support into testing.

In general, Microsoft seems to manage its people well, especially for a company that has grown so much so fast, with little "professional" management along the way. In a 1991 survey in the applications division, most employees felt Microsoft was one of the best places to work in the industry. (See Appendix 4 for a summary of these data.) There were complaints about inadequate training for new employees and some lack of cooperation among the divisions, problems that Gates and other managers are working to rectify. There was also some grousing about low salaries (but not total compensation) and a conflict between demands for "quality" versus "quantity" in work. But the survey suggests that Microsoft provides a very good, if imperfect, atmosphere in which to work. There are capable and accessible managers, little internal politics or bureaucracy, interesting and varied assignments, a strong teamwork culture, and plenty of opportunities to learn and make decisions as well as a few mistakes. Chapter 3 now discusses the wide variety of product offerings Microsoft people have created and how the company uses these products to compete in a growing number of mass markets related to PC software.

3
Competing with Products and Standards

Pioneer and Orchestrate
Evolving Mass Markets

To compete in a growing variety of related segments in the software industry, Microsoft follows a strategy that we describe as *pioneer and orchestrate evolving mass markets*. We break down our discussion of this strategy into five principles:

- Enter evolving mass markets early or stimulate new markets with "good" products that set industry standards.
- Incrementally improve new products and periodically make old products obsolete.
- Push volume sales and exclusive contracts to ensure that company products become and remain industry standards.
- Take advantage of being the standards provider with new products and product linkages.
- Integrate, extend, and simplify products to reach new mass markets.

None of these principles is unique to Microsoft, although few

127

firms have combined all these principles in a single industry over more than one product generation. We believe that Microsoft as a company is unique in its ability to implement this combination of principles consistently; this ability is a key reason for its current market power.

Creating or entering a potential mass market—not as the inventor, but as one of several pioneers—and then incrementally improving a good product that becomes the market standard, describes the behavior of Japanese firms in the VCR industry. Sony, Japan Victor (JVC), Matsushita, and Toshiba followed Ampex's invention of the video recorder in the 1950s by introducing a series of machines for the home; these firms also created a new market for video tapes. Microsoft's use of high-volume exclusive contracts for MS-DOS and Windows resembles the way Japan Victor and its parent company, Matsushita, lined up high-volume contracts with original equipment manufacturers in order to make VHS into the world VCR standard. Intel deployed a similar tactic to garner support for its microprocessors. Microsoft has also capitalized on its position as the standards provider to push new products into the marketplace, very much like VHS manufacturers and Intel have done.[1]

Not all industries involve platform standards (like an operating system, a microprocessor, or a video recorder), and complementary products that must be compatible (such as computer applications software, computer hardware components, or videotapes). And although platform technologies and complementary products enable their provider to lock customers and suppliers into architectural standards, components, and particular products, this advantage does not always last forever. Companies such as Japan Victor and Matsushita (with the VHS video recorder) and Intel (with the microprocessor) are now under pressure from competing standards, such as digital systems and reduced instruction-set computing (RISC) microprocessors.

There are other well-known examples of temporary market dominance based on product standards and complementary products: Xerox once monopolized the original plain-paper copier and various copier supplies and services. IBM controlled computers as well as related hardware peripherals, operating systems, languages, and development tools. RCA dominated color television with replacement components as well as licensing fees. Sony invented the 8-millimeter camcorder and leads in sales of these machines and 8-millimeter tape cartridges. Nintendo and Sega dominate their industry with home video-game machines and their video-game cartridges and licensing arrangements. Sony and Philips control the standard for the compact audio disk and its extension to computer CD-ROMs.

Becoming the standards provider is not necessarily easy, though there are two more elusive challenges. One is to sustain this position long enough to take advantage of it with more than one generation of products. Another is to extend this dominance (for example, through product or marketing linkages) to new markets. Though two decades old, Microsoft is still relatively young; it has been the top PC software company in sales only since 1988. It has dominated critical tools and platform technologies—languages and operating systems—for more than one generation (both character-based and graphical computing), but it has only dominated some applications segments. Nonetheless, Microsoft is one of those rare firms that has sustained and extended its market power. We think two of the principles we cite in this chapter explain how.

First, Microsoft frequently makes incremental improvements and occasionally introduces major advances in its products. While often doing little more than packaging many incremental innovations, these major changes make older product versions obsolete. With a continual cycle of incremental and occasionally more radical innovations, competitors have little opportunity to challenge the market leader. Microsoft has accumulated enormous financial and technical resources that enable it to sustain this level of R&D. It has also followed somewhat of an unusual strategy: Dominant firms generally hesitate to introduce new products that steal sales from their existing product lines.[2]

For example, Microsoft sustained the dominance of MS-DOS with Windows 3.1. As both a graphical user interface and a set of new operating system functions, Windows 3.1 has made sales of MS-DOS alone and DOS applications largely obsolete. Similarly, Windows 95 and Windows NT—and new applications written for these systems—make Windows 3.1 and older Windows applications outdated. Visual Basic, a graphical version of BASIC that greatly simplifies the writing of screens and menus for Windows applications, has replaced the traditional version of this language in the marketplace because nearly all new applications development is for Windows and other graphical systems. The Office applications suite, for both technical and pricing reasons, has practically eliminated the sale and use of individual applications programs. The Microsoft Network may even make obsolete some of Microsoft's multimedia products now sold on CD-ROMs.

Second, Microsoft is continually integrating, linking, repackaging, and often simplifying its products. The main objectives are to enter new markets with products that combine multiple functions that were once separate, and to make products more accessible to broader sets of users. This pattern of competition and innovation has enabled Microsoft to extend its reach to the enormous mass markets of the computer novice and the home consumer.

Again, this is not a unique strategy. VCR producers have combined their machines with TV sets as well as made the VCR and the camcorder extremely easy to use. What Microsoft is doing also resembles Apple's efforts beginning ten years ago; Apple made the Macintosh computer extremely easy to use, bundled this with different applications, and has continuously offered new software products and even an on-line service. Nintendo, Sega, Sony, and other consumer electronics firms are extending the video-game machine to perform other functions. Telephone, cable TV, and wireless communications companies are all developing new uses for their networks and thus extending their influence to new markets. Microsoft is doing the same thing: It is leveraging existing technologies and products as well as impressive capabilities in new product development. It is entering new but related mass markets by creating linkages among products and taking advantage of a vast customer network.

PRINCIPLE   *Enter evolving mass markets early or stimulate new markets with "good" products that set industry standards.*

In the mid-1970s, the first mass-market products for personal computing were computer languages, which people needed to write software to make the new PC hardware work. The next were operating systems, which are special programs that control the primary operations of the computer. Then came a still-growing number of applications for the desktop computer, such as word processors and spreadsheets. More recent mass markets include network operating systems for distributed computing (usually for corporations or other large organizations), as well as multi-user communications and applications products. There are also on-line network systems and applications available for the home consumer. A typical PC user has several applications, one operating system, and one network communications program, each depicted as layers in Figure 3.1.

Two trends, however, have made this picture of PC software more complicated. One is that companies have increasingly been adding functions from one layer of software to another. This practice makes it difficult for producers of simpler products to compete. For example, as we describe later, Microsoft has added many small applications functions, including a primitive word processor and calculator, to the Windows 3.1 operating system. Windows also includes some basic network communications functions, and Microsoft has added more sophisticated network communication features to Windows 95. Similarly, Novell has distinguished its NetWare operating system by building in extensive networking capabilities. Lotus (now owned by IBM) sells a product called Notes that has aspects of a sophisticated database management application, operating system, and network communications program.

The second trend is that, to distinguish their products and sell

Figure 3.1   Major Types of PC Software

User 1:	User 2:	User 3:
Application A,B,C, etc.	Application A,B,C, etc.	Application A,B,C, etc. . . .
Operating System	Operating System	Operating System . . .

Network Communications Software   . . .

more of them both to individual users and to corporations, PC software companies have introduced many more types of systems, applications, and network software. Table 3.1 lists nine different sublayers, along with representative products from Microsoft. As seen in these product examples, Microsoft competes in each major software layer, although with varying degrees of effectiveness. We have noted that Microsoft began with the BASIC programming language and then moved into mass-market operating systems for desktops and more recently into network operating systems for corporations. Operating systems now account for about one-third of Microsoft's revenues (see Table 2 in the Introduction). It also diversified early on into desktop applications and then other types of applications products, which now account for more than 60 percent of revenues. In the 1990s, the second and third software sublayers have constituted the largest mass markets for the overall industry, although the seventh and ninth sublayers may be the largest segments in the future. Firms competing in the latter can charge fees for access to their on-line networks as well as for enabling the user to buy products and services or gain access to other databases and networks. The fifth and sixth sublayers are also important markets because of the growing usage of PC networks and communications programs (such as Lotus Notes) in office settings.

We will explain more about these different types of products and Microsoft's strategy later in this chapter. What is important to understand here are four key points about how the company has competed. First, Microsoft has aggressively moved from one type of software and mass market to another, as well as from one generation of products to another. Sometimes it has achieved this diversification or evolution by technically linking products and certain enabling technologies. Examples that we talk about in this chapter include MS-DOS with Windows, DOS applications with MS-DOS, the Office applications suite with Windows, Object Linking and Embedding (OLE) with Windows and Windows NT as well as applications, and Windows 95 with the Microsoft Network. Microsoft has also used relationships with hardware and software retail vendors and similar marketing practices to promote new products and new product generations.

Second, Microsoft has created standards that have themselves

Table 3.1   Layers of PC Software and Microsoft Products

Systems Software

1. *Programming languages and other development tools* (e.g., BASIC, C, Visual Basic, C++, OLE; used to write other software products)

2. *Desktop operating systems* (e.g., MS-DOS, Windows 3.1, Windows 95; used to run PC applications and other software products)

Applications Software

3. *Desktop applications programs* (e.g., Word, Excel, Office, Access; used to perform a variety of tasks)

4. *Corporate applications development and server tools* (e.g., Microsoft SQL Server, Microsoft BackOffice; used to create database systems for networks of PCs)

Network Software

5. *Network operating systems* (e.g., Windows for Workgroups, Windows NT; used to connect one PC to other PCs, and to enable connected PCs to access information or applications through client-server functions)

6. *Network communications programs* (e.g., Microsoft Mail, Microsoft Exchange, Microsoft At Work; used to allow PCs to communicate and share information with other PCs and programmable devices)

7. *On-line network systems* (e.g., Microsoft Network; used to allow PCs to access electronic information and products over telephone lines or cable-TV systems)

8. *On-line network tools and servers* (e.g., Microsoft Tiger Video Server, based on Windows NT; used to create and send information and other on-line products and applications over networks)

9. *On-line network applications* (e.g., applications available through Microsoft Network as well as products such as Microsoft Money for home banking; used to provide a variety of products and services to networked PC users)

stimulated new mass markets. For example, MS-DOS for IBM-compatible computers created the IBM-clone market for PC hardware manufacturers. The availability of these inexpensive PCs then expanded the markets for operating systems as well as applications and other types of software. MS-DOS and Windows created their own applications markets. Visual Basic has created a market for custom programs. OLE has created a market for OLE-enabled Windows applications. The Microsoft Network, we believe, will create a new mass market for on-line network applications; at the least, it should greatly expand the existing set of relatively sophisticated users of on-line networks. The markets Microsoft standards have created or expanded enhance the growth opportunities for Microsoft as long as it competes in these new arenas.

Third, aggressive expansion has been important because Microsoft's early mass markets have become saturated. With some exceptions (for example, Visual Basic), there is not as much innovation in PC programming languages as in other software areas, such as applications and network systems. Moreover, computer users for years have been able to buy operating systems and then packaged applications programs "off the shelf." These have made programming languages unnecessary for most people, and languages thus have ended up as a very small part of the overall software market. Operating systems and then stand-alone desktop applications like word processors and spreadsheets have also become commodity products. This fact has encouraged Microsoft and other companies to create applications suites as well as move into various types of office and networking software, home-consumer products, multimedia publishing, and on-line ("information highway") products and services.

Fourth, Microsoft is now a leader in blurring the distinctions among the different layers of software and different types of software within these layers. This tendency to combine or "integrate" features in a smaller number of products makes it easier for Microsoft to market products and attract large numbers of new customers. Adding more features can also help retain an existing base of users: Customers are likely to buy product upgrades and new products from Microsoft, and they may never need to go to other companies for different types of software as their needs change over time. (We will talk more about this mode of competition in Chapter 7 as part of Microsoft's strategy to "attack the future.") There are, for example, the many features that Microsoft has added over time to MS-DOS and Windows 3.1; the creation of the Office suite of integrated applications; the creation of the simpler "Bob" suite of home applications, which includes networking features; and the linking of the new Microsoft Network product with the Windows 95 operating system.

Market Data: Various market data reveal the extent (and limits) of Microsoft's position in the very broad PC software industry. Between 1993 and 1995, Microsoft accounted for at least 80 percent of new operating system sales for desktop PCs, which have been selling at the rate of 40 million per year. (IBM's OS/2 accounted for about 10 percent of this market.) Windows and MS-DOS are the two best-selling systems products, respectively. MS-DOS also leads in installed base, appearing on 140 million out of 170 million PC users' machines worldwide; about 70 million of these MS-DOS users also run Windows. Although Microsoft has incorporated MS-DOS within Windows 95 (which had a ship date of August 1995) and will no longer sell many copies of it as a separate operating system, MS-DOS has served as a virtual gold mine since 1981. It has provided billions of dollars in revenues and as much as 25 percent of company profits in many years, with minimal support and development costs. In 1994, Windows and MS-DOS together brought in about $1 billion in sales to Microsoft; about 80 percent of these came from stable OEM channels such as Compaq and Dell Computer. Office or one its major components (Word and Excel) had about 30 million users and together brought in another $1.7 billion, as well as about half of Microsoft's profits.[3]

Microsoft has had a lower market share, as well as a slower start, in applications and networking products. It only had about 10 percent of the spreadsheet market and 15 percent of word processing before the introduction of Windows 3.0 and the Microsoft Office suite in 1990. By 1995, however, Microsoft accounted for approximately 60 percent of new sales in these two major PC application categories, with Word and Excel leading for both Windows and Macintosh computers. Office alone has about 70 percent of the rapidly growing applications suite market.[4] Microsoft has only a few percent of the markets for more sophisticated database management tools and applications, and for networking operating systems for corporations. It has only recently entered these segments, however, and various products aimed at corporate users (such as Windows NT 3.5) are now selling well.

Overall, Microsoft has the broadest product portfolio in the PC software industry by far. Its products range from programming languages to an on-line network system, and include sophisticated office systems as well as products for children and computer novices. Its approximately $6 billion in sales for the fiscal year ending in June 1995 dwarf those of competitors dedicated solely or primarily to PC software. (Revenues in calendar 1994 were approximately $2 billion for Novell, including the WordPerfect division, and just under $1 billion for Lotus.) Microsoft does not have dominant positions outside the major mass-market applications; nonetheless, the company is mounting serious challenges to competitors in nearly all important areas that extend the PC. Microsoft's objective, as stated by Mike Maples, has been to focus on new markets where potential sales and profits are especially large: "We're going to build some number of things that we think we can make a good buck on, and even though you need some other things, you're not going to get them from us. . . . We're in a phase where we want to start making trade-offs and making wise investments. We're too big a percentage of the business. We've got to develop new businesses. We're getting to be too significant a part of our industry, so pretty soon we'd only grow to the industry growth rate, and that's not satisfying to us."

From Languages to Operating Systems: In 1975, Bill Gates and Paul Allen helped start the PC software industry by introducing the first PC computer language, BASIC. An acronym for "beginners' all-purpose symbolic instruction code," BASIC is a relatively simple language invented at Dartmouth College in 1964 for mainframes and minicomputers. Gates and Allen took a publicly available version of the language and adapted it to MITS Computer's Altair PC, the first inexpensive personal computer. They followed this product with other languages and made them available on all the inexpensive PCs that appeared after the Altair, such as the Commodore 64, Apple II, and IBM PCjr.[5]

Gates and Allen continued selling programming languages until 1981, when IBM asked them to provide an operating system for its new PC. (They had never built an operating system before, but Microsoft's founders had pursued the deal with IBM anyway.) Instead of developing a system from scratch, Gates and Allen bought a prototype product called Q-DOS—which was short for "Quick and Dirty Operating System"—from a small local company, Seattle Computer, for $75,000. They used this as the basis for the first version of DOS. Though not a commercial product, Q-DOS was itself a pioneering technology in that it was the first operating system designed for new 16-bit Intel microprocessors. (The newest microprocessors for PCs and video-game machines handle information in chunks of 32 and even 64 bits.)

To some extent, IBM's decision to buy an operating system from Microsoft was no more than a stroke of good fortune for Gates and Allen; indeed, IBM tried but failed to reach an agreement with Digital Research, whose 8-bit CP/M (for Control Program/Monitor) had provided the model for Q-DOS. But IBM went to Microsoft at least in part because Gates and Allen had a good reputation for delivering BASIC, already the standard programming language for PCs. Furthermore, in creating BASIC, Microsoft demonstrated that it had the simulation tools and programming skills to make a reliable, shippable product. In contrast, IBM managers were uncertain whether their programmers could quickly write a small operating system to fit the severe memory constraints of the PC (a task dramatically different from writing mainframe software), and other PC software companies had poor reputations for quality and delivery.[6]

Desktop Applications: Just as Gates and Allen did not invent the BASIC programming language or the core of the DOS product, Microsoft did not invent the spreadsheet or the word processor, its first applications for the PC. These had their origins in applications programs written years before for mainframe and minicomputers as well as for the Xerox Alto PC prototype and the Xerox Star workstation. (Xerox designed these in the 1970s, but never made them commercially successful.) Other companies also led Microsoft in introducing products for personal computers during the late 1970s and early 1980s. Nonetheless, once the IBM PC and PC-compatible markets began taking off, Microsoft began introducing good competing products and marketed them aggressively. It also continuously added useful and foresighted features as Bill Gates and then other managers went after new markets. (See Appendix 2 for an overview of Microsoft's major desktop and business applications products.) Though clearly an exaggeration or perhaps simply wishful thinking, the extent of Microsoft's ambitions in applications development can be seen in another quote from Mike Maples: "If someone thinks we're not after Lotus and after WordPerfect and after Borland, they're confused. My job is to get a fair share of the software applications market, and to me that's 100 percent."[7]

Spreadsheets. When Microsoft began work on spreadsheets in 1980 (with a project called "Electronic Paper"), Gates hired a consultant to study the two products that had started the market. One was VisiCalc, introduced in 1979 for the Apple II by Software Arts (which Lotus later acquired). The other was SuperCalc, developed for CP/M machines by a company called Sorcem (later acquired by Computer Associates). Charles Simonyi, who had done some preliminary work on spreadsheet concepts at Xerox PARC, took over the project when he joined Microsoft in 1981. (Doug Klunder, the MIT computer science graduate who would later run Microsoft's boot camp for programmers, also joined the company in 1981 and became a key member of the five-person development team.) Simonyi's team created novel features such as menus and submenus that appeared at the bottom of the screen and allowed the user simply to select commands (such as "print" or "save") and utilize simplified formulas. Microsoft released the first version of its new spreadsheet, dubbed Multiplan, in August 1982 for the Apple II, followed by versions for CP/M computers and the IBM PC. Multiplan received excellent reviews in industry publications, as well as Apple's public endorsement.[8]

Multiplan quickly became the leading spreadsheet in sales, although Microsoft was slow to introduce an upgrade that took full advantage of new PCs coming out with more memory. This delay allowed Lotus to overtake Multiplan with its 1-2-3 spreadsheet in 1983. Lotus went on to take 80 percent of the U.S. spreadsheet market and remained the leading PC software company in annual sales until Microsoft regained the top spot in 1988.[9]

Lotus 1-2-3 provided the main inspiration for the successor product to Multiplan, called Excel. Klunder offered this comment on the team's development strategy: "Our mission was do everything 1-2-3 does and do it better."[10] Microsoft began the project with a three-day retreat (attended by Gates and Simonyi) to figure out how to compete with Lotus. The output of the meeting was a rough specification of ideal features that the new spreadsheet should have; this was the predecessor document for what Microsoft now calls the "vision statement" for a new product. Klunder compiled these ideas into a twenty-page memo that served as an outline specification. Fulfilling a role that would later become that of the program manager, Jabe Blumenthal—who had studied features in VisiCalc, SuperCalc, and Lotus 1-2-3 while working on marketing Multiplan—took charge of writing up the product specification and worked closely with the developers to flush out the details of each feature. The final product combined the best aspects of Multiplan with good features from both Lotus 1-2-3 and another competing product, Framework. Microsoft then translated the new program over to the Macintosh platform.[11] As we describe below, Microsoft based its software sales comeback on graphical programming skills refined while working on Macintosh versions of Word and Excel.

Word Processing. A company called MicroPro started the PC word-processing mass market in 1979 with a product called WordStar, written for 8-bit CP/M machines.[13] Because WordStar was difficult to use, there remained an opening for such other early entrants as WordPerfect Corporation (founded in 1979) and Microsoft. Simonyi had designed a graphical word processor called Bravo while at Xerox PARC; he took over Microsoft's word-processing development in 1982 and wrote a new product, Word, specifically for MS-DOS and the 16-bit IBM PC. Microsoft then launched the product in 1983 with a brilliant mass-market promotion that gave away 450,000 demonstration diskettes in a special issue of *PC World* magazine.[14]

More so than Multiplan or the early version of Excel, Word attracted buyers because it had innovative features. These included elements of a graphical user interface, "what you see is what you get" (WYSIWYG) on-screen typefaces, and a laser printer driver, which Gates had insisted on adding.[15] Microsoft also used much of the same code for its Macintosh version of Word, introduced in 1984. The Mac version did not have as many features as the PC version, but it was the only word processor available for the Macintosh other than Apple's MacWrite, which at the time could not handle documents longer than about eight pages. Microsoft Word thus filled a major gap in Macintosh software; along with Excel 1.0 (introduced in 1985), it helped the Mac succeed as a commercial product.[16] The Macintosh versions of Word and Excel also helped lay a foundation for Microsoft to compete with graphical applications products for the new Windows PC platform. The PC version of Word did not receive as much attention from Microsoft as the more advanced graphical applications, however, and it soon fell far behind WordPerfect in sales for DOS machines. Later versions of Word would compete directly with and then surpass WordPerfect in sales for Windows machines and eventually for total word-processor sales.

Applications Integration. Microsoft followed its spreadsheet and word-processing programs with a host of other applications (such as for presentations, database management, project management, electronic mail, personal scheduling, and desktop publishing), usually for both Macintosh and Windows PCs. The company initially concentrated on stand-alone products, like Word and Excel, but soon found that it could attract more customers by bundling products together and lowering prices. As a result, Microsoft has gradually been trying to replace individual desktop applications with application "suites" such as Office.

The first version of Office came out in 1990 as a bundle of discounted applications containing Word and Excel as the main attractions and PowerPoint as a presentations package. Microsoft Mail, an electronic mail product, also now comes with the suite.

Access, a database management product, is available with the more expensive Professional version. Microsoft has gradually integrated the features of these different products and made Office into a low-priced applications product in itself. Gates explained this strategy in October 1993 with the launch of Office 4.0: "For the first time, we're positioning our primary application as being Office as opposed to the individual applications. . . . Now this is not to say that the individual applications are not important. They are. But already today we sell over half the units of Excel and Word as part of our Office package. And so we've turned Office into far more than simply a way of marketing a group of applications at a discount and rather into an individual product."[17]

Graphical User Interfaces: As Microsoft diversified from one mass market to another, it moved from character-based interfaces to the most mass-market interface of all: the graphical user interface (GUI, pronounced as "gooey"). Character-based interfaces such as in MS-DOS and old applications written for this operating system primarily show letters and numbers on the computer screen. Users communicate with the computer programs mostly through English-like commands or through a series of keystrokes, many of which are difficult to remember. In contrast, graphical user interfaces rely on "icons," symbolic pictures that allow people to use the computer simply by moving a pointer controlled by a device such as a "mouse" or a "trackball." Graphical interfaces make computers much easier to operate, since users only have to point to and "click on" particular icons to begin a program and initiate other actions. (Some DOS applications, like WordPerfect 5.1 and 6.0, now have primitive graphical interfaces, as do recent versions of MS-DOS. But these products do not contain icons and are still essentially character-based.)

GUI programs require much more hardware processing power and memory than is needed by MS-DOS or DOS applications. But this fact has enabled the Windows standard to stimulate two new mass markets: one for fast PCs with lots of memory, and another for GUI applications compatible with Windows. Growth of these markets, in turn, has stimulated demand for more copies of Windows and new Windows applications, creating a profitable cycle for Microsoft and other applications providers.

Developers in Microsoft also learned to build GUI products from working with Apple on applications for the Macintosh, introduced in 1984. Microsoft signed a contract with Apple in January 1982 to design spreadsheet, database, and graphics applications when the Macintosh was still under development. This allowed Microsoft developers to become intimately familiar with the Mac's user interface and internal workings. The contract prohibited Microsoft from introducing a GUI or mouse-based program for any other machine, but only for one year after shipment of the Macintosh or until January 1, 1983.[18] Thereafter, Microsoft was free to develop similar applications for PC-compatibles, which it did—albeit slowly, because of the limitations of DOS compatibility and the PC hardware.

Microsoft leveraged these graphical programming skills when building the Windows operating system. The first version (in 1985) and a second (in 1987) had many problems, including the memory constraints of MS-DOS; they failed as commercial products. Microsoft persisted, however, and version 3.0 (in 1990) broke through MS-DOS memory limitations and sold in the millions. An enhanced version 3.1 in March 1992 quickly sold in the tens of millions and became the new market standard for graphical computing on PCs compatible with the original IBM PC and Intel microprocessor standard. Gates, like his predecessors at Xerox PARC and Apple, recognized in the early 1980s that GUI operating systems and applications were the future of mass-market computing:

> Microsoft bet the company on graphical interfaces. . . . It took much longer than I expected for the graphics interface to move into the mainstream, but today we can say that it is the dominant way that people use their personal computer. We can just look at the sales of DOS applications as compared to Windows applications and see that, over the last two and a half years, character-based applications have gone from being about 80 percent of the market to now less than 20 percent. . . . Even that 20 percent will drop very dramatically when the last major character-mode application updates are shipped and all of the industry's resources move finally to doing graphical applications.[19]

While Microsoft tried to hone its GUI skills, people in Apple realized that they would lose their distinctive advantage if Microsoft succeeded with its Windows development effort. In particular, Apple protested that the second version of Windows had copied the "look and feel" of the Macintosh too closely. After $9 million in attorneys' fees, however, Microsoft had a lawsuit by Apple dismissed in April 1992, arguing that Xerox had really invented the technology and failed to commercialize it.[20] After denying previous applications, the U.S. Patent and Trademark Office in August 1994 also approved Microsoft's long-standing efforts to receive a registered trademark for the label "Windows."[21] This decision recognizes Microsoft not as the inventor of graphical computing but as the developer of the graphical computing standard for Intel-compatible PCs.

Networking Systems for the Corporate Mass Market: Another PC software market that has been growing along with increases in the capabilities of PC hardware is networked computing. Initially, these users worked on powerful computers based in corporations or other large organizations (such as universities or government facilities). Since the 1960s, these organizations have been able to link people who want to share the same databases or communications systems by using terminals—or, since the 1980s, personal computers—connected to mainframes or minicomputers. More recently, various organizations have created networks of powerful desktop PCs or workstations. Some of the machines act as "servers" of information or communications control, and they connect a larger number of computers acting as "clients" or receivers of the information. These networks frequently run on operating systems based on UNIX, such as Novell's NetWare.

To move into this high-end but still potentially very large market, Microsoft followed the lead of AT&T (which invented UNIX), as well as Novell and other companies, such as DEC and Sun Microsystems. It developed Windows NT and introduced the first version in August 1993 (numbered 3.0 to correspond to Windows 3.0) and then an upgrade (NT 3.5) in 1994. (See Appendix 3 for a description of Microsoft's operating systems.) Windows NT requires powerful machines with lots of memory and computing power, but it offers special features to attract corporate users.

Unlike UNIX-based systems or proprietary operating systems (such as from DEC), NT can run Windows and DOS applications programs, and it has the same user interface as Windows 3.1. NT can also run on computers other than Intel-compatible machines; a special version can operate as a server in a network linking Macintoshes, PCs, and workstations. Like UNIX and other advanced systems, it has security functions that prevent one user from getting into another user's files without permission.

In addition, like UNIX (as well as NetWare and OS/2), NT is "multithreaded": It can divide itself into several processing tracks (called "threads" or "virtual machines"), then run different tasks or applications programs separately as well as simultaneously. The separate threads protect one application if another fails. Windows 3.1, in contrast, can run multiple tasks and applications but only on a single thread; if one application fails, the whole system can shut down. Single-threaded applications also must share the computer's time, and one power-intensive application (such as a multimedia program) can cause other programs sharing the processor at the same time to operate extremely slowly. These deficiencies (which are primarily artifacts of the single-threaded MS-DOS) have caused considerable frustration among Windows 3.1 users and make it difficult for Microsoft to sell Windows 3.1 to corporate customers.

The origins of NT go back to 1988, when Nathan Myhrvold started a small project to write an operating system that would succeed OS/2. (OS/2 is an operating system initially designed by IBM and Microsoft in the mid-1980s to replace DOS, but marketed and developed solely by IBM after the two companies ended their partnership in 1989.) Myhrvold wanted the new system to run on RISC workstations as well as on Intel chips and multiprocessor computers; he decided to license and study Mach, a UNIX-type system developed at Carnegie-Mellon University in the 1980s under Rick Rashid (now Microsoft's vice president for research). Meanwhile, David Cutler, one of the chief designers of the VMS operating system for DEC's popular VAX minicomputers, had been working on developing a RISC operating system at

DEC's office in nearby Bellevue, Washington. After DEC management canceled his project, he quit and joined Microsoft to direct NT development.[22] Microsoft continued to work on the mass-market version of Windows in a separate group, although the two product units have shared some components and design concepts, including the user interface.

Windows NT had a slow start gaining followers: Gates announced that he expected to sell a million copies in the first year, but sold only about 300,000. Reasons included the expensive hardware upgrades required to run NT, a severe shortage of application programs available to take advantage of NT's 32-bit processing capabilities, and some other inadequacies common in a new product. Nonetheless, NT has provided a new architecture and many features for Microsoft's next generation of operating systems and upgrades, including Windows 95 and the popular Windows NT 3.5, released in September 1994. NT 3.5 sold 700,000 copies in four months and brought total NT sales to about 1 million as of December 1994.[23] Microsoft is also using NT as a server technology for information highway products and services such as interactive TV and video-on-demand over cable TV lines and telephone wires.[24]

PRINCIPLE   *Incrementally improve new products and periodically make old products obsolete.*

Microsoft has preempted the competition, as well as dramatically expanded its market coverage and penetration, in two main ways. First, by channeling hundreds of millions of dollars into R&D each year and steadily refining its products, Microsoft makes it extraordinarily difficult for competitors to keep up. We can see this in the many versions and flavors of Microsoft's operating systems, spreadsheet, and word-processing products, and the Office applications suite. Microsoft even saved MS-DOS from obsolescence by taking several years to build the graphical Windows interface layer and then gradually making this into a full-scale operating system (with MS-DOS embedded within it).

Second, Microsoft periodically introduces new product generations rather than complacently watching existing products decline in sales relative to competitors. These new generations (represented by Office, Visual Basic, Windows NT, and Windows 95, for example) still depend heavily on previous products and, in a sense, represent no more than a bundling of many incremental enhancements. When put together with a few new technologies, however, these many small improvements result in new products that make old products almost obsolete. As explained by Chris Peters, vice president of the Office product unit, Microsoft's strategy has been to combine incremental improvements with major changes every three to five years. The idea is to parallel and even anticipate the "exponential growth" in the processing power of computer hardware:

> Everything that we've ever done won't matter three years from now. In terms of products, the amount of computing power that will become available in the next five years will be equal to all the computing power ever made before. What it basically means is that you always have to be jumping well ahead. If you internalize that exponential growth, everyone else thinks that the thing will be like last year only a little different, which of course is true for a very short period of time. When you look at the industry in a two-year little chunk, it does look very linear and you have to step back and find out that it's always exponentially growing. And then, when you do that, you do make bigger bets and a little bit different kinds of bets. . . .
>
> I think it's an underlying principle for Microsoft. I think it's something that Bill always understood and internalized, that you [must] . . . radically change things and really have big plans. . . . A classic example is, DOS was doing great. [We could have said,] "Let's just come out with new versions of DOS. Why make Windows?" And, well, Windows takes up so much more hardware and computing power. . . . In a sense, [though, an innovation like] Office makes the individual apps obsolete. Just when our competitors are trying to be good in Windows [applications], now [they] . . . have to make a good word processor *and* a good spreadsheet *and* a good database. You have to be that kind of a software company now.

Incremental Improvements: Critics have claimed that Microsoft rarely has "hit" products initially and usually takes two or three versions to create products that match its top competitors.[25] For example, the first two versions of Windows had very limited functionality, and even version 3.1 trails the Macintosh operating system in ease of use and other technical characteristics. Windows NT originally did not sell well in the corporate market compared to Novell's NetWare, although NT 3.5 is catching up. We can see a similar pattern of improvement over time in Microsoft's spreadsheet (Multiplan, Excel) and word-processing (Word) offerings, integrated applications suites (Office), and home consumer lines (multimedia titles as well as personal finance and other product offerings.) Microsoft Money, introduced in 1991, took two versions to approach the functionality of Intuit's Quicken, though it has never come close in sales. (Quicken, introduced around 1985, has about seven million users, compared to about one million for Money.) Even highly innovative products and technologies such as OLE and Visual Basic have undergone significant evolution between their first and later versions; they also await further enhancements.

Over time, continually adding new features and changes results in increasingly competitive products. A reading of industry critiques, for example, indicates that Microsoft products now tend to be strong in standard features, ease of use and learning, and documentation and technical support. Some products lag in advanced features, although in many cases Microsoft is simply targeting mass-market users or is still in the process of adding features in small increments over multiple versions.[26] Most Microsoft products now do well not only in sales but also in technical evaluations, and they have been receiving industry design awards with increasingly frequency. *PC Magazine*, for example, gave Microsoft Office for Windows its 1994 award for technical excellence in applications software, and it recognized three of Office's components—Word 6.0, Excel 5.0, and Access 2.0—as the year's best new products in their respective areas. In addition, the editors gave Windows NT 3.5 the award for technical excellence in the systems software category and named it the best operating system introduced in 1994.[27] These are impressive achievements, given that Microsoft does not specialize; it competes in just about every PC software mass market.

MS-DOS: The company's first operating system has gone through six versions since 1981, with remarkably few major changes to the basic program. DOS 2.0, introduced in 1983, mostly added support for hard disk drives that came with the IBM PC-XT and compatible machines, as well as primitive multitasking when the user is printing. MS-DOS 3.0, introduced in 1984, supported the more advanced hardware available in the IBM PC-AT and compatibles, which had faster Intel 286 microprocessors. (DOS gradually became known as *MS*-DOS after Microsoft began selling the operating system to companies other than IBM, and after IBM and Digital Research introduced their own DOS systems.)

Version 3.1 added networking capabilities in 1985. MS-DOS 4.0, introduced in 1988, offered a simple graphical interface or "shell" designed for use with a mouse, but this found few buyers. MS-DOS 5.0, introduced in 1991, accessed more memory for applications and improved the limited multitasking capabilities, making it possible to load more than one application (but not to run them simultaneously). This upgrade, which proved to be an excellent platform for launching Windows, has sold tends of millions of copies.[28]

Microsoft introduced another version in 1993, although managers probably wish they had not. MS-DOS 6.0 primarily added a data-compression feature called DoubleSpace as well as some new memory-management features and diagnostic tools. This product suffered from early troubles, including a patent infringement suit (won by Stac Electronics) that forced Microsoft to withdraw and then replace its initial data-compression technology.[29] According to *PC Magazine*, based on surveys of several thousand users, MS-DOS 6.0 also scored "significantly below average" compared to DR-DOS, IBM's OS/2, and DESQview in product support and several other technical features.[30] More seriously, reviewers complained about problems with the DoubleSpace data compression (see Chapter 6 for a fuller discussion). Microsoft, however, remedied these difficulties with minor updates. The latest, MS-DOS 6.22, is now a solid product and has sold in the millions, usually bundled with Windows 3.1.

Although critics like to disparage MS-DOS for technical shortcomings, it has been a remarkable product. It has made billions of dollars for Microsoft while serving as a platform technology for an entire industry. MS-DOS offers relatively powerful features for a very low price, yet requires only a small amount of memory and processing power. These traits have made it possible for inexpensive PCs to run thousands of useful applications. Microsoft has also been able to expand the capabilities of MS-DOS, and it survived into the GUI era as a platform to launch Windows.

But the era of MS-DOS as a stand-alone operating system and platform for Windows is quickly drawing to a close. Microsoft has not put many resources into its development since the mid-1980s, concentrating instead on Windows and NT systems. Consequently, in some areas, competitors have surpassed MS-DOS in features, even though they have not made much headway in market share. Because it incorporates or mimics the code needed to run the old DOS applications, Windows 95 does not come bundled with MS-DOS. There may yet be another version of MS-DOS if Microsoft people think there is a large market for it, but Windows 95 essentially makes MS-DOS obsolete as a separate product, except for people without enough computing power to run graphical programs.

Desktop Applications: Not until Excel 2.0 in 1988 do industry reviews suggest that Microsoft matched the skills of the Lotus Development Corporation in spreadsheet design. But Excel 2.0 took such excellent advantage of the Windows interface that it saved the fledgling Windows product and helped make it a new standard for the PC, much like Lotus 1-2-3 did earlier for the IBM PC and DOS. The new Excel also drew rave reviews from industry observers, attracting comments such as "one of the landmark products of its time . . . a work of art, a masterpiece."[31] Later versions of Excel have sometimes ranked average or below average compared to Windows competitors (Lotus 1-2-3, QuattroPro, and SuperCalc), but they have generally garnered top honors on the Macintosh.[32] Excel 5.0 is now the best-selling Windows and Mac spreadsheet.

Word had a slower start as a product. Despite innovative features, PC Word 1.0 (introduced in 1983) and Mac Word 1.0 (introduced in 1984) sold modestly, and they received a mixed response from industry critics because of too many bugs. The early Word versions apparently were also somewhat difficult to learn, though easier than WordStar.[33] But the major problem holding back sales was the rapidly growing popularity of WordPerfect, which had many rich features as well as excellent customer support over toll-free telephone lines. By 1986 the latter had become the top PC word processor, with approximately 30 percent of the market—about three times Word's market share.

As with spreadsheets, Microsoft had something closer to a success on its third try. Word 3.0, introduced in 1986 for the PC, was more refined and had an on-line tutorial that greatly simplified learning the program.[34] Microsoft still ran into problems. As discussed in Chapter 1, a 1987 version for the Macintosh became a commercial and public relations disaster after hundreds of bugs forced Microsoft to send customers a free upgrade. Microsoft also took four years longer than it initially estimated to finish a version of Word for Windows. Nonetheless, when Word for Windows arrived in 1990—with a new version more carefully ported over to the Macintosh—Microsoft passed WordPerfect to become the market leader in word-processor sales. It has occasionally trailed WordPerfect for DOS and Lotus' Ami Pro for Windows in surveys of customer support satisfaction and technical features. But Word 6.0 (introduced in late 1993) is the second best-selling Windows application, behind Excel, and it is also the best-selling Mac application. More than half of Word (as well as Excel) sales, however, now come through the Office suite.[35]

We should add that while Word has about 65 percent of the Macintosh word-processor market (compared to about thirty percent for WordPerfect), Mac Word 6.0 has been very poorly received.[36] This is the first version of Mac Word that consists almost entirely of "core code" from the Windows version, with only a small amount of customization for the Macintosh. Microsoft has done this successfully for years with Excel. As we discuss in Chapter 4, however, Excel contains a special layer isolating it from the Macintosh and Windows operating systems. Because Word does not have such a layer, Microsoft ended up with a large and extremely slow Macintosh version. In order to ship the Macintosh version as soon as possible after the new Windows version, Microsoft also decided not to take extra time to tailor Word 6.0 code for Mac hardware. Developers eventually had to trim down the code and offer Mac customers a special upgrade. In the long run, merging the Macintosh and Windows versions of Word—as with Excel—is the right thing to do from Microsoft's perspective. It means that Microsoft only has to build and support one version of the product. The incident with Word 6.0, though, reflects Microsoft's lack of concern for Macintosh users and preference for Windows users. If not corrected, this attitude will clearly hurt Microsoft in Macintosh applications, especially word processors. This market is significantly smaller than Windows, although Mac users have traditionally led the broader market as well as bought a lot of software.

The new versions of Excel and Word, as well as other new Microsoft applications (such as PowerPoint), contain several innovative features that have proved attractive to customers and helped the products gain market share over specific competitors. In particular, Microsoft has been able to overcome technical and psychological factors that have often kept software customers from switching to other products. For example, Excel contains "Help for Lotus 1-2-3 Users," and Word has "Help for WordPerfect Users." These features provide instructions in response to keystrokes that would have activated functions in Lotus 1-2-3 or WordPerfect. Excel and Word also have the ability to read and convert files from a huge number of competing products. In addition, both products contain built-in tools that simplify and automate common tasks and, to some extent, anticipate what the user is trying to do. Word's AutoCorrect will automatically correct spelling errors or typographical mistakes, capitalize first letters of a sentence, capitalize *I* when it stands alone, or insert curved "smart" quotes in the right places. (It also, annoyingly, likes to change *PCs* into *Pcs*.) Users can also set up AutoCorrect to type out full words or phrases in place of an abbreviation, like *New York Times* for *NYT*. The AutoFormat feature formats documents in certain styles, while "wizards"—or step-by-step help screens—assist users with detailed instructions for complicated tasks.[37]

And now Office is making individual desktop applications obsolete. This product works in combination with the Windows operating system and interface, and it employs technologies such as

OLE, dynamic link libraries (DLLs), and other design approaches. The result is that Office (and similar suites introduced by Novell-WordPerfect and Lotus) allow their component applications to share features and data in ways that were inconceivable on PCs just a few years ago. MS-DOS machines and applications now seem especially out of date. The application suites also provide an inexpensive way for customers upgrading to Windows to replace these old applications.

Windows: We have noted that early versions of Windows sold poorly and were clumsy to use, especially given the limitations of PC hardware at that time. To look right and run fast enough to be acceptable, Windows requires a color monitor as well as a more powerful processor and more memory than were commonly available before the late 1980s. In addition, few graphical application programs existed in the mid-1980s. Writing applications for Windows is more complex than writing for the DOS standard, and Microsoft took several years to introduce programming tools such as Visual Basic. Applications developers in other companies also hesitated to learn and write for Windows because they were uncertain when and if this would become the market standard.[38]

As with Excel and Word, Microsoft kept working on the product. It introduced a second version of Windows in October 1987, specifically designed for the new Intel 80386 microprocessor and developed with the cooperation of Compaq (whose market share for PCs surged due to its aggressive introduction of 386-based computers). The new Windows still seemed slow and awkward to many reviewers (and users), but it was clearly a more refined program. Most importantly, Windows created a new market for easy-to-use graphical applications, which were now becoming available. Microsoft led the way itself by writing Excel 2.0 specifically to work with the new Windows program. Excel helped Windows' sales and propelled Microsoft into a closer competition with Lotus for the lead in spreadsheets. Windows 3.0, introduced in May 1990, sold nearly four hundred thousand copies in five weeks and was already a successful product when Microsoft replaced it with the more refined and debugged Windows 3.1 in April 1992. Within a year, nine out of every ten personal computers being sold came bundled with this version, and Microsoft has continued to ship more than two million copies per month.[39]

In early user surveys, Windows 3.1 did not score well in customer support, although Microsoft introduced more phone lines, support personnel, training, support tools, and other measures to address this problem. (See Chapter 6 for a discussion of Microsoft's product support services.) Windows 3.1 ranks considerably higher than OS/2 in technical satisfaction among users and in ease of use, and it usually runs applications much faster, although it has scored lower than OS/2 in some other categories. Many industry reviewers have long wished for technical improvements, such as better memory management and protection, true multitasking, and an improved program and file manager.[40] At least for new 32-bit applications, however, Microsoft has fixed these problems with Windows NT and Windows 95. And both of these make Windows 3.1 more or less obsolete.

Windows NT: The first version of NT brought many complaints from users. NT required a large amount of disk space and computer memory to install and use the program. It also ran many applications slowly, was difficult to install, and had problems with device drivers and compatibility with some applications. For many customers, OS/2, NetWare, NeXTStep (a version of UNIX built around Mach), and other versions of UNIX were preferable systems; they had been through multiple versions and ironed out most bugs. NT 3.0, in contrast, was a totally new product in a category—high-end corporate operating systems—where Microsoft had not competed before with any serious commitment.[41]

A slimmer version of NT introduced in fall 1994, numbered 3.5, fixed many of the initial problems and requires fewer hardware capabilities while adding more features. In particular, 3.5 incorporates design changes that make it more reliable when running Windows applications, and it has improved workstation graphics and networking capabilities. In addition, it makes fuller use of OLE, allowing separate applications or objects to interact with each other through a standard interface.[42]

Also widely discussed in industry publications and within Microsoft is the next major version change, referred to internally by the code name "Cairo" and outside the company as Windows NT 4.0.[43] Cairo is not a tightly managed project; it is more like an open-ended research effort. Nonetheless, the project is developing important technologies. In particular, Cairo utilizes a network version of OLE and includes other new features that will give NT much broader capabilities for connecting multiple computers on a network. For example, Cairo will allow users to share applications programs as well as place and track data and other types of objects across a series of linked computers. (This is in addition to supporting applications and objects of data or information on one person's computer.) Cairo also contains a new file management technology that does not simply store files by names; it keeps an index of the contents of files and enables users to search for or arrange these by different criteria. (Users can ask the operating system to arrange all files relating to a particular topic or that originated on a particular date. This is useful for sophisticated customers who create thousands of separate files, and for "groupwork," where people need to share large amounts of information and access it easily.) Interface components are also OLE objects, which means that users can add or subtract them—in other words, customize the computer screens—as they desire. Industry observers expect Cairo to appear as a commercial product in 1996 or 1997, although Microsoft has not formally announced the product or a ship date.[44]

Windows 95: Once code-named Chicago, Windows 95 brings Microsoft's mass-market operating system closer to the ten-year-old Macintosh in performance and ease of use. This new system runs with the same relatively modest hardware requirements as Windows 3.1: four to eight megabytes of random-access memory (RAM) and a fast 386 processor, compared to the twelve to sixteen megabytes of RAM and a fast 486 processor required as a minimum by NT or IBM's OS/2 (and preferred for Windows 95 as well). Windows 95 is an incremental improvement technically in that it incorporates and builds on advanced architectural features that already existed in Windows 3.1 (and 3.0). But it also adds new design concepts and features, some of which have come from Windows NT and other Microsoft projects.

For example, as with NT and the enhanced mode of Windows 3.1, Microsoft has built Windows 95 around a 32-bit application programming interface called Win32. (Win32 is central to Microsoft's systems software strategy. As long as applications developers adhere to this standard, any of their applications will run on any of the Windows family that supports the interface.) More like NT than 3.1, however, Windows 95 has a layered architecture surrounding a "micro-kernel." The kernel does memory management and multithreaded task switching, with separate subsystems to handle tasks like display management and file input and output. (See Chapter 4 for a more detailed discussion of the Windows 95 architecture.)

Perhaps most important in terms of performance, Windows 95 bypasses MS-DOS in the same way NT does, at least for new 32-bit applications. This is useful because, when running MS-DOS directly, the operating system cedes control to the individual DOS applications and can only run one application at a time. Windows 3.1 gets around this limitation by "cooperative multitasking." The operating system alternates tasks or applications, making it appear to the user that the computer is running multiple tasks or applications simultaneously. The time-sharing becomes tediously slow, however, if one of those tasks consumes a lot of processing time, because the alternating occurs evenly among the running applications or tasks.

Windows 95, like the NT family, uses "preemptive multitasking" for new 32-bit Windows application programs. This allows the operating system to determine which tasks or applications are consuming the most power, and it can stop one application to run another or a particular task. As in NT, MS-DOS and 32-bit applications also get their own "protected" space in Windows 95. If the computer is running multiple applications and one encounters problems and terminates, the others usually remain unaffected. This is a major improvement over MS-DOS and Windows 3.1, which contain only one processing track and are more vulnerable to application "crashes."

Another enhancement in Windows 95 is the interface. Though Windows 3.1 is much easier to use than any of the MS-DOS versions, industry critics have described the screens as "a confusing mishmash of icons, program groups, lists, and menus."[45] Users must also maneuver through files and applications using two separate subprograms called Program Manager and File Manager. The Windows 95 interface is simpler and more "integrated" (a term Microsoft likes), similar to IBM's OS/2 Workplace Shell and Apple's Macintosh. On the Windows 95 "desktop" (the main computer screen) are folders that hold icons representing an application program or files. A new TaskBar at the bottom of the screen tells users which applications are running; it also lets them switch tasks or applications without entering, exiting, and reentering the separate programs (as required in Windows 3.1). Using technology borrowed from the Cairo project, Windows 95 also lets users customize the screens they see and automate applications by combining features from different programs.

Some features in Windows 95 contain all-new code and involved substantial architectural work. In particular, the plug-and-play feature enables the operating system to determine what hardware devices users have plugged into the system, then automatically activate the appropriate software "drivers" for that equipment. (The Macintosh has offered a similar capability for years, to the extent that the operating system incorporates device drivers for Apple hardware.) In addition—and again like the Macintosh—Windows 95 handles long file names, rather than the maximum eight characters plus a three-character extension in MS-DOS and Windows 3.1. It also includes fax and electronic mail capabilities, as well as basic networking features found earlier in Microsoft's Windows for Workgroups 3.11 and Microsoft At Work. There is even a button feature that provides a simple connection to the new on-line Microsoft Network without shifting to a separate communications program.

Windows 95 has been available in beta test versions sent to as many as 400,000 customer sites since May 1994. The 1995 shipping target fell more than a year and a half behind the original schedule; Microsoft needed extra time to make Windows 95 more compatible with existing applications, as well as to complete and test new features (especially plug-and-play and multitasking).[46] This delay does not reflect well on the ability of the Windows group to estimate how much time they need to build a complex new operating system, even if earlier announced schedules were far too ambitious. Nor has Microsoft been in a hurry to ship: Bill Gates and other managers clearly want to avoid the type of quality problems they used to experience in the 1980s and which Intel recently encountered with the Pentium. (Apple has also become reluctant to rush new products out. It has delayed shipment of its long-overdue upgrade to the Macintosh System 7.5 operating system for a full year, to mid-1996.[47])

PRINCIPLE   *Push volume sales and exclusive contracts to ensure that company products become and remain industry standards.*

As long ago as 1981, in a talk at a public conference, Bill Gates discussed the strategic connection between volume and standards:

> Why do we need standards? . . . It's only through volume that you can offer reasonable software at a low price. Standards increase the basic machine that you can sell into [the market]. . . . I really shouldn't say this, but in some ways it leads, in an individual product category, to a natural monopoly: where somebody properly documents, properly trains, properly promotes a particular package and through momentum, user loyalty, reputation, sales force, and prices builds a very strong position with that product.[48]

More than a dozen years later, this comment serves as an apt description of what Microsoft has done since 1975. It prices, markets, licenses, and supports products in a way that aggressively promotes volume sales. It offers huge discounts on the assumption that it is far better to collect a small sum for each copy of a product if lower prices lead to exponential growth in the market. Over time, these and other tactics have given Microsoft overwhelming leads in such key markets as programming languages (BASIC and Visual Basic), character-based operating systems (MS-DOS), graphical operating systems for the PC (Windows), and desktop application suites (Office). Selling millions of copies of Windows and Office has also helped make OLE into a de facto standard for applications developers.

Volume sales have been essential to keep the cycle going and the company growing. Large-scale revenues and profits—first from BASIC and MS-DOS, and then from Windows and Office—have enabled Microsoft to finance the continued refinement and marketing of its products, as well as its huge recent investments in R&D and new ventures. No dedicated PC software company can now match Microsoft's financial resources. (The company spent $830 million on R&D in fiscal 1995 alone and has between $4 billion and $5 billion in cash.[49]) Gates offered this comment on Microsoft's strategic advantage: "It's all about scale economics and market share. When you're shipping a million units of Windows software a month, you can afford to spend $300 million a year improving it and still sell it at a low price."[50] Executive vice president Steve Ballmer concurred: "Software businesses are all fixed-cost businesses. And so volume is absolutely everything . . . because you've got to amortize that fixed cost very broadly."[51]

BASIC and MS-DOS: Microsoft first promoted volume sales by selling inexpensive licenses to hardware companies in 1975. These provided the right to bundle BASIC with the computers they sold. In the initial pricing scheme for Altair BASIC, for example, MITS Computer paid Microsoft a small royalty for every copy that MITS delivered, with a ceiling of $180,000. MITS also received the rights to relicense BASIC to other companies, in which case MITS and Microsoft shared the royalties. Initially, MITS charged $75 extra to ship BASIC to people who purchased the Altair PC and $500 to people who just wanted the language. (The Altair computer itself, without BASIC or an operating system, sold for about $400 unassembled.) The MITS prices were extremely cheap, given that mainframe and minicomputer languages usually rented at fees of $400 or more *per month*.[52] In some other OEM cases with high potential volumes, Gates agreed to inexpensive flat-fee deals, such as with Apple (for the Apple II) and Radio Shack (for the TRS-80). Then he did not have to worry about piracy and collecting royalties.[53]

Microsoft received $200,000 from IBM to adapt Q-DOS to the IBM PC and $500,000 instead of royalties for DOS, BASIC, and several language compilers. In contrast to the MITS agreement to relicense BASIC, this new contract prohibited IBM from licensing

DOS—but placed no restraints on Microsoft. Microsoft then licensed MS-DOS cheaply to other hardware vendors, thereby establishing it as the PC industry (not merely IBM) standard. It first charged other OEM customers $95,000, but since then has sold MS-DOS at half this price to get as many companies as possible behind the standard. When it charges a royalty, Microsoft asks for a low fee (usually bundling MS-DOS and BASIC); this is generally between $1 and $15 per copy, depending on the number of copies.[54] Retail prices are considerably higher and offer room for significant profit margins for hardware manufacturers and retail stores. (MS-DOS 6.22 upgrades have recently sold for about $50 in national software chains.) As Gates commented:

> Our restricting IBM's ability to compete with us in licensing MS-DOS to other computer makers was the key point of the negotiation. We wanted to make sure only we could license it. We did the deal with them at a fairly low price, hoping that would help popularize it. Then we could make our move because we insisted that all other business stay with us. We knew that good IBM products are usually cloned, so it didn't take a rocket scientist to figure out that eventually we could license DOS to others. We knew that if we were ever going to make a lot of money on DOS it was going to come from the compatible guys, not from IBM. They paid us a fixed fee for DOS. We didn't get a royalty, even though we did make some money on the deal. Other people paid a royalty. So it was always advantageous to us—the market grew and other hardware guys were able to sell units. . . . Subsequently there were clone competitors to DOS, and there were people coming out with completely new operating systems. But *we had already captured the volume*, so we could price it low and keep selling.[55] [italics added]

A variety of nonpricing tactics further decreased the likelihood that competing products would challenge MS-DOS, or Windows later on. For example, Digital Research's CP/M-86 (developed in the early 1980s) might have become the dominant PC operating system; reportedly, it had better memory management features and other advantages over MS-DOS. Microsoft, however, was the leading languages producer, and it did not rush to deliver versions of its languages compatible with CP/M-86. When it did ship compatible languages, Microsoft priced them 50 percent over DOS-compatible versions, and they sold in low volumes. Microsoft also sold only an inferior version of BASIC, stripped of graphics. As a result, applications developers found it difficult to write for anything but MS-DOS, and CP/M-86 failed as a competing product.[56]

Microsoft introduced perhaps its most effective, and controversial, marketing innovation—per-processor licensing—in a way that warded off challenges from CP/M-86's successor, DR-DOS, as well as from IBM's OS/2 and in-house DOS version, IBM PC-DOS. In 1988 Microsoft began offering hardware companies a specially low royalty fee for MS-DOS if they paid something *for each computer* they shipped, regardless of whether the hardware company bundled each machine with MS-DOS. Dave Moore, Microsoft's director of development, claimed that one reason Microsoft did this was to simplify its own accounting and forecasting. Microsoft provides hardware companies only with a master copy of the software; the latter can easily copy the master and keep no records—and pay no royalties. But Microsoft can track how many computers (processors) they ship, and it can forecast sales simply by totaling up manufacturer estimates of how many Intel and compatible microprocessors companies plan to ship. Whatever the intent behind this practice, the Microsoft products quickly became so popular that hardware companies were reluctant to bundle any other software, and they usually wanted the volume discount.

After DR-DOS version 5.0 appeared in 1990 and 6.0 in 1991, Microsoft seems to have become particularly aggressive in pushing per-processor contracts. DR-DOS, marketed actively by Novell (which purchased Digital Research in 1991), actually passed MS-DOS during early 1992 in retail sales. Even though retail is a very small percentage of MS-DOS sales, most of which come through OEM hardware vendors, Microsoft responded quickly to the challenge.

First, directly after DR-DOS 5.0 came out in April 1990, Microsoft announced that it would upgrade MS-DOS to version 5.0. It took until June 1991 to introduce a product, but the early announcement may have discouraged hardware vendors and other customers from buying DR-DOS. (Industry critics often refer to products announced far in advance in order to preempt competitors as "vaporware," although it is common industry practice to let customers know in advance what products are forthcoming.) Second, Microsoft appears to have stepped up pressure on hardware vendors to accept the per-processor contracts. Third, Microsoft in 1992 let it be known publicly that DR-DOS might not be fully compatible with Windows (by then on 90 percent of all new PCs), because Microsoft had not tested it. (Microsoft did not use Novell as a beta test site for Windows 3.1.) Microsoft even inserted a message warning users who tried to run Windows on top of non-Microsoft versions of DOS that they might encounter compatibility problems, although instances of this proved rare.[57]

Windows and Windows 95: Microsoft has used equally low prices and aggressive marketing and licensing tactics to promote Windows. When it first appeared in 1985, Microsoft priced version 1.0 at $90 wholesale per copy, but charged its largest customers as little as $8 "per processor" or $24 a copy. Microsoft claimed to have sold half a million or more copies of Windows 1.0 by spring 1987, but it did this by bundling Windows with MS-DOS; probably no more than 20 percent of users installed these copies on their machines.[58] Recent versions of Windows 3.1 have sold for about $35 wholesale and $95 retail and Microsoft is pricing the Windows 95 upgrade comparably. Hardware vendors can reduce the OEM price by as much as $30 if they agree to install Windows 95 on 50 percent of their PC shipments or adopt the Windows 95 logo and sign a contract by a particular date.[59]

Long-term contracts with hardware vendors, even apart from per-processor licensing conditions, make it particularly difficult for competitors to introduce competing products. For example, Microsoft's contracts with leading PC producers in effect isolated IBM when it tried to introduce such alternatives to Windows as Presentation Manager and then OS/2.[60] Microsoft has also secured early commitments from hardware producers to license Windows 95. An industry journalist commented on the likelihood of this new product (referred to here as Windows 4.0) failing in the marketplace: "You might as well put your money on Wile E. Coyote to finally catch the Roadrunner. Microsoft's secret weapon is its stack of contracts with just about every PC maker in the world. Thanks to those deals, you can be sure that Windows 4.0 will be preloaded on more than 70 percent of all PCs sold in 1995. . . . And look for Microsoft to do everything but sell the new Windows door to door in an effort to get you to upgrade."[61] Though late to market, most industry analysts expect Windows 95 to sell at least 30 million copies in its first year.

Again, as with MS-DOS and early Windows versions, Microsoft is not leaving the success of a major new product to chance. It has announced that it will spend as much as $100 million on the Windows 95 marketing campaign.[62] This is in addition to another $100 million campaign to advertise the Microsoft name and product lines such as "Microsoft Home" to the general consumer. Furthermore, as discussed below, Microsoft has instituted licensing conditions that greatly discourage applications developers from producing any more products for Windows 3.1. These measures will ensure that Windows 95 and its successors eventually replace Windows 3.1 as the desktop operating system standard.

Applications Marketing and Bundling: The popularity of MS-DOS and Windows has given Microsoft at least an indirect advantage in marketing applications. The company has close relationships with many hardware vendors and retail software stores, and millions of customers see the Microsoft name every time they start up their computers. These marketing relationships appear to have helped the company sell formerly unpopular or new applications, such as Works, PowerPoint, Mail, and Access, in addition to Microsoft's multimedia titles. In particular, Microsoft made the initially unpopular Works into a best-selling product by selling it to OEM vendors who have bundled it with their PCs, as they have done with BASIC, MS-DOS, and Windows.

Millions of users have also switched to Word and Excel—and tried the far less popular PowerPoint and Access programs—because Microsoft has bundled (as well as technically integrated) these into Office. Retail customers can buy the standard version of Office for approximately $250, a huge discount compared to a list price of $300 or more for *each* of its three main programs. Tens of millions of MS-DOS users upgrading to Windows make a simple (and inexpensive) purchasing decision by buying the latest version of Office—a product from a manufacturer they all know. Bundling these applications into Office has also enabled Microsoft to ship more copies of its presentation software, PowerPoint, and expand market acceptance and usage of this previously low-volume product category. Bundling applications together, lowering prices, advertising the Microsoft name, or selling aggressively to retail stores, however, are not enough in themselves to sell applications. Products have to be close to or as good as the market leaders, *and* they have to be relatively early to market. The low sales of Microsoft Money compared to Quicken attest to this reality.

Overseas Markets: Much of what it has achieved in the United States, the world's first and largest PC market, Microsoft has replicated overseas. Charles Simonyi offered the economic logic: "We realized from day zero, or at least day zero of applications, that international is key. It makes the product 3 to 5 percent more complex, and it doubles your market. It at least doubles." Following this rationale, Microsoft designed MS-DOS 2.0, released in 1983, for easy internationalization.[63] Since then, it has designed most new versions of its major products for international sales and has established thirty-six subsidiaries around the world. Not surprisingly, more than 40 percent of Microsoft's revenues now come from overseas, mainly Japan and Europe (see Table 2, p.3). The strategy to compete in these markets has been the same as in the United States: Form alliances and use a variety of pricing and nonpricing tactics to obtain long-term agreements whereby companies bundle Microsoft software with the local hardware.

In Japan, Microsoft established an early position in the PC operating systems market by building relationships with NEC and other Japanese PC manufacturers. Microsoft began with MSX, an 8-bit operating system introduced in 1983. It followed this with a Japanese version of BASIC that ran on machines made by NEC, the Japanese market leader in PC sales, as well as on IBM-compatible machines. Microsoft started licensing a Japanese version of MS-DOS in 1983, although this became popular only with the rise in sales of 16-bit machines after 1987.[64] Microsoft now builds Japanese versions of Windows, Windows NT, and all its major applications. Its Japanese subsidiary (which is part of the desktop applications division) also oversees the translation of key applications products into Chinese and Korean as well as Japanese.

In Europe, Microsoft set up a marketing company in 1982 in the United Kingdom and soon moved into France, Germany, and other countries. Apple then had 50 percent of the European market, but Microsoft convinced several European PC manufacturers to ship MS-DOS and BASIC as software products bundled with their PCs. Microsoft helped its cause by quickly translating the BASIC manual into European languages and producing European-language versions of Multiplan. European sales of the IBM PC after 1983–1984 also greatly encouraged European PC companies to adopt MS-DOS as their operating system standard.[65]

Antitrust Concerns: A huge shadow hanging over Microsoft's success has been concerns about potential antitrust violations. The U.S. Federal Trade Commission (FTC) began an inquiry into Microsoft's practices in June 1990; at Novell's insistence, the European Union launched a similar investigation. Although the FTC deadlocked in August 1993, the U.S. Justice Department continued the probe and reached a consent agreement with Microsoft in July 1994. At the same time, Microsoft reached an identical agreement with the European Union.

In February 1995, however, a U.S. federal judge, in an almost unprecedented move, refused to ratify the Justice Department settlement. He decided this on the grounds that the agreement was too narrow, applied only to future practices, and did nothing to remedy Microsoft's current domination of the operating systems business. In particular, the judge was concerned that the agreement did not deal with Microsoft's use of a common industry practice of pre-announcing new products ("vaporware"), which can deter sales of competing products. Nor did it deal with Microsoft's ability to leverage "its near-monopoly in operating systems into the more competitive field of applications software."[66] The Justice Department had agreed to relatively narrow terms, because it is difficult to prove broad anticompetitive practices in a court of law. Microsoft and the Justice Department appealed the court ruling and won. Even prior to this decision, Microsoft had been complying with the original agreement in the United States and Europe.[67] (The European agreement did not need court approval.)

The July 1994 settlement contains three key elements. First, Microsoft agreed to stop granting large discounts to licensees if they pay a royalty per processor or computer shipped, rather than per copy of the software shipped. This type of contract covers about 60 percent of Microsoft's operating systems sales. Second, Microsoft agreed to abandon long-term contracts that commit computer vendors to buying particular volumes of software several years in advance. Third, Microsoft agreed to end its policy of strict nondisclosure agreements with independent applications software developers. (Microsoft had required that beta testers and other companies not disclose details of its operating systems for three years after the system was introduced into the market. This restricted the activities and mobility of applications software developers in other companies, whereas Microsoft was free to recruit developers from anywhere and have them work on applications sold by Microsoft.) In these negotiations, Microsoft also reaffirmed that it would not withhold information on new products from competitors or customers, although it retained the right not to license or publish its source code.

Even these relatively mild restrictions have increased competition in operating systems and added some volatility to Microsoft's operating systems sales, as they open the way for hardware vendors to purchase competing systems. This is already occurring in Germany, for example. Europe's largest PC vendor, Vobis Microcomputer, started in the fall of 1994 to ship PCs with OS/2 and Windows, but not MS-DOS. As a result, approximately 20 percent of European PCs now come with OS/2 (twice the number in the United States); this figure is about 40 percent in the German market. Since these machines come with Windows as well as OS/2, it is not clear which operating system people are actually using. No other PC vendor followed Vobis's lead, and Vobis also plans to ship PCs with Windows 95 when this arrives, but Microsoft now faces at least a slightly more difficult task to establish new products as de facto standards.[68] (Vobis also negotiated a change in Microsoft's per-processor licensing policy for Windows 3.1. As of March 1995, it is paying Microsoft only for copies of Windows 3.1 that it ships with its PCs.[69])

We also believe, however, that the terms of the consent agreement will probably have little impact on Microsoft's worldwide market share or financial earnings. Nearly all hardware vendors continue to bundle MS-DOS and Windows on their machines, even if they also load OS/2. The Microsoft products have a huge installed base and thus are already de facto industry standards. Furthermore, Microsoft can still use volume discounts and exclusionary licensing terms to push Windows 95 and future versions of this and other products. Users who adopt a competing product have to worry about potentially losing access to the thousands of existing DOS and Windows applications. (Not even Windows NT and Windows 95 run all old applications perfectly.) For these reasons, whatever the terms of any antitrust agreement, only a few hardware vendors are likely to risk not offering Windows 95 or future enhancements of it on their PCs.[70]

At the same time, however, Microsoft is altering its behavior as a result of government antitrust actions. In particular, company executives decided in May 1995 to abandon their efforts to acquire Intuit (which Microsoft first announced in October 1994) after the U.S. Department of Justice filed a suit to block the merger.[71]

PRINCIPLE   *Take advantage of being the standards provider with new products and product linkages.*

Pricing, marketing, and distribution arrangements that promote volume sales have helped establish Microsoft as a company and some of its products as industry standards. But to maintain and extend its market positions, or to sell new products in new markets, a standards provider may also try to take advantage of its influence over the product "architecture." Being the standards provider may also give it an advantage over the network of players that adhere to a particular architecture, such as the technical standards that define how products work with MS-DOS and Windows. In Microsoft's case, this includes makers of applications software as well as producers of software development tools, hardware peripherals and drivers (such as printers and monitors), and other products designed to work with Microsoft operating systems. A 1994 quote from innovation columnist Michael Schrage captured the aims, and achievements, of Bill Gates and Microsoft as the standards provider:

Who understands the business of standards better than anyone? Probably Bill Gates and Microsoft. Microsoft really isn't in the software business; it's in the standards business. Microsoft succeeds not because it writes the best code but because it sets the best standards. Microsoft Windows—the personal computer software that made Gates a septibillionaire—was nurtured and developed to be a standard, not just another operating system. Microsoft's goal was emphatically not the maximization of revenue or even market share; it was creating relationships with customers, software developers and microprocessor firms like Intel to give as many good reasons as possible to support—strategically, financially and technically—Microsoft's operating systems. These networks of relationships are what makes a standard something more than a product. The standard is not the product of a company, it's the byproduct of these networks. Managing the standard means managing these networks.[72]

Providing the Standards: There are four main elements to the hardware and software architectural standards for a personal computer: the microprocessor, the operating system, the data controller (called a "bus"), and the video graphics system.[73] These determine interfaces for sending and receiving data and commands between the operating system and the hardware logic and memory chips, between the operating system and applications programs or network communications software, and between peripheral device drivers (the software that runs the printers, monitors, keyboards, mouse pointing devices, and so forth) and the operating system and applications programs. Because users demand backward compatibility, no one company can arbitrarily change any of these elements today, as opposed to earlier days in the PC industry. Microsoft, for example, cannot change elements of Windows that maintain compatibility with existing applications, including DOS applications and those written for Windows 3.0 or 3.1. Senior vice president Brad Silverberg (a former developer at Borland and Apple) pointed this out as one of the key reasons why his group at Microsoft did not improve Windows earlier:

[Windows] 3.0 was pretty big and pretty slow; 3.1 made a lot of improvements. . . . [But] at some point you can't break compatibility, either. It's the interfaces. Some of them define the APIs through the applications. In some ways, if we could do them over again, we know how we could do it so we could write the system faster. But once you have those interfaces, you're pretty much locked. You can't just change them and break applications. A system like we have, we don't own it; the ISVs [independent software vendors] own it. We [the Windows/MS-DOS group] exist for one purpose, which is to run applications. And [if] you break an application, you don't have a reason for being any more.

Nonetheless, the providers of the key hardware and software technologies—Intel and Microsoft—both exert tremendous influence over the evolution of their de facto standards for the PC microprocessor and the PC operating system. And Microsoft is especially well placed to take advantage of its position: It produces complementary products (applications) as well as key enabling technologies, such as OLE. Thus it can and does create technical and marketing linkages that support sales of every major type of software product (see Table 3.1).

Complementary Products: Windows is complex, but it is the environment to which nearly all software applications writers (as well as makers of printers and other peripherals) adhere. Microsoft releases enormous amounts of detailed information about its new products, even before selling them commercially, at industry conferences as well as with beta releases to customers and software development kits to applications programmers. Microsoft people answer questions from applications developers from any company.

But Microsoft designed Windows as well as MS-DOS, and its developers understand the intricacies and idiosyncrasies of these systems better than anyone else. From 1988 to 1995, both the systems and applications groups also reported to the same executive, Mike Maples. He as well as Bill Gates openly encouraged the movement of people and sharing of technical knowledge. (Gates also admitted in a March 1995 interview published in the *Wall Street Journal* that "there is no Chinese wall" between the applications and systems groups, saying, "We don't block input going in either direction."[74]) There is no substitute for having the designers of the standard right across the hall or the lunch table, in the next building, or on the same development team.

Some industry observers have claimed that Microsoft applications programmers have a particularly unfair advantage in the form of "undocumented calls" or low-level application programming interfaces (APIs) found in Windows as well as in MS-DOS. APIs are code routines that activate functions in the operating system; they are necessary to write applications programs. The concern is that Microsoft developers probably have access to these lists of calls and probably use them when writing applications.[75] This may be true in some cases, although how important these are for applications development is unclear. Dave Moore argued to us that many undocumented calls exist simply because developers have decided not to use them. He also explained that many calls are there so that operating systems developers can perform internal debugging or test different functions, rather than to assist applications programmers.

Even without considering the issue of APIs, however, Microsoft has utilized its position as the provider of Windows. It has made particular investments and commitments, as well as adopted particular standards and policies, that mutually reinforce its applications and systems products. For example, Microsoft managers made an early commitment to Windows as their new standard environment and quickly authorized graphical versions of Microsoft's main applications. These products successfully challenged Lotus and WordPerfect in the spreadsheet and word-processor markets. Both of these competitors had been the market leaders by far when Windows first appeared, but both also hesitated to adopt Windows and delayed introducing graphical versions of their products. Their DOS versions worked with Windows, but were not as easy to use or as powerful in features. Gates recalled the advantage this gave to Microsoft: "At the time that Windows came out, our competitors in applications paused. And in doing that, it took them a long time to come out with their first Windows version that many people would have deemed adequate. And it's only recently that they either have come out with or are about to come out with decent Windows versions. So we've had all that time to continue to move ahead and lengthen our lead."[76]

Microsoft has also designed the Office suite and the Microsoft Network to work well with Windows 95 and Windows NT, and it has every intention of building more applications that take full advantage of features in these operating systems. Gates made this intention public in the fall of 1993: "We fully exploit all the user interface capabilities in Windows as we enhance desktop Windows through a project that's code-named Chicago [Windows 95]. We'll be there first taking advantage of it. . . . We see a lot of opportunities to integrate our applications in the shell, not only in Mail but all the workgroup functions, the file searching functions. The advances in user interface will be there right with Chicago, updating the applications in a rich way. Likewise for the high-end version of Windows. We're committed to fully taking advantage of that with our applications."[77]

Key Enabling Technologies: Object Linking and Embedding (OLE) provides an excellent example of how Microsoft can take advantage of its position as the standards provider, in this case by creating a key enabling technology and bundling it with an operating system. Microsoft also leads the industry in OLE usage, both for applications and operating systems development. OLE is, again, a complex and still-evolving technology; nonetheless, Microsoft has made this into a critical element of the applications programming environment for Windows.[78] As with MS-DOS and Windows, Microsoft developers are the providers of OLE, and they understand its intricacies and idiosyncrasies better than anyone else. As long as they maintain compatibility with older products, they are in an excellent position to direct OLE's evolution and lead the way in taking advantage of new capabilities in the technology. The most recent example of this is distributed networking in a version of OLE now under development, and Microsoft's plans to use this in the forthcoming Cairo upgrade to Windows NT.

Microsoft made an early version of OLE available to outside developers in the Microsoft Foundation Classes C++ library. It also held numerous specification reviews, as well as an OLE developers conference (attended by one thousand people), before releasing OLE 2.0 to the public in 1993. In addition, Microsoft has published volumes of detailed technical information on OLE[79] and continues to hold conferences for developers to discuss the future evolution of the technology.[80] Nonetheless, as the providers of the standard, it is not surprising that Microsoft first used the technology, incorporating OLE 1.0 in PowerPoint during 1990 and in Excel during 1991. These were to some extent just early experiments, and Microsoft people have disagreed internally over how much to invest in OLE because the current technology has many technical limitations. In any case, outside developers did not widely use the technology until Microsoft included OLE 2.0 as a set of extensions to the Windows APIs and made this available with an updated software development kit for Windows.

OLE 2.0 is particularly important because it lets software developers create products that can manipulate or share objects and information in extremely useful ways. For example, users of "OLE-enabled" applications can edit different kinds of objects (for example, a block of text, a spreadsheet filled with data, or a drawing) within the context of the original document they first opened. The menus and tools of the "host" application change to that of the object being edited, but the context remains the host document. In addition, OLE 2.0 lets users "drag and drop" OLE objects from one application to another. For example, users can take a spreadsheet of data from Excel or Lotus 1-2-3 and insert this into a report written in Word or WordPerfect; they can then edit the spreadsheet while in the word processor but still use the spreadsheet's features.

Perhaps most important, OLE 2.0 objects can pass data and messages between applications. This makes the objects programmable and allows applications developers to create an integrated set of programs that share functions (like text processing or drawing). The result is that application interfaces and functions appear more consistent to users and take up less disk space, because the software producer does not have to duplicate the same features in the different applications. (Both Excel and Word do text processing and printing, for example, and can share these as well as other features within the Office suite. See the discussion of OLE and Office in Chapter 6.)

OLE 2.0 has already become a standard technology for Windows applications developers. This is because of its technical benefits as well as Microsoft's adoption and publicity, inclusion within the Windows Software Development Kit, and current availability (in contrast to merely *proposed* competing standards for sharing objects, such as from Apple and IBM). Outside users include Lotus, with the Lotus Smartsuite as well as Lotus Notes (which relies heavily on OLE 2.0 to create distributed database objects). Novell also uses OLE 2.0 in five applications, including the Word-Perfect Office electronic mail and scheduling product as well as the flagship WordPerfect word processor for Windows. To make OLE into more of an industry standard, Microsoft is developing a Macintosh version and has teamed up with DEC to try to define a next-generation "Common Object Model." This incorporates technical specifications for distributed objects from the public Object Management Group and Open Software Foundation.

Still, Microsoft appears to be the most enthusiastic and expert user of OLE. Visual Basic for Applications (which Excel incorporates) utilizes OLE to allow users to automate tasks and customize applications by mixing and matching different functional objects. Windows 95 and Cairo also make extensive use of OLE. Cairo, for example, will allow users to create documents and applications by mixing and matching local objects (those on the user's computer) with remote objects (those on other people's computers linked through a network). It will similarly handle multimedia objects. Again, as the provider of both the NT and Windows 95 operating systems as well as the OLE technology, Microsoft seems to have an advantage in commitment, technical understanding, and technical influence on future versions. This is true even if it shares all preliminary specifications and volumes of documentation with other applications developers.[81] To be fair, however, one can also view both OLE and Visual Basic as extremely useful standards and technologies that Microsoft has provided the software industry. In addition to Microsoft, thousands of applications developers are effectively using these tools to build commercial software products and custom applications.

Product Linkages: Perhaps the most striking examples of Microsoft's potential ability to leverage its position as the standards provider involve Windows 95. As we explain in more detail later, Windows 95 will allow users to access the new Microsoft Network directly from within the operating system. Microsoft will then offer its customers a variety of on-line products and services. In addition, Microsoft has already used the expected popularity of Windows 95 to boost sales of Windows NT, as well as to make it difficult for IBM's OS/2 to compete in the future.

Microsoft initially had trouble marketing NT 3.0, for a variety of reasons mentioned earlier. In particular, since Windows 3.1 has been the de facto mass-market standard and only runs 16-bit applications, Microsoft could not convince many hardware vendors or customers to load their PCs with NT. (NT runs 16-bit Windows applications slowly and needs specially tailored 32-bit applications to take full advantage of its advanced capabilities.) In turn, applications developers have hesitated to write 32-bit applications, because NT did not sell well at first.

To solve this chicken-and-egg problem, Microsoft has pushed applications development for Windows 95—both within its own groups and in outside companies—so as to support NT. Both NT and Windows 95 have 32-bit architectures based on Win32, so they have the same compatibility standards for applications. Thus, if applications developers write programs for Windows 95, then they automatically write for NT. These new products should help Microsoft sell more copies of NT to customers who want features and networking capabilities not available in Windows 95. To meet this twofold objective (ensuring the success of Windows 95, and boosting sales of Windows NT), Microsoft has used the lever of Windows compatibility and the Windows logo. At the same time, reducing incentives for applications developers to write for Windows 3.1 will hurt IBM. While OS/2 can run applications written for Windows 3.1, it cannot run applications written only for Windows 95, even though both OS/2 and Windows 95 are 32-bit operating systems.

Having the "Microsoft Windows" logo on a company's applications product certifies that it works with Windows 3.1. Approximately 75 percent of the companies that write applications for 3.1 have licensed the logo for their packaging. In late 1994, however, Microsoft announced that only applications products fully compatible with both Windows 95 *and* Windows NT 3.5 will be able to use the Windows logo. Microsoft then introduced new licensing terms that require applications developers to upgrade their products to 32-bit architectures, adopt the Windows 95 user interface, demonstrate compatibility with the Microsoft plug-and-play standard, and rework applications to handle long file names. In February 1995 Microsoft partially backed down on the logo issue, allowing applications producers who wrote programs for Windows 3.1 to use the "old" Windows logo for a certain period of time. To use the new "Windows 95" logo, however, companies must meet the new compatibility requirements. Microsoft has also established an independent testing facility run by VeriTest to check whether applications producers are meeting its architectural standards.[82]

Because most applications developers will want their products to run on the latest version of Windows, they have little choice but to write for Windows 95 and Windows NT. In addition, companies such as WordPerfect (now part of Novell) and Lotus both delayed developing products for Windows 3.1 when this came out and saw their market shares decline drastically. It was therefore unlikely that they would delay efforts to build products compatible with Windows 95. In fact, they decided to design 32-bit versions for Windows 95 simply to keep pace with Microsoft, which began shipping 32-bit Word and Excel products in November 1994.[83]

PRINCIPLE   *Integrate, extend, and simplify products to reach new mass markets.*

Microsoft has devoted enormous resources during the 1990s to developing products that bring formerly distinct functions together and are much easier for customers to use. With low prices and easy delivery mechanisms—one box, or one telephone call over an electronic network—these new products can reach ever-larger numbers of potential customers. The Office applications suite, for example, packages functions once separated in Word, Excel, and PowerPoint, and costs about the same as just one product did several years ago. Windows 3.1 and MS-DOS, and now Windows 95, combine in one low-priced package many features that users once had to buy separately: a screen saver, terminal emulator, clock, calculator, calendar and schedule, data-compression program, anti-virus utility, diagnostic tools, e-mail, fax, networking software, and others. More of this type of packaging is under way in other new products, such as for the novice home consumer.

This is no accident. Microsoft is building up its expertise in areas such as office equipment networking and multimedia titles. It is also experimenting with how to merge functions once separated in operating systems, applications programs, and network communications software. Along with its ease-of-use research and experimentation, these efforts are moving Microsoft closer to the computer novice and the average home consumer. The underlying strategy is simple: If computers are easy enough to use and if software is easy enough to obtain, then there will be *billions* of potential new customers, and unthinkable numbers of potential applications, services, and individual transactions for which people will pay money.

To be sure, Microsoft is not the first company to offer products or do research in these new areas. Many large and wealthy companies are also already present in or entering fields such as office networking, consumer software products, and information-highway services. Nonetheless, Microsoft is again entering relatively early—certainly before the mass market has truly arrived. And this time it comes with tens of millions of existing Windows customers, billions of dollars for R&D and acquisitions, an aggressive but flexible strategy, and thousands of talented research scientists, software developers, program managers, software testers, and marketing specialists.

In the Workplace: The Windows operating system has scalable capabilities; in theory, smaller versions of the program can run on machines ranging from tiny hand-held devices to networked PCs linked through products such as the Windows NT server. In practice, this scaling has been difficult to achieve. Nonetheless, since around 1992 Microsoft has been laying the groundwork to connect, through Windows, any device with a microprocessor. It has made the most progress to date on connecting office equipment. This is an area that Xerox and IBM have experimented with unsuccessfully, but it still represents a potentially huge opportunity to extend the Windows technology to another large group of users.

The key effort, initially called Microsoft At Work, is a collection of networking and interface technologies that aim to connect telephones, fax machines, printers, copiers, and hand-held devices, then control them through a Windows PC. A separate team now located in Microsoft's personal operating systems division has built a system for fax machines, which Microsoft began selling in January 1995. Although the effort has not turned out as well as Microsoft managers had expected, more than seventy major office-equipment manufacturers (including Compaq, AT&T, Ericsson, Intel, Motorola, Philips, Sharp, Toshiba, Hewlett-Packard, NEC, Northern Telecom, Ricoh, and Xerox) have signed up to license Microsoft At Work. Windows 95 incorporates this standard as well.[84]

Another growing workplace market is "groupware," pioneered by Lotus Notes. This connects multiple PCs over telephone lines or direct wiring, letting them share the same information databases as well as automatically updating and replicating files that users have changed. Notes also provides advanced electronic mail capabilities, handling both text and graphics. Notes has about 1.4 million users, and a large new owner in IBM. But the number of networked computers—30 million in 1994—leaves plenty of room, and time, for challengers to enter.

Microsoft's strategy is to extend its electronic mail product to include some Notes-like features while adding better networking and communications functions to the NT operating system and to Windows 95. To build and integrate these products, Microsoft has 250 employees in its business systems division working on a system it calls "Microsoft Exchange." Unlike the more comprehensive and expensive Notes product, Exchange takes a modular approach. Customers can build up groupware capabilities gradually, adding functions such as for electronic mail, electronic forms generation, and scheduling of meetings one by one, as needed. If customers want these capabilities all at once, Microsoft will offer them a discounted package. Microsoft shipped a beta version of Exchange in February 1995 and should make a finished version available by late 1995 or early 1996.[85]

The company is also well positioned to improve its market share in more integrated and advanced corporate software systems. Another product called BackOffice packages together the Windows NT Server, Microsoft's popular SQL (for Structured Query Language) Server for database systems management, Systems Network

Architecture Server (a product that connects old and new software systems), Systems Management Server (a product for installing software from remote locations, such as over the network), and Mail (for electronic mail services). Customers can also combine BackOffice with Exchange and Office for groupware capabilities.[86]

In the Home: More promising than the office is the home, where an almost infinite variety of potential uses for the PC or smaller devices exists. Sanjay Parthasarathy, a group product manager in the advanced consumer systems division, explained how Microsoft is extending its reach to a new (for Microsoft) method of gaining revenues from average consumers. The idea is to offer products and services and then charge customers for each activity or transaction, rather than relying on one-time sales of packaged software:

> I run a group of business development people, about eight, who work with me to determine how Microsoft plays in interactive digital networks. We're looking at networks as different as cable, telephone, wireless, power. . . . We're going from a company that builds packaged products for an up-front fee to more of an annuity revenue stream, at least in this new area, where you charge rental for your software. You give it away and then whatever the software enabled in terms of transactions or capabilities you charge per use. . . . And typically a home uses anywhere from 350 to 500 activities. . . . Our role in life is to spread computing to the masses—masses who never used a computer, never want to use a computer. And you really have to take a very different approach to them: not just in the way the product looks, but in the way it feels and in the way to collect money.

Microsoft began its entrance into consumer software in the early 1980s, when it started experimenting with video games and other multimedia technologies. It was also the first large PC software company to enter multimedia publishing. Microsoft's first title came out in 1987 on CD-ROM—the text-only Microsoft Bookshelf, a collection of reference works. In 1988, Microsoft established a multimedia systems group and began work on new products as well as a technical standard, which it called the Multimedia PC ("MPC"). This allows any MPC machine to play any

MPC CD-ROM disk. Microsoft also organized a consortium, including AT&T, CompuAdd, NEC, Olivetti, Tandy, Zenith, and Philips, that continues to support and update this standard.[87]

The multimedia system group has since evolved into what is now Microsoft's consumer division, which had 1994 sales of about $300 million. These numbers are tiny by Microsoft standards, but this is the fastest-growing part of the company. The division owns the Microsoft Home brand name, ships a product a week, and covers everything from personal finance software to multimedia products distributed mainly on CD-ROM laser disks but coming soon over the on-line Microsoft Network. Microsoft now has some fifty multimedia titles and ranks fourth as a publisher of this type of material. The top seller is the under-$100 Encarta encyclopedia, followed by Cinemania, a $50 interactive guide to 19,000 movie reviews, and Art Gallery, a collection of famous art works. Complete Baseball is another popular new product, offering current statistics on players and teams.[88] CD-ROM multimedia publishing in 1994 only accounted for about $30 million in sales, but Microsoft is clearly cultivating skills that will be useful in home products that manipulate video images and sound, such as interactive TV and on-line information databases.

As a foundation for bringing versions of its desktop applications, device-networking technology, multimedia titles, and other new products and services into the home market, Microsoft's consumer division has also been developing what it calls a "social interface" (earlier code-named "Utopia"). This presents a living-room setting to the user, rather than the loosely organized assortment of icons in Windows 3.1 or the desktop environment in Windows 95. It also contains "intelligent agents" in the form of cartoonlike characters (selected by the user) who appear on the screen. The intelligent agents observe and then adjust to the needs of different users, and they give spoken instructions to guide users through different tasks. These are similar in many ways to the automated assistance and "wizards" that Microsoft employs in products such as Word and Excel, but now they have smiling faces, personalities, and voices.

The first usage of the new social interface is in a Windows product called "Bob," which went on sale in March 1995 for under

$100. Bob bundles together eight introductory applications, including a letter-writing aid, checkbook, address book, schedule, financial guide, and electronic mail. Reviews of a pre-release version found the product disappointing: The applications have limited features, the "chatty" advice from Bob and other guides can be annoying to some people, and the amount of computer memory required (8 megabytes) is substantial. In its use of intelligent agents and icons, though, even critics admit that this "social interface" appears to surpass the Macintosh in ease of use and learning for novice computer users.[89] In other versions of this type of interface, VCR and TV icons, among other symbols, appear on screen and are relatively easy to identify and program through the PC, with "intelligent" helpers. These should help Microsoft extend the Microsoft At Work style of technology to the home.

Microsoft is also developing an operating system that will control home appliances or utilities, such as heating and air conditioning systems. This may use a new "wallet PC" as the controlling device, or a regular Windows PC. The wallet PC should also be able to handle bank transactions and other information-access tasks via wireless networks. In addition, new software for cable TV set-top boxes, under development by Microsoft with Intel and General Instrument, will deliver interactive digital TV services on existing TV sets.[90] In yet another project (called "Tiger"), Microsoft's research division is developing a network server system that runs on Windows NT. This will allow cable TV or telephone companies to provide video-on-demand (this allows users to view movies any time they want) and interactive TV. Microsoft is not finding this new software easy to build. Nonetheless, it has hired specialists in the technology, entered into agreements with companies such as Sony and NTT in Japan, and scheduled trials for 1995 with leading cable TV and telecommunications companies in North America, Europe, Japan, and Australia.[91]

Another important product for the home is personal finance software to keep track of budgets, checkbooks, and taxes, as well as pay bills electronically and access investment data such as mutual fund or stock accounts. Quicken is the leader in this product category, but Microsoft has been more successful in making arrangements with banks and other companies such as Visa International to facilitate electronic payments. Microsoft Money can also read and convert Quicken files, and it contains most of the same functions. Microsoft would have preferred to acquire Quicken and its large customer base. Nonetheless, Money can serve as a basis for building up Microsoft's expansion in the home finance market, particularly if Microsoft bundles the software's features with other widely selling products. It has already set a precedent for bundling multiple features and applications products together with MS-DOS, Windows, Works, Office, and Bob.

On the Information Highway: Linking the desktop PC, office, and home markets is the information highway—a growing and increasingly interconnected hodgepodge of on-line services, databases, and multimedia networks. These services include electronic mail, home banking, interactive television, and video on demand from special cable or telephone lines. There are also databases covering everything from electronic versions of newspapers and airline schedules to Hubble Space Telescope pictures from NASA. The information highway is not now a coherent system, and it may not become one; there are various carriers and multiple modes of access to independent systems. But Microsoft plans to extend everything it does to the information highway, as Steve Ballmer explained in a recent talk:

> We're in five businesses today, and we're trying to extend them all for the highway. We build desktop operating systems. We're trying to evolve Windows effectively to be the thing that runs in the [TV] set-top. We build server software through our Windows NT offering. We're trying to extend it to be able to be the server at the backbone of these networks. We build development tools. We recently bought a company up in Montreal called Softimage, whose tools were used to produce [the movie] *Jurassic Park*. Why? We need to evolve our development tools to make it easy to offer this kind of content. We build applications for the home today. Why do we build products like a baseball product or a basketball product? Because they're just starts. They also should hopefully pay for themselves today. But they are starts at getting a franchise to be the company that delivers . . . information. . . . Every time you publish rich information on a CD, you're simulating a lot of what that highway experience will start to be like.[92]

Microsoft's technical experts have experimented with designing "intelligent" fax machines and telephones. They have also observed the efforts of competitors to enhance existing single-function devices (such as telephones, fax machines, set-top cable TV boxes, and home game machines) and make these more like personal computers. They have concluded, however, that it is far easier and cheaper to make a PC that can receive a telephone call, send a fax, or view a home movie than to make a telephone, a fax machine, or a television set that can do word processing, calculate spreadsheets, or perform all the other functions possible on a PC. (New home video-game machines can more easily take on functions similar to a PC. In fact, in 1994 Microsoft announced a partnership with Sega to develop operating system software to extend the functions of home video-game machines.) Because usage of PCs or similar devices will likely become more prevalent in the future, Microsoft executives and researchers see themselves as in a key position to package a variety of consumer technologies into PC software. Microsoft needs to extend Windows, however, as Ballmer elaborated:

> When you talk about all of this convergence going on from a technical perspective, it's wonderful, from the point of view of a software company . . . because you can write standard pieces of software. . . . We can isolate 98 percent of all of the work we do from the particular medium or the particular way that this information is traveling. So it's a very leveraged investment for us across quite a variety of different network types, as long as we take a long-term model of what things will converge against. . . . We have a brand name called Windows that means a certain set of things. And our guys who work in the convergence area say, "Don't tell anybody that it's Windows that we're putting in set-top boxes." . . . But if it's not Windows, there's absolutely no reason for Microsoft to be making the bet. We get no sharing, no synergy, no nothing. So unless we can use 80 to 90 percent of that software, it makes no sense.[93]

Encouraged by Bill Gates's personal enthusiasm for information-highway technologies, Group vice president Nathan Myhrvold is leading Microsoft's effort to launch new products and services, as well as create more exotic technologies not now available in the product divisions.[94] He is also supervising a large and growing number of alliances, partnerships, and acquisitions. (See Appendix 5 for a listing of recent initiatives.) The scope of activities suggests that Microsoft is following an incremental but aggressive approach to entering a variety of new markets with enormous potential:

- Build up skills in developing and marketing basic multimedia applications products.
- Build up skills in basic networking and telecommunications software needed to link PCs and other devices to outside networks.
- Gradually add more multimedia and networking capabilities to Microsoft operating systems and relevant applications products in the hopes of transforming a large portion of the Microsoft customer base into Microsoft information-highway customers.
- Acquire access to content providers or sources, such as rights to movies, art works, or movie reviews.
- Form alliances or make acquisitions in pursuit of the above goals.
- Put the pieces together by offering multimedia products and interactive services to millions of Microsoft customers and non-Microsoft customers over on-line networks as well as cable TV lines and phone systems.

Many pieces of this strategy are already in place. We noted earlier that Windows 95 includes a connection to the Microsoft Network, which users can link into through a modem and a telephone line or, in some cases, through a cable TV line.[95] This new on-line service (done in partnership with Tele-Communications, Inc.) will differ from the competition. It will have simplified access, a very low price (such as $5 per month, about half of competing services), few or no per-minute additional charges (these will probably be per product, service, or transaction), and a wide variety of easy-to-use features. It will include the usual electronic mail and access to the Internet, the gateway to most on-line networks. But the way to get onto the Microsoft system should make it especially suitable for the mass market.

Most PC users today must exit their regular operating system and applications programs, then enter network communications software to gain access to an on-line network. With Windows 95, users just click on a button on the computer screen and the operating system automatically connects them to Microsoft, which then provides a registration application. If the users register, Microsoft will later bill them for the network and any special services and products (such as checking stock quotes or paying the gas company). AT&T and Sprint in the United States, British Telecommunications in the United Kingdom, and Unitel Telecommunications in Canada have all agreed to help Microsoft carry the service to thirty-five countries (in twenty languages) for access through telephone lines. Tele-Communications, Inc., will carry the network through cable TV lines as well as provide some video programming. In addition, General Electric's NBC television subsidiary will cooperate with Microsoft to create multimedia products as well as interactive TV programming.

Customers of Microsoft products will also be able to receive support (for example, answers to common problems, or replacement software) through the network, as well as updates of products such as the Encarta encyclopedia, Complete Baseball, or Cinemania. There will be news, sports, weather, business, and technology information databases as well. Customers will have access to digital copies of art works to display on their computers and eventually in their homes (as Bill Gates plans to do). Customers will be able to purchase products and services from other companies, including the Home Shopping Network and dozens of other companies. Microsoft is enticing them into its network by cutting prices and providing inexpensive, simplified tools to get their information databases or catalogs into on-line formats. To offer home banking and on-line financial services transactions, and on-line stock quotes, Microsoft has established relationships with Chase Manhattan, First National Bank of Chicago, Bank of Boston, and other major banks. It is also developing software with Visa International for electronic shopping and theft-proof on-line payments with credit cards.

If the expected 30 million or so people upgrade to Windows 95 or receive it pre-loaded on new computers, and just a few percent of these register for the Microsoft Network, Microsoft will instantly become a giant in the $13 billion on-line services industry. This industry is growing at 30 percent annually and has tremendous potential: Only 5 percent of U.S. households subscribe to on-line networks, and customers on existing services from America Online, Prodigy, CompuServe, and other leading companies *to-gether* totaled no more than 8.5 million in 1995.

To some people, Microsoft may seem to be going too fast in too many directions; the idea behind these many moves, however, is to cover all logical bases. No one knows specifically how the new communications and multimedia technologies will evolve and in what time frame, although they are clearly coming together to reach ever-greater numbers of people. And, as Steve Ballmer ad-mitted, Microsoft does not need to make money in the short term with these new ventures, or to formulate very specific plans. Mi-crosoft executives are simply forming strategic relationships and placing bets to make sure that the company's revenues and tech-nological skills do not decline on their watch.

> In terms of convergence in the highway, we're really out looking and seeking and trying to form the relationships that will be key. In our com-pany, in the position that we have today, really the single biggest risk is that something comes out that makes obsolete what we're doing techno-logically in the same way that something attacked what was going on in the mainframe and minicomputer world, and stole away that customer base. . . . It's both a scary and an exciting proposition because it forces us to continue to push and invest in some things that, frankly, from time to time, you can think are a little crazy and a little bit in advance of their time. We like to say that we did our first CD-ROM conference seven or eight years ago, and we're now making the first profit—on the margin, not on the investment—on CD-ROM titles that we develop. . . .
>
> Our view is that, for much of the investment that people typically talk about under the rubric of convergence, it's going to be a long time before anybody makes any money. And we're certainly prepared for that. . . . We go into this without a very clear-cut plan of how everything is going to happen. We just know that, with our current circumstances, it is not pru-dent for us not to be at the leading edge of investing in this technology. And it's not about technology. It's about what kinds of scenarios we can describe for how people will access and use information *if* somebody makes the infrastructure investment behind these technologies.[96]

Microsoft brings to these new markets more than just a growing variety of applications, extendible operating systems, enabling technologies such as OLE, creative and talented technical people, and the resources to form dozens of partnerships and new ventures. As we outlined earlier, in recent years Microsoft has been introducing techniques that allow product development teams to analyze how users actually behave in great detail, figure out which features are most important to the largest number of people, and then build software products that appear relatively easy to use, even to the novice home consumer. Other key tools and techniques allow teams to evolve features incrementally and frequently synchronize as well as periodically stabilize their components during the development process. This entire approach is particularly useful in applications projects where program managers and software developers cannot fully anticipate or control what final products and individual features should look like. Chapters 4 and 5 now discuss the specific techniques and tools that make up Microsoft's synch-and-stabilize process for software product development.

4

Defining Products and Development Processes

Focus Creativity by Evolving Features and "Fixing" Resources

To define products and their development processes, Microsoft follows a strategy that we describe as focus creativity by evolving features and "fixing" resources. We break down our discussion of this strategy into five principles:

- Divide large projects into multiple milestone cycles with buffers and no separate product maintenance.
- Use a vision statement and outline specification of features to guide projects.
- Base feature selection and prioritization on user activities and data.
- Evolve a modular and horizontal design architecture, with the product structure mirrored in the project structure.
- Control by individual commitments to small tasks and "fixed" project resources.

Microsoft's approach to defining products and development

processes is not particularly new. Companies that have adopted similar incremental development methods include computer hardware vendors (such as Hewlett-Packard and Digital Equipment Corporation), computer systems integrators (EDS and SAIC), aerospace and defense contractors (TRW and Hughes), and electronic equipment manufacturers (Motorola and Xerox). Microsoft has been extremely effective, however, in creating a strategy for product and process definition that supports its competitive strategy.

Microsoft tries to develop products for mass markets and set de facto standards. Its products also have relatively short development times and life cycles, and these factors exert tremendous influence. In particular, product development needs to be flexible as well as structured, and it must move forward as quickly as possible. State-of-the-art engineering methods or tools are of secondary importance. In slower markets, companies might also try to create a complete specification and then "freeze" the specification, along with a schedule, before they start writing code. Microsoft teams work more in parallel, as Chris Peters explained: "I guess that's the thing that is different about high-speed consumer software development. Everything is being done in parallel right through development. As soon as you have any kind of a spec or you start on any kind of a schedule, then the schedule's being refined while the spec's being refined, while the test cases are being redefined. But all this stuff is moving absolutely forward as fast as possible. You're not stopping."

First, Microsoft teams try to understand users' needs and structure those needs into individual features. Then they assign priorities to these features and allocate them to subprojects that break up a development project into three or four milestone periods. To sharpen and focus creativity in product specification and product development, Microsoft managers also try to "fix" project resources—limiting the number of people and amount of time in any one project. The fixed project resources thus become the key defining elements in a product development schedule; in particular, the intended ship date causes the whole development team to bound its creativity and effort. The team must define intermediate steps and milestones that work backward from the target ship date, and coordinate product delivery with other Microsoft projects, product distributors, and third-party system integrators. Projects accomplish these goals even though the intended ship date almost always changes.

There are some differences, though, in how Microsoft applies these principles of product and process definition to applications as opposed to systems products. Applications like Word and Excel, or consumer products like Works or Complete Baseball, tend to have shorter schedules, smaller teams, and more precise estimates of delivery dates than do systems products (such as operating systems). In particular, new systems products can have many new functions and require years and hundreds of people to specify, develop, and test. For example, to develop the first version of Windows NT, Microsoft needed over four years and a team of more than four hundred people at its peak. Version 5.0 of Excel required a group of one hundred to one hundred twenty-five people over an eighteen-month period. Many applications products, such as Excel and Word, also tend to be in their "Nth" (rather than the first) release. This facilitates a more regular product development cycle and schedule estimation process.

In terms of functionality, systems products tend to have more of an inseparable "core" set of functions that projects must complete and demonstrate as reliable (called being "stable") before they can ship the product. It can be very difficult to delete unfinished functions from an operating system in order to accelerate product shipment. The need to develop and refine a central set of functions that execute correctly and efficiently drives the releases of systems products like Windows NT and Windows 95; the target ship date is of secondary importance. Applications and consumer products tend to have more independent features that projects can add or delete to meet competitive pressures, resource constraints, and delivery schedules. The vision statement and specification document for systems products, therefore, are more complete and detailed earlier in the life cycle than they are for applications in order to define essential groupings and interdependencies among features.

Systems products also tend to have longer testing periods, including extensive beta testing. This is because of their greater need for stability and compatibility with numerous application products, networking systems, computing vendor platforms, and peripherals such as printers. Application products tend to have more stand-alone functionality and fewer product interdependencies, although this is now changing with an emphasis on sharing components (such as in the Office suite of applications).

Microsoft's increased use of shared or common components has begun to reshape the structure of its applications. They were once stand-alone products, but they are now increasingly becoming compartmentalized and sharable. For example, projects can now flexibly arrange OLE-integrated components into various operations or separate "threads of execution." These components provide users with specific packages of functionality, such as for graphing, printing, or mathematical calculating. Users can also combine functions and objects of information from different products—for example, writing a letter containing graphics and spreadsheet data.

Marketing and program managers, rather than developers, tend to drive the functionality required in applications products. They also apply user-scenario modeling techniques, such as activity-based planning. Developers have more of a say in the functionality for systems products. Groups within divisions also have differences. Excel and Word are very similar, although Microsoft does not manage small consumer applications as tightly as it does these large revenue generators. In the systems and languages areas, for example, Windows NT was generally more carefully organized and managed than Visual Basic or Windows 95. Nonetheless, applications and systems products at Microsoft have a great deal in common, as do product units within each of the divisions. Most of what we write in the following sections applies to both types of software, as well as to all of the major products that Microsoft builds.

PRINCIPLE   *Divide large projects into multiple milestone cycles with buffers and no separate product maintenance.*

At Microsoft today—particularly in comparison to the 1980s—people try to be realistic but still ambitious in scheduling. A project's schedule incorporates flexibility but also provides a highly structured mechanism for communicating expectations and interdependencies both within and outside the project. Typical desktop applications projects, such as the next release of Office, Word, or

Excel, are about 12 to 24 months in duration. Microsoft is moving toward alternating 12- and 24-month schedules for applications products, with the 12-month projects offering minor feature enhancements and the 24-month projects offering major feature and architectural changes. Both schedules might begin at the same time for a given product and run in parallel for the first 12 months, so that Microsoft ships a product release every 12 months.

Major new operating systems products such as Windows NT or Windows 95, however, can require schedules of 3 to 4 years. Rather than trying to put as much as they can into the 12 to 24 months for a typical project, Microsoft managers try to determine how much time and how many people they actually have for new development. They also try to allow for unknown changes or problems, then scale the product to fit the period and available personnel. In this way, Microsoft structures project schedules into planning phases and multiple iterations of product development and release, test and stabilization, and unallocated contingency or "buffer" time in between the milestone junctures. Each project has its own individual schedule, but there is an increasing emphasis on coordination of release schedules across products. For example, Office has an integrated schedule including Excel, Word, and the other products that are part of this applications suite.

The program managers, developers, and testers who specify, implement, and test a new release of a product are the same people who correct bugs, modify, and enhance previous versions of the product (called product "maintenance"). There is no separate group for this activity. In many other companies, such maintenance consumes much of the time that developers could be spending on new product development. In contrast, Microsoft's product units have created continuous "release cycles" for new product versions. Not only is MS-DOS in version 6 and Windows in version 4, but Excel is in version 5, Word is in version 6, and so forth. Microsoft groups determine what they need to fix in a product and what they would like to add and change based on marketing and customer inputs, then they do this work as part of the next product release. Next releases can also contain features that a project had to cut because it ran behind schedule, especially in the case of applications products.

Project Scheduling and Milestones: Microsoft's synch-and-stabilize approach to product development (which Chapter 5 describes in more detail) originated in the late 1980s. This focuses around the key concepts of milestones and daily builds (to strive for "zero defects"). Publisher 1.0, which the former Entry Business Unit shipped in 1988, was the first Microsoft project to use milestones in its schedule; Excel 3.0, in 1989 and 1990, was the first large project to adopt them. A few other small projects, such as Works, also moved to milestones around 1988–1990. Some groups did daily builds at this time, but they had only a weak notion of using the builds to continuously find and fix defects. Milestones, as well as daily builds and more rigorous quality control practices, gradually became more common in Microsoft after the 1989 retreat (see Chapter 1).

The life cycle of typical Microsoft projects today contains three phases. *Planning* concludes with a functional specification and final schedule, *development* concludes with the code complete release, and *stabilization* concludes with the product release to manufacturing.[1] Microsoft calls the three critical points at the end of these phases "schedule complete and project plan approval," "code complete," and "release to manufacturing." (The concept of manufacturing applied to software products means the replication of diskettes and documentation.) These three general phases and the underlying iterative approach differ from the sequential "waterfall" life cycle phases of requirements, detailed design, module coding and testing, integration testing, and system testing.[2] They are more similar to the risk-driven, incremental "spiral" life cycle model, which is being increasingly followed by software development organizations.[3]

Microsoft's planning phase produces vision and specification documents that explain what the project will do and how. These force discussion and thought on design issues before managers prepare the schedule or developers write code. The development phase revolves around three major internal product releases; the stabilization phase focuses on extensive internal and external (beta site) testing. Throughout the product cycle, Microsoft uses the concept of buffering. This allows teams to recover from unexpected problems or changes affecting the schedule, and it also provides balance between aggressive shipment goals and accurate prediction of the ship date.

The planning phase can take as little as three months for an update to an existing product, or more than a year for new products. In typical past projects, the development and stabilization phases have taken approximately eighteen months, and may be divided as follows:[4]

- Six to twelve months development time, generally consisting of three or four major milestone product releases
- Two to four months of buffer for development time, allocated for each of the 3 to 4 major milestone product releases
- Three to eight months of stabilization, including testing, buffer time, and six weeks of preparation for final release and customer support (The target date for completing the final testing phase and the on-line documentation is approximately six weeks before the release to manufacturing; the target date for completing the printed documentation is approximately four weeks before the release to manufacturing.)

Of the total number of months allocated for development and stabilization, a project will generally spend about two-thirds of the time in the development phase and one-third of the time in the stabilization phase. Chris Peters, vice president of the Office product unit, described a general scheduling guideline: "Classically, in the overall schedule, you write features for half the time, and you leave the other half for debugging or unexpected things. So, if I was going to work on a two-year project, I would create estimates for one year. . . . If things don't work out right, I'll just cut features I think are less important." This milestone process generally enables Microsoft managers to stay in close touch with the progress on a product and preserve the flexibility of trading off features late in the development cycle.

Figures 4.1 and 4.2 summarize Microsoft's (a) product cycle phases, (b) documents or intermediate products, (c) reviews, and (d) milestones at intermediate points or completion of phases. These figures and the following sections focus on the roles of program management, development, and testing in the product cycle. Figure 4.3 provides a comprehensive summary of the typical prod-

Figure 4.1   Overview of Synch-and-Stabilize Development Approach

Planning Phase: Define product vision, specification, and schedule.

• **Vision Statement** Product and program management use extensive customer input to identify and prioritize product features.

• **Specification Document** Based on vision statement, program management and development group define feature functionality, architectural issues, and component interdependencies.

• **Schedule and Feature Team Formation** Based on specification document, program management coordinates schedule and arranges feature teams that each contain approximately 1 program manager, 3-8 developers, and 3-8 testers (who work in parallel 1:1 with developers).

Development Phase: Feature development in 3 or 4 sequential subprojects that each results in a milestone release.

Program managers coordinate evolution of specification. Developers design, code, and debug. Testers pair up with developers for continuous testing.

• **Subproject I** First 1/3 of features: Most critical features and shared components.

• **Subproject II** Second 1/3 of features.

• **Subproject III** Final 1/3 of features: Least critical features.

Stabilization Phase: Comprehensive internal and external testing, final product stabilization, and ship.

Program managers coordinate OEMs and ISVs and monitor customer feedback. Developers perform final debugging and code stabilization. Testers recreate and isolate errors.

• **Internal Testing** Thorough testing of complete product within the company.

• **External Testing** Thorough testing of complete product outside the company by "beta" sites such as OEMs, ISVs, and end-users.

• **Release preparation** Prepare final release of "golden master" diskettes and documentation for manufacturing.

Source: Same as Figure 4.2.

Figure 4.2 Synch-and Stabilize Life Cycle for Program Management, Development, and Testing

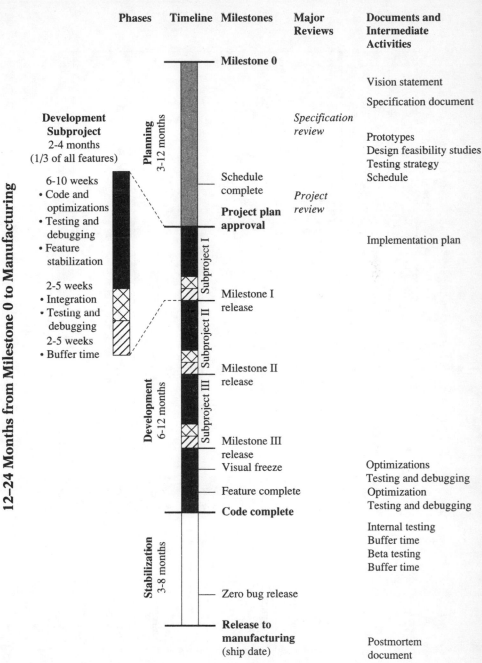

Source: Interview with Dave Moore, Director of Development, 3/17/93; and Microsoft Corporation, Office Business Unit, "Scheduling Methodology and Milestones Definition, unpublished internal document, 9/1/89.

Figure 4.3 Product Life Cycle Model with Product Management and User Education

<table>
<tr><th rowspan="2">Role</th><th colspan="3">Product Cycle Phase</th></tr>
<tr>
<th>Planning
Final milestone: Project plan approval (incl. schedule complete)</th>
<th>Development (3-4 milestones)
Final milestone: Code complete</th>
<th>Stabilization
Final milestone: Release to manufacturing</th>
</tr>
<tr>
<td>Product Management (marketing)</td>
<td>• Market research
• Marketing plan
• Vision statement</td>
<td>• Pricing, promotion, packaging</td>
<td>• Beta-test sites
• Launch</td>
</tr>
<tr>
<td>Program Management</td>
<td>• Vision statement
• Design & prototype features
• Write specification
• Activity-based planning
• Contextual inquiry
• Create master schedule</td>
<td>• Manage project status and communication</td>
<td>• Provide input on bug decisions
• Ship sign-off</td>
</tr>
<tr>
<td>Usability Lab Testers</td>
<td>• Establish usability goals
• Exploratory testing</td>
<td>• Iterative testing (prototypes/ early code)
• Complete product testing</td>
<td>• Activity-based planning scenario testing
• Field testing
• Test for next version</td>
</tr>
<tr>
<td>Visual Interface Design Group</td>
<td>• Begin user interface design
• Consult on user interface specification</td>
<td>• Finalize user interface designs
• Create icons and bitmaps</td>
<td>• Visual interface design review</td>
</tr>
<tr>
<td>Development Group</td>
<td>• Feature vision and feasibility
• Feature design</td>
<td>• Write and optimize code
• Daily product builds
• Testing and bug fixing
• Product releases</td>
<td>• Testing and bug fixing</td>
</tr>
</table>

Inter-operability Design Group	• Common feature set designs	• Support code sharing • Consult on test plans	• Plan common feature for next release
Localization Group *(non-U.S. versions)*	• Localization plan	• Create and approve glossaries • Visual and functional verification • Documents to translation • Review/check run-time user interface	• In-team testing and debugging • Print production cycle • Final testing
Software Testing	• Testing strategy	• Create tests • Run test suites	• Internal testing • Beta testing • Final release testing
User Education *(printed documentation)*	• Conceptual design and strategy document	• Define terminology • Writing, editing, and creating online links • Technical review • Finalize content and graphics	• Final page-layout proof • Prepare and transmit to vendor • Print documentation • Documentation release to manufacturing
User Education *(online documentation)*	• Same as user education for printed documentation	• Same as user education for printed documentation • Finalize run-time user interface help	• In-team testing and debugging • Final testing and debugging
Product Support	• Collect customer data • Forecast support costs	• Identify support issues • Determine support strategy • Training	• Product support services (PSS) beta and evaluation • Customer support knowledge Base sweep • Take telephone calls

Organizational

Source: Interview with Dave Moore, Director of Development, 3/17/93; and untitled internal Microsoft document.

uct cycle, including other company functions such as product management (marketing) and user education (creation of documentation or manuals for customers).

Planning Phase: The planning phase is the time for all pre-development planning in a project life cycle. This period produces the vision statement, marketing plans, design goals, an initial specification, interface standards for integrating components developed in other groups, initial testing plans, a documentation strategy (printed and on-line), and a list of usability issues. The planning phase begins with the *vision statement*. This comes from product managers and program managers in each product unit; it is the marketing vision for the product, and it includes an analysis of competitors' products and a projection of future releases. The vision statement may also discuss problems to fix from the previous release and key functions to add, based on customer or market analyses and data from the product support services (PSS) group. Managers consider long-term product planning issues as part of a three-year planning cycle, as discussed in Chapter 1.

The *specification document* begins in outline form and then defines and assigns priorities to the new or enhanced product features. As discussed in Chapter 2, the program managers coordinate the writing of the specification, but other groups of people contribute to the document, especially developers and testers. The specification document is only a preliminary outline of the product features; it grows and changes 20 to 30 percent from the start of development until the end of the project. Changes late in the life cycle tend to be minor, however, and developers increasingly need to have very good reasons to make late changes.

Program managers create extensive prototypes using the Visual Basic tool. They also conduct design feasibility studies to understand design trade-offs and accelerate decisions related to the product specification. John Fine, formerly the director of program management and now the group program manager for Excel, explained that the specification document needs to define and package product features that ordinary users can describe in a single sentence: "You invent the features of a product, feature by feature. . . . All is from the user's standpoint. That's everything—just never worry about anything else except 'What does the user perceive?' When you use a product, what the product does should be understandable enough so that any user can say in a sentence what it does. There have been products that in my opinion haven't done very well because—although they had a lot of cool features—believe it or not, no one could say what the product did."

As discussed in Chapter 1, Bill Gates and other senior executives conduct the specification reviews for major products and delegate this task to division managers for less critical products. The outline specification document, developer time estimates, and the strategy for testing, documentation, and customer support provide the basis for defining the project schedule. Gates also holds a project review for major projects in order to approve the project plan and schedule. "Schedule complete" with an approved project plan is the project status at the completion of the planning phase.

Development Phases: The plan for the development phases allocates specific subsets of features to each of the three or four *major milestone releases*, defines feature details and technical interdependencies, and records developers' individual tasks and schedule estimates. During the development phases, the developers write code guided by the functional specifications, testers write *test suites* that check if features and areas of the product work properly, and user education staff produces draft *documentation*.

Rather than waiting until later, developers fix errors found by testers and automated tests continuously throughout the development phases. This improves product stability and makes the release schedule more predictable. After a certain point in the project (for example, 40 percent of the way into the schedule), team members attempt to "lock in" the major functional requirements or features of a product, allowing only minor changes thereafter. If developers want to make significant changes after this point, then they have to negotiate with program managers and the lead development manager, and perhaps with the product unit manager as well.

Major Milestone Releases. A project organizes the development phases around the three or four major internal releases, or "milestone subprojects." Microsoft intends these releases to be very stable. Theoretically, projects could ship them to customers, as Chris Peters observed: "Milestones are something we used for the first time [on a large project] in Excel. I think all the other groups are using them now. . . . What you do is you essentially divide a project into three [or so] pieces . . . and you pretend to ship the product after each piece."[5] Developers may need to make several preliminary releases prior to each major release in order to meet the acceptance criteria of the testing group and achieve the milestone of a major release. Mike Conte, formerly a program manager for Excel and now a senior program manager for Office, described how a project works on a major milestone release: "We actually break our development into three separate milestones. They might be six-week milestones, [or] they might be ten-week milestones. . . . At the end of the milestone, our goal is to get all the features that have been implemented . . . for that milestone at zero bugs. . . . And then, when we get to the point where we get to 'ship quality,' we can move on to the next milestone. The point of this is so we never get so totally out of control that we're at the end of a project and we have so many thousands of bugs that we can't ever tell when we're going to finish it."

Projects spend approximately two to four months developing each major milestone release. Each of these releases includes its own coding, optimizing, testing, and debugging activities. Projects reserve about one-third of the total development period for unplanned contingencies or "buffer time" allocated to each of the milestone subprojects. For example, there were thirteen-week milestones for each of the three major internal releases in the development phases on Excel 5.0 (see Table 4.1). The initial scheduled time within each milestone period was eight weeks for development and two weeks for integration (making sure features and pieces of features work together properly); the Excel group also allocated three weeks of buffer for each milestone. The group did not use all the buffer on the first milestone, so the project added an extra week to the second and third development periods, making these nine instead of eight weeks. After the second milestone, however, Excel used up all the buffer, mainly because of a problem after switching the compiler used on the Macintosh. On the third milestone, the buffer was not enough: Developers required an additional six weeks, mainly due to Excel's dependencies on OLE and Visual Basic for applications (VBA). OLE was six months late and VBA eight months late, resulting in added complexities and delays for Excel 5.0 (as well as Word 6.0). As Mike Conte commented: "Well, the reality is we wanted to ship on the 27th of September and we ended up shipping on the 22nd of December, so we were three months off. VB and OLE were big problems for us."

As another example, the development phases on Office have four major internal releases, with a total of twenty-one months for development and stabilization. The first milestone release is an architecture definition subproject, and the managers view it as a special case. The other three milestone subprojects are each sixteen to eighteen weeks long; each subproject spends an equal amount of

Table 4.1   Predicted Versus Actual Schedule for Major Internal Milestones on Excel 5.0

Major Internal Milestone	Predicted Schedule	Actual Schedule
Milestone I		
	8 weeks development	8 weeks development
	2 weeks integration	2 weeks integration
	3 weeks buffer	1 week buffer
Milestone II		
	8 weeks development	9 weeks development
	2 weeks integration	2 weeks integration
	3 weeks buffer	3 weeks buffer
Milestone III		
	8 weeks development	9 weeks development
	2 weeks integration	2 weeks integration
	3 weeks buffer	3 weeks buffer
		6 weeks delay
Total	39 weeks	45 weeks

Source: Interview with Jon De Vaan, Development Manager, Office, 4/15/93 and 9/29/94.

time in development and an equal amount of time in buffer, while adding an additional week for each successive integration phase.

Systems products, as well as consumer products and new types of software built in the research division (such as the Tiger video server), follow a similar process. There are, however, some differences related to the nature of the product and its customers. Brad Silverberg, senior vice president for personal systems (Windows/MS-DOS), outlined the four types of milestone completion requirements for systems products and contrasted the incremental Microsoft development approach with his experiences at Apple and Borland:

> When we reach milestones, we have not just functionality but size, performance requirements, and quality requirements. . . . So that milestone isn't met until we've added these functions, we've met these performance goals, and we've reached this level of quality. If we were at a previous milestone, we may have relaxed some of the performance goals just to get that functionality in and still keep the milestone relatively on track. Then the next milestone is going to be primarily size and performance over function. And then beyond that, size and performance is just an integral part of adding function. . . .
>
> If what we did at Apple is conventional, then this is a departure from that. [Apple had] separate, independent teams develop pieces. At the end, three months before you want to ship, you say, "OK, let's integrate it all together." Borland broke it up into small pieces and would always keep things running, this incremental philosophy. . . . It appears that this incremental approach takes longer, but it almost never does, because it keeps you in close touch with where things really are.

Visual Freeze, Feature Complete, and Code Complete. After testing and stabilizing the last major milestone release, the product undergoes a "visual freeze." The term denotes that the product's major user interface components—such as menus, dialog boxes, and document windows—will not undergo any further major changes, even though minor alterations are certain. Projects use the visual freeze for the benefit of the user education group that writes the product documentation. The product becomes "feature complete" when it is fully functional and testers can run test scenarios against it. At this point a product is still not fundamentally stable, probably has many bugs, and needs considerable performance improvements in terms of speed and memory usage (called optimizations). The final development phase ends when the product is "code complete," which means that all features work as described in the specification and user documentation. No tasks remain except debugging and opportunistic optimizations. After code complete on Excel 5.0, for example, Jon De Vaan, formerly the development manager for Excel and now the development manager for Office, spent two months rewriting poorly implemented code. Chris Peters has a rule-of-thumb to determine when a project has reached code complete:

> Code complete . . . is difficult to define for a thirty- to forty-person project. For example, if someone spends three days fixing a bug, they . . . are in effect writing code. They were never code complete to begin with. . . . So, what happens is, as you rush to finish the project, the bug count will climb. Then, as people transition off to truly fix bugs, which are bugs that they can fix in a few hours, you'll finally reach a point where the bug count . . . will decrease every day until you ship. The path will absolutely be downward at that point. When that happens, that's when you know you're code complete . . . and there's no way to lie about that.

Stabilization Phases: The stabilization phases focus on extensive testing and debugging of a product in order to work toward release. Projects try not to add any new features during the stabilization phases, but they can add some if competitive products emerge or other market factors change. Microsoft organizes the testing process into a series of phases that are each, for example, four weeks in duration. Testers and developers find and fix bugs continuously in order to get the product ready for release as early as possible; schedules include buffer time here as well in order to accommodate any unforeseen problems or delays. A project distributes the last major milestone release of its product to a variety of test groups internal and external to Microsoft. External testing groups (called beta sites) include a mix of individual users, large corporate customers, independent software vendors, and distributors.

A "zero bug release" comes after an extensive testing process finds no more high-severity bugs and project managers have decided to fix all remaining known bugs in the next product development cycle. The developers then produce a "golden master" diskette and release it to manufacturing. This is the copy of the product from which Microsoft will make all others. Shortly after the product release to manufacturing, the project team generally writes a postmortem document—an extensive summary of what worked well and what did not on the project. (Between half and two-thirds of all projects actually write the reports, which range in length from fifteen to more than a hundred pages. See Chapter 6 for a further discussion.)

Buffer Time in Project Schedules: Microsoft uses a buffering scheme to balance peak efficiency with better predictions. This contingency time is part of each major milestone during development and stabilization. Buffer time absorbs slips caused by incomplete understanding of features or technical issues, tasks inadvertently not scheduled, or unexpected problems. Problems often include delays in dependent projects or time needed to coordinate unplanned changes in features shared across more than one product. Primarily, however, buffer time helps a project accommodate unanticipated events. As Chris Peters recalled: "The big secret that we did when we finally started shipping things on time [is that] we finally put time in the schedule. Not the 'lazy and stupid' buffer, but a sufficient amount of time for unexpected things to happen. Once you admit you don't know everything about the future, it's like an alcoholic that says, 'Yes, I have a problem.' Once you admit you have the problem that you can't predict the future perfectly, then you put time in the schedule, and it's actually quite easy to ship on time—if you're hard-core on cutting features or scaling back features."

Projects should use buffer time exclusively for uncertainties, and not for such routine or anticipated tasks as feature development, testing, or document reviews. Project teams also use internal product milestones as their goals and do not assume the added buffer time. Internal milestones set by the project leaders in consultation with the development teams, such as the "Milestone I release" in Figure 4.2, thus reflect the date of the major milestone minus the buffer time. Internal milestones are for use within functional groups only and do not appear on published team schedules; groups outside the project team use the published schedules to do their scheduling.

In applications products, buffer time typically constitutes 20 to 30 percent of the schedule. Peters confirmed this: "On Excel [3.0], which I think is the current state of the art in doing this stuff, we had 20 percent of the schedule as buffer time."[6] Since systems products have relatively longer schedules and less divisible feature sets, these projects tend to need more buffer time. Convincing traditional project managers of the need for lots of buffer time can be difficult amid pressures to shorten product development times. Microsoft, however, regularly applies this concept across its projects. Brad Silverberg described resistance from senior managers and his unshakable belief in the "50 percent buffer rule" for systems projects:

> A lot of the times developers naively say, "It'll take me a week," so you schedule a week. We've learned how to ask better questions to size a task as well as to incorporate buffer space into the schedule. In the past, a lot of people didn't incorporate buffer space into the schedule. I've been in situations earlier in my career where you present a schedule to the president with some buffer space and he says, "What, are you guys just going to go fishing or something? What are you going to do in that buffer space?" "Well, based on experience, we're going to need it to fix bugs." "Well, tell me what exactly you're going to do." "Well, if I could tell you exactly what I was going to do, I'd tell you what the tasks are, but trust me—it's going to be needed." It's a leap of faith for many traditional managers to see buffer space in a schedule, so a lot of times it gets beaten out of the development manager: "No, let's tighten it up. We need to ship. We can squeeze some of that buffer space down." So you have a schedule which is unrealistic. I don't know what it's going to be needed for, but time and time again, I know it's needed. Whether it's to fix bugs, or you have some idea along the way and you say, "We really should have this feature." . . . So, if you have two months, you'd allocate one month for buffer. [A] fifty percent buffer rule . . . turns out to be accurate. I can't always explain why.

Beyond helping make product schedules more realistic, the inclusion of buffer time also gives a project an opportunity to respond to competitors' product announcements or unforeseen industry events. Chris Peters contrasted the concept with older methods of project scheduling:

> Now I don't know about perfect specs and perfect estimates, but there's no way in hell we're going to have perfect knowledge about what the competition is doing [or] . . . which way this very, very exciting industry is moving. The old scheduling method is just adding up all the stuff you know about and saying that's the date—that's all we know about. Are we at all surprised that it generates a date which is too little, considering how little we know about the future? . . . The way you do an accurate ship date is that you add buffer time, which is time that says the future is uncertain, which it clearly and obviously is. This isn't being not hard-core or being a wimp. This is just saying the future is the future. It's self-evident.[7]

Review and Checkpoints: To create some pressure from top management to keep projects under control, Microsoft also holds weekly, biweekly, or monthly project reviews at key junctures, particularly before determining the implementation plan. As described in Chapter 1, Bill Gates participates in this process by meeting frequently, sometimes even weekly, with key projects. For example, the Excel 5.0 project had four reviews; these usually consisted of two-hour meetings attended by Gates, Mike Maples, Pete Higgins, and other key developers and program managers, as well as the test manager, Marc Olson. For other projects that are more routine, Gates may only approve their schedules and specifications via e-mail.

Product Maintenance and "Milestone 0": At most software development organizations, separate teams—who often have little product development experience—usually perform product maintenance activities. We noted earlier that this is not the case at Microsoft, where development of the next version of a product includes building major new functions, as well as fixing bugs from the previous product version. In addition, Microsoft sets up a separate product support team to answer telephone calls from users, basing the size of this team on the estimated volume of calls. For emergency problems, however, some product groups do have quick-fix maintenance teams who may also create an intermediate "point release" of a product to send to customers (for example, MS-DOS 6.2 to replace MS-DOS 6.0).

Another concept that Microsoft has recently begun to deploy is "Milestone 0." Jon De Vaan described this as the work that occurs after the completion of one product version and before the official start of the next development cycle: "The rule of thumb is people are responsible for making their own code work. . . . It sounds like chaos at first, but in the end, actually, people do learn the right way to do things. And we make a little time. We're starting to euphemistically call this 'Milestone 0.' This is the time between finishing one version of the product and the actual official start of coding on the next version, where people go through and clean up the things that they know weren't right. . . . If there's something that we really don't like a lot, then that'll become part of the schedule, and we'll formalize it more." For example, between Excel 4.0 and 5.0, developers spent one or two months doing this patching and fixing up.

During Milestone 0, developers also work with program managers to refine the specifications for the next version and build estimates for the schedule. Projects thus have opportunities to incorporate time into the schedule for the next version to correct major problems. New projects now spend about 10 percent of their time redoing existing features, including some user interface changes, rather than working on new features that are part of the next product version. There are also cases—such as with Windows 3.1 and Windows NT 3.5—where Microsoft introduces an intermediate product version that does more than fix minor problems. For key products, however, it is becoming more common for Microsoft to develop in parallel both a minor change (such as a twelve-month revision) and a major change (such as a twenty-four-month revision).

PRINCIPLE *Use a vision statement and outline specification of features to guide projects.*

For individual projects, the key task for Microsoft and other PC software developers is to give enough structure to the development effort so that work can proceed, but allow enough flexibility to accommodate change during the development process. In order to do this, Microsoft uses a high-level vision statement and outline specification to get projects going, rather than trying to write a complete and detailed specification at the outset. The vision statement, a very short document written by product planners from the marketing group and program managers, defines a set of goals that drive the product development process, but does not outline detailed product requirements. For example, the vision statement for Word 6.0 was only one page, and its counterpart for Windows 3.1 was only one sentence. For a totally new product, though, the vision statement is usually much more detailed and actually comprises a rough specification document. Overall, Microsoft's goal is to have statements that are as short as possible and focused on describing clearly "what the product is not" as opposed to "what the product is." This is because deciding what functionality to leave out of a product is much more difficult than deciding what functionality to put in.

Program managers use the vision statement to begin defining the functional specification document, which explains what the product's features do and how they interact with other features and products. Program managers start with only an outline specification document and then add more details as the project evolves, because they know it is unrealistic to freeze the features and their details too early. In a project's lifetime, competitors' products, customers' needs, and market opportunities will change; therefore, the specification document needs to be flexible enough to accommodate changes and exploit new opportunities. At the same time, the specification document needs to be specific enough to estimate the project schedule and enable developers to make progress without having to redo and rework their features continually. Moreover, developers need to have the freedom to determine how to accomplish the feature objectives in the actual code.

Over the course of a project, program managers are responsible for developing, updating, and evolving the specification. The complete specification document becomes one of the outputs of the project, like a user manual, rather than existing only as an input to development. Consequently, the complete specification serves not only as a final description of the product functionality, but as a central basis for testing and evaluating a product before release to manufacturing and shipment. Early in the specification process, program managers also establish a formal on-line location for the specification and use a version control tool to keep track of successive revisions; the specification document is not printed until the end of the project. In addition, they are supposed to involve the developers and interoperability group in contributing to the specification, use the document and schedule to reserve testing facilities (primarily the usability lab), and set up a tracking system for recording information for the postmortem report.

Vision Statement Helps Decide What Features to Cut: The Excel 5.0 vision statement is about five pages long. It concentrates on themes that the marketing group wants the product to focus on in priority order: special functionality, hardware and software required to run the product, special dependencies (such as OLE), overview of the business unit plan, and aspects of the schedule. The Excel 5.0 vision also defines "areas" (broad categories of functionality used to group features) and assigns these areas to individual program managers. Because Excel 5.0 is a relatively complex application with a broad range of functions, the vision statement defines goals for the current release as well as five-year product objectives. It also contains separate, smaller vision statements for some of the individual areas.

In contrast, the vision statement for Office emphasizes the harmonious use of multiple applications together to perform a single task: for example, creating a compound document containing text, numerical data, graphics, and automatically inserted scheduling information. The Office vision statement also views the PC as having "one major application," rather than the more complex scenario of PCs with many individual applications that users have to make fit one another.

A major problem in specifying a product is that the marketing people generally want more features than are feasible to develop within a tight schedule. To deal with this, Microsoft groups use the vision statement to help crystallize the defining themes for a product version; then they can use these themes to include or reject candidate features. Chris Peters described what occurs if a project does not have a clear defining vision for a product, and the difference between a good vision statement and a bad one:

> Classically, the program managers will create a rough spec with way too many features than could be done. The developers will roughly estimate the time on each of those features. And knowing what the desired ship date is, there's a very cantankerous meeting where people barter and yell and scream, and try to cut it down. Hopefully, you have some single vision of what you want the product to do. That helps you in the ever-present argument about whether this one ought to be in or that one ought to be in. . . .
>
> There can be good and bad vision statements. A good statement tells you what's not in the product; a bad vision statement implies everything is in the product. In order to give you guidance on what's in and out, you have to kind of explain what the thing isn't. And too often marketing will decide that it's best if everything's in. . . . The hard part is figuring out what not to do. We cut two-thirds of the features we want to do in every release off the list. If we could actually write down everything we wanted to do, it would be a fifteen-hundred-page document. So the vision statement helps you in the chopping mechanism, not in the creation mechanism.

For example, the vision statement for Excel 3.0 stated that the goal for the product was to make Excel 3.0 "the most analytical spreadsheet ever created." In the subsequent discussions during the specification process of which features to add and delete, this vision translated into a decision not to include three-dimensional (3-D) graphs and other objects. When project members had to make decisions on which features to cut, they favored mathematical or data analysis features over those that supported graphical capabilities, although Excel 3.0 added one drawing function.

Product visions, however, can change. It turned out that marketing modified the theme to "power made easy" when Excel 3.0 finally shipped. This marketing theme focused on the product's powerful capabilities, as well as its ease of use. The product actually supported the new marketing theme quite well, but the change of theme did cause some confusion among program managers and developers.

Writing a Specification Document: According to John Fine, a specification document should be very much like a cooking recipe. He gave the example of a recipe—or initial specification—for apple pie:

"Pies can be many things to many people. This apple pie will have the best characteristics of all the pies in the world today. It will contain whipped cream, apples, flour, sugar, and a number of other key ingredients. It should be so big that everyone is satisfied. We will improve its size significantly from version 1. To make this pie: Mix the apples, sugar, lemon juice. Enclose with the crust. Bake hot enough to make sure the pie is cooked to an acceptable degree."[8]

An outline specification document should serve as a cookbook for developers, testers, user education personnel, and marketing personnel. The specification communicates the product vision and requirements to all members of the product team, other product groups within Microsoft, and management. These groups are the "customers" of the specification document. Because projects base all the schedules for development, testing, user education, and non-English versions on information in the initial specification, it must describe features and assign priorities clearly enough so that projects can create meaningful schedules. We should also note that some program managers have felt increasing pressure to make these "recipe" specifications as complete as possible before development begins. A key reason for this pressure is the rising interdependency among product components, such as in Office (see Chapter 6). As a result, the specification documents that program managers create can be very detailed and lengthy (a thousand or more pages) for complex products.

Since the specification builds on the vision statement, it contains a superset of the information in that document. The outline specification document should have an executive summary that clearly states a vision for the product. It should also contain the following items: a one-sentence project objective, a list of what the product is and is not, a definition of the customer, and a definition of competitive products.[9] It should describe the system requirements for the product, including the operating system version, minimum memory, hardware disk space, processor speed, and graphics. In addition, the specification should list any dependencies of the product on third parties (such as printer drivers), and on other groups or components (such as the visual interface design group or OLE). The primary content of the document, however, is a functional description saying what the product features do, not how they do it. It also groups the features into general functional areas and subareas, as in the example for Excel seen in Tables 4.2 and 4.3.

A feature description generally follows a standard format. Each feature has one to several pages in the outline specification that describes how it is supposed to work and look and interact with users from their point of view. If the feature has a user interface associated with it (such as a panel, menus, or buttons), then the specification includes a mock-up diagram of how the interface should appear. Scenarios that illustrate how people would use the feature are particularly helpful to understand how to build the feature efficiently.

The outline specification also describes the problem that the feature tries to solve. (The linkage of features to specific user problems and activities is discussed in depth in the next principle, on feature

Table 4.2   Feature Areas in the Excel Specification

Add-ins	Macro
Benchmarks	Mail
Calculation	Names
CBT	Outlining
Charting	Print
Configurations	Projects
Data	Q+E
DBCS (Far East)	R2L (right to left)
Display	Search
Edit	Setup
Format	Startup
Formula	Toolbar and objects
Function	User interface
Help	Utilities
Links	What-if
Load/Save	Window
Lotus compatibility	

Source: Interview with Marc Olson, Test Manager, Excel, 4/13/93; and "Excel Test Areas," undated Microsoft document.

Table 4.3   Example Subareas of Features in Excel 5

Area	Subareas	Area	Subareas
Charting	General	Charting	Edit series
	Arrows	(cont.)	Terminology
	Axes		Text
	Complex references		Preferred
	Draggable chart points		Chart editing
	Format main and format		Radar charts, series line
	Overlay		Volume-open-high-low-
	Format pattern		close charts
	Gallery		Surface charts
	Data point labels		3D charts
	Legend		3D bar charts
	Data series markers	Links	Apple events
	Chart creation		DDE
	Overlay axes titles		OLE
	Picture charts		Publish/subscribe
	Plot area		General

Source: Interview with Marc Olson, Test Manager, Excel, 4/13/93; "Excel Test Areas," undated internal Microsoft document.

selection and prioritization.) For example, Word for Windows has a feature that quickly saves a document even if it contains subset documents stored in separate files; this is common in desktop publishing and book publishing. An example of the outline specification describes the feature's problem definition as follows:[10]

Feature Problem Definition

The Activity of Publishing Books.
Professionally published documents that are longer are typically created by a group of people. The group members work concurrently on separate parts of the document, but the publishing is done as one single publication. While the 'book' is only published once, it gets printed many times for iterative reviews. Thus the consolidation and printing of the pieces as one master document is done many times.

The Problem with the Current Product.

The master document support through 'include fields' is weak and fragile. Consolidation requires re-saving of the data at every level. Thus the master document has all of the data of the supporting documents duplicated. Since the master document ends up being a mega-sized document that takes tons of time to save, you want to do it as few times as possible, but without doing the full resynchronization every time you risk having the master out of synchronization with the supporting documents.

The feature descriptions in the outline specification document are essential for user education personnel to write documentation and for localization personnel to write non-English product versions. Program managers try to avoid changing the terminology that appears in a feature's user interface (such as a dialog box or a menu), because it is difficult to keep track of changes in the documentation for non-English versions. When writing specifications for user interfaces, program managers can also facilitate the non-English versions by watching out for word length, abbreviations, date formats, currency formats, cultural differences, sorting sequences, paper size, right-to-left orientation, and other elements that might differ among languages or countries.

Program Managers Coordinate and "Write Down" the Specification: Clearly, program managers are at the hub of the information wheel during the lifetime of a product. They write down the specification, help define the user interface, and coordinate interoperability issues. According to John Fine, they ask questions like the following:[11]

- What is the point of this feature?
- What does the user really want to use this feature for?
- Does this feature make sense?
- Is there a similar feature in the product or in any Microsoft product?
- Is this really the product that end users want?
- Is development really creating what we planned?
- What issues have slipped through the cracks?
- Is the intra-group communication satisfactory?

As discussed in Chapter 2, a program manager is a leader, facilitator, and coordinator for the developers, but not their boss. Because developers usually become closely involved in creating the specification, it is most accurate to say that program managers write down the specification rather than create it themselves. Mike Conte discussed the role of the program manager:

> I'm going to give you a false impression when I say the program managers author the spec. Maybe more accurately, the program managers type the spec; the features are actually authored by the group in some ways. As a matter of fact, the challenge of the program manager is to try to get everyone to think that they designed it. . . . Developers are very, very involved with the design. It's very unusual for a program manager to create a spec out of thin air, type it up, hand it to a developer, and it just gets implemented. More often than not, there's a bunch of iteration . . . [and] haggling that goes on, probably because the developers have points of view about how they think features ought to be implemented. And part of it is because they'll give us cost information: "Well, if you do it this way, with a separate window type, that's going to be sixty-four weeks. And if we don't do it, if we do it with a dialog box, it'll be sixteen weeks. Maybe we should do it in the dialog box." And also, if you go talk to a developer and they say, "Well, that'll cost a thousand weeks," maybe what the developer is really saying is, "I think it's a stupid idea." The estimates usually have an awful lot to do with how much the developer likes the feature.

Specifications for major products like Office (including Excel and Word) or Windows are usually defined by ten to twenty program managers, coordinated by a "group" program manager. Some of the program managers work on the product subelements, such as purchased spell-checkers or foreign-language releases. Chris Peters illustrated the interaction between program managers and developers: "[Program managers] try to . . . allow developers to be developers. It's important to understand that the developers don't work for [the program managers] and that they don't have any control over developers in any sure way. In other words, if they write it in the spec, the developer may or may not implement it the way he wrote it. . . . The programmer reads [the feature descriptions in the specification document], understands the code, and then does something pretty darn close to that. Often, there is a lot of talking back and forth, and a lot of screaming and yelling in the hallways."

Tool Support for Managing the Specification: To communicate and manage the specification during its evolution (adding details of the functions of the features as well as changes in the feature set), team members make heavy use of electronic mail. They previously used Word to create and update one large specification file, but now commonly use an Excel spreadsheet to manage the contents of the specification. The specification documents have also grown to the point where they now have separate large files for each specification area or subarea. The spreadsheet lists the following:

- the feature number
- the feature title
- the primary program manager contact
- the development contact, user education contact, marketing contact, international contact, and so on
- schedule estimate for each feature versus actual time spent
- testing release document information
- change (revisions) log for the specification

Of course, a user can move information from electronic mail to an Excel spreadsheet to an actual document written in Word. As an alternative to spreadsheets, Microsoft also has internally developed specification tools that manage structured Word files. Program managers primarily use these specification spreadsheets and files.

On some earlier projects, Microsoft groups used a tool to handle "concurrency control" for the specification files. This allowed only one user to make a change to a file at a time, although multiple users could read it. It required too much hard-disk space on each program manager's machine, though, and proved unnecessary. Now Microsoft handles this access control simply by having people send comments via electronic mail to the program manager who "owns" the particular features. Only the program manager who owns the specification can actually make changes to the files.

Prototyping: Prototyping has become a basic activity of program managers when they specify a new product or version. This allows predevelopment testing from many perspectives, especially usability, and helps create a better understanding of user interaction. It also leads to tighter product specifications. Brad Silverberg noted that program managers even build prototypes for systems products: "Absolutely, they will build prototypes, or they'll work with the developers to build the prototypes. The actual . . . writing [of] the spec, [the] decision making of this feature or that feature goes in, tends to be in program management over development."

Visual Basic is the prototyping tool of choice for user interfaces. Program managers commonly use this in the specification process for a wide variety of products. Another popular prototyping tool, Paintbrush, allows program managers to create computer-screen mock-ups of the product. These static pictures of screens are especially useful for minor modifications of the current product, such as changing how a dialog box appears. If program managers need to create a prototype from scratch or have a prototype that actually works, then Visual Basic is more useful. (An analogous tool to Visual Basic is Apple's HyperCard, which the Excel program management group has used for prototyping in the past.) Visual Basic does not run on the Macintosh (although a Mac version is coming), however, and it sometimes requires more time and effort than a program manager wants to expend if changes are simply incremental. Visual Basic is excellent for prototyping dialog boxes but not very good for other things, like designing new charting metaphors.

Recipe Specifications Become Living Documents: The specification should not be so detailed that it constrains invention. Products that Microsoft builds require invention and creative adaptation. As Chris Peters noted, specification documents have to be flexible enough to accommodate this evolution:

> The spec absolutely changes during development. A spec is a living document. It's the current best description of the features in progress. It gives plenty of latitude to the developers to invent. Hopefully, it's thought through the hard issues, like how this feature interacts with other features. But something that we do differently here that I don't think is done in big defense department projects is [that] the industry is changing so absolutely fast that the spec must change as you're developing the prod-

uct. You gain so much information while it's under development. You gain information on your customers. You gain information on your competitors. You gain information on how easy something is to implement. Or you actually implement one feature and then you suddenly realize that, with a small extension, it could be used in this whole other area of the product that you didn't realize when you first started. You now see it, it's obvious. If you somehow said, "Okay, here is the spec, and then we're going to lock coders—which is a very insulting term for a developer—into this room and they're going to write the spec," then you'd have terrible morale, the thing would be junk, and it wouldn't come out on time.

Early versions of specification documents grow and change considerably during a project. For example, the initial specification for Excel 5.0 was 1,500 pages before the start of coding, and the complete specification when the product shipped was 1,850 pages. (Some people in Microsoft consider this to be much too long.) Word 6.0's initial specification was approximately 350 pages, and its complete specification was about 400 pages. A very early version of the latest Office specification was about 1,200 pages; Microsoft has not printed it recently, but it is now too large to bind as a single document.

In addition to the growth in size, about 30 percent of a specification document changes (or "churns") after the beginning of the first major milestone phase. As Mike Conte observed:

> If you read the spec prior to our starting development . . . and then at the end of the project went back and looked at the spec, I would say at least 30 percent of the spec would be inaccurate. . . . The spirit of a feature might still be there, but it might change. . . . We had this idea, when we started, that this dialog box was going to have five options. Well after we started developing it, we realized that three of those options were too expensive, but we need these other two because we haven't thought about them. . . . So by the time you actually get done with it, it's a different feature.

Conte also noted that projects delete about 20 to 25 percent of the features included in a product's initial specification.

Many projects now try to describe 100 percent of the features thoroughly in the early draft of the specification before the first major milestone phase begins. In practice, though, Microsoft groups seem to achieve this goal for only about 70 percent of the features. The exact details and trade-off decisions of implementing a feature are often not clear in advance, so program managers deliberately leave parts of the specification incomplete. As the project continues, developers provide further information about the behavior of a feature as well as implementation options and performance trade-offs. Chris Peters emphasized that there is an inherent need to see the source code firsthand in order to make the appropriate feature decisions:

> The spec will always be incomplete, and you always, as a developer, want it to be incomplete. A program manager can never see the code in the product. They never will; it's not their job. And to do the feature right requires you to look at the code and to make those engineering trade-offs in the code. In addition, these features that we're working on are extremely complex features, so that again it's impossible without actually seeing the thing in action to know exactly what it should be. We've seen in IBM the horrors of writing directly to a spec, because nobody is that smart. What you have to do is see what the spec looks like, change it, and make it perfect—make it something that people want.[12]

Projects sometimes add major new features that are totally absent from the early specification. Lou Perazzoli, software engineering manager for Windows NT, commented on changes made during the NT 3.0 project:

> The thing we ship has to have the functionality: run Windows, be compatible, be a 32-bit platform, be enabling technology, support network interconnectivity, and have the quality. What has really lengthened the time [to release the final product version] is the additional functions that have come in. The NT product is now going to have services for Macintosh, so you can hook your Mac client to an NT server. You can put [Mac] files up there, put folders up there, click on icons on the Mac, and see folders on an NT machine. That was never in the product two years ago . . . yet here it is in the product. All the remote access servers over telephones lines [are] in; we are going to get the ISDN driver into the product so you can have your 256K line coming to your house, plug that into your PC, and talk to your server over ISDN. We would never have

dreamed of putting that in, yet corporate pressures caused this to be added. So there is a lot of "Let's add these neat things," like Mail. There was no Mail in the product two years ago, but now we are shipping Mail.

Developers, however, need to know as early as possible what part of the specification is changing and what part is stable. They do not want to invest time in developing, refining, or utilizing a feature that the project later discards or changes to the point where work becomes obsolete. A developer on a large project never knows the status of a feature completely. Microsoft's approach to this is to stagger work, concentrating first on features that do not have much of a user interface. These are less likely to change, because it is not necessary to see how users react to the feature before completing development.

For example, developers might first work on a feature that increases the number of fonts a word-processing program supports, or "optimize" the internal data formats for storing a file on a disk. Later on, they might work on a frequently used feature, such as the tool bar for drawing. Very late resolution of user interface appearances, though, can threaten the timely production of documentation and shorten the time available for usability testing. Jon De Vaan recalled some problems in Excel 4.0 that occurred because they firmed up the specification too late in the project. The Excel 4.0 development phases began July 8, 1991, and the first release—the Windows version for the United States—shipped on March 27, 1992:

> The decision to go with a short development project occurred very late— so late that . . . we had to start coding right away. This was a mistake in that it introduced a lot of undue stress into the entire business unit. . . . From the strictly development perspective, we ended up making many implementation decisions long after the schedule was completed. This meant the schedule was not as accurate as it could have been. Since we were making some decisions very late, other parts of the program could not be implemented in synch with other new features. For example, since Workbooks were designed and implemented so late, it was impossible to have Lotus 3-D Sheetloading implemented according to the final design. This resulted in a large number of late-breaking bugs against [worksheet] loading, which could have been avoided. In general, these bugs tended to be concept bugs, rather than simple errors.

The programming team did a good job of making substantial changes very carefully right at the end of the project. Because of the late design decisions being made, it was nearly impossible for testing to generate good test cases. . . . The lack of an up-front design period caused stress between functional groups in the business unit. The relationship between program management and development was affected the most. Because so many decisions had to be made in a short amount of time, some program managers resorted to being autocratic. This caused developers to feel that the program managers weren't "on our side."[13]

Visual Freeze for Documentation: If projects finalize most of the user interface details too late in the project, then the user documentation may be incomplete or inaccurate because insufficient schedule time remains to make the documentation changes. To guard against this problem, Microsoft instituted the target of "visual freeze" to allow user education personnel to write documentation in parallel with the final debugging and testing. But this target becomes almost meaningless if developers continue to make changes or hold user interface features until the end of the project.

Despite their best efforts to freeze the visual appearances relatively early, developers usually make late changes to product features that affect what users see; the user education personnel have little choice but to redo the documentation in the end to accommodate the changes. This reflects the dominant position of developers versus testers or documenters at Microsoft. Chris Peters acknowledged the problem: "Sticking to the visual freeze is the hardest thing in the world. . . . All the stuff always gets done at the end, and the user ed people are always screaming. It's the classic battle. . . . You always hose the documentation. . . . What I mean is, the document is still [basically] correct. What happens is those people have to work twelve-hour days and lots of weekends near the end. . . . [They] have to redo a bunch of work."

Flexible Specification Documents: A fundamental cause for product delays at Microsoft (and elsewhere) is continual change in the specification document or feature set of a product during development. All too often, once a team agrees to change something in the specification, then everything becomes subject to change and the original specifications and schedule slip beyond recognition. Mike Conte elaborated on how specification changes lead to schedule delays:

> When you look back at why those [schedule delays] happen, there's a whole bunch of places where you can point the blame, but there's some fundamental things that could be a problem. One is if you keep changing the product definition—if every time something comes up you say, "Well, we need to change our plans; we need to add this feature"—that has a tremendous effect on the product. Every change takes all this time to implement, [and] now you slipped the whole product out. It affects people's decisions in terms of, "Well, if that's open for debate, let's open everything else up for debate also." The other thing was that you had a product development schedule where you would start development. You had some vague idea when you were supposed to be done, and then you had to debug the product. This is still the way, actually, most applications are written.

Microsoft has relatively flexible specification documents. Some projects, however, have instituted controls over major changes in the spec after certain points in the project, such as 40 percent into the schedule. They allow minor changes afterwards primarily to get features to work properly, but not to add new features. This type of control is easier to accomplish with products like Word or Excel because these are in multiyear version cycles, with new versions appearing every twelve to twenty-four months. If these projects discover during development that they should have made a major change, they will postpone the change until the next version rather than ruin the current schedule. Conte was proud of how the Excel group has been able to avoid making major changes to the specification after a certain point:

> It also means we try to be very disciplined, that we actually don't start development until the spec has been frozen and we have a balanced development schedule with all the features we're going to do. If we want to add features in the middle of that process, it is really, really hard for us to do. So . . . if we learn something in the middle of a product—too late, next time. The reality is that there always are some small things that you're going to sneak in that are really opportunistic. But it is a difficult thing, because they have to walk through the process. There are a lot of groups that are involved.

Late feature additions not only cause development delays, they also squeeze the time available for testing. A willingness to allow a specification to evolve, however, can help a product succeed in the marketplace. This may be especially true with products that have long development periods, because market needs and company needs change over time. It may also take unusually strong technical leadership to keep a project with a significantly evolving specification under control. At some point, managers have to say no to any more changes, or become extremely selective in what they agree to add to a product. Windows NT provides a good example of this flexibility and strong control.

We noted in Chapter 3 that NT began in the late 1980s as a replacement for OS/2, which Microsoft and IBM were developing jointly (until 1989) to replace MS-DOS. Microsoft hired Dave Cutler from DEC to manage the project; he was not familiar with the new Windows type of interface, but he wrote a specification and then a detailed design for a solid operating system for the corporate market. The divorce from IBM and the explosive takeoff of Windows 3.1 then convinced Bill Gates, Paul Maritz, Steve Ballmer, and other senior Microsoft people to bring NT into the mass-market Windows family. In particular, Microsoft's top management wanted NT to adopt the Windows 3.1 graphical user interface, as well as become fully compatible with Windows 3.1 applications. These and other requests required dramatic changes in the product. Before NT shipped in 1993, it underwent three major design changes after the original detailed design. Cutler and his team oversaw all of this work and kept the project relatively well under control.[14] They also demonstrated considerable discipline in resisting additional changes to the product over time. For example, Lou Perazzoli recalled the decision not to support DoubleSpace data compression, because adding this feature would not have allowed them enough time to test the product thoroughly:

> When considering the DoubleSpace stuff that DOS 6.0 has, we just said no. We can't afford to do that in a file system that takes three months just to test. So if it takes six months to develop it, add three months to test it, and then—would you trust your data in a file system that has only been used for three months? I wouldn't. On the file systems we use now like NTFS,

which is our latest file system, I have been using it personally on my machine since July, and I have never lost a file. I feel really good about telling people they can run on that. I could never tell people they could run on a file system that I haven't personally used for at least three months.

Difficulty Understanding and Prioritizing Features: As Microsoft products grew in size and in functional complexity, the number of features expanded dramatically. As a result, projects needed a way to assign priorities to features. One way to prioritize was to focus on features in the next product version that would minimize calls from customers, which cost Microsoft about $12 each on average. Program managers also looked at market research data. Mike Conte described how the Excel group dealt with the problem of determining what features users wanted most:

> There was a bewildering array of features. . . . As the product grew and the industry matured, there were a couple of trends. First of all, you end up in this pointless features war, which is a lot like an arms race. You keep adding more and more "2 percent" features that very few people are going to use. We really knew that wasn't the way that people were going to choose and use products. Nevertheless, it had always been the way of the industry, because it used to be an important measure of what customers wanted. But that trend [is] changing. We have market research from five years ago; if you asked people what they want[ed] in a spreadsheet, they said power. Well, if you ask them today, power is like fourth or fifth most important; most important is ease of use. As the bell curve spreads out, you have people who are less interested in features, who have less time to spend with spreadsheets, less emotional attachment. To them, it's like a fax: They just want it to work, and they don't want to learn it. Products were becoming much more capable, so we had to make them work better.

Program managers used to think of products and organize the specification documents in terms of features that were independent, corresponding to how they would break up the developers. As the specification grew in length and complexity, this feature-breakdown approach became a poor way to think of the product. It also became an increasingly difficult description of the product for program managers and marketing to evaluate. Conte recalled problems obtaining feedback from the marketing group on a detailed specification document:

> We used to print and catalog the spec in terms of functional areas of the product, so we'd have database features, compatibility features, and analysis features. We would have them all broken up roughly according to how the developers were broken up. But it was very, very hard to evaluate. . . . I would give [the spec] to marketing and say, "Please give me your feedback. Is this the right set of features to do?" And marketing would either read or not read it, because it was way too long. Or, if they did read it, they would get lost in it, because it's a super-technical thing. And if they did comment on it, . . . they would say, "Well, we think this dialog box is laid out wrong. You should really have the check boxes on the left," or something. It's not the feedback you want as a program manager. You want the marketing guys to come back and say, "Wait a minute. This product is not going to work for lawyers, [who are] a key part of our marketing strategy," or "It's not going to work for small business." . . . The high-level feedback you really would like to get from marketing is things like, "This is not going to satisfy our strategic direction." And it was very hard for them to do that reading a granular document like the spec. It's a little like reading the ingredient list for an automobile and trying to figure out, is this thing a sports car or what?

The program managers also attempted to use large meetings of developers, testers, user education personnel, product support personnel, marketing personnel, and program managers to discuss the specification and evaluate feature trade-offs. Conte recalled the difficulties in clarifying issues and making decisions based on those large meetings:

> You have a big group now, and you can't just rally around a motley collection of three hundred features. There has to be a vision for it . . . a strong theme . . . that everyone can understand. . . . The bigger the group got, the more features we had to debate, the more irrational the process got. So we'd get in a big room and yell about things. . . . Whoever shouted the loudest about their particular feature would usually get it in. If the feature was . . . some new 3-D chart or some very 'cool' thing, that would get in. And if it wasn't very cool but certainly was important, nobody would rally behind it. Printing is very, very important, but it's not

very glamorous, so people wouldn't want to do it. And it was real easy for there to be snipers in the room. One smart person would say, "That's a stupid idea," and then everyone would lose interest in the idea. So it was working out not to be a process we felt very comfortable about for designing our future versions. So we decided, "Well, let's kind of invert the process a little bit. Let's not even think about features."

Finally, program managers faced a challenge when they wanted to present the essence of a new product to Bill Gates. Conte noted that relying on a preliminary specification hundreds of pages long did not work: "It was actually somewhat precipitated by a Billg [Bill Gates, referred to by his e-mail address] program review. It's the question of, 'Here's this really smart, really busy guy. How are we going to communicate to him what we're doing in the next version of the product and why we're doing it—is this a smart thing to do?' We could give him the spec and argue about the features, the way we usually do, but that isn't going to be very valuable. It was clear to us that we had a really lousy system for doing this sort of evaluation." All of these factors—large numbers of features, the need for feedback from other groups (especially marketing) on feature evaluation and prioritization, and the need to communicate the essence of a product to the group and to senior management—helped lead to the formulation of activity-based planning, as well as the other techniques discussed in the next principle.

PRINCIPLE   *Base feature selection and prioritization on user activities and data.*

In Microsoft's early years, as Mike Conte related, what features got into a product often depended on who shouted the loudest at design meetings. There were more ideas for potential features than projects could develop in time for the next release; the most difficult question thus became which features to leave out. Strong-willed developers or program managers often got features into a product that customers did not really need or could not figure out how to use properly. To solve these problems, Microsoft adopted the principle of basing feature selection and feature prioritization in the development schedule on a technique the company calls *activity-based planning*.

Activity-based planning is similar in concept to "activity-based costing" in accounting. The latter tracks expenses by what companies do (such as the expenses a multifunctional team incurs in designing a new product), rather than by formal departments or traditional functions. Microsoft people appear to have named their planning technique independently of the cost-accounting literature, although many other firms study users intensively in similar ways. With regard to the promotion of activity-based planning in Microsoft, Mike Conte is one of the three original proponents, in conjunction with Sam Hobson and Chris Graham. (At the time the concept was suggested, Sam Hobson was an Excel product planning manager, and Chris Graham was the group program manager for Excel.)

Activity-based planning begins with a systematic study of user activities for actions like writing letters or doing a budget. It then evaluates features in terms of how well they support important or frequent user activities. The benefits are more rational discussions of feature trade-offs, better rankings of what customers want to do, more focused debates on whether a particular feature facilitates a particular task, more readable specifications, and better synchronization among marketing, user education, and product development.

Activity-Based Planning for Feature Selection and Prioritization: The key concept in activity-based planning is to analyze a product in terms of user activities, product features, and interrelationships between activities and features. Program managers and product planners break down the user tasks or scenarios that a product intends to support into approximately twenty "activities." Then they try to map the activities (and any subactivities) to current features in Microsoft's product, as well as to features in competitors' products. They also map activities to different customer profiles—for example, novices versus advanced users, or different market segments.

The activity-based planning approach has helped program managers and developers focus their energies and creativity when specifying new versions of a product. In practice, projects such as Excel try not to add more than four major activities with each new product version. Most new features map directly to these activities. The Excel group even lists how many activities each feature supports as part of the specification document, a practice that enables the project to rank features in terms of their value to the user. Mike Conte outlined how the Excel group evaluates activities in order to focus the next product version on just a few features:

> The net of all this was, as a business unit, to agree on essentially what were the important activities for us to focus on for a future release. Let's pick four—I thought four was a nice number, no more—and let's prioritize them. And that would be our focus for the next release of Excel. We still have these big meetings where we all get together and yell at each other. But now, instead of yelling about . . . which feature we're going to do, we would be arguing about the activities. We'd say, "I really think the most important activity is switching from 1-2-3, and here's my data, and here's the reason why I think it's strategically important." And somebody else would say, "No, I think basic usage is more important because more people use it, and we've got to focus on new users." . . .
>
> The end of that process was that we had a ranked list of four activities that we wanted to focus on for the next version of Excel. . . . Now we go back to that big list of features that we had, and we said, "Okay . . . We've got feature number one. How does it support our activities? Well, let's see, it helps building templates, it helps scenarios—this guy gets a 2. Let's do feature number two. It helps templates, it helps scenarios, it helps printing—this guy gets a 3." We were never as simplistic as this, but we did actually go through scoring each feature.

One effect of this "scoring" is that it creates competition among program managers and developers to make their features support as many activities as possible. This is good competition—good for users, and good for the productivity of the specification and development effort. Scoring also makes it possible to select what features to put in a product, what to leave out, or what to leave to a future version that might target a particular activity. Conte described how activity-based planning has encouraged projects to create more general-purpose features:

It had a couple of interesting effects. First of all, people still had to think of features that they want in the product. So they would think, "Okay, I'll cheat, actually. If I change the feature by just 10 percent, it will support more activities, and then it'll get in the product." And that's exactly the kind of cheating you want people to do, because we do want features to be more general. We want them to support as many activities as possible. It also gave us a way to take a whole lot of good ideas and say no to them, which is actually one of the hardest things to do as a program manager.

Gathering Data for Customer Activities, Not Product Features: With activity-based planning, the project planning phase focuses on activities first and features second. Rather than thinking about and picking favorite features and crafting a vision statement around them, program managers and marketing personnel make a list of what activities their customers are doing. Then they center the product vision statement on features that support those activities.

Microsoft product managers and program managers started to research exactly how people used spreadsheets, for example, and specifically what activities they did with the spreadsheet to accomplish particular tasks. They noticed that lots of people used Excel to make budgets. These users also followed specific activities: They might first make a template, distribute it, and ask people to fill it in. Then they might run scenarios on the template, and send the results to a boss for auditing and comments. Perhaps they would later do some sensitivity analysis, and eventually consolidate the information and print it. People also tended to do budgets twice a year. In addition, it turned out that large and small companies both go through a roughly similar budgeting process. In small companies, however, one person often does the budget; in larger companies, people specialize in parts of the budgeting process.

As Microsoft people probed just this one task—budgeting—they found about twenty basic customer activities. Furthermore, they noticed that the current version of the specification did not adequately cover several of these. They also found that many activities used in budgeting resembled other activities, such as writing expense reports or forecasting sales. As a result, they created a more fundamental activity called "data roll-up." Another activity that people making budgets did was to switch from Lotus 1-2-3 to Excel, including moving files from Lotus as well as simply switching programs. It turned out that 65 percent of Excel users had prior experience with Lotus 1-2-3, but Excel did not take this into account and make it easy for former Lotus users to make the transition.

Chris Peters gave this account of how activity-based planning has helped teams focus their creativity:

> We have this technique called activity-based planning, and that basically involves going to people and the customers and doing research on exactly what they're doing. If you ask people what features they want and what improvements they want, you always get this filtered through what they think is possible. And if a company tries to invent features based on the customer, they always filter it through what they think the customer wants. I think it's easier for us to try to understand what steps the customer is doing than it is for them to understand what we can write or invent. So we went out and did stuff . . . like in word processing, like how typographic errors are made, or how do people do mailing lists. . . . It turns out that the way most companies do mailing lists is that they have this . . . list with all their customers' names and addresses, and they put that in the copying machine and make labels, and they run the exact number. Well, if you just ask people what features they wanted in a word processor, you wouldn't get that answer.
>
> You often hear, "I want a drawing package. . . ." "And so, what are you going to do with the drawing package?" "I'm going to do an org chart." . . . So only if you understood what kind of things they are making at some fine level, and if you break these down to the activities that make up the different tasks, and you create your features this way, you can see . . . [if] you have all the subactivities necessary to complete the actual activity. And also you can focus on creating things that have maximum utility; in other words, "This feature is used by seven different activities." It allows you to be just as creative as you were before but . . . in a fairly focused way, because you haven't abdicated creativity. You haven't said, "Tell me what feature you want." All you've done is fundamental research on what's really occurring.

Focusing on Activities Promotes a Holistic Product Approach: Use of activity-based planning started with the planning phase for

Excel 4.0 in early 1991. Microsoft also used this on Excel 5.0 and has promoted the approach among other groups, particularly where activities affect or require features in other products. The Word and Mail groups, as well as some systems and languages groups, have all adopted some form of the methodology. Microsoft has not written down the methodology or tried to make it into a science, however, in order to allow the techniques to evolve more easily. As Conte observed: "It's certainly popping up all over. . . . We were kind of intentional about not writing it down and making it very scientific, so that it sort of spreads through the company and evolves a little bit in the process. . . . We thought if we got any more than twenty [basic activities], you just can't keep track of them, and it becomes a mishmash. It's not a very scientific thing."

Activity-based planning appears to have spread among groups because it helps project personnel think about the product in a more holistic way. This whole-product viewpoint helps project members from different functions understand what a product does, as well as how corresponding features in other products might support activities that cut across or require different application products. Conte commented on these benefits of the technique:

> One of the things we tried to do is evangelize the methodology to other groups. There were some selfish reasons for doing that. This was originally designed as something only to help us essentially "spec the exe"— spec the actual code itself. But it turned out a lot of times you would look at one of these activities, like switching from 1-2-3, and say, "Well, you know what? We need a marketing program to support this. We need a chapter in the documentation to support this." And so it became something where suddenly we could now take a more holistic approach for building the product. We also would find that there are cross-application activities, like creating a compound document, where there's a feature— not a feature that we need in our product, but a feature that we need the Word guys to add in *their* product. . . . Traditionally, those kinds of cross-application features would be relegated to some appendix and easy to cut.

Marketing Research to Support Activity-Based Planning: To support activity-based planning, product managers from marketing conduct some joint research with program managers and developers, such as direct studies of users. In general, however, product managers do most of the research. As Conte described, this research is now a year-round activity:

> Traditionally, product planning research was this really specialized thing that would happen only in this five-week window right before we froze the spec. . . . So after we'd finish, let's say Excel 4.0, the program managers would now want to do Excel 5.0. They would say, "Okay, we need all your product planning research, and we're going to freeze the spec in eight weeks, so get it all in to us." And the marketing guys would be totally busy launching this new version, and they would have no time; by the time they had time to think about it, it was too late, because we'd frozen our spec. Because the activities-based planning research is more generally applicable, it's actually something we do year-round.

Activity-based planning has also led to a broadening of the type of marketing research Microsoft does to support product development. Initially, program managers placed no constraints on what kinds of research people should do to gather information on activities, although they did make suggestions. Conte has preferred quantitative research to qualitative research or very small-sample studies, because it is more difficult to extrapolate from the qualitative research. One good example of a large research project consisted of a market segmentation survey done through random-digit telephone dialing to U.S. households. The marketing group used this survey to ask what activities people did with the product, and it realized that Excel needed a new activity for list management. (See Chapter 6 for a fuller discussion of customer feedback and product improvement.) Microsoft groups have since gone beyond any one type of research; their studies now extend from visiting customers directly to asking customers to use "instrumented versions" of the product that record all of their keystrokes. Conte continued:

> That research varies from customer visits to special research projects. We did do some longitudinal studies of users. We would visit them every three or four weeks and see how they were getting along with the documentation, how they were getting along with the product. . . . We have one activity called basic usage, which is sort of a fake activity. It's selecting and scrolling and entering formulas, and stuff that people do all the

time that isn't necessarily part of doing a budget or whatever. For that we have a special version of Excel called the instrumented version, where it records every action the user does, and we can go back and analyze it.

In general, activity-based planning has given the marketing group a mechanism for more clearly affecting the evolution of Microsoft products. As Conte concluded: "We [program management] find we get much better info from them [marketing] than we ever did in the past. Instead of getting a list of pet features that they would like for the launch demo, we now get real information: 'Well, this activity is not that important; don't focus on it. This activity is very important to us; focus on that activity.' It's also allowed us to get much better info from some of the partners who don't have the resources of [Microsoft's group for] U.S. marketing, like [Microsoft's] international [divisions]."

Contextual Inquiry for Studying Group Activities: Microsoft projects also use a technique called "contextual inquiry" to help understand the activities of users working in groups or teams, although activity-based planning can capture activities of either individuals or groups. Contextual inquiry evolved at the Digital Equipment Corporation during the late 1980s from techniques anthropological researchers use to study group and social dynamics. Office, Money, and Cairo have applied contextual inquiry to help refine existing specifications and features as well as probe for new types of activities that these products should support.

Contextual inquiry encompasses a whole series of disciplines, exercises, and attitudes, and it is much more involved than activity-based planning. The basic model is an immersion process. First, a project team chooses a focus, such as creating compound (text and graphics) documents with the Office product. Second, team members visit customer sites; these are not really interviews, but are more oriented toward simply observing the customers and their activities. As a third step, which occurs during and after the site visits, observers take extensive notes and draw diagrams and models that record activities in terms of physical environment, work context, activity flow, and dependencies.

Finally, the team members conduct a data extraction session

back at Microsoft, where a dozen or so members discuss the site visit. In the data extraction session, people use hundreds or thousands of labeled Post-It notes to build an "affinity diagram," which attempts to capture the activities they observed and their associations. A site visit usually lasts two to three hours, and the subsequent data extraction session two to three hours. Projects conduct a series of site visits and extraction sessions over three to four weeks. Mike Conte summarized the process: "It's almost like an Outward Bound thing: They come to this consensus, but they are not exactly clear how they did it. . . . The people who didn't go on CI [contextual inquiry] don't [come to a consensus]."

Conte also noted other limitations to the technique: "The problem is that CI doesn't really have an output. . . . There's no quick one-page-of-what-we-learned outcome. . . . It's very hard for other people to absorb. So it is an awkward thing to try to spread widely." Another problem is that contextual inquiry is very time-consuming and can require project representatives to attend a series of visits over a three- to four-week period. Some of the results are also ambiguous; for example, a contextual inquiry study for the Office group led to the conceptual separation in the user interface among "places for finding things, ways for opening things, and places for making new things." Conte pointed out that in the usability lab, however, users had trouble distinguishing between opening and finding objects.

PRINCIPLE   *Evolve a modular and horizontal design architecture, with the product structure mirrored in the project structure.*

A key concept in Microsoft product design is that the underlying structure of products—especially applications with rapid life cycles—should become flat or horizontal over time (rather than hierarchical or "top-down"). When they build the first version of a product, development groups use more of a top-down structure in order to define an initial skeleton for the product design. Over time, however, they move toward a flatter structure that allows projects to focus on feature competition. Projects need to add and delete features incrementally, change and evolve features over

time (such as move from character-based to graphical user interfaces), and increase the consistency of how features appear and
operate across products. As discussed further in Chapter 6, an increasing emphasis at Microsoft is to share features across different
products. Sharing helps to harmonize the "look and feel" of different products; it also facilitates user tasks that require more than
one application, reduces redundant writing of code, and cuts
down the size of individual applications.

As discussed in Chapter 2, Microsoft also structures projects in
a way that mirrors the structure of the product—it organizes products by features, and organizes projects by feature teams. This approach makes it easy for everyone to understand how teams relate
to the overall product. Projects begin by defining an outline specification in terms of a prioritized list of relatively independent features to develop for the next version of the product: Office, for
example, has features such as editing text, manipulating tables,
and formatting data. These are not completely independent, because the edit text feature relies on the print feature to print and
the file management feature to save text. These and other activities
also utilize features that Word and Excel used to separate. Nevertheless, related groups of features are sufficiently distinct so that
projects can develop them in separate feature teams.

Program managers and developers divide a project into subsets
of features for each feature team to produce during each of the
three or four major internal project milestones (see Figure 4.2).
For Office, Microsoft also divides the project into Excel features,
Word features, PowerPoint features, and features common to all
these products (usually built by the Office development group).
Chapter 5 analyzes the techniques that developers use to coordinate and evolve the product as a whole, such as daily builds and
synchronizations. This feature-driven product organization and
development approach allows Microsoft to increase product functionality incrementally simply by adding more developers to a project and creating a larger team. As Chris Peters observed: "We had
a very large development team [on Excel 3.0]. . . . First of all,
which may come as surprise to a few people, is that it does work.
You actually can write lots of features. Let's say we had approximately thirty people. Did we do three times as many features as

ten [people]? No, we probably got twice as many features as ten. The development costs on Excel are . . . minuscule compared to the revenues which are generated by Excel. So the fact that we used thirty and got the work of twenty, that we actually got twice as many features in it than we could have, is a huge competitive advantage over Lotus."[15]

Features (and Functions) as Building Blocks: The features in Microsoft products are relatively independent units of functionality visible to end users. They are like building blocks, especially for applications products. Examples are printing, automatically selecting a column of numbers and adding them, or providing an interface to a particular vendor's hardware device. Features in systems products, such as Windows NT or Windows 95, are often less visible to the end user; Microsoft and other companies sometimes simply call these "functions."

Program managers take on a set of features (or functions) to manage from specifications through testing and documentation. They must coordinate with the developers, who are responsible for estimating schedules and refining the functionality of each feature. Developers also keep the program source code for a feature in one or a small number of files stored on-line on a development computer.

The development or enhancement of most features requires only one developer, although some large features require a small team. This variation exists because the level of abstraction for a feature is subjective; developers decide the appropriate level. An example of a feature for one person to work on is to add character styles to Word. In a recent product, some features were so large that individuals worked on them (one per feature) for an entire year, although this is unusual. Most features consume about three person-weeks—that is, one person working for three weeks. The smallest features may take just three days or so. One very popular feature, the "auto-sum" feature in Excel, took one person only one week to develop.

Product Architecture—A Flexible Internal Skeleton for Features: A product architecture is the skeleton that is internal to a product; it defines the major structural components and how they fit together. A product architecture and the components that fit into it provide the backbone for implementing the product features (that is, doing the detailed design and coding). The architecture for a product is generally not directly visible to an end user; only the features that the architecture implements are visible. The product architecture is also the skeleton that determines the long-term structural integrity of a product. Any evolutionary change in a product's functionality should not cause the underlying product architecture to unravel.

Microsoft groups intend their product architectures to be very flexible in order to facilitate the incremental addition, deletion, refinement, or integration of product features. Good product architectures reduce the amount of interdependencies among groups, including developers within and outside Microsoft. Bill Gates emphasized this in our interview:

> If there were a hundred people involved in [Windows] NT development, then there were ten thousand, because all those people outside the company who were writing NT software were working to the same type of architected interface that the guys who were writing utilities were and the guys who were writing user interface applications running on top of the thing were. So there's a whole spectrum of how interdependent work is. Good architecture can reduce the amount of interdependency within even a development group here.

Product Architectural Layers: We may also describe an architecture in terms of horizontal "layers" and interfaces between the layers. A layer provides a set of functions and capabilities to the next higher horizontal layer in the architecture. Software companies usually call the lowest layer the system "kernel"; the highest layer provides the functions and capabilities—the features—that end users see and use. Sometimes functions and capabilities from layers below the highest layer are also visible to the end user. As a rough analogy, a layered architecture resembles an onion. An onion is made up of a central core (or kernel); it has many successive layers surrounding the core; but the consumer only sees the outermost layer. The creation or definition of clean abstract interfaces between layers of functionality helps insulate the product's functions from underlying details. These details include dependencies on particular hardware platforms like the Macintosh or PCs running MS-DOS and Windows.

The central defining concept in a software architecture is the definition of the interface between each of the layers. Chapter 3 referred to these as application programming interfaces (APIs). An API defines the published entry points that a layer makes available for calling by parts of the product located in higher layers in the architecture. A layer of a product can consist of hundreds of "subroutines" or sets of instructions in computer code; developers usually only make a few of them available for other parts of the program to utilize or call. Typically, when a project breaks a product up into pieces for different teams to implement, they agree to define what types of functions and capabilities each of them will provide to the others. Those definitions are usually in the form of APIs, which can be lists of procedure names, what parameters each accepts, and a brief description of what each does. Well-defined architectural layers and APIs greatly facilitate the flexible addition, deletion, and enhancement of product features.

Excel's Architecture Uses a Generic Layer for Portability: Each of the Excel architecture layers, for example, has an application programming interface that defines the functions and capabilities in that layer. The APIs for the top four layers are the same for the different versions of Excel that execute on different operating system platforms. The API for the lowest Excel layer will differ depending on the underlying platform (such as Macintosh, Windows, OS/2, or Windows NT), but Microsoft insulates the bulk of the Excel code from these differences because of a platform-independent API for the generic portability layer.

The Excel product architecture illustrates the concept of horizontal product architecture layers. We list Excel's five architectural layers here from highest to lowest:

1. Formulas and formula manipulation
2. Format table (well-defined ways to create a format or display of data)
3. Cell table (well-defined ways to put data in cells, enumerate cells, and so on)

4. Generic portability layer (an Excel-specific miniature "operating system" or kernel).
5. Operating system (such as Windows 3.1, Windows 95, Macintosh, or OS/2).

Excel's generic portability layer is an important technical strategy for the product's architecture. This facilitates the usage of major portions of the application code on different hardware and operating system platforms. In a sense, the generic portability layer is like a miniature "operating system" that specifically serves as an interface between the Excel application features and basic operating system software, such as Windows or OS/2. As Jon De Vaan commented: "We write Excel to our [generic] layer, which is our version of an operating system. We've implemented it on Macintosh, Windows, OS/2, and now Windows NT as well, although that one's pretty darn easy. It's almost the Windows version, just compiled for Win32. It's a pretty straightforward virtualization of graphical environment concepts. We did Mac Excel 2.2 and OS/2 Excel 2.2 from that layer."

Not every Microsoft application product has a generic portability layer like that in Excel. Word does not, for example. Word 6.0 used the Windows API to approximate a generic layer, although this first effort resulted in the noticeably poor performance of the initial Macintosh version (see Chapter 3). The Excel group wrote their generic layer relatively early in the development of the product in order to facilitate use of the same code on both Macintoshes and PCs. De Vaan summarized the development status of a generic portability layer for Word:

> Word, for example, is just working on getting there [having a generic layer], and they're going to use the Windows API as their layer. We [Excel] did ours a long time ago. It was actually an experiment because, when we were thinking about it, there were definitely skeptics among us. Could you even make a decent program, within performance constraints, with this kind of approach? So we got to do the experiment on Excel. At that time we thought there wasn't a way to make a good Macintosh program using the Windows API as that abstraction. . . . And part of it is we knew both APIs, having done Mac Excel 1.0 on the Mac API and Excel 2.0 on the Windows API. They're a lot similar, and they're a lot dif-

ferent. I think at times we were focusing a lot on the differences and saying, "Wow, these differences are not overcomeable directly, so we don't think we could do that." But as you get more familiar with stuff, you get some different perceptions.

Product Architecture for Windows 95: As another example of a product architecture, Windows 95 uses specialized layers to support a wide range of applications, including 32-bit, 16-bit, and DOS applications. These layers, called "virtual machines," provide separate processing threads and protected areas; each looks like an individual computer to the programs running on top of it (see Figure 4.4). All Windows applications, including the 16-bit Windows 3.1 applications and the 32-bit applications for Windows 95 or Windows NT, execute in the System Virtual Machine layer. Within the System Virtual Machine, each 32-bit application has its own private "address space." A private address space prevents the

Figure 4.4   Windows 95 Product Architecture

System Virtual Machine				DOS Virtual Machines	
32-bit Windows application	32-bit Windows application	User . . . interface shell	16-bit Windows application		
			16-bit Windows application . . .	DOS Virtual Machine	DOS Virtual Machine
Windows Subsystem (Defined by Windows API)				DOS application	DOS application
• Windows user (window manager)					
• Windows Graphics Device Interface (GDI)					
• Windows kernel					

Base System
- File management subsystem
- Network subsystem
- Operating system services
- Virtual machine manager subsystem
- Device drivers

Source: Adrian King, *Inside Windows 95* (Redmond, WA, Microsoft Press, 1994), pp. 64, 105.

application's data from interfering with another application's data or causing the other application to halt abnormally (or "crash"). All 16-bit applications share a single common address space in the System Virtual Machine, so they may still interfere with one another (just like they do in Windows 3.1). The Windows Subsystem supports the System Virtual Machine, and the Windows API defines the capabilities in the Windows Subsystem. Each DOS application executes in its own DOS Virtual Machine and uses its own private address space.

The Windows 95 Base System provides the lowest layer in the product architecture, and the Base System supports the System Virtual Machine, Windows Subsystem, and DOS Virtual Machines. The Base System includes a file management subsystem (disk files, CD-ROM files, and so forth), network subsystem (including remote computer access and data sharing protocols), operating system services (plug-and-play configuration capabilities, date/time functions, and the like), virtual machine manager subsystem, and device drivers (keyboard, display, mouse, and so on). The virtual machine manager subsystem in the Base System constitutes the heart of the Windows 95 operating system. The virtual machine manager subsystem implements the basic system functions for process scheduling, memory operations, and program starting and termination.

Product Subsystems: A horizontal layer in a product architecture can have several distinct subsystems or subsets of functions and capabilities. Each subsystem has an API that is a direct subset of the API for its architectural layer. For example, Windows 3.1 developed the concept of a "universal print subsystem"; this has a simple API and enables third-party vendors to write printer drivers in a much more straightforward way than in past Windows versions. (Printer drivers are small vendor-specific programs that control the printing of a document or data on the vendor's printer.) Brad Silverberg described the usefulness of the universal print subsystem approach and how Microsoft is applying the same concept to a universal video subsystem and elsewhere:

> With Windows 3.1, we went to a new printer driver architecture, which we called the universal driver. It's a powerful generic printer driver en-

gine that allows them to use small snap-on modules, which we call mini-drivers. In the simple case, they [the persons writing the printer mini-driver] basically just describe a table of the escapes that are needed to talk to the printer—all the rasterization [such as computing line positioning] and all the device management is done in the piece [subsystem] that we supply. . . . So that turned the act of writing a printer driver from having a very skilled person take six months to write a monolith to someone who could read a printer manual, look up a table of the escapes, and spend a two- to three-week effort. As a result, with Windows 3.1, we got great printer drivers and coverage for a lot more printers. The issue of printer drivers dying is no longer a problem. We got a lot of that information from PSS. . . . And we're taking that same philosophy with most of our other drivers now. We didn't do the universal driver approach for video in Windows 3.1, so video drivers were a problem and people had buggy video drivers that crashed the system. So, for Chicago [Windows 95], we're going to a universal video driver architecture with small snap-on mini-drivers for individual video cartridges. We're doing the same for universal modems drivers, with small snap-on modems. We're doing the same for hard disk drives and so on.

Feature-Driven Versus Performance-Driven Product Architectures: Many existing Microsoft products, such as Office and Excel, embody a "feature-driven" product architecture. Such emerging products as the video-on-demand Tiger project or other multimedia projects, however, require "performance-driven" product architectures. The architectures differ because, for example, delivering video and audio requires consistent real-time system behavior under heavily loaded conditions. ("Real-time" means that a product must perform some operation, such as delivering video or audio, almost instantaneously by a fixed deadline, or else the information is useless.) According to Rick Rashid, vice president for research, these inflexible performance requirements do not fit into the traditional Microsoft notion of a product feature:

> There might be goals in products like Word and Excel to perform this operation within this amount of time, but . . . they're not hard statements that it has to do precisely this; they are statements saying that it should

do about this. When you think of delivering video, for example, over a cable-TV network or a telephone or even in a standard computer network, you have very, very strong guarantees that have to be given as to when information arrives and how quickly it has to be processed to have it function correctly. And the behavior of the system under load has to be completely specified. It can't be the case that the system under load behaved dramatically differently from the system in lightly loaded situations. It has to be the case that the system under load behaves exactly according to its specification and refuses to accept additional load beyond a certain point, so that it can maintain its guarantees.

Microsoft's development process for building these types of performance-driven systems includes mathematical and algorithmic design for guaranteed behavior under all possible load situations. This development process emphasizes "fault tolerance," which means that the system can recover automatically from failures during operation. For example, the Tiger video-server project discussed in Chapter 3 started out as a research activity, and it had an extensive up-front analysis and simulation phase. Now it has moved into the advanced consumer systems division, with Rashid acting as the director of interactive TV and video systems development. The project took about six months of work to define the basic system ideas and produce an initial working version. The research group also used processes such as frequent builds and milestones and allowed the specification to evolve, although they had to specify critical performance elements of the system before they began coding. This emphasis on performance first (rather than on features or functions) and the need for analysis and simulation up front are probably the critical differences between these new types of systems versus the other kinds of products Microsoft usually builds. Rashid continued:

> I think that's one area where the greatest difference may occur, whereas a more traditional path might be, for example, to first get functionality there and then deal with performance issues. . . . When you have significant constraints, you have to first resolve those constraints . . . algorithmically, by analysis and by modeling, and then you worry about what other features you may want to add on top of that or what other things

you wanted to do. . . . I think the difference may be one of bringing up issues of performance and quality divisions in behavior early in the process, rather than leaving them for later in the process, which is probably more traditional in any computer project.

Little Architectural Documentation: Source Code Is the One Document: True to the "hacker" tradition, other than the API documentation, Microsoft does not produce much written documentation on the architectural structure of its products. Sometimes senior developers write down the higher level architecture, but this depends on the development manager. For complicated features, many individual developers write down and review the architectural details specific to their features at some point, but this is up to their discretion. A few groups have documentation for new programmers that lays out a level of structure beyond code files and features; for example, an eight-page document goes over Word's internal structure (major data structures, how they work, and so on). People do not update these regularly, however, and managers do not require projects to produce such internal documents.

The specification, in turn, does not talk about implementation; developers should know how to do the implementation or be able to learn it. Chris Peters explained that there is so little written architectural documentation because "a developer's job is to write code that we sell, not to spend time writing high-level design documents." Bill Gates supported this view, emphasizing that design documents should not be separate from the source code: "[There is] some methodology where you have a document that's independent from the source code. [If you think] that you're going to gain greater efficiency by going off and spending a lot of time on that [other document]—that's ridiculous. A lot of rules that are fairly rigid in nature are pretty ridiculous. So there're a lot of pragmatics that go into building great designs and building great software. . . . One document. One. It's the *source code*. It's the one place you go. You learn everything there, and you know everything there."

Compartmentalizing Code and "Keeping It Simple": Instead of relying on documentation of the product architecture, Microsoft depends on developers to compartmentalize code. This usually works, but not always. Jon De Vaan described the reliance on developers: "We don't do—and we always get into discussions where this might be a liability—a lot of overall design stuff, like 'that feature should be grouped in this module, and this should be the interface for that.' We don't do that. We rely on people's judgment that they properly compartmentalize things. Sometimes people don't, and that can be a problem." De Vaan emphasized that Microsoft also tries to keep the design and code as simple as possible: "The other kind of guiding principle we have is 'keep it simple.' Things don't need to be complex unless they need to be complex. Surprisingly enough, and I'm not sure if it's the way computer science is taught or other things, people like to make things complex even when they don't need to be."

One example of compartmentalization and simplicity is a "revert to save" procedure that De Vaan worked on for Excel 5.0. The original procedure was very complicated, affecting as many as twenty different parts of the program. Since people did not commonly use the feature, developers would often forget it existed and "break" the feature when making an unrelated change. As a result, it has been historically riddled with bugs. De Vaan replaced this with a much simpler design that centralizes the function in one place in the code, so that developers working on other parts of the system do not have to worry about it. Ben Slivka, development manager for MS-DOS 6.0, gave another example of poor compartmentalization and an overly complex design in a portion of his product:

> The split between the user interface of DoubleSpace Manager and the Compression Engine Library (CEL) was conceived to allow a Windows-based UI [user interface] to be written without requiring changes to the CEL. CEL would understand all the details of the CVF [compressed volume file] format, restartability, et cetera. Unfortunately, this concept was not carried out, and so major aspects of restartability, robustness, and CVF limits and properties are spread throughout both [DoubleSpace] Manager and CEL. . . . In the future, we should make sure all team members have practice at object-oriented design, focusing on data-hiding and minimal interfaces, to ensure that code will be modular, decoupled, and maintainable. A two- to four-week teaching period where [a] project is designed and implemented would be a very, very good thing.

Growth in Product Size: Microsoft and other companies use product size metrics to make sure that developers are aware of how large their products are becoming from one version to the next. The continual addition of new features and graphical capabilities can cause substantial growth in the number of source lines of code in a product and in the size of its executable file. For example, the number of lines of source code in Mac Word increased 68 percent from version 3.01 (152,525 lines) to version 4.0 (256,378 lines). Other products whose size metrics indicate substantial growth include Word for Windows (31 percent between versions 1.0 and 2.0), Excel (31 percent between versions 3.0 and 4.0), Project for Windows (85 percent between versions 1.0 and 3.0), and Windows NT (109 percent between Preliminary Developers Kit 2 and Beta 1; Table 4.4).

Additional features may justify the size increases. Developers and testers, however, pay the penalty of having to understand, mod-

Table 4.4   Product Size Metrics

Product	Source Lines of Code	U.S. Release Date	Percentage Increase
Mac Word 3.01	152,525	1987	—
Mac Word 4.0	256,378	1989	68%
Word for Windows 1.0	249,000	1990	—
Word for Windows 2.0	326,000	1991	31%
Excel 3.0	648,531	1990	—
Excel 4.0	851,468	1992	31%
Project for Windows 1.0	134,225	1990	—
Project for Windows 3.0	248,025	1992	85%
Windows NT PDK 2	1,821,719	1991	—
Windows NT Beta 1	3,800,000	1992	109%

Source: Chris Mason, "MacWord 4.0 Development Postmortem," 5/19/89; "Preliminary Postmortem Data on WinWord 2.0;" Jon De Vaan, "Microsoft Excel 4.0 Postmortem," 6/8/92; Glenn Slayden, "Microsoft Project for Windows Version 3.0 Development Postmortem," 3/16/92; Lois O., "WinProj 3.0 Post Project Analysis," 4/2/92; David Anderson et al., "NT Test PDK 1 and PDK 2 Critique," 4/92; David Anderson et al., "Windows NT Test PDC and Beta 1 Critique," 1993.

Table 4.5   Product Executable Size Metrics

Product	Source Lines of Code	Executable Size (Bytes)
MacWord 3.01	152,525	349,000
MacWord 4.0	256,378	668,000
Word for Windows 1.0	249,000	775,000
Word for Windows 2.0	326,000	1,268,000
Project for Windows 3.0	248,025	1,629,568

Source: Same as Table 4.4.

ify, test, and debug ever-larger amounts of code. As the code grows, developers generally try to compartmentalize features and localize the dependencies between them. Tracking these measures helps keep the length of time required to change, debug, and test features manageable. In some cases, project groups have to change their development style; for example, Office has adopted a two-stage build process in order to accommodate its large volume of code and decrease the time spent in product builds (see Chapter 5).

Developers should also try to keep down the amount of disk space that a product requires. This is the size of a product's "executable file." It has ramifications for packaging the product on floppy disks as well as for assessing aspects of the product's memory usage. A product's executable file size, however, is not easy to manage or predict. It depends on the amount of code and data specific to a product, as well as the amount of reusable or shared code included in or "linked" to one product from other products. For example, Word, Excel, and PowerPoint share some features as part of the Office suite; Office also links with some files directly from the Windows operating system. The individual executable sizes of the applications, if installed separately, are larger than if a user installs the three products as part of the Office suite running on Windows. For this and other reasons, there is no direct correspondence between lines of code and executable size. Another illustration is Word for Windows 1.0 and Project for Windows 3.0 (Table 4.5),

Figure 4.5 Example Executable Size Growth Metrics for Word for Windows 2.0

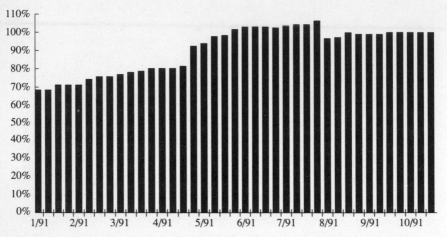

Source: "Preliminary Postmortem Data on WinWord 2.0," Microsoft internal document.

which have similar numbers of source code lines but dramatically different executable sizes.

Microsoft projects use both actual numbers and graphs to keep track of executable size, and developers will spend some time trying to reduce these numbers by making the code more concise and efficient. Figure 4.5, for example, displays the growth in the size of the executable file for Word for Windows 2.0. The large jump from May to July of 1991 and the subsequent decrease from August to October of the same year reflect the addition and deletion of features, the enabling and disabling of debugging code, code optimizations, and other factors.

Feature Teams and "Content Experts" as Team Leaders: In Chapter 2, we described feature teams as small groups of usually three to eight developers who work on related areas of features under the direction of a feature team lead. Team size often depends on how experienced or capable the team lead is. (More experienced leads take on larger teams.) Feature team leads report to the project's development lead, who has a broad view of the product and can best see interconnected problems; he or she is in charge of all the development work for the project. Jon De Vaan felt that the feature team leads are key to Microsoft's development process and ability to integrate new people: "Feature team leads are very important. I think that they're the most important thing in making the whole process work because, when push comes to shove and people need guidance, they're the ones who have the job title and responsibility to give it. They're also responsible for writing a lot of code as well."

Several groups moved toward feature teams at about the same time during the late 1980s. Excel was one of the leaders, adopting the feature team concept while building version 3.0 during 1989 and 1990. The group had only a few teams at this time, although the number has increased significantly since then. For example, Excel 5.0 (shipped in late 1993) had ten feature teams: Eight worked on the basic Excel product, one worked on a separate Graph product, and another worked on the Query Tool product. In comparison, Word 6.0 (shipped in early 1994) had six feature teams.

The Windows 95 project also centers around feature teams. Because of its size (more than one hundred developers), managers initially grouped the feature teams into three larger self-contained teams: one team for the Windows 95 base, one for networking, and one for mobile components. (The project later consolidated networking and mobile.) As Brad Silverberg explained: "There are two feature teams under the mobile. Under networking, there are probably half a dozen. Under the base, there are probably ten. The base is the biggest group and they have the most number of people by far, and really the most number of pieces of the product. They're building the file system, the shell, the underlying kernel, the device drivers, and so there are probably ten to twelve different teams. Each has a feature team lead and program manager in charge of that area. And again, for each area . . . if the feature team lead is really strong, he drives that area forward. If the program manager is really strong, he drives that area forward. If they are both strong, they tend to drive it together." Silverberg considered the people in charge of the major self-contained teams for Windows 95 as "content experts":

Within my group, I break them down into . . . three major teams. They are pretty well self-contained in that they have program management, development and testing—all the development parts of the puzzle—

within the group. One for the base piece, one for the networking pieces, and one for the mobile pieces, because that enables those teams to still be relatively small and keep the hierarchy flat. And the person in charge of that piece will be a *content expert*. . . . If you look at successful software products, the ones I've been associated with at Borland or here at Microsoft, people in decision-making positions—program managers, testers, developers, marketing guys—are also content experts. They know that product. They know how to use the product, they know the competitor's product, they know where the future is going. They know technology. They are product people; they're not just the managers. . . . They are content experts. And when you know the products, you can make the right decisions. When you don't, when you're just trying to build off some product spec, you just lose track of what's important. There's no sense of priorities or sense of what's really important or exciting, what's important to really do right.

Silverberg also stressed the need to keep feature teams small with close working relationships because products tend to resemble the organizations that create them:

The software tends to mirror the structure of the organization that built it. If you have a big, slow organization, you tend to build big, slow software. If you have a small and nimble group that talks together well . . . then the pieces that they write tend to work together very well. If you have two teams that have to deliver tightly coupled software, but the two teams don't get along together well, what you end up with usually are very formal interfaces between the two groups and between the two components. . . . So I can often look at a piece of software and tell you about the company that built it, and with pretty good accuracy. You put fifteen people on a compiler, you tend to end up with a fifteen-pass compiler. And fifteen-pass compilers tend to be pretty slow.

Everyone Is an Expert for Some Functional Area: Many Microsoft products are now so large that managers encourage developers to become experts in parts of the code. As a result, developers often consult with other developers—the "local experts"—to make coding or architectural decisions that might affect other features. Windows NT, for example, has hundreds of functional areas where some individual has become the expert. Products such as Excel and Word are smaller, but they also have dozens of functional areas and experts for each area (see Table 4.2). Lou Perazzoli commented on this: "One of the things we do is to try to make sure that everybody has an area of expertise. . . . I think that does two things. One, it gives you someplace to go when you have a problem; you can go to a person who is the expert in that area. And two, it lets people feel really good about themselves because they are the expert in this area. And we don't encourage people to be experts only in one area."

As in all software companies, some developers are far more skilled and experienced than others. Microsoft projects take advantage of these differences by assigning the most difficult tasks and areas to the most capable people. Usually, only the more experienced or talented developers make changes that affect many parts of the product simultaneously, such as altering the kernel code in NT or the recalc engine in Excel. Chris Peters observed: "The old model that some developers are ten times better than the others is true no matter at what level of development you are. There's always a guy that's ten times better than you. If you're this hot-dog guy, you would get huge responsibilities—it's almost assigned based on how many tentacles that the actual feature has. If it's a fairly small self-contained feature, we will tend to give it to a very junior person. And if it has all sorts of side effects and ramifications, it tends to be given to a more senior person."

The next principle describes how the feature-based product organization and feature-team project structure also form the basis for project scheduling.

PRINCIPLE   *Control by individual commitments to small tasks and "fixed" project resources.*

Estimation for product development and delivery schedules is a very challenging task, especially in software projects. There are many factors that affect the schedule, and development progress is difficult to measure. Microsoft managers deal with these difficulties by pushing responsibility for schedules and work management down to the lowest level, the individual developers and testers. This ensures that everyone takes individual responsibility in addition to acting as part of a team. Individual developers set their own schedules, and program managers aggregate the individual schedules and add buffer time in order to formulate an overall project schedule. Top executives also "fix" the basic resources—people and calendar time—to make sure that projects focus and limit their effort and creativity.

The key goal, particularly in applications, is to specify a target ship date for the product and try to stick to it as long as possible. Program managers and developers then work backwards from the ship date and define the dates for the intermediate project milestones. This fixed-ship-date approach centers on developers; the motivation is to reduce the number of situations where projects have no defined end point and go on for a year or more in ultimately useless iterations among design, redesign, and testing. These seemingly endless iterations and wildly inaccurate schedules used to be common at Microsoft, and they still occur occasionally on projects that managers do not tightly control. Such uncontrolled projects frustrate personnel, managers, and customers. In the words of Bruce Ryan, a program manager: "Fake schedules, whether intentional or not, help no one."[18]

Developers Make Their Own Schedule Estimates: For the past decade or so, Microsoft has scheduled projects by asking the developers who will code the features to estimate the time they will need. Senior managers do not generally hand people schedules and tell them to complete their work by a particular date. Many companies in the United States, Japan, and Europe do their scheduling in this autocratic manner, although usually after consulting with the developers and reviewing historical data from other projects. Bill Gates emphasized that Microsoft lets developers and teams set their own targets: "All these dates are the dates of the group. There's nobody else who's trying to set a date. We got away from that about ten years ago, of setting the date in some top-down approach."

Developer-based estimation brings with it the problem that managers have to guess how overly optimistic developers are and adjust project schedules accordingly. Similarly, managers have to add buffer time to solve problems that may arise due to imperfect information. This kind of scheduling is not as accurate as, for example, keeping detailed records on what each developer does on particular types of projects, compiling statistical averages or "standard times" for different activities, and then using these data for project estimation and control. (This more factory-like style is common among large Japanese software producers.[19]) Microsoft's developer-based estimation approach, though, has two major benefits: It gets more cooperation from people because the dates are *their* dates, not the manager's dates; and the schedules are always aggressive because developers invariably underestimate how much time they actually need.

In the past few years, Microsoft projects have improved their ability to adjust estimates as well as add appropriate amounts of buffer time. Many developers now keep their own records on past projects, to see how accurate their estimates have been. Project members, team leads, and development managers usually have access to data from past projects to help them adjust their own estimates, although managers do not require that projects keep and analyze such historical data. Microsoft's style of scheduling thus makes some sacrifices in accuracy, although it gives developers what Chris Peters termed a greater "illusion of freedom":

> It's important psychologically that the developer who is writing the feature estimates the feature. . . . That's the only way you can get the buy-in necessary, if you want to ship on time. Because if you hand estimates to a person, then that isn't really their ship date. It's your ship date. So, if they take longer to do a feature than you said that they ought to, then you were just dumb. You just didn't know much about the way it was going to turn out. You never have to fear that estimates generated by developers will be too pessimistic, because developers will always generate a too-optimistic schedule. So you can give the illusion of freedom, while still having a very ambitious ship date, simply by giving people the option of estimating their own feature schedules. . . . At least in this place [Microsoft], you never have to fear. . . . The schedule is done by development, and development owns it completely.

Schedule Estimates for Fine-Grain Tasks: A second Microsoft scheduling approach tries to "force" more realism and avoid wild underestimates (as occurred on Word for Windows in the 1980s and many other projects) by asking developers to give their estimates for implementation activities based on a very detailed consideration of tasks to complete. The level of granularity for the tasks is usually between four hours (a half day) and three days. Some groups, such as Excel, are in between, as Jon De Vaan noted: "When we do scheduling, we try to get the schedule refined to no longer than two-day tasks. Depending upon the feature, it could have one task, it could have twenty tasks." This push for more fine-grain scheduling is important because developers tend not to be very good at thinking concretely about how much time particular tasks should take. Chris Peters, who has promoted more accurate scheduling in the Excel, Word, and now Office groups, explained:

> Any task that takes longer than a week, it's almost certain that the person has not thought it through well enough. And any task where the guy has estimated it at less than half a day . . . he's thought about it too much; he ought to spend more time programming and less time thinking about it. The classic example is, you ask a developer how long it will take him to do something and he'll say a month, because a month equals an infinite amount of time. And you say, "Okay, a month has twenty-two [working] days in it. What are the twenty-two things you're going to do during those twenty-two days?" And the guy will say, "Oh, well, maybe [it will take] two months." Even in the task of breaking that down into twenty-two tasks he realizes, "Oh, it's a lot harder than I thought." So we usually try to get them down to less than three days.

Scheduling for systems products is more difficult. It is not as easy to cut features; moreover, the reliability and functionality of the product are usually far more critical than shipping on time. Nonetheless, projects like Windows NT emphasized fine-grain scheduling (days or half-weeks of work) early on, and later paid more attention to integrating components and staying focused on finishing the product. As Lou Perazzoli recalled: "When we do our initial schedule, we really try to schedule things down to days or half weeks . . . and then we try to have integration periods. Obviously, estimating software design is a real black art. One of the big problems we have is, you never get the functionality level that people want. You do what you promised to deliver and then people say, 'Oh, but look, you didn't handle this.' Or 'On this machine their interfaces are slightly different, and you have to handle these three cases.' So we have a lot of fudge factors at the end that we build in for integration through testing."

The Psychology of Scheduling Developers and Teams: We have noted that as projects have grown larger, Microsoft has broken up work by teams. Managers then push down responsibility and ownership of the schedule as low as possible, to the teams and individuals; this creates for both a sense of ownership of the work. It also generates intense peer pressure among the teams, individuals, and especially team leaders to keep to the estimated schedules, because managers can rebalance the schedule and take work away from individuals or teams that fall behind. Peer pressure thus makes it less necessary for managers to try to tightly control the progress of individuals or individual teams.

Excel 3.0 (and recent versions of Word) used this scheduling psychology, for example. Several feature teams did their own schedules and worked relatively autonomously; they ended up competing fiercely with each other to stay on track. The result was that even a large team (the entire Excel project) ended up working like small autonomous teams who set their own goals and time hurdles. There was no single coordinated schedule, and yet the project shipped only eleven days late. Chris Peters recalled the experience:

> In order to push responsibility as low as possible, we had each of the feature teams do their own schedule. Not only did the ship date matter to each individual, it means that each feature team lead wants to make sure they ship it on time. . . . There was actually no coordinated schedule. In other words, if you had five feature teams, as people slipped and features didn't quite work out, you'd actually end up with five different ship dates. And then at each milestone time, you would rebalance the schedules: You would either chop features or move them between feature teams until the thing became balanced again, and then you'd proceed on another milestone. You ended up with all sorts of neat things where a feature team guy would be even less willing to slip, because it was showing him as being not a very good new manager in a company where managers were picked to be feature team leads, and his direct peers were presumably doing better or worse. This had an even stronger effect on

ownership of the ship dates than it would be if all these people just sort of rolled up and said, "Well, I'm a little late." . . . We were basically trying to come up with methods for having the same behavior modes as we did in smaller teams.

The "Fixed" Ship Date: Of course, the potential for disasters is large when managers delegate so much authority to individuals and teams. Mike Conte, who kept track of the schedule for Excel 5.0, recalled how bad scheduling disasters have been in Microsoft: "One of the big problems with software development is that you have very uncertain schedules. That was always a problem. . . . It's been the experience in some embarrassing cases in Microsoft that it took eight years to develop a product that was supposed to take about two years." A fundamental cause for project schedule slippage at Microsoft, according to Conte, has been starting a project with no fixed ship date and thus no limits on what the project attempts. There has also been no understanding of how to assure the quality of the product during development. We noted in Chapter 1 that this situation can lead to a state that Microsoft people have called "infinite defects"—projects that continue to generate huge numbers of bugs even after developers think they are finished because each line of code they write to fix one bug tends to generate another bug. Developers then face years of debugging and rework, with no ability to predict when they will finish.

As a result, to bound creativity within time limits, Microsoft now tries to fix ship dates—or at least, the internal targets for ship dates—in advance for new products or new product versions. This keeps pressure on people to cut down on features and stay focused on one project. It forces them to think hard about the key features that absolutely must go into a new product. Developers and teams still set their own schedules, although senior executives might set the delivery target for the final product. Chris Peters elaborated on these benefits of the fixed ship date:

> The reason why we try to do fixed-ship-date releases is that it forces creativity and hard decisions that would not be made otherwise with a floating ship date. You can imagine, "Should I do thirty features or twenty features?" If the ship date is not fixed, the answer is always thirty.

"Should we do the big complicated version, the medium version, or the small, lean version?" "Well, I think we should do the complicated version; we'll just move the ship date." . . . So the ship-date fix is usually done in order to force people to come up with that essential 20 percent [of a product] that gives 80 percent of the benefit. . . . Remember, the problem is not lack of ideas; the problem is too many ideas. So what do you do to give you the discipline to find the essential ideas?

Peters viewed his "crowning achievement" as the nearly on-time shipment of Excel 3.0 in 1990. This project holds the Microsoft scheduling record for an application of this complexity, although smaller products have shipped on time: "In general, we used to ship products six months to a year late, and certainly there are parts of Microsoft that still routinely do that. But a few years ago we tried to create a feedback loop and understand what was causing the delays and try to improve on it. We were able to get pretty good; even disasters now are [usually] within only sixty days of the original schedules. But no one's beat the eleven-day [record] yet."

The fixed-ship-date concept applies to a much lesser degree to systems products. A big negative is that rushing the ship date generally leads to less time for testing and quality assurance activities at the end of the project. These activities tend to be more demanding for systems products as opposed to applications due to the huge number of user scenarios (different combinations of equipment and applications software) with which an operating system has to work. Ben Slivka summarized both the positive and negative aspects of the fixed-ship-date approach for the MS-DOS 6.0 project (we discuss this further in Chapter 6):

The product team really kept a strong focus on the ship date throughout the project. We all shared a clear understanding of where we were going, and kept in mind the trade-offs we had to make to get there. The shared goal was a strong unifying force for the team. . . . Unfortunately, to a degree we became captives to the ship date. More time for creative testing and tracking down non-readily-reproducible bugs might have helped avoid some of the problems customers are now experiencing. While it isn't clear that we would have found or corrected any of the problems encountered since release, a less rushed atmosphere at the end would have given us more of a chance.[20]

Tracking and Announcing the Ship Date: Compared to what they did in the 1980s, group program managers, development managers, product unit managers, and senior executives now keep relatively close track of where major products are on a development schedule. This is true even if managers do not try to intervene or rebalance work until the milestone junctures. Most groups also now have similar metrics to record data on estimated times versus actual progress, and use either Microsoft Project or an Excel spreadsheet to collect and map out the data. (The Office group and its constituent product units prefer Excel to Project; this is mainly because the Office people are more familiar with Excel. Chris Peters also claimed that Microsoft Project is more appropriate for managing the design of airplanes and buildings, rather than individual tasks like software development.)

Figure 4.6, for example, displays a project schedule chart for PowerPoint 3.0. The original delivery date was March 1992; the group revised this several times before shipping the product in May of the same year. One major revision to the target date occurred around 1/1/92, approximately when the project reached the code-complete milestone. A product tends to ship about four to five months after it reaches this point.

Microsoft does not usually like to announce a planned ship date until just before a product is actually ready for commercial release. As noted in Chapter 3, however, there are some cases where Microsoft and other companies announce new product plans very early for strategic reasons. Early announcements (referred to as "vaporware" in the industry) can signal a move into new markets or the intention to challenge a particular competitor, and thereby deter customers from buying products from another company. In general, however, announcing a planned delivery time too early decreases flexibility to change development plans, gives competitors a chance to react, and causes negative press coverage if the date slips (which it usually does). Mike Maples commented on this:

> We also have gone pretty conservative, at least in all but the systems products, on not announcing our products before they're ready to ship. The marketing guys always have good reasons why announcing early is helpful, but almost every time it turns out that it really wasn't helpful in a marketing sense. Secondly, you always give the competitor some infor-

Figure 4.6   Tracking Predicted Versus Actual Schedule for Power Point 3.0

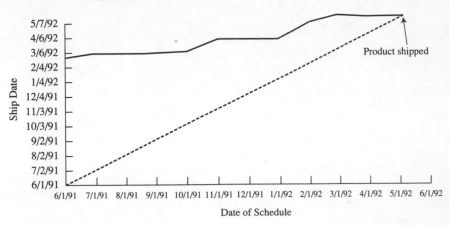

Source: Microsoft internal document.

mation and you give them more time to react. Thirdly, you totally mess up your business model. Fourth, if you're not on schedule and you decide to change something, you have the world helping you manage your schedule. The last thing I need is the *Wall Street Journal* telling me how to run a development process. If it ships in June, hopefully they'll never know it was supposed to ship in April. And if we decide to change it for some set of reasons, I don't want to have to explain that to five hundred people. That's an element that a lot of our customers and a lot of our competitors haven't figured out.

Many companies announce ship dates for their products and then "slip" the dates to allow for additional development or testing time. Microsoft schedules have become more accurate but, as seen in the case of Windows 95 or totally new products such as Microsoft Exchange (see Chapter 3), they clearly continue to slip. It is our impression that Microsoft managers now want to be extremely comfortable with the quality or reliability of a product before shipping it. There is some risk of alienating customers with late deliveries, but a much larger risk of alienating them with a buggy product. In Chapter 5 we further discuss the basis for making product ship decisions, as well as examine the details of how Microsoft actually builds and tests its products.

5

Developing and Shipping Products

Do Everything in Parallel, with Frequent Synchronizations

To develop and ship products, Microsoft follows a strategy that we describe as do everything in parallel, with frequent synchronizations. We break down our discussion of this strategy into five principles:

- Work in parallel teams, but "synch up" and debug daily.
- Always have a product you can theoretically ship, with versions for every major platform and market.
- Speak a common language on a single development site.
- Continuously test the product as you build it.
- Use metric data to determine milestone completion and product release.

These principles outline a remarkably simple approach to product development, with many steps that are incremental and concurrent, as well as coordinated and automated. Yet none of these principles (or the tools and methods Microsoft uses) is highly innovative in itself. Many software-development organizations have

261

practices that facilitate teams or individuals working in stages and in parallel, and numerous companies and research laboratories exhibit more advanced software design and development technologies. As in defining products, Microsoft distinguishes itself primarily in execution: Product development supports a mass-market strategy that relies on the incremental evolution of product features. At the same time, people work within a corporate culture inherited from the loosely organized world of PC software. Microsoft teams try to work quickly and deliver lots of products and features at low prices to a broad variety of customers.

Several principles provide structure and facilitate coordination and problem solving in Microsoft projects, but allow enough flexibility for products to evolve in stages within a usually fast-moving schedule. Perhaps most important are the methods, procedures, and tools that we have labeled the synch-and-stabilize process. Microsoft uses this approach to tackle small as well as large projects and still retain the benefits of nimble small teams that communicate easily and quickly. The key idea is that one large team can work like many small teams if developers synchronize their work through frequent "builds" and periodic "stabilizations" of the product. This incremental building also enables Microsoft groups always to have products theoretically ready to ship to customers.

Several other factors promote structure and flexibility in Microsoft projects. Different groups use common programming languages and tools, and they work predominantly on a single geographic site. It is relatively easy, therefore, for individuals and teams to communicate face-to-face or switch projects. Managers pair developers with testers so they can work together to test, debug, and integrate features concurrently, as they go along. Projects are also becoming easier to control, since project managers are learning to rely on metric (that is, quantitative measurement) data and statistical trends when making decisions such as when to move on to the next milestone or when to ship a product.

In contrast, more sequential approaches to software development may require very long periods of time because they schedule work in sequence, not in parallel. Managers may also find it difficult to assess progress accurately because they tend to schedule major testing very late—often too late—in the development cycle.

Sequential types of processes also do not facilitate doing frequent product builds. Sequential development is thus a mismatch for Microsoft, especially in groups developing subsequent versions of a product, such as Excel 5.0 or Word 6.0. If a project is creating a totally new product with no existing base of features, then the team usually adopts a hybrid development process. It starts with more traditional sequential phases; once the first subset of features is complete, however, the team quickly moves to a frequent build process to synchronize and stabilize the evolving components. For example, Windows NT, as a new operating systems product, followed this type of hybrid process in its four-year development cycle. It began with specification and detailed-design phases, and then adopted incremental milestones and daily builds.

Again, though, there are differences in how Microsoft applies its development principles to applications and systems products. The product builds tend to be less frequent for systems because of their code volume and large number of parts. The process can take overnight for systems, as opposed to only several hours for applications. The "always have a shippable product" concept thus applies more to applications than to systems products.

Microsoft projects simultaneously build product versions for different hardware platforms (PC and Macintosh) and foreign-language requirements more frequently for applications. Systems products tend to target a single platform (such as Windows) and have fewer features visible to end users that contain native language (for example, English) and cultural conventions (for example, currency formats). Applications projects emphasize usability testing more because they have many features that non-expert users need to understand. Systems products make more extensive use of very large beta test periods because they need to work properly with a wide range of hardware equipment and applications programs.

PRINCIPLE   *Work in parallel teams, but "synch up" and debug daily.*

Daily Build Process: The daily build process consists of several steps, because many different people can be making different changes to the same source code (the finest-grain components of the product) in parallel. For example, the Excel 3.0 project at its peak had thirty-four developers actively changing the same source code—the one Excel executable (.EXE) file—on a daily basis.[1] Table 5.1 outlines the steps that Microsoft developers go through to create the daily build and keep everyone "in synch":

Table 5.1   Daily Build Process

1. *Check Out.* Check out private copies of the source code files from a centralized master version of the source code. Only the developer who checked out these private copies will modify these private copies of the source code. Other developers can check out separate private copies of the same files.

2. *Implement Feature.* Implement the feature by making changes to, adding code to, or deleting code from the private copies of the source code files. A developer uses an interactive source code editor tool to make the changes. The feature implementation could take less than a day or several days to complete.

3. *Build Private Release.* Build a private version of the product, called a "private release," using the private copies of the source code files that include the changes implementing the new feature. The developer may build one private release of the product for each target platform, such as Windows and Macintosh. The build is usually executed overnight.

4. *Test Private Release.* Test the private release of the product to make sure that the newly implemented feature works correctly.

5. *Synch Code Changes.* Compare the private copies of the source code files that include the changes implementing the new feature to the current centralized master version of the source code files. (This comparison process is called synchronizing or "synching" the changes.) A developer uses a "diff" tool to compare files and determine differences automatically. The current centralized master version of the source code files could have changed since the developer checked out his private copies of the source code files in step 1; since then, other developers implementing other features have changed and checked in some of the same source code files that he has checked out. The developer should do the comparison between his private copies of the source code files and the current master version of the source code files in the late af-

Table 5.1   (continued)

ternoon. Then he is sure to use the most recent centralized master version of the source code. No one can make changes to the centralized master version of the source code after a certain time each day. For example, the daily deadline for changes to the Excel source code is 2:00 P.M. If an Excel developer wants to synch his code on a particular day, he would do so after 2:00 P.M. that day.

6. *Merge Code Changes*. Update the private copies of the source code files so that the private copies of the files incorporate both the developer's changes as well as any changes that other developers have made to the same files. (This update process is called "merging.") The Source Library Manager (SLM) tool does this merging automatically. It also warns the developer of any inconsistencies (called "merge conflicts") between the files that he needs to resolve manually. On Excel, for example, synching and merging usually take about 5 to 20 minutes, depending on the nature and degree of the changes.

7. *Build Private Release*. Build a private release of the product using the private copies of the source code files that include the changes merged with other developers' changes. The developer may need to build one release of the product for each target platform, such as Windows and Macintosh. The build is usually executed overnight.

8. *Test Private Release*. Test the private release of the product to make sure that the developer's newly implemented feature still works correctly. The developer does this feature test in the morning on the day after he did steps 5, 6, and 7.

9. *Execute Quick Test*. Execute a highly automated test, called a "quick test" in most groups (other names include "smoke test"), on the developer's private release of the product. This makes sure that basic functionality in the product still works correctly after he has added his feature. The quick test does not test his new feature directly; it just makes sure that his changes do not interfere with some other features of the product and cause errors indirectly. The developer does this quick test in the morning on the day after he did steps 5, 6, and 7. On Excel, for example, executing the quick test usually takes about 30 minutes.

10. *Check In*. If the feature test (step 8) and the quick test (step 9) are successful, then the developer can officially check in his private copies of the source code files into the centralized master version of the source code files. The first

Table 5.1   (continued)

part of the check-in process is to synch the private copies of the source code files again with the current centralized master version of the source code files using the "diff" tool (just like he did in step 5). The second part of the check-in process is to resolve any merge conflicts between the private copies and the master files using the SLM tool (just like he did in step 6). The final part of the check-in process is to physically update the master version of the source code files so that they contain the changes the developer made to implement his feature. Some other developers could have checked in changes to the same source code files earlier in the same day; this could have been before the developer checked in his changes to those files. That is why the developer needs to synch and merge again in this step as part of the check-in, in addition to the previous synch and merge that he did as part of steps 5 and 6. On a day when a developer checks in changes, he must watch the other check-ins later that day to make sure that they do not affect his same-day changes in an indirect way. If there is some interaction effect, he may need to withdraw or "back out" some of his changes until the developers can resolve the incompatibility in both sets of changes. Each project has a daily check-in deadline, so developers must complete all changes to the centralized master version of the source code files before a certain time each day. For example, if an Excel developer wants to check in his changes on a particular day, he would do so before 2:00 P.M. that day. He does the check-in on the day after he did steps 5, 6, and 7. This is the same day that he does steps 8 and 9. On Excel, checking in can take from 5 to 60 minutes, depending on the number of files.

11. *Generate Daily Build.* Each day after the check-in deadline (for example, 2:00 P.M.), a developer designated as the project "build master" generates a complete build of the product using the centralized master version of the source code files. The new internal product release resulting from this build is called the "daily build." This is a relatively stable snapshot of the evolving product as it gains increasing functionality. Projects generate the daily build each day regardless of how many developers checked in their source code changes that day. The build master monitors the build process until all the code compilations complete successfully and the build finishes. This may require staying late that evening or coming in early the next morning, depending on the length of time required to complete the build. After a successful build, the build master executes a series of automated tests. These assure that

Table 5.1   (continued)

---

basic functionality works correctly and that the build is reasonably stable. The build master then makes the daily build available to all project personnel, including program managers, developers, testers, and user education staff, for their use and evaluation.

The daily build process has several key steps. First, in order to develop a feature for a product, a developer "checks out" private copies of source code files from a centralized master version of the source code. He implements his feature by making changes to his private copies of the source code files. He then "checks in" the changes from his private copies of the source code files; these go back into the master version of the source code. The check-in process includes an automated test to help assure that changes to the source code files do not cause errors elsewhere in the product. A developer usually checks his code back into the master copy at least twice a week, but he may check it in daily.

Regardless of how often individual developers check in their changes to the source code, a designated developer—called the project "build master"—generates a complete build of the product on a daily basis, using the master version of the source code. Generating a build for a product consists of executing an automated sequence of commands called a "build script." This creates a new internal release of the product and includes many steps that "compile" source code. Compiling automatically translates the source code for a product into one or more "executable" files. (An executable file can perform particular operations directly on the computer, as opposed to a file that, for example, simply contains text or a list of data.) The new internal release of the product built each day is the *"daily build."* Jon De Vaan, former development manager for Excel and the current development manager for Office, explained the rules and logic behind the daily build process that the Excel group followed (also see Table 5.1):

> The idea is, we always want the checked-in code to be as high quality as possible. So, to do that, we've established some rules. The first rule is: If

you're going to check in today, you have to check in by two o'clock. The code that you checked in must compile and link. For Excel 5.0, it has to do that for Windows Excel, Macintosh Excel, Windows Japanese Excel. We also do a program called Graph, which is based on a lot of Excel source code. So Windows Graph and Macintosh Graph also have to compile and link. Windows and Mac Excel have to pass a quick test macro; this is a macro that exercises . . . parts which tend to get broken often. People have to download their versions to their machines and start the macro, but after that it's automated, so you can get checked in by two o'clock. When I say that you have to be able to compile and link, that means you must have—the night before—synched to the project, resolved all your merge conflicts, and have been able to build from a clean state all the things that I've said. A lot of people synch every day, [but] you really only have to synch the day before you check in. I'm sure we probably average better than every other day, for everybody.

Daily Builds—A Rigid Rule to Keep Teams Coordinated: Doing daily builds gives rapid feedback to the project team about how the product is progressing. Lou Perazzoli, software engineering manager for Windows NT, saw daily builds as painful but useful: "Doing daily builds is just like the most painful thing in the world. But it is the greatest thing in the world, because you get instant feedback." Although Microsoft has very few rules, projects strictly apply the frequent build process because this ensures the day-to-day stability of the evolving product and pulls together all the development activities. As Dave Maritz, former test manager for MS-DOS and Windows, commented: "This is absolutely rigid military discipline, that exactly at five o'clock each day a snapshot is taken of the build. My philosophy is that there are certain things that are inviolate rules. You always take a snapshot every day; it doesn't matter what happens. Even if it's a holiday the next day and you know no one's going to use it, everybody just gets to know the rhythm and feels that there's control of the project. A weekly build gets taken come hell or high water, even if you know that the build two weeks behind [the current one] is still not stable. It doesn't matter."

Ed Fries, development manager for Word, argued that the daily build process is critical for the development teams to function effectively. A major Microsoft project tries to work like a collection of small autonomous teams; even subgroups should have no more than a handful of people—as in the early days of building PC software. But major projects are no longer small teams in the aggregate. They are also very dependent upon many other groups and individuals for pieces of the product. Even individual developers within a feature team need to work with source code that other people are changing. Fries described how the daily build process ensures team coordination: "It's really important. We couldn't have this big a group without that [the daily build process], because we are still cooperating. We're trying to work like a small team. But we're not a small team. And we need the work that other people are doing. We need the product to be basically working all the time, too, or it's going to interfere with your area. You can't have the guy who's working on drawing break typing, so that no one can type, so that they can't type in to get to the area that they're trying to work on."

The daily build process makes it possible for many project members to function as an integrated team because it provides a code control mechanism that almost always produces a version of the product that works. To keep track of code changes and detect conflicts, Microsoft uses an internally developed tool, referred to as SLM, as a source-code library manager. (Microsoft people affectionately call this "Slime.") Microsoft projects use SLM as well as automated testing to help assure the consistency and stability of the evolving product. As Fries summarized: "We rely on the breadth test to do that, or the quick test to do the same thing. We rely on our source code control system; when it goes, we're in a bad way. It lets multiple people change the same files, and it deals with conflicts and merges them together. Before you can check in, you have to merge with the checked-in version, and the conflict will show up in your local build immediately. Then you have to resolve that conflict before you can check in."

Stay in Daily "Synch" with the Product: We have emphasized that the daily build process makes sure that the basic functions of the evolving product are working correctly most of the time. In order to assure this high level of stability, Microsoft likes to have developers synchronize and merge (but not necessarily check in) their source code files every day (see steps 5 and 6 in Table 5.1). Fries, for example, believes it is important to get into the habit of "synching up" every night before leaving the office: If a developer waits a longer time, problems to synchronize and merge usually increase.

Developers frequently synchronize and merge their checked-out source code files with completed source files that other people have checked in after modifications. As a result, developers always have an up-to-date version of changes. The daily synchronize-and-merge steps help coordinate source code changes among the different developers and prevent large, error-prone merge conflicts later in the project. Fries explained: "We still think it's important that everyone synch every night, that everyone stays in synch with the project, so that they are getting the changes that everyone else is doing. . . . If you try to hold off and wait, then . . . you tend to have huge merge conflicts . . . when you get back in synch with everyone. So we try to keep everyone working off the same set of source [code] basically all the time."

There are actually several reasons why people want to check in frequently. First, the less frequently a developer checks in, the more time other developers have to change the source files on which they are working. Therefore, a late check-in means the developer is likely to face more problems merging his files. Second, checking in creates a central backup copy of the source files. This is valuable to have in case a developer's machine runs into mechanical problems or other circumstances arise that make it difficult to retrieve the files. Third, checking in creates a history of all files that developers have changed, and their differences. This "diff history" is useful for tracking down problems if they occur later, as Fries described: "You can see who changed what when." People often check in simply to take advantage of this feature of the tool.

Breaking the Build: A crucial rule for developers is to make sure their checked-in changes compile correctly. Changes should not clash with other features or cause an architectural incompatibility in the product that stops the automatic build process. "Breaking the build" is especially problematic for large projects that execute their build processes overnight, because no one discovers the breakdown until the next morning. The team loses valuable time. It must correct whatever caused the build to fail, restart the build, and, in the meantime, fall back to the previous build for testing. Because developers cannot see the effect of the most recent changes, they may postpone their check-ins, and this hinders overall progress.

At mid-afternoon every day, the build master starts the master build for the product using the centralized master version of the source code. He usually waits until the build completes successfully before going home; the resulting release then becomes the daily build for the product. Applications groups generally pass the role of build master to the next person who checks in code that prevents the build from completing successfully. Marc Olson, Test Manager for Excel, explained: "That's the fundamental rule, that you can't break the build. . . . If you hose the build that day, you are the person that docs the build until someone else hoses it. So there is a penalty if you screw up the process."

Groups usually impose a penalty for breaking the build. In applications, the guilty person becomes the build master. Systems, however, usually have a dedicated build team of two to four people; in these groups, the developer may have to pay a fine of five dollars or so. Microsoft people also like to tease developers who break the build. They often have a special hat for them to wear, such as a WordPerfect hat in the Word group. Lou Perazzoli recalled the ritual of checking in code on Windows NT 3.0:

> We used to have goat horns. The rule was, if you broke the build, you wore the goat horns, and then the next guy who broke build, you gave him the goat horns. . . . Now you just pay five bucks. One of the guys the other day was making a massive check-in of about 150 files and he . . . posted a fifty dollar bill next to it, so there is some humor in this. I told my debugger guys, if they have a whole lot of bugs they want to fix and they have a massive check-in they want to do . . . [then] they have one shot at it. They should post a hundred-dollar bill on the board. If it goes without problems, they get to keep their hundred-dollar bill; if they have a problem, they lose their hundred-dollar bill. So they should do all the testing they need to, because it is about forty minutes to build the debuggers.

Minimizing the Build Process Overhead: The synchronize, merge, and check-in process is a relatively unproductive period for developers, because they keep their machines pretty heavily loaded. A developer cannot really do any other computer-based activity during this period. As a result, developers try to keep the overhead of the synchronize, merge, and check-in process small. They need to use their time effectively and implement changes quickly—especially late in the project, when testers need rapid bug fixes. Late in a project, developers often do a "one-day pass," checking in code changes—often bug fixes—on the same day the changes were made. Jon De Vaan talked about the need to reduce overhead in the build process and get a quick turnaround on bug fixes: "Well, it's okay for people not to check in every day, because typically the feature area that they're working on isn't the one-day pass. The time where it really gets expensive is at the end of the project, when you are doing one-day passes—in fact, less than one-day-pass bug fixes. You want to turn around to the testers those fixes as quickly as possible, because they're inevitably blocking getting coverage on other areas in the feature. So that's the time when that checking-in overhead really starts to kill. . . . Once we get to the bug-fixing time, it's really important to get that turnaround to the testers."

The amount of time required to synchronize, merge, and check-in source code files is roughly proportional to the number of files changed and the degree of the changes. On Excel and Word, the time needed for the daily build is relatively small, usually less than one hour. De Vaan gave a breakdown: "In terms of how long does it take to do the overhead, synching can take five to twenty minutes, depending upon how many files you have checked out. Compiling happens overnight, so I count that as a cost of zero. Downloading and running the quick test probably takes about a half hour to do all the stuff. And then checking in can take five minutes to an hour, depending upon how many things you have checked out. An hour is very long."

Microsoft does not use the exact same daily build approach with Office. This is because the number of files that a developer has to synchronize, merge, and check in has more than doubled, and this would more than double the required time. Faster PCs and development tools are making the size of the product less of an issue for the daily builds. Nonetheless, for a large project like Office, one way to minimize overhead is to check in less frequently. Since this can defeat the advantages of frequently checking in, Microsoft has structured the Office source code files so that a developer has to change only a few files to implement his features. A developer then does not need to do a complete rebuild of the product; he can just rebuild portions of Office that relate to his changes.

Beyond reducing the number of files that a developer needs to change for feature additions, the Office group has also established a two-stage process that further reduces the time required to synchronize, merge, and check-in source code files. Stage one of this process allows a developer to check changes to source code files into a testbed version of the system, called Limestone. A build of the Limestone testbed system does not require a rebuild of the whole Office product; therefore, it does not need the quick tests of all the individual applications, nor a full "regression test" of the whole product. (A regression test determines if previously working features or functions continue to work.) The Office group still builds the Limestone testbed release daily, and it has its own automated regression test.

In the second stage, the build masters periodically move the changes from the Limestone testbed version of the files into the master version of the Office source code files. They move changes from Limestone to the Office version when developers have completed particular features. This usually occurs at least weekly and certainly before the milestone release. For the milestone release, they move all the source code changes from Limestone to Office. This process requires the full overhead of building all the component applications (Word, Excel, PowerPoint, Access, and Mail) and executing all the quick tests and application-specific and Office-specific automated tests.

Posting Before Check-In: Some check-ins for Windows NT 3.0 were huge and included as many as eight hundred changed files at a time. These tend to be simple component name changes or additional data exchanges among components. Many smaller check-ins, which were much more common, involved complicated changes to the product. As a result, the NT group added an additional step to the daily build process. Prior to checking in source code files (step 10 in Table 5.1), a developer walks to the project white board and writes on the board what files he wants to check in. He posts this intent in advance so that other people know what to expect, because his changes might cause incompatibilities or affect other parts of the source code. After a short time, the developer receives a phone call from the build master that says to check in his code. The developer does the check-in, then sends electronic mail to the Windows NT build master with a specific description of which parts of the product depend on the newly checked-in code and need rebuilding. This additional step before check-in gives other developers extra time to prepare for changes, allows centralized coordination of the build process, and minimizes chances of breaking the build.

The build master for a large systems product, such as Windows NT, has a small team to help him. NT 3.0 had four people on the build team; Dave Cutler, who directed the project, often joined as well. Windows NT also handled multiple build requests by staggering them and executing them in parallel and overnight. Lou Perazzoli explained:

> This is the daily build process. You get a phone call saying, "Okay, we are ready to take your check-in." You check it in, and then you send [electronic] mail to an alias called NT-build that describes exactly the operations to do to get that into the source [code] pool. So, you go synch this file, build these things, go here and synch this file, build this. Now go to this directory and link this, and you will get a new kernel, a new [Windows executable file or] whatever. You are going to get a new editor. And, of course, you can only do so many things a day. You have one machine that can compile eight, ten, twelve hours a day. . . . So a lot of times what we will do is at eight o'clock at night we'll say, "Go check in all your stuff." There are people that have checked it in during the day, but we won't build until night. We'll go home with five windows running clean builds of various components, like a clean building of the whole kernel. Let's say we changed the size of a process object; to rebuild a kernel takes about an hour and half. . . . We don't like to do that during the day, but at two o'clock in the morning it works just fine.

Frequency of Build Cycles: Microsoft uses a range of build-cycle frequencies depending on the particular needs of a project and the amount of time required to complete a build successfully. Systems products generally take longer to build because of their size and the number of files and interdependencies included. Microsoft builds Excel, Word, and a testbed version of Office daily; it builds the full version of Office at least weekly. Windows 3.1, Windows NT, and MS-DOS had monthly and weekly builds early in their development cycles, and daily builds for the several months prior to a release. Windows NT started full-time daily builds in July 1992, approximately twelve months before the product shipped. Microsoft built Windows 95 weekly during its extended testing phase.

Some other firms also do frequent builds. On the VMS operating systems project at Digital Equipment Corporation, for example, the development team did weekly and biweekly builds, according to Lou Perazzoli, who was part of that team. Some major software development projects at IBM and AT&T now build biweekly or monthly. Large operating system or custom software projects may have no periodic builds for most of the project and then adopt biweekly or monthly builds later on during integration and system testing. Among PC software companies, Lotus tends to do monthly builds,[2] while at least one team in Borland (Turbo Pascal) has done daily builds. Brad Silverberg, who used to manage this group at Borland, thought that his former company most resembled Microsoft in development methods:

> At Borland the products and the teams were a lot smaller, so things went amazingly quickly. . . . We built things on a regular basis. Turbo Pascal was probably daily, although it was only half a dozen programmers so it was easy to stay in synch. When they did a build, that was it. The beta test cycle on that product . . . only needed six weeks because the [lead] developer was just so good. . . . Borland does a super good job, too. They're smaller [than Microsoft], a little more flexible, and not as well organized. At the top level, they are probably the most similar to Microsoft than any others, but I don't know anybody who does it better [than] Microsoft. . . . I don't look at any other development organization and say, "Boy, I wish we did things their way."

The next principle describes how the daily build process helps Microsoft constantly prepare to ship a product.

PRINCIPLE   *Always have a product you can theoretically ship, with versions for every major platform and market.*

A major benefit resulting from the daily builds is that a project constantly has a stable yet evolving product with a flexible set of features. The incremental feature development, frequent synchronization, and continuous testing help force the project to try to establish and maintain a version of the product that is always at or near the level of quality needed for shipment to customers. Of course, the reliability of a new daily build that contains extensive feature additions is uncertain; theoretically, though, Microsoft could ship each of the three or four major milestone releases (as well as a majority of the weekly builds) to customers. The ship-readiness nature of the evolving product builds allows Microsoft to add or delete features relatively late in the product development cycle. This makes it possible to ship on time, or to change features to respond to customer feedback or competitive pressures. Projects also have great flexibility in deciding when to release their products to customers. Throughout development, the projects build simultaneous versions of their products for different platforms (such as Windows 95, Windows NT, and Macintosh), as well as for different markets (such as the United States, Europe, and Asia). These simultaneously evolving versions enable Microsoft to introduce products for the different PC platforms and markets within a very short time of one another.

Knowing Where You Are: The incremental milestone approach and the daily build process allow Microsoft teams to follow closely their progress in developing products. They also make the overall product development process more visible and predictable. As a result, a project team always knows where it stands relative to completing the features or functions it wants to build. After completing the development phase for a product, Microsoft projects also insert a relatively short stabilization period prior to the actual product release to customers. This contrasts with conventional software development approaches, which routinely spend 50 percent of their schedule in final testing phases after completing development. Mike Maples summarized how the milestone process helps Microsoft people evaluate if they are ready to release a product:

> The older concept of "Write the spec, write the code, test the code, maintain the code" as a life cycle idea is very misleading as to how near completion you are. You see lots of projects that stay 80 to 100 percent complete for 80 percent of the time. So we've developed this idea of a . . . milestone process, where you try to pick out some of the more difficult things to do, you finish them 100 percent, and then you reevaluate where you are. . . . You do all the . . . things that, if that set of features was the product, you'd be ready to ship it. . . . If you do it right, the time from when you finish the product to when you can get someone the whole product is very short. . . . It does make the process much more predictable. You know much earlier in the process when you're in really bad shape. . . . You know where you are.

The ability to quickly release a product that has greater or fewer features relative to what a team originally specified is a significant competitive advantage for Microsoft. Other companies such as Lotus and Borland, however, have adopted this same principle. At least Borland has used this approach to compete against Microsoft by coming to market earlier than planned with a new product. (We know of no cases where Microsoft has shipped a product sooner than planned because of the daily build process, although projects often cut features to ship on time or reduce their lateness.) According to Brad Silverberg, Borland was developing Turbo Pascal in multiple stages and had to ship it at least five months early in order to counter a competitive Microsoft product, Quick Pascal. Borland had kept Turbo Pascal at a high level of ship-readiness throughout its development, and this enabled it to move quickly and successfully against Quick Pascal. Silverberg recalled the competition between these two products from Borland's perspective:

> It also gives you the chance in competitive markets to be a lot lighter on your feet if you always have something that's working. If your competitor comes out with something that you're not expecting it to do, you are

then in a position to [take] your intermediate product and ship it. In fact, a very good example happened to me while I was at Borland. We were building Turbo Pascal, which was really the foundation language product Borland had. We had the franchise, and there was a lot of company esteem tied up in Turbo Pascal. We heard rumors Microsoft was coming out with a product called Quick Pascal. . . . And so we put together this war team and we said, "Okay, if I were Bill, what would I do to compete with Borland's building a turbo language product?" So I drew up a spec of what I thought Quick Pascal was, and then used that spec to drive what I thought the next version of Turbo Pascal should be.

It was a good thing that I was developing Turbo Pascal in stages, because we had been planning for the next version to come out in nine months. But we heard Quick Pascal was due out in just four months. We needed to get something out at the same time that countered it, and we were in a position to do it. I had guessed right; I basically had the spec 98 percent right on what that product was. I was in a position to . . . counter what they thought was going to be a surprise product announcement that would take the Pascal leadership away from Borland. We, in fact, came out with a superior product—and, well, how many people have heard of Quick Pascal? Not many. We won, because we were able to always stay in a state of readiness.

"Grow" Rather Than Design Software: Rather than trying to create a complete specification and detailed design for a product before starting to build it, Microsoft now implements features through a continual process of prototyping, testing with internal and external users, and debugging. Projects also frequently replace old pieces of products with new components when developing a new product version. Developers often refer to this practice of prototyping individual product functions and evolving them systematically into full capability features as "growing" software. (Fred Brooks, formerly of IBM, also used this term in a well-known 1987 article on software development.[3]) Lou Perazzoli described how projects prototype and evolve features: "I have this theory that you grow software, and if you look at the app groups, that's what they are doing. That is also what we [the systems groups] are doing. You get something that starts working, and then slowly but surely you evolve it, and you find out where it is weak and where it is strong. It evolves because people see it and say, 'Boy, this would be great if it only did this.' Then you grow that part, or people say, 'This stinks.'"

Microsoft groups extensively apply this iterative prototyping approach. For example, Perazzoli described how they rewrote major subsystems in the Windows NT 3.0 project, such as the file system, several times before finally releasing the product:

> This is something that I really believe in. You want to get stuff prototyped as quickly as possible, so you can find what is stupid and wrong and fix it before you get so involved that you can't. To give you an example, our file-system guys have had the luxury of doing four file systems, and they have had even the greater luxury of redoing two of them. So two of our file systems have been rewritten because, as we wrote more file systems, we learned things that we were doing not so well. Then we integrated those concepts into the earlier file system. Our serial driver was written twice. For a whole lot of stuff, we just go back and say, "The heck with it. We are going to rewrite this." And you don't rewrite it overnight. You . . . incrementally rewrite it, and when you are all done it is brand new.

Short Half-Life of Code: Various developers pointed out that teams continually rewrite software and tend not to overrefine particular pieces of code. Dave Moore estimated that the "half-life" of a piece of software in Microsoft is as little as eighteen months, meaning that teams change or replace 50 percent of the code in their products every eighteen months or so. Since Microsoft releases a new version of a particular product approximately every twelve to twenty-four months, this half-life concept suggests that 50 percent of a product's code changes between each release. In fact, Chris Peters acknowledged that Microsoft has not placed too much emphasis on writing reusable code because it becomes obsolete so quickly: "You can spend so much time making something sharable, only to have it be obsolete two years later. In a world where things change so fast and so furiously, you tell me what part ought to be shared."

The pace of change, or "churning" of code, becomes extremely quick in some groups. In Excel, for example, Ed Fries asserted that developers change at least part of every source code file at least once a week. He cautioned that the frequent code changes make it difficult to keep detailed design documentation that is separate from the source code: "The program [Excel]—it's huge, but it changes at a very fast rate. In a week, pretty much every C file will be touched. If you wait a week to synch, almost every single file in the whole project will be different when you have this many people running around making different changes. Sometimes they're making big global changes that affect lots of files. And that's the problem with documentation. Taking something out of the process, it quickly becomes stale. So I'd really worry if I were taking something out and saying this is an example of how to do something."

Features Need to Be Twice as Good to Justify Being Different: Over the years, Microsoft projects have learned to restrain themselves from introducing relatively small changes in products that bring only a little improvement for the user but require lots of effort or lead to inconsistencies. The objective with Windows applications, for example, is to make products work with Windows. The object is not necessarily to change Windows itself—unless, of course, the change makes a major improvement.

Microsoft learned this lesson when working on OS/2. As Chris Peters recalled: "OS/2 was an attempt where they tried to change things. . . . They tried to make things 10 percent better but completely different, and nobody wanted 10 percent better. We have a rule of thumb that things have to be twice as good before they can be different, if you're trying for consistency." Peters recounted the example of the "undo icon," a feature that existed first in Word. The Excel group developed an undo icon that works differently and tests 10 percent better in the usability lab. This is not good enough to warrant a different undo icon in Excel as opposed to Word, because of the large number of people who use both programs; nor is it enough of an improvement for Word to adopt the Excel format. As Peters commented: "Obviously, if it's a lot, lot better, then maybe we ought to think about it. If it's only a little bit better, then the lack of consistency becomes an issue as well."

Twenty Percent Tax for Rewriting Code: Another aspect of keeping products ready to ship is to invest in rewriting code in between projects. (This resembles "maintenance" or product "reengineering" work in some other software companies, although Microsoft has no separate groups for this work.) As an informal guideline, development managers try to allocate about 20 percent of their developers' time to reworking weak parts of the product. If they do this consistently over multiple versions, the product will consistently improve; if they do not, the overall quality may deteriorate as developers add different features and as users demand more functionality from the product. Chris Peters said that "we have this thing called the 20 percent tax, which is related to rewriting or re-architecting certain parts of the product. If you don't pay the 20 percent tax, then you end up in a bad situation. So you try to pick the part that's the worst." Often, projects use this time to rework parts of the program that are important but not highly visible to the user. Examples are storing names in Excel, moving from 256 fonts to 4,000 fonts in Word, rewriting how a program prints, or making more fundamental changes in the way features operate or interact.

Microsoft people consider this work a "tax" in the sense that projects reserve about one day a week of the developers' time to make improvements in the fundamental structures of a product, rather than to add new features. Developers often spend this time during the period immediately after they release a product (called "Milestone 0" in Chapter 4) and before the official beginning of the development phase for the next product version.

Build Multiple Product Versions Simultaneously: It is also critical for Microsoft's competitive strategy to have versions of each product simultaneously ready for different hardware platforms, as well as for different markets around the world. Projects leverage resources by trying to maximize the common code shared across product versions for debugging, final release, different hardware and operating system platforms, and different end-user languages. Such sharing allows projects to develop and test all these versions at the same time. The Excel group, for example, built twenty different versions of the Excel 4.0 product to accommodate five different language areas—United States, German, French, Spanish, and Far East (Japanese, Chinese, and Korean)—Windows and Macintosh operating platforms, and both a production (or ship) version and a "debug" version (which contains extra code for testing and error detection) for each language/platform combination. (Microsoft releases only ten of these versions to customers, since projects use debug versions internally.)

Excel provides a good example of how projects prepare to ship these multiple versions. During a project, developers separate the language-specific portions of the product (such as text for error messages and dialog boxes) into a separate file. This separation allows them to translate these portions into a foreign language by simply translating the contents of a single file; Microsoft groups call this translation process "localization." Developers can then focus on the language-independent portions of the code that all language versions will share. Marc Olson commented on the separation of the language-independent code and the language-dependent portions in the product: "The U.S. version is the one we spend most of our time on. All of our language-specific parts of the product, like all of the UI [user interface] that gets localized or translated, gets put into a separate DLL [dynamic link library file] that we call a language DLL. So we will just build a single Excel .exe [executable file], and then have a DLL for each language. The code is the same in the French version as in the U.S. version, but the UI specifics are taken into a DLL."

The translation of the language-dependent localization files happens relatively late in the development phase, when the user interface is stable. Projects want the features to stabilize first so they do not have to retranslate user interface text as the features change. The actual translation of the localization files occurs just before a project releases the U.S. version or shortly thereafter. The separation of the language-dependent localization files from the language-independent code allows testers to spend their time efficiently by focusing primarily on testing the localized portions of an international product. Olson explained how this process works:

> That allows us to separate the localization of the product, the testing of the translation and the localization in terms of dialogues, menus containing strings, and sort order. We do that testing last. And the testing we do along the way is to make sure things like country settings don't matter, so the code accounts for country settings as part of the core code.

There is nothing special we do in the French version; it's all part of the same code base. So, for each feature, people have to understand the implications of changing the code page or changing the country settings on their feature. For some features, it doesn't matter at all. For a feature like format number, where you're looking at currency formats or date separators or list separators, you have to make sure you're getting the information from the right place. Nothing is hard-coded.

The Office project creates a similar number of versions of its product suite. Office builds a Win32 (32-bit) version and one or two Macintosh versions (for the PowerMac and the older Macintosh products based on the Motorola 68000 processor chip family); they also build a production and debug version for each platform, and they have different localization files for each language. The Far East version for Office will eventually require a separate build—and not just a localization file—because Microsoft is adopting the UNICODE standard. UNICODE uses two bytes for each character (as opposed to the existing approach of one byte per character, supplemented with special extensions) in order to provide broad support for Kanji characters.

Releasing Products for Multiple Platforms and Markets: The real benefit of building multiple versions of a product simultaneously is that Microsoft can ship versions for different platforms and markets within a short time of one another. The company goal is to have a simultaneous shipment (called a "sim ship") for every major product on each major platform and for each language market; this means releasing the versions within about 30 days of each other. Releasing different versions within a narrow period of time is essential to marketing products successfully. Foreign customers tend to stop buying old versions of a product if they hear that a new version is available in the United States, just as Macintosh customers tend to stop buying old versions of Excel and Word if they hear that a new Windows version is available.

Although shipping versions within thirty days of one another is the goal, Microsoft will release some minor language versions over a longer period. For example, Excel 4.0 shipped in the U.S. Windows version first. The French and German Windows versions came thirty days later, but the Spanish Windows version came sixty days after the U.S. version. Excel 4.0 shipped in the U.S. Macintosh version about twenty days after the U.S. Windows version, and the international Macintosh versions came out with the same thirty- and sixty-day delays that the Windows versions had. For Windows 95, the goal is to ship the Kanji version within three months of the U.S. version. (The Windows 95 code also provides the basis for a Middle East version and a Far East version.) These staggered releases mostly reflect logistical delays and testing, according to Marc Olson: "Everything is spread out, partly because of the need of some last-minute logistical details. There's things that you don't think about. The Software is pretty much ready to go. It's getting the documentation done; it's getting the "read me" files that go on the disk done; it's getting the set up program finalized; it's getting all the example files and . . . any add-ins we ship finally done. It's just maintaining that list of files to make sure they're the right ones, and that they have all had a chance to be looked at."

The sales volume is not yet too large in some international markets, but Microsoft invests in foreign language versions when managers believe these markets will eventually be substantial. For example, the Hebrew version of Word sells relatively few copies. Yet Microsoft people want to have a presence in many Middle East countries, and they view China as a huge eventual market as well. Chris Williams, Microsoft's director of product development, described this investment strategy:

> [The] Middle East [group] is there [outside of the product business units] because we wanted to isolate our investment in that area. If we were to put the development of Hebrew Word in the Word group, and all of its 1,200 copies or whatever that it will sell, the Word people would completely ignore it . . . or they would put more effort into it than was appropriate. The point is that you couldn't judge . . . how much effort was being put into it. So we have allocated those people to that market space, with the charge of providing the products necessary for us to have a presence in that market space on an investment basis.
>
> Right now, they have horrendously bad intellectual property laws, so that people steal the software 90 percent of the time. But we know that 20 percent of the world speaks Arabic, and sooner or later, we'll make

some money in that market space. So right now we have a strategy that says we will spend just about as much as we make. We have a very concrete investment, and it just about exactly pays for our income in that neighborhood. . . . The people in Japan, the Far East, are managing the China effort, which is the other significant one that we are investing in on a cost basis. We're just flooding that market with copies. . . . The goal is . . . that when people actually end up having to buy software, they [will] already know our software and it's the one they will buy when the laws get passed. We're basically getting market share. As soon as we start to get a return on that investment, it will be humongous.

PRINCIPLE   *Speak a common language on a single development site.*

To help people communicate across and within groups, Microsoft groups do their development work at the company headquarters outside Seattle. They also speak a common "language"—that is, they adopt a small set of development languages, conventions, and tools. This common base of understanding how to create products helps Microsoft personnel communicate and solve problems relatively quickly and effectively.

Single-Site Development: Microsoft has continued to honor the tradition of doing all major development efforts at the Microsoft headquarters. There are only a few exceptions to this rule. There are some overseas adaptation projects (like the Japanese version of Windows, which Microsoft later moved to the United States), and certain applications products and tool development work (like PowerPoint and Softimage) are off-site because they originated as Microsoft acquisitions. As noted in Chapter 1, however, Bill Gates in particular wants groups to be able to solve problems and technical interdependencies face-to-face. Despite the benefits of electronic mail and its extensive usage at Microsoft, single-site development allows project personnel to get together physically on a regular basis and explore ideas interactively. Frequent and easy communication can prevent major problems from getting worse. Dave Maritz emphasized the benefits:

Location—single-site development—is so, so important. One of the reasons that Win[dows] 3.1 still hasn't got off in Japan is that it was [developed] across in Japan. And there was just the Japanese mentality of trying to hide what was going on from us, because that's how they want to work and their managers do not let two people speak together. That's why it's now been brought across to here. In Chicago [Windows 95] . . . [we've] just been able to get up and walk down the corridor and find out what's going on. [It's] what I call the "whites of your eyes": If you can't see the whites of a person's eyes once a day, then you have got a problem. And that was one of the problems with OS/2 [the Microsoft-IBM joint project done in the 1980s], this multi-site development.

Microsoft managers have also been willing to invest in the infrastructure to support people at the Microsoft headquarters. Nearly everyone—except for summer interns and an occasional new hire—gets an individual office. Many offices have windows, because of the layout of the buildings in an "X" configuration. Product units also generously provide project personnel with whatever computers and tools they need, including several different desktop machines (usually one Windows PC, one Macintosh, and a third of either type) fully loaded with software and networking capabilities.

The C Programming Language: Microsoft projects implement (code) their products using the C programming language, as well as a limited amount of C++ and assembler. Many companies use the C language in commercial software products because it is very portable across different hardware platforms, runs efficiently, and provides great implementation flexibility. The C language itself is independent of any hardware platform—unlike assembler—but the underlying system functions that a C program uses (called "libraries"), especially the user interface libraries, are platform-specific. Writing programs in C thus helps but does not ensure portability; Microsoft has achieved success in porting its code to many platforms (Windows, DOS, and Macintosh) because it also uses internally developed tools to evaluate code portability, and it develops "core code" for certain products that it can recompile on different platforms without making major changes. Excel 4.0, for example, contained about 69 percent core code shared across the Windows and Macintosh platforms.[4] (Core code has many benefits for the producer. As we noted in Chapter 3, though, the first attempt to use Windows–Macintosh core code in Word 6.0 caused some performance as well as "look and feel" problems on the Macintosh.[5])

In spite of the portability, efficiency, and flexibility advantages of the C language, some people in the software development community feel C is too primitive and encourages developers to use unnecessary implementation tricks. Bill Gates acknowledged the disadvantages of C, but maintained that Microsoft developers work to generalize (or abstract) their code: "Like everybody else, we haven't figured out how you write code in anything other than C. Now C is a very low-level language, and we're using C++ for a lot of things. We're abstracting a lot of things." The C++ language encourages developers to write highly structured code that abstracts general concepts and hides details. Microsoft has adopted C++ where appropriate on selected projects (for example, some new components of Office and Windows NT), but C is still dominant.

Gates also emphasized that Microsoft was using object abstraction and reuse concepts (called "object-oriented programming") long before a language like C++ directly supported them. This attests to the general skills of Microsoft developers. He also argued, however, that Microsoft does not promote these implementation or methodology details as an advantage of its products:

> Many people will say, "Oh, object-oriented programming is going to cause a factor of ten [improvement]." . . . Yes, it's a benefit, because the tools are going to encourage it more and it's going to allow for more sharing, and all that. But the pieces of code we wrote ten years ago used those same abstractions. We passed procedural pointers around so you can have different data structures and use common subroutines; it's only a matter of degree. And, frankly, there's a lot of potential abuse that comes with that in terms of understanding efficiency, and really knowing that you have factored things in a way that it's appropriate to share those things in the future. A lot of people are going to fall into the trap of that promised land.
>
> That's why you haven't seen us out, even though we write massive amounts of C++ code, acting like, "Oh, customers should buy our detergent, because it has objects in it." If it runs faster, if it has more features, yes, you should buy it. It doesn't matter if we used squirrels to create the

thing. So we don't brag about what methodology we did or didn't use in terms of end users of the product.

The "Hungarian" Naming Convention: Many Microsoft applications projects, as well as a few systems projects, use a Microsoft code-naming convention called "Hungarian" after its originator, Charles Simonyi, who was born in Hungary.[6] (Microsoft Hungarian is unrelated to the Hungarian language spoken in Europe.) A naming convention is an explicit name usage pattern or style that a developer can use for procedures and variables in source code; it should increase the readability and understandability of such code for developers who are trying to modify or reuse the code. (A common problem in software development is that source code is often not comprehensible by anyone other than the person who originally wrote it. Yet many people have to be able to read, understand, and modify product source code reliably so that developers can work in parallel as well as reuse, change, or fix other people's code.)

Use of Hungarian at Microsoft started when Simonyi arrived from Xerox PARC to work on Multiplan in 1981 (see Chapter 3). He and others, such as former senior developer Doug Klunder, heavily promoted its use among the applications groups, where Simonyi and Klunder worked during the 1980s.[7] The Hungarian naming convention gives developers the ability to read other people's code relatively easily, with a minimum number of comments in the source code. Jon De Vaan estimated that only about 1 percent of all lines in the Excel product code consist of comments, but the code is still very understandable due to the use of Hungarian: "If you look at our source code, you also notice very few comments. Hungarian gives us the ability to just go in and read code. . . . Being fluent in Hungarian is almost like being some Greek scholar or something. You pick up something and you can read it. . . . I remember starting at Microsoft thinking, 'What's this? This is crazy, it doesn't make any difference.' But it really does."

In Hungarian, variable names have three parts: prefixes, a base type, and a qualifier.[8] For example, the variable name *pch* is a pointer to a character; the *p* is a prefix that means "pointer," and the *ch* is a base type that means "character." The name *pchFirst* is a pointer referring to the first element of an array of characters; *First* is a qualifier that means the first element in a set. While this may seem straightforward, names can get more complicated. The variable name *mpmipfn* is an array of pointers to functions indexed by *mi*'s, which could be menu items. A developer could use such an array for command dispatch. The *mp* is a base type that means "array," *mi* is the index type of the array, and *pfn* is the type of elements contained in the array, which are pointers (*p*) to functions (*fn*). In Hungary, people write the family name first and the given name second, just as Microsoft developers write the base type before the qualifier in their Hungarian.[9]

Most of the Office applications products continue to use Hungarian extensively. Only a small amount of old Excel code carried over from an early version of Multiplan does not use it. Practically all Word code uses Hungarian, except for some code that summer interns have written (although someone eventually goes over their code and rewrites it in Hungarian). Ed Fries noted that some people are very particular about the proper way to use the naming convention: "It's like any language. It sort of has dialects, and some people are very strict about their Hungarian use, and others are a little less so. But it's such a part of our culture that I don't even think about it."

Systems projects, however, do not use Hungarian very much. This may be because Hungarian, and Charles Simonyi, have not been part of the culture of the systems division. Lou Perazzoli preferred not to debate the merits of the language convention too extensively, but he described his doubts as well as the experience of another developer on his team:

> Hungarian merely got in his way, didn't help him read the code at all, didn't help make the code more maintainable. The code that he looked at had as many bugs as other code he had seen. . . . The applications people think it is great. We don't discourage people from using Hungarian, but nobody on my team [Windows NT] . . . is working on the system proper using Hungarian. This is because it is not as descriptive as it seems. We never have . . . somebody say, "Oh, gee, I didn't know that was an unsigned byte. I thought that was a signed byte." Those aren't the problems we have. The problems we have are synchronization problems. . . .

I think if I did an application, I wouldn't use Hungarian either. I think it is a religious issue, and you shouldn't debate religious issues. I personally grew up in a non-Hungarian world. We wrote huge systems. The system we worked on in NASA . . . was a couple million lines of code and it all worked. They did it by a top-down approach and very small . . . procedures, even though it was written in FORTRAN.

Common Tools That Support Projects: Microsoft people also communicate well because projects use a common set of tools to help manage and develop products. Many tools are commercially available as Microsoft products; the bulk of the remainder are specialized internal tools or augmentations of commercial products that would not be viable in the marketplace due to lack of volume. Some of the internally available tools have also provided a major competitive advantage to Microsoft over the years. For example, Microsoft has been able to develop languages and applications very quickly for different hardware platforms and operating systems, such as the MIPS Altair, CP/M, the Apple II, DOS, the Macintosh, and Windows (see Chapter 3). Bill Gates emphasized the virtues of creating and using your own tools:

> We have control over our tools because we use our own tools. . . . There's a lot to bragged about in this area. Why could we write software for the Macintosh and nobody else could? We wrote our own tools. . . . Why does the company exist in the first place? We wrote our own tools. There were no tools nearly as good. It was a massive competitive edge. . . . You just take simple things like the way we did memory-pointer handling in our . . . compiler for protect-mode architecture. The one challenge this software company has is, we write for real machines. When it was the 8088, we wrote for the 8088. When it was the 286 protect mode, we wrote for that machine. Then it was the Apple II. . . .
>
> We make our software work. In terms of size and speed, there's no software company of any size that's even close on that. And controlling our own tools has been extremely helpful. Even today, we have things that do certain types of analysis. We just choose not to release those as products, because they are a competitive advantage to us.

There is no official list of a common Microsoft tool set, and any list would change over time and vary somewhat by product group. Most projects, though, use similar tools that we can describe here. Program managers often use Excel to manage a product specification and either Excel or Microsoft Project to track schedule information; they will use Word if they need to write and print a project document. Program managers generally use Visual Basic for prototyping product features. (A version of this serves as a macro language in applications products, such as Excel, so that users can tailor the products to their needs.)

Developers often use Microsoft's commercial Visual C++ compiler for writing in C++, and Microsoft also has its own C compiler. Several projects have specialized internal code debuggers and analyzers to help understand and evaluate code. Editors vary by project and product; for example, Word uses a tool called the Brief Editor that includes many specialized macros to browse code and identify variable usage and function-calling relationships. Developers currently use SLM for source code management, synchronization, and merging; Microsoft sells a commercial version of this called Delta. (Microsoft also acquired the Source-Safe configuration management tool from One Tree Software when it bought this company in 1994. Some projects may switch to this instead of SLM or Delta.) In the past, many developers used OS/2 as their operating system platform when doing development work, primarily because of its multitasking capability. (This allows several processes to execute at the same time.) Now, however, most projects use Windows 95 or Windows NT. For example, Office builds on Windows NT, although it will later build on both Windows NT and Windows 95 to facilitate automatic testing.

Testers use the internal RAID tool to record and track the status of product errors or bugs. Products that have extensive user interface testing often use Microsoft Test to capture and replay keyboard events automatically. Several projects use an internal test case manager (TCM) tool, which combines Visual Basic as a "front end" with a Structured Query Language (SQL) database. The tool organizes test scripts and logs test-execution information.

Having a common set of tools and development methods helps people adapt quickly when they move from product to product within the company. Gates felt that this was especially important:

Well, we try not to let the way people use tools diverge too much from group to group, because we want people to be able to move between groups with great ease. We really encourage lots of moving around between groups, so people can do a fresh new thing and can understand what the other groups are up to. We don't have much divergence in terms of the tools that people use nowadays. They all are equally good in some cases and bad in other cases. Once upon a time there was a boundary—systems had certain tools, and apps had certain tools—but now that's basically resolved.

Of course, in spite of Microsoft's strengths in tool development and usage, there is room for improvement. Some developers tolerate poor tools simply because they have become familiar with them, and they prefer to spend their time building products. Gates admitted that Microsoft has not invested as fully in some types of development tools as it should have:

We've had cases where we didn't invest enough in tools, and sometimes there's actually an outside tool that would be better. . . . Many years ago, our debuggers weren't even that good. . . . And we have some tools now that have to do with dynamic feedback, where you watch the profiles, and you go back and you change the compilation and memory organization based on that. Why didn't we do those years ago? I happen to think our source code control system is pretty crummy, although people use it. A lot of them stick up for it. But it's terrible, really. So people just get used to this stuff, even us, with all of our appropriate philosophy about investing in tools and being willing to take a long-term approach by investing in tools and all. On balance, it's been a huge asset. [But] . . . we haven't executed on that fully the way that we should have. So that's a big negative.

Even Microsoft's relatively crude tools, though, have had their advantages. Jon De Vaan acknowledged that some of their tools, such as compilers and debuggers, look rather backward relative to what people studying computer science in universities are using. But he also argued that more sophisticated tools may not be as reliable. Furthermore, he has found that the Microsoft tools generate the best code for commercial purposes:

Our tools are pretty primitive compared to what I think people are used to from school. . . . For Excel 4.0, actually, it was the first time we had source-level debugging, believe it or not. And mostly I think that's a comment on the fact that the Microsoft tools have been kind of lagging. We use the Microsoft tools because they generate the best code of any of the other tools that we've evaluated. And to us, the punch line is the code that goes on the disk that we sell, and that's why we do that. Then you have a lot of people like myself; I prefer to use the assembly language debugger, because it's faster and it works more reliably.

Understand Products at Assembly-Code Level: Most Microsoft developers have another ability in common: Like Jon De Vaan, they can understand how their software works at a very low level. They may not always choose to take advantage of this ability, however, for all users. In particular, sharing code between Windows and Macintosh versions often means that Microsoft developers give priority to the Windows code and try not to write low-level code for the different platforms. In general, however, it is extremely useful for developers to understand code at the deepest possible level; then they can compensate for the limitations of Microsoft's compiler tools and make sure to ship code that executes as efficiently as possible given the objectives of the project. De Vaan emphasized that in the Office and Excel groups at least, the senior people insist that developers be able to read assembler. Managers will not simply let developers write code in a higher-level language, such as C or C++, and run it blindly through a compiler. (A compiler automatically translates the high-level code into assembly code and then an even lower-level machine code that the computer can understand directly.) On Excel 4.0, for example, the language composition was 75.7 percent C code, 10.8 percent assembler code, and 13.5 percent other code (such as include files and token files).[10] Microsoft also used to write approximately 80 percent of Word in C and port this across the PC and Macintosh platforms, with 20 percent of the code in assembler.

Increased use of assembler language can improve execution speed. For example, an evaluation using an automated macro test of new 32-bit versions of Excel and Word ran in seventy-four seconds on Windows NT 3.5; the older 16-bit product versions that contain more assembler code ran in seventy seconds.[11] In addition to enhancing the speed of a product, some developers also need to understand the early MS-DOS code, which Microsoft and IBM wrote in Intel assembler to minimize memory requirements and maximize processing speed.

This deep product understanding also involves learning the constructs where the compilers generate bad code, then writing code to avoid or replace those constructs. De Vaan estimated that his developers read the assembly code generated by the compiler for more than 50 percent of the source code. He also complained that Microsoft has to teach developers to understand systems at this low level. The courses in computer science at universities generally do not adequately emphasize how to assure efficient use of memory and execution time, which has been critically important for selling software products for personal computers. De Vaan elaborated on these points:

> We do encourage people to understand how the system works at the very lowest level. . . . Unfortunately, your tools don't work often enough, and things like Windows and the Mac system don't work often enough. So you have to get into that level to figure out why it doesn't work. That's one of the primary motivators. The other primary motivator . . . is we're very interested in making sure that the best code goes out in the product. When you're looking at the machine instructions, you know what the quality of the code is. You also get to learn—it's the only way to learn. You can write good code in C, but you have to know how your compiler generates its code to be able to do that. And if you're always stepping through the source-level debugger, you have no clue.
>
> That's an attitude that we have to teach people. What people learn in school is that stuff doesn't matter. But when you're making a product that people want to buy, that stuff really matters. . . . The idea is to learn the constructs that the compiler is bad at. We can ask the compiler guys to fix it, but to the extent that that's a long-turnaround thing, we know just to write code which doesn't have that problem.

PRINCIPLE   *Continuously test the product as you build it.*

Several principles guide testing in Microsoft, and each helps teams continuously test their products as they build them. This notion of continual testing done concurrently with development distinguishes Microsoft; too many software producers emphasize product testing primarily at the end of the development cycle, when fixing bugs can be extraordinary difficult and time-consuming. In addition, Microsoft groups now test their products from a wide variety of perspectives.

For example, projects create automated tests that developers can run every day on their code and *must* run before checking in their code changes to the master source code version. The test suites execute automatically by using a product's macro language or simulating keyboard strokes. Developers create "debug versions" of their products that contain special routines to help detect and locate bugs as well as check for special conditions, and they also conduct code reviews to detect errors through code reading. Usability tests ask people "off the street" to evaluate the ease of use of product features in dedicated laboratories. Projects also pair testers with developers (there is about one tester for every developer at Microsoft). The testers read specifications to start preparing test cases and testing strategies early; developers give private releases of their code to their "testing buddies" to test before they check in their code.

Testers then use multiple approaches. One consists of highly structured test scripts (called "scenario-based testing"). Another is "gorilla testing," where testers do not follow a script but try everything they can think of to "break" the product. In addition, Microsoft projects hold "bug bashes," which are parties where various people come by to try to find bugs. Project members also use the products they are building, distribute early versions internally, and send out thousands of beta copies to lead users—all in an effort to find bugs before releasing a product to the marketplace.

In order to test as quickly as possible and encourage testers to acquire expertise in functional areas, projects organize a typical product test group into parallel teams that each focus on particular feature areas. For example, the Excel 5.0 testing team consisted of 45 people responsible for testing Excel, MS Graph, and Query Tool; they also developed and tested the internal TCM test case management tool. The project organized the 45 people into six testing teams of 6 to 9 people each.

Of course, due to the complexity of software products and the constraints of time schedules and manpower budgets, testing is as much an art as it is a science. The inability to test a product completely is also, unfortunately, part of the business. Microsoft products have improved continually but they are certainly not perfect, especially in their first versions or when they contain totally new features. In the past, Microsoft has also introduced some products to market without adequate testing; this has become much less common with its new development approach and the gradual refinement of metrics to determine when a product is ready to ship. Microsoft will also now extend beta testing and delay the final release, especially with systems products, if features are not working fully or if bug levels are higher than desirable at the target ship date. (Windows 95, which has a large amount of new code and complex new features, such as plug-and-play and the multitasking of applications programs, is a recent example of this type of delay.)

Quick Tests: A key tool in making the daily build process work efficiently is a highly automated set of tests called a "quick test." After a developer has implemented a new feature, but before he has checked in the source code changes to the master version of the source code files, he builds a private release of the product (see step 7 in the daily build process described in Table 5.1). He then executes the quick test on his private release. This makes sure that basic functionality in the product still works correctly after he has added the new feature (see step 9).

A product's macro language provides an effective mechanism for automating these quick tests in addition to its use as a way for users to customize and extend the product functionality. The quick test does not test a new feature directly; it just makes sure that a developer's changes do not interfere with some other features of the product and cause errors indirectly. If the quick test is successful, the developer then checks in his code changes. The fact that Microsoft has automated the quick test is critical because many developers execute the test a large number of times, and it checks for many special cases that developers may forget. Nonetheless, developers cannot rely completely on the quick test and need to talk with other experts in their area, as Ed Fries described:

From a testing point of view, one way to do it is a lot of automation. . . . From a developer's point of view . . . it's very rare that you're doing something truly new. And hopefully, when you go to put something in, you look for something similar in the code and you imitate it. There you'll see all these special cases, like pieces of code saying "If the recorder's on," and I'm doing something special to the recorder, [and you think] "What about undo?" and here's some undo stuff. That's really the best way to catch cases that might not be obvious to you. Then the other thing is that we rely a lot on experts in the group. There are various experts in various areas. A lot of stuff has to happen just with people talking.

Testing "Buddies" and Private Releases: The principle of continuous and concurrent testing also means that testers must work literally side by side with developers as they are writing code. At the same time, to ensure some detachment from the code, Microsoft's philosophy is that testing must remain a separate function from development. As we described in Chapters 1 and 2, testers do not report to the development group or the program managers. They report to the test manager, who reports to the product unit manager. But projects achieve this side-by-side closeness by assigning developers and testers to work together in teams on particular features. In addition, testers not only test new code but also have the opportunity to review specifications as they evolve and write test cases in parallel with the evolution of the code. Chris Peters stressed the importance of this close interaction between developers and testers: "You need separate but equal organizations in development and testing, so that it keeps you from shipping bad stuff. Development and testing need to be deeply intermingled or else you have this terrible 'inspector 12' phenomenon, where developers throw things over the wall. What we do now is testers and developers, at least test and feature teams, are usually assigned to each other, so they tend to work with each other quite closely."

As we outlined earlier, many Microsoft developers generate a personal daily build of the evolving product each day, regardless of whether they plan to check in code changes that day (see steps 3 and 7 in Table 5.1). The resulting "private release" incorporates the latest version of a developer's changes before he has checked these into the master version of the source code. The developer shares his private release with his assigned "testing buddy." This lets testers gauge the progress of features and also prevent many errors from entering the master version of the source code. Marc Olson pointed out how this technique in itself creates a close working relationship between developers and testers. It also gives developers more time to spend on writing code and fixing problems:

> The goal of private release testing is to find defects before they get into real production code, or into code that is part of this main source code library, before it is shared with all of the other developers on the team. They have to work around the problems you have introduced by checking in your code. So there are some pretty strict rules about private release testing. . . . It is just developer and tester, and they develop a working relationship. . . . Depending upon the level of trust that gets developed there, they can be a really tight team. The developer can focus on writing code and fixing problems, and the tester can focus on getting this feature really quickly stabilized.

A developer will put a feature through private release testing at least once before checking in his code, and often will do this on a daily basis. Ed Fries believed that informal private release testing reduces the time between when a tester discovers a bug and a developer corrects it: "We like to try to make a private release to testing before we move off from one feature to the next. That means writing up a testing release document and making a special version of your feature available for testing. This is for a kind of pretesting that doesn't go into the bug database, to make sure that things are stable. It lets you go through a lot of the quick bugs. We get faster turnaround than when you go through a more formal bug-database process."

Debug Code: We mentioned in the discussion of multiple versions that in the development phase for a product, Microsoft developers create "debug versions" of their products. These result from inserting various forms of specialized tests, or "debug code," into the product's source code. When a developer does a build, he switches on the debug code as part of the debug release. He switches it off for the production release, so the version that ships to customers does not include the extra code. (Developers usually access the debug code via an invisible menu on the product user interface; for example, Word's invisible menu is next to the "Help" selection.)

Developers must write their own debug code as part of their regular work. Fries noted that they have to plan to develop debugging aids; otherwise, people do not do them: "Whenever we're scheduling out all the new features for the product, we try and think, 'Well, what are the infrastructure things that we should be doing as well? Let's make sure we save some time and schedule some time for that work, too, or it's just not going to get done.' . . . We try and schedule a few things every version that are . . . infrastructure-type things that will add to the whole program. We schedule those along with normal features." The debug code mainly provides automated built-in tests for monitoring the execution of the product and checking for exceptional conditions. These help developers tune and improve the memory usage and execution speed of the product. When using the debug code, developers can also use the source code or an assembly debugger tool to view internal data structures while a program is executing. Fries described an example of dual, redundant implementations of features in Word. The team has implemented one set of routines in the C language and another set of routines in the native computer's low-level assembly language (they do this for efficiency and portability trade-offs):

> Something that's really right that we do in our apps is, we build a lot of debugging code into them. This is true in both Word and Excel. When the apps are so big, that's part of a nice framework that you want to build for supporting it, for making it easier to track down problems. One example is Word has C and native versions. It has C versions for all of its assembly versions of routines. So if we have a routine that we've written in hand assembly, we also have the C version. And in our debug version, we include both; we can switch, just on the fly, between using the C versions and using the assembly versions. A common problem when you have C and assembly versions of the same thing is that they get out of synch. It helps to keep them in synch. In fact, you can turn on a verify mode where it runs both, one right after another, and makes sure that the result is the same.

There are actually many examples of debug code that Microsoft developers use to improve quality or efficiency in the products they are building. In total, these can amount to tens of thousands of lines of code even on a small product. Of particular importance are memory and data structure checks, assertions, and instrumentation (instrumented product versions). Debug code also plays a particularly important role in weekly releases of the product build to the testing groups.

Memory and data structure checks. "Memory checks" account for every byte of memory that a program uses or allocates. For example, if an automated audit of the memory fails, then a "MIF" (memory integrity failure) message appears. A similar technique, called "data structure checks," uses special routines that validate the consistency of nearly every data structure in the product. These make sure that the program has stored the data properly and can retrieve it. They are a type of default "idle-time" process, which does the checks automatically when the computer's processor has idle time.

Other similar types of debug code simulate resource allocation failures. For example, Excel can simulate failures for nearly all calls to operating system functions. It does this by adding a repetitive "loop" to the program and "bottlenecking" most Excel functions through a command dispatcher. The loop sets the threshold for resource allocation failure, then calls a particular function from the operating system. The function eventually fails at some point (due to the defined threshold) and returns a failure status. The loop then does memory allocation checks and data-structure consistency checks. If there are no problems, the debug code increases the failure threshold to the next highest level and continues testing. If the operating system function fails, then the debug code has detected a problem, and it shows an error message to the developer. Other debug code examples are movable memory checks, dynamic relocation (called "shaking") of the memory allocated in the "heap," and forced failures. (The heap is the region of memory that a program allocates and deallocates for data storage while it is executing.)

Assertions. Very common examples of debug code are "assertions." These are "if-then" tests in the code that must always be true, regardless of the input data from a user. For example, a banking application product may use an assertion that tests the balance of a checking account after a transaction. It might say, "if the balance is greater than or equal to 0 dollars, then OK else FAILURE." This assertion statement should always be true. Many Microsoft products tend to have a "global state" of information that they share throughout the program. Developers often use assertions to check their assumptions about the global state of the program or particular "arguments" passed into or out of a function. Many bugs occur when people write code without fully considering the program's global state or these arguments. As a result, many projects have an informal rule that developers must include assertions when they make assumptions about data stored elsewhere in the program. Jon De Vaan explained that assertions make it possible to track down bugs relatively quickly: "Assertions are pretty important because . . . one of the big sources of bugs is people writing code when they don't understand the global state, or they're assuming something about the global state. . . . We try to build the habit that if you assume something about global state, you have to assert it in the code you are writing. And the same thing with arguments. . . . If you're assuming something about the arguments to your function, you have to assert it. . . . With enough assertions, you get to see the bug right away."

Instrumentation. Developers also insert probes into the code that capture which commands users select, and which corresponding statements in the source code get executed. Microsoft calls a product release containing these probes an "instrumented version." With the users' consent and agreement to send back the results, these versions can become a valuable addition to internal testing, usability testing, and field beta testing. The data resulting from the instrumentation allows developers to recreate users' actions easily, understand their problems, and avoid being unable to reproduce errors. For example, developers were able to reproduce 96.6 percent of the reported errors in Works for Windows 2.0,[12] and 91.4 percent of the reported errors in Windows NT PDK 2.[13]

The amount of data that instrumented versions of products can generate is enormous. In fact, Bill Gates boasted that Microsoft has databases containing millions of commands that users have executed: "They [developers and testers] also take what's called the instrumented version. That's the version that records what commands people are using, what errors they get, what sequence that's done in. . . . We can do a lot of analysis of what's going on: Why do people get error messages? What commands do they really use commonly? What commands do they use in a sequence, so that we might be able to capture that at a task level? We have literally millions of commands that users have given in the instrumentation database."[14]

Instrumentation also indicates which parts of the source code users have exercised heavily or lightly; software developers call this "execution coverage." Testing that forces 100 percent execution coverage helps reveal bugs lurking in seldom-exercised parts of the source code. De Vaan observed that projects commonly do execution coverage testing late in development using automated tests (such as a small set of programs written in a macro language that combine many operations): "Some amount of the final debugging time will be spent with developers helping the testers get their auto test to cover a higher percentage of code."

Weekly testing releases. During the development phase, developers give the daily build for the product to the testing group once each week. This "weekly testing release" tends to use the debug version because the facilities in this version, like assertions, show problems sooner. As the project approaches the ship date, the developers will do weekly releases of the production version (which does not contain the extra thousands of lines of debug code) more often than the debug version. Testers may also write their own routines to test code and then add them to the program, according to Fries: "We have some pretty sophisticated testers. There's a group who are basically programmers. They usually know what they want and come and say, 'Do we have permission to go in and insert a few [built-in tests] in your code here and there that we're going use to test it better?' And of course we say, 'Sure.'"

Code Reviews: Before implementing features, Microsoft groups do a limited amount of formal, intensive design reviews. These try to detect cases of missing code or consistency problems earlier than the later testing activities that require a running product. Generally, however, Microsoft groups do not do deep, comprehensive design or code reviews for their products, because they specify only an outline of the product functionality before they start writing code. (See the discussion of the outline specification approach in Chapter 4.) Moreover because specifications and code also change a great deal during a project, it is sometimes difficult to determine when to hold reviews.

With the pressure of their short development cycles, Microsoft people have not had the time to study if it is better to spend more time up front doing more reviews and design work, or to devise better ways of checking for these problems later. Jon De Vaan, for example, tries to think of all possibilities and contingencies that might cause problems when he is implementing a feature, but he does not necessarily do this when he is designing the feature. "We've kind of given up on thinking that we can think of all the cases ahead of time. That's why we leave a fair amount of flexibility for when you're actually [implementing] the [feature]. . . . We could probably reduce the number of cases by having more formalized design reviews, [but] no way would we eliminate it. And so then the question is, how do you find them faster? Do you find them faster by testing? Or do you find them faster by thinking ahead of time?"

Senior developers do tend to review the code of new people or people working on a new area of a product to check their quality and to help them learn. Usually, the best expert available—sometimes the team leader, and sometimes the person's mentor—will review a new person's code before that person checks it in. The code reviews provide an effective peer-to-peer mechanism for learning implementation tips, as De Vaan related: "New people, we review their code. When someone's working on a new assignment and maybe someone else was the expert in that area, then before they check in code, they'll have the best expert review their code. He'll tell them, 'This was done right,' or 'This is a better way to do this thing.' The idea is that everyone is going to learn by doing, and so people do. Mentors will answer questions and stuff to help them get along. But then when they think they're done with the code, they'll get a code review to get tips."

Testing Releases and Test Release Document: We noted that projects periodically make a testing release of their evolving product available to the product's test group. Testers record errors detected in the testing releases in a bug database managed by the RAID tool, and managers use these bug data for progress tracking. A group will usually build a testing release each week throughout a project, and attach a test release document, called a TRD, to the release. Excel 5.0, for example, built its weekly testing release on a Monday night and made it available on Tuesday.

The test release document describes each feature at the time of its initial completion and hand-over to testing. Developers generate this document for their testers, and developers generally write their portions of it prior to testing their private releases. The size of the document varies with the size of the features; it explains to the testers how the features work so that they can test them effectively. The testers also use the specification document as another source of testing information. Ed Fries explained the role of the test release document: "There are some documents that we do require the programmers to generate, and those tend to deal with how they interact with other groups. When they create a new feature and they're ready to move on to the next one, they have to submit this to testing and work with testing. They need to come up with a test release document that explains to them how this feature works, what kinds of things they should look at, and what kinds of things they should be testing."

Usability Testing: A very different kind of testing that Microsoft projects do mainly during the development phase is usability testing of new features in a formal laboratory environment (also see our discussion of this in Chapter 6). This testing is especially appropriate for user interfaces and features in applications products; both should emphasize ease of use. Microsoft has a dedicated, centralized staff of thirty to thirty-five specialists to evaluate almost all applications products and some of the systems products by various usability criteria. Since this testing goes on continuously, it represents an enormous investment of time but generates invaluable customer feedback *during* a project. Bill Gates commented on the extensive usability testing process for Office: "We take the proto-

type that we build based on all this work and we put it into our usability labs, where we watch people actually sit in front of the application. Once again, that's feedback—we use that to refine again
and again. For [Office 4.0] . . . there were over eight thousand
hours of usability testing done before we decided we had it right
and we wanted to put it out to the marketplace."[15]

Other companies have usability labs that they use to test new
product ideas, or improve existing products. Microsoft takes this
idea to an extreme, however, and has made evaluating features for
usability a regular part of the development process. When developers think they are done or almost done with a feature, program
managers schedule the feature to appear in the usability lab. Sometimes developers do a special version or a mock-up of the feature if
they have not finished but want to test a prototype in the lab anyway. Generally, every feature in an application product that affects
the user goes through the usability lab. Each feature team lead
manages the team's schedule, and there is also a master schedule
for the whole project; program managers use this information on
feature availability to schedule features into the usability lab.

During a typical usability test, the lab staff recruits groups of ten
people from "off the street" to represent different types of users.
They sit in special, individual rooms. The lab staff asks them to do
a specific task using a product (for example, to create a new document or organize financial data into quarterly summaries), and the
usability specialists watch and videotape the user actions from behind one-way mirrors. Many times the people do not receive much
guidance, so if the product is not easy to understand they will be
unable to complete the task. The usability testers document problems that the users have and the percentage of users that complete
each task successfully without referring to a manual. The testers
do about two lab tests a week for a particular product, and they
evaluate about three features in each half-day session. Developers
see the reports on problems people had in the lab and discuss reactions to them with program managers and the usability testers.

The usability lab does not generally support overall product
planning, such as helping projects make major decisions on activities; that is the purpose of the activity-based planning technique
discussed in Chapter 4. Rather, Microsoft uses the labs more to

provide almost instant feedback to help developers decide how to make new or existing features simple to understand. Developers, for example, often have to trade off more than one appearance or behavior for a feature. They also have to resolve detailed user interface design issues, or choose between a small set of features that do similar functions to see which feature is easiest to use. Most developers visit the lab to witness their features in action. This lets them learn about problems firsthand, as Ed Fries explained: "The programmers tend to go out [to the usability labs] when their individual features are usability tested. They watch people use it, see what kinds of problems they're having, and come up with ideas on their own for making things better. So usability testing probably has a bigger influence [than other testing] from day to day on what we're producing."

The labs however, have some limitations: They tend to model the new user much better than the experienced user, and they work best on well-defined questions. Nonetheless, there are important advantages to usability testing. It allows Microsoft to continue to add new powerful features and avoid less useful ones (sometimes critically called "feature creep"), as well as continue to make added features easy to use. The usability lab also has several advantages over beta testing, which provides information very late and often lacks detail. As Chris Peters elaborated:

> In that laboratory setting, you actually have the data that you need to change the features, and you could do it while you were developing a feature, while beta test couldn't. We never had the data [before introducing the usability lab], first of all. You'd get some guy complaining that something didn't work very well; it was hard, but you wouldn't know why. . . . We'd often see where we would think we understood a problem. We would put in a feature and no one would use it. Everyone would be twice as mad at us because it would do 80 percent of the task, but it would do zero percent of the whole task. It's because we filtered too much from what the customer said he wanted to do. . . . There's often a very big gap between what people say they do and what they actually do—that was the other thing we noticed.

While developers do usability testing throughout the development process, more time remains for program managers and developers to redefine how particular features look and work if they do the testing early in development. But many Microsoft products have extensive graphical user interfaces, and testing these products often results in changes late in the life cycle once developers better understand how users interact with the product. Mike Maples observed: "We don't start off in a project and say, write the specs and build it to the specs. We know that things are going to change. Whenever you have a very interactive user-interface-driven product, things at the end sometimes just don't seem to work as [well] as you thought they would. . . . You're better off fixing it than not fixing it."

Performance Benchmarking and Gorilla Testing: Systems products should deliver extremely high levels of performance (executing functions so that the response time to the user, memory usage, and disk usage are as small as possible) and high levels of reliability (executing functions so that the number or frequency of failures is zero or very small). One example of performance testing is the use of industry-standardized yardsticks—called benchmarks—to evaluate the execution speed of a product. Various computer industry organizations have agreed on the importance of certain types of operations or sequences of computations, and they have formalized them into standard benchmark tests to facilitate detailed comparisons among products. Brad Silverberg summarized the benchmark tests in use on systems products: "We have complete, very extensive performance tests that test a very wide range, whether it's interrupt latency [for low-level switching between processes] or end-to-end [for complete user commands]. They can be on a very micro level—say, interrupt response time—or a very macro level, running this suite of applications. There are the Babco tests or the Winstone test, or some of the well-known application test suites. We run a whole battery of test suites, performance suites, and see how we do. We track them and measure what our working set size [subset of memory needed] is, and we have certain working set goals that we need to meet."

One type of reliability test that systems projects use is gorilla testing. Here, dedicated testers set up and execute automated tests that purposely try to "break" the product by exercising features at extreme levels. The gorilla testers supplement the regular testers, who managers assign in a one-to-one ratio with developers for systems products, just as they do for applications products. Lou Perazzoli recalled the testing on Windows NT 3.0: "There is probably . . . pretty close to one-to-one tester per developer. . . . Maybe you might have two or three testers testing security or testing file systems, or testing the memory management function. But then you have . . . gorilla testers, or system functional testers. And their job is to find things that just break. So they will write a command procedure that loads and unloads the same driver overnight and see if it is still running the next day."

Another example of reliability testing for systems products is the testing of the low-level application programming interface (API) that provides a mechanism for applications products to access the operating system functions directly. The reliability of the operating system API functions is critical to the reliability of an application. Many software applications vendors want to have their products already available on an operating system by the time a company such as Microsoft releases it. Therefore the Microsoft testers must make the operating system API functions stable and reliable early in the project, so the vendors can use the API to "port" their applications. Jonathan Manheim, test manager for Windows 95, described the testing process for his product:

> Testing operating systems is a multi-phased process, and depending on where you take a snapshot of the process, you may have a focus in different areas. For example, early in the development process, you're focusing very heavily on testing the API directly. You're doing low-level testing of the kernel and the [application] programming interface partly so that you can find those low-level bugs before they show up in higher-level functions of the operating system, and partly so that you can get the development interface well tested and out to the ISVs [independent software vendors] so they can start developing the applications for an operating system prior to release. . . .
>
> Then, later on in the process, you move to higher-level testing, user interface testing, application testing—all these things that you really can't do very well early in the process. . . . At this point in the process, we are very much at that higher-level phase, the application tests. The direct

API tests are not finding too many bugs anymore. The systems are pretty well trained to them, and we're finding most of our bugs by running applications and finding bugs in the user interface.

Internal Usage and Self-Hosting: Another extremely important form of continuous testing is for projects to use a new product, or a new product under development, within the company as soon as possible. Microsoft people strongly believe in doing this and sometimes refer to this practice of internal usage as "eating your own dog food" (see Chapter 6). Internal usage also turns out to be a very cost-effective mechanism for a first-pass testing of a product. Microsoft has thousands of employees using computers daily, so why not have them run the latest release of a product as part of whatever their job is, and report any bugs they see? When a project uses its own products to build its own products, Microsoft people use the term *self-hosting*. This practice is especially relevant to operating systems. For example, developers of Windows 95 ran the latest internal release on their machines, so they used Windows 95 to build more features for Windows 95.

Brad Silverberg explained that self-hosting keeps developers in close touch with their end users. He contrasted this with "cross-development," where a project develops a product using a platform that is different from its target platform (such as using OS/2 to develop Windows 95): "We're completely self-hosted. We make sure that the developers use the systems that they're building, and not do cross-development. I think I've seen more products fail because of cross-development than probably any other development technique I've seen. You lose complete touch for your target environment; you lose complete touch for what your users see." As we discuss further in Chapter 6, however, there are limits to the benefits of self-hosting and internal testing using Microsoft employees, because they are not always the most representative customers. Even Bill Gates admitted this: "Microsoft is not the most typical user of all of Microsoft's products. And so you can miss out on certain things if you just do [testing] with these groups."

Beta Testing: The many testing approaches Microsoft uses to evaluate products prior to release are still insufficient to detect all errors due to the very large number of combinations of product usage scenarios that can occur. The various commands, data inputs, and underlying system configurations can cause a possibly infinite number of combinations. For example, assume the following: A systems product has 100 features. Each feature has 1 normal execution completion, and 2 error messages it could generate. The product runs on 20 different vendors' disk drives. It should run in 4, 8, 16, or 32 megabytes (MB) of memory. The product should run with 15 different vendors' printers, and 5 different vendors' video cards. It should support 100 of the most popular applications, and the 50 most frequently used commands for each of these applications. In order to simply begin testing this product, testers would have to set up a lab that could support over 9 billion combinations of usage scenarios (because 100 x 3 x 20 x 4 x 15 x 5 x 100 x 50 is equal to more than 9 billion). Even if such a lab were practical, it would not be cost-effective—and this list of combinations is incomplete by far.

The use of a large field test, called a beta test, helps address the problem of testing products with very large numbers of possible usage combinations. Systems products in particular commonly use this type of test and may spend six months to a year, or more, in beta testing. Brad Silverberg recalled how Microsoft came to see the need for large-scale beta tests for systems products: "Another thing that we've done in this [systems products] group, which has really changed the way software development is done, is our beta testing procedures. We realized, starting with Windows 3.0 and then with MS-DOS 5 and Windows 3.1, that the system software is used on so many different machines and so many crazy configurations. There's just no way you can predict, in this business, what somebody's going to plug into a PC. There's no way we can internally test all those configurations, under all the circumstances. We do have to rely very heavily upon very extensive beta tests."

Beta testers numbered 7,000 for MS-DOS 6.0, 15,000 for Windows 3.1, and 75,000 for Windows NT 3.0. The number of beta testers for the June 1994 Beta-1 release of Windows 95 was 15,000, and Microsoft planned to have up to 400,000 beta test copies of Windows 95 in the field by August 1995. Silverberg recalled how difficult it was to get his management colleagues in Microsoft to increase the size of the beta tests. The benefits of large tests were so obvious, however, that Microsoft expanded the practice, at least for systems software:

> In the past, and this is still probably pretty true with applications, a beta test is 300 sites, 500 sites, maybe 1,000 sites. A huge, inconceivable beta in the past would be to have a 1,000-site beta test program for an application. But we realized that what we needed to do to get the kind of coverage is to really rely on outside beta testers. . . . With MS-DOS 5, we went to 7,500 beta sites. When I came on board, I looked at the original beta test proposal and saw it was 300 sites. And this was after MS-DOS 4, which was a huge disaster because it was buggy. I proposed to Stephen [Ballmer] . . . that maybe we go to 2,000 or 3,000 and that was like, . . . "What, are you crazy—3,000 beta sites? Nobody's ever done that before. What are you thinking?" And it worked so well, and there was so much demand for the beta, that we ended up with 7,500 sites. As a result, the product was absolutely solid. It worked so well that for Windows 3.1, we ended up going to 15,000 sites. As a result, the product really, really was solid, and compatible, both with hardware and software.

Many software companies use beta testing, although the number of beta testers that Microsoft engages tends to be substantially greater than other vendors due to its enormous installed base and product sales. Microsoft has also been increasing the number of beta testers over time. This is not surprising given the technical benefits of beta testing. In addition, however, beta tests generate excitement about a new product in the user community. This helps to garner support among key industry players—for example, encouraging applications producers to get an early start in building products for new operating systems like Windows NT or Windows 95. Many Microsoft distributors, value-added resellers, and independent software vendors, including companies such as Lotus, are regular beta testers of Microsoft systems software.

In a beta test, participants receive a pre-release product version (called a beta release) and use it themselves. These beta testers become an informal extension of the testing team. They evaluate and test the beta release, then report any errors or problems back to Microsoft. Generally, Microsoft's beta testers receive no compensation and pay no fee for the software or only a minimal fee; they also have to sign an agreement not to tell competitors about the product features. The 75,000 beta testers for Windows NT did not have to sign an agreement, but had to pay a small fee for the beta release (so they, in effect, purchased the software). Beta testers of Windows 95 signed agreements, although only later testers had to pay a small fee for the software.

Avid PC users tend to be eager beta testers, because they like to try out the latest product features and evaluate how well the software works on their particular machines before making a purchase. Microsoft tries to get a broad range of beta testers, however, in order to adequately represent many different hardware, software, and networking combinations. The testers submit error reports before Microsoft finalizes the official product releases. In recent years, beta testers have been receiving the beta releases—as well as sending their errors and suggestions back to Microsoft—using telephone dial-up accounts and electronic mail on CompuServe.

Microsoft projects designate personnel to supervise the electronic mail traffic and respond to the beta testers directly. Silverberg commented on this: "I want to make sure that the forums get properly supported, so everybody who gets the beta gets an account on a private [electronic mail] forum at CompuServe. We have a large number of people assigned to managing and answering questions, and strongly encourage the developers to spend time up on the forum so that they answer the questions themselves as well as see for themselves what the issues that are getting raised are." Silverberg personally spends time reading the electronic mail feedback from beta testers: "And myself, for the last two, three months before a major product shipped, whether it was MS-DOS 5, MS-DOS 6, or Win 3.1, I probably spent two to three hours a day on CompuServe, just answering questions, just getting a feel for the product. You could think of it as checks and balances on the rest of the system. I get the bug reports from my test manager and my development manager. But when I'm up on CompuServe, I see firsthand what's being reported. So if there's no correlation, then I know we need to do something."

Data from Windows 3.1 illustrate how effective beta testing can be. The so-called Final Beta resulted in the detection of 22 percent of all bugs found in the product prior to release.[16] All the external tests of Windows 3.1, including the Final Beta and all earlier beta releases, detected 27 percent of the total bugs. ("External" here means anyone outside Microsoft, such as beta testers, or people inside Microsoft who were not part of the Windows 3.1 project.)[17] Nonetheless, Microsoft still has trouble testing some products. Windows NT and Windows 95, and even the sixth version of MS-DOS (the DoubleSpace data compression feature in particular), have proved to be extremely difficult to test adequately before release because of the huge combination of different computer brands, applications, and peripherals (especially printers) that customers use with an operating system. As a result, Microsoft projects continue to rely on multiple methods of testing. They also continuously evaluate their tools and techniques to find better testing methods.

Comparing the Effectiveness of Testing Techniques: Microsoft reports reveal some of the metrics that projects use to characterize the effectiveness of various testing techniques for detecting bugs. On the Windows NT 3.0 project, for example, the most effective technique was the usage test, which detected the highest percentage (15.0 percent) of all bugs.[18] Usage tests detect bugs through simulating the everyday use of a product. Application programmer interface (API) tests detected the second highest percentage (12.8 percent) of bugs. These tests exercise a particular API function by calling it directly. API tests contributed heavily to the bugs detected early in the project, and then their contribution diminished later in the project. The applications tests, especially the 16-bit applications (Apps-16) tests, started out with a small contribution to the bug count, but their effectiveness increased later in the project as testers more heavily exercised applications. Some testing techniques were extremely helpful because they found a relatively large number of high-severity bugs; for example, stress tests detected only 3.8% of all bugs, but the bugs were generally quite severe. Table 5.2 defines the testing techniques used on Windows NT 3.0.[19] Table 5.3 then summarizes the effectiveness of these various techniques.

Table 5.2   Product Testing Techniques Used on Windows NT 3.0

Usage tests	Bugs detected in everyday use of the system.
API tests	A test written to exercise a particular API function by calling it directly.
Ad hoc, other tests	Tests that do not meet any of the other criteria.
Apps-16 tests	Tests using 16-bit applications.
Gorilla tests	Tests where people explicitly try to break the system by using it in extreme conditions.
User interface tests	Tests of the user interface, including Command Line, File Manager, etc.
Stress tests	Stress test scenarios. Does not include API tests that are also stress tests, but does include scenarios that use them.
Apps-32 tests	Tests using native 32-bit applications, both large and small.
NT verify tests	Bugs detected while trying to get a periodic build to usable quality levels.
Applets tests	Tests of the various system "applets," which are small applications, especially the control panel applets.
Non-NT tests	Tests from outside the NT testing group, but still from inside the NT project. Includes developer unit testing, documentation writers figuring out things, developers discovering their code is broken, and program managers making sure the product is correctly packaged.
"Bug bash" tests	Tests from parties held to detect bugs.
SGA tests	Bugs found using the SGA (Synthetic GUI Application) tool. SGA automatically records function calls between 16-bit apps and the operating system and converts them so Win32 operating sys-

Table 5.2 (continued)

	tem function implementations are used instead of the Win16 implementations.
RATS tests	Bugs found using the RATS tool. RATS is an automated test "engine" (tool) that executes API tests and stores the results in a centralized location.
Unspecified techniques	The field in the bug report form did not specify the testing technique used to detect the bug.

Table 5.3 Effectiveness of Testing Techniques on Windows NT 3.0

Testing Technique	Percentage of Bugs Detected
Usage tests	15.0%
API tests	12.8
Ad hoc, other tests	8.0
Apps-16 tests	7.6
Gorilla tests	6.8
User interface tests	5.5
Stress tests	3.8
Apps-32 tests	2.8
NT verify tests	1.7
Applets tests	0.7
Non-NT tests	0.6
Bug bash tests	0.3
SGA tests	0.3
RATS tests	0.2
Unspecified techniques	33.9
Total	100.0

Note: Percentage of bugs detected by testing technique for Windows NT project through 12/19/92. The Beta 1 release shipped 10/92.

Source: David Anderson et al., "Windows NT Test PDC & Beta 1 Critique, "1993, pp. 17–18.

PRINCIPLE *Use metric data to determine milestone completion and product release.*

Similar to how they evaluate the effectiveness of testing techniques, Microsoft projects commonly use empirical measurements and statistical data, called metrics, to understand, track, and visualize progress within a project. For example, program managers and developers have to determine whether to move to the next milestone, or to ship a product on or after the original ship date. To make these decisions, they rely on specific metrics as well as accumulations of data on error (bug) trends and their severity. They must also rely on personal judgment and experience to interpret these data. Bug data drive the milestone progress assessment, milestone completion, and final shipping decisions, and test managers must agree with the decisions that developers, program managers, and other people make. Relying on metrics and data prevent one person—such as the marketing manager, the development lead, or even the product unit manager—from being able to ship a product before it is ready. The objective is to avoid or minimize the type of disasters that occurred in the past, where products contained fatal flaws and Microsoft had to recall them.

Using Bug (Error) Data for Evaluating Milestone Completion: Microsoft managers use error data, generally called bug data, as the basis for deciding when a product has achieved the quality necessary for completing a major milestone. A *bug* occurs whenever an executing program does not do what its specification says it should do. Bugs occur as a natural part of the software development process; developers correct as many as they can prior to releasing the final version of a product. The bug data have a positive correlation with the overall quality of the product, as well as with the degree and rate of improvement in product quality during development and testing. Project personnel track the bugs found (called "opened"), corrected (called "fixed"), resolved (which means postponed, duplicate, etc.), and active (which means the bug has been found but not yet fixed or resolved). Developers fix bugs that testers report, and they follow the daily build process to incorporate their changes in the master version of the source code.

The use of daily builds strongly encourages developers to complete additional bug fixes each day.

Figure 5.1 displays a typical bar graph used for bug tracking. The bug data reflect bugs opened, fixed, resolved, and active during the integration portion of the second milestone for Excel 5.0 (which also included Graph 5.0). The figure illustrates that projects continually test the product, find bugs, and fix bugs as they approach the end of a milestone. The bars with slanted lines depict new bugs found, and the solid bars depict bugs fixed. Managers and developers look for a steady decrease in the number of active bugs to indicate progress. The line with solid boxes shows a downward trend in the number of active bugs; the number decreases even though ongoing testing is continually finding new bugs. (In Figure 5.1, the number of active bugs is not a simple running total because it can also include or exclude information from other sources.) In order to evaluate actual milestone completion, the number of active bugs that can cause a system to shut down or destroy data should be zero (or very near zero) while testing still continues.

Detecting and Fixing Bugs Full-Time: The portion of the development cycle that comes after the code complete milestone but before the scheduled ship date is a stressful time for the project team. They are trying to detect and correct as many defects as possible, yet still release the product on the scheduled date. Ed Fries recalled the final stages of Word 6.0:

> We've got a lot of bugs to fix here, to finish this thing off. This is always a tense time. You're trying to get the bug count down before ship. . . . You've got two immovable objects. Basically, you have a number of bugs that are out there, and they have to be fixed—and there's not much you can do at this point to change the number of bugs that you put in [the product] over the last year. And you have a ship date that you want to meet. You're just hoping that those two come together, because all you can do is fix bugs as fast as you can and hope that works out well. . . . It'll be good, though; we won't ship it until it's good. Hopefully, we'll ship it when we want to ship it.

Testers report the bugs they detect to developers continuously

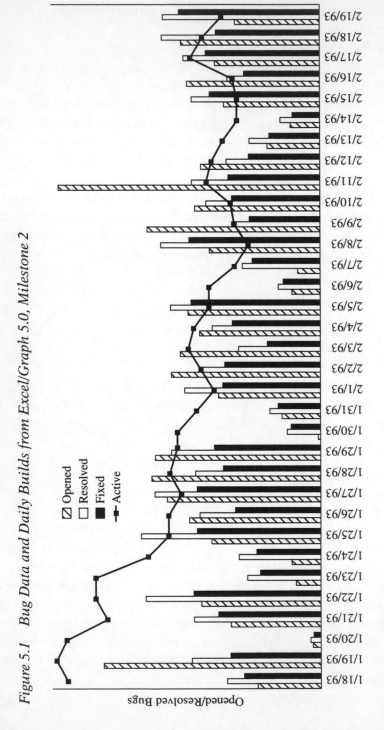

Figure 5.1   Bug Data and Daily Builds from Excel/Graph 5.0, Milestone 2

Source: Microsoft internal document.

318

throughout the project. After the code-complete milestone, developers work full-time fixing bugs. Some developers may fix a relatively large portion of the bugs because they have more experience, because the bugs affect code they are developing personally, or simply because they are just excellent bug fixers. On Excel 4.0, for example, eight of the thirty-seven developers fixed 50 percent of the total bugs, and one developer fixed almost 10 percent of the bugs.[20] (Not all of the developers were full-time on the project, however.) The Windows NT 3.0 developers were fixing bugs full-time in the spring of 1993, and each bug fix required changes to three to five files on average. Many bugs resulted from compatibility with Windows 3.1 and existing applications. Lou Perazzoli gave this account:

> We fix on a good week 1,200 bugs. . . . You figure the average bug takes changes in three to five files, but we also have these big ones . . . where you just check in minor changes to sixteen, twenty, or thirty files. . . . Now for the bad news. About 1,000 [bugs] get opened. And the question is, how the hell can anybody developing software have so many bugs? It turns out that it is called "compatibility." If we didn't have to be compatible with Windows [3.1], we wouldn't have so many bugs. It turns out if your printout doesn't look exactly like Windows, then that is a bug because Windows is right, regardless. If this WoW 16-bit app—we call it WoW, for Windows on Windows—doesn't run, then that's a bug.

Metric-Based Checklists for Feature and Product Completion: Microsoft projects have also been compiling metric-based checklists to help determine feature and product completion. For example, Excel has a six-page list of criteria entitled "Am I Done Yet?" This groups completion criteria into twenty-six categories, such as menu commands, printing, interaction with the operating system, and application interoperability (see Table 5.4).[21] A program manager, developer, or tester uses the checklist to help evaluate whether a feature is complete. Another metric-based checklist helps determine whether a product is ready to ship to customers; Table 5.5 summarizes the ship-readiness criteria checklist for Excel 5.0. This checklist states, for example, that the various test types should be 100 percent completed, and the highest-priority bugs

Table 5.4   Example Section from "Am I Done Yet?" Checklist

Interactions with Operating System

- Activate/Deactivate Excel (with keyboard and mouse)?

- Non-standard control panel window colors?

- Do colors track when application is running?

- System 6 mono-finder and multi-finder?

- Operating system filename length restrictions?

- Desk Accessories on Macintosh?

- Non-color QuickDraw?

- Dual monitors on Macintosh?

- Does Excel work on localized operating system?

Source: WesC, "Am I Done Yet?," Microsoft internal document.

should be corrected and then retested at least twice (this is called regression testing). Also, the bug detection rate and bug severity should be decreasing, and there should be no must-fix bugs detected during sustained testing in the last week prior to release.[22]

In addition to checklists, projects sometimes use specialized completion criteria to evaluate a product's readiness to ship. In the case of Windows 95, for example, the product had to correctly upgrade a certain number of corporate customers before Microsoft considered the product ready. Windows 95's plug-and-play feature is supposed to automatically determine what types of hardware a user has installed on a computer. The operating system must be able to detect successfully the widely varied hardware configurations on several thousand machines. As Jonathan Manheim explained: "Chicago [Windows 95] has advanced hardware detection configuration functionality. That's a strong area of focus for us right now, so we're doing a lot of focus set up testing and

Table 5.5   Metric-Based Checklist for Determining Ship Readiness for Excel 5.0

Testing is Done:

• Automated auto-test runs without errors

• Manual test cases have been run

• Each test area defined in the master spreadsheet [that outlines the product features] has been declared "done"

• Ad-hoc testing for each area by primary and secondary testers completed

• All bugs regressed and closed

• Last 200 priority 1 and 2 bugs regressed again

• Set up and all components (except Excel.exe) have been frozen [unchanged] for a month prior to the release-to-manufacturing (RTM) ship date

• The ever-popular "gut feel" survey shows that the testing group feels like we're ready to ship

Bug Find/Fix Data:

• Bug find rate shows a decreasing trend prior to the zero-bug release (ZBR) and is maintained after our ZBR

• Bug severity distribution changes to be more severity level 3 and 4 bugs, and there should be a continual decrease in severity level 1 and 2 bugs reported

• All bugs reported after the first release candidate (RC1) go through a "maybe meeting" (where a reported bug will be classified into "yes," "no," or "maybe" to indicate whether it will be corrected in the current release or postponed to the next release), and extensive comments are added to the bug report when resolved to aid in bug regression testing

• No "must fix" bugs are reported during the last week prior to the release-to-manufacturing (RTM) date under sustained testing

---

Source: Excel 5.0 Test Plan, 4/13/93, and "Testing at Microsoft," Microsoft internal presentation.

hardware detection testing. One of the things that we're doing now, in addition to testing set-up explicitly here, is that we're going out to external sites and upgrading corporate sites that volunteer for this program. Our objective is to do ten thousand corporate upgrades by the time we ship."

Systems products have a general formula for the release decision, based on the length of time that the product has gone unchanged. First, a systems product needs to meet its various functionality, quality, speed, and size criteria. Then project managers evaluate the thoroughness of the testing effort (especially beta testing), the number and severity of the known bugs, and the length of time the current release has gone unchanged. In general, before shipping the product, a project has to have a two-week period where people are testing full-time, finding no new severe bugs and not making any changes to the source code. Bill Gates commented on the complex set of issues they considered in the Windows NT 3.0 project:

> [Paul] Maritz and I talked through what the key criteria were in terms of how long he had to go at zero bugs. We had spent, of course, massive time on what features were necessary—how far did . . . OS/2 have to go, how far did Windows compatibility testing have to go? What about speed? It's slower than Windows 3.1; is it too much slower than Windows 3.1? How does it compare to OS/2 doing these things? So we spent a lot of time on speed criteria, spent a lot of time on size criteria. Was it okay to require 8 [megabytes of memory]? There was an early time when we thought 8 or 12 [megabytes of memory] would do, and we ended up being more like 16. Was that okay? We went through and we looked at lots of data to decide that.
>
> When it came to the release . . . nobody was calling me at home at night saying, "Can we ship this thing?" Everybody knows that you get all the bugs out and then you wait—depending on how complex the project is—either a week or two weeks, where you haven't touched the code at all and nothing's come up. You just make sure the internal testing and the beta testing is very comprehensive, and you go ahead and ship. So nobody's in contact with me during that period, because there's never that much pressure to ship a product, honestly. This is a company with lots of money in the bank. We can take a very long-term approach to

doing things. So what's the pressure to ship? If somebody thinks we shouldn't ship, the default case is we're not going to ship the thing.

Rules of Thumb for Bug Data and When to Ship: Before a product is ready for release, program managers, developers, and testers are working full-time testing code, detecting and evaluating bugs, and correcting defects. While all these people test the code, only developers change the code, and developers check in their code changes almost every day. The daily build process (see Table 5.1) is the backbone that keeps the product stable and steadily improving. Without such a systematic process, the sheer number of developers changing the code at this stage would cause chaos. When developers have completely caught up to the testers and corrected all of the known bugs (or at least all of the known severe bugs), Microsoft people call this project event "touching zero bugs." When an applications project first touches zero bugs, then it is about six weeks away from shipping the product. Chris Peters summarized the rules of thumb that he uses to determine when a product is ready to ship:

> We're much more interested in figuring out when code complete happens as a predictor of our ship dates, more than just to . . . say "You can't change stuff." . . . In the olden days, we used to say it [shipment] would happen two months after we were code complete, but from past performance we know it actually happens between four and five, so in modern schedules we usually put four and a half months. And that's one of the things that allows us to ship on time. . . . Another thing that happens is, you first touch zero bugs on the active bug count about six weeks before shipping. . . . Classically, when you're first darn sure that you're going to go to manufacturing, you're probably two weeks away from going to manufacturing.

Rules of thumb for ship readiness also utilize metrics that capture the rate of detecting new bugs. The rate should be approaching zero as the project nears the target ship date. Figure 5.2 displays a sample graph for Word 4.0 for the Macintosh; it indicates the average rate of bug detection per tester per week throughout the project. The brief periods of high detection rates occurred early in the

Figure 5.2   Example Bug Detection Rate Metrics for Mac Word 4.0

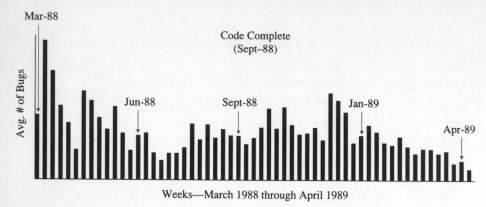

Weeks—March 1988 through April 1989

Source: Phil Fawcett, "Mac Word 4.0 Postmortem Report," 5/25/89.

project and about five months before release.[23] Even though these rates can vary widely, managers can use them to gauge testing resource requirements. On the Money 2.0 project, for example, the average bug detection rate per tester was 1.9 bugs per day.[24] The project had ten testers, and the number of testers was ramped up and down as needed throughout the project. The time an individual tester spent testing the product ranged from 21 to 203 days. On the Works for Windows 2.0 project, the average bug detection rate was 1.4 bugs per tester per day.[25]

The Unforgiving Market: After some past bad experiences when projects shipped their products too early, Microsoft groups have learned to use bug data as the primary means for deciding when a product is ready to sell to customers. Of course, there are a variety of market-timing considerations that affect the shipping decision. Ultimately, however, Microsoft managers have to weigh the decision against the chances of a product update or recall.

If a product has a fatal bug that destroys users' data or prevents some critical feature from working, then Microsoft has to send out a product update release to correct the problem. These product update releases are unusual, but costly in several ways. They cause overhead in another product cycle, drain resources away from the next major product version, and require a repeat of the full diskette manufacturing and distribution process. Fatal bugs and the resulting updates also damage the reputation of the company and may result in lawsuits. Users sometimes pay a small fee to receive the updates, but companies like Microsoft frequently issue these at cost, depending on the severity of the problems. As Bill Gates commented: "We're in a unique situation. When we send something to manufacturing, we just build [lots of copies]. DOS 6 got released to manufacturing, and they built two million copies. And we're selling the product into the channel at about $45. If we had to do an update of that product, boom, all the profitability of that thing would just disappear like that. It's a ridiculous thing to ever have to go through a product recall."

Quality has become an issue of rising importance to Gates and other managers primarily because of pressure from customers and competitors. Nonetheless, Microsoft people still tend to view quality in a relative and pragmatic, rather than absolute, sense. For example, Dave Moore insisted that quality has to include being market-focused and flexible: "Our viewpoint is that an obsession with quality has to map to customers. There has to be utility. There is a certain amount of quality in being flexible, being adaptable to changing customer needs, changing market conditions. And so your standards for quality must not hinder that."

At the same time, as seen in Intel's experience with the Pentium chip, PC customers are no longer willing to tolerate defects; there is too much at stake. Jonathan Manheim admitted this when explaining why Microsoft delayed the Windows 95 release to complete features and test more thoroughly: "We're not going to ship it out when it's buggy. We feel that the market will forgive us for being late, but they won't forgive us for being buggy." Gates acknowledged a similar deep concern with Microsoft's reputation. He seemed quite willing to delay critical new products like Windows NT or Windows 95 if they are not ready by the promised ship date: "You never want to release a bad product into the marketplace. Our reputation is a huge asset. And so it's important that I get involved in that final decision on whether this thing is exciting enough or good enough to release. We have this huge sales force that just assumes everything we hand them is just great. . . . So we've got to make sure that we don't hand them a dud."

Chapter 6 discusses how Microsoft is building an organization that learns from itself and from its customers. Not only have people reflected on past mistakes, but they have effectively learned how to channel customer feedback directly into the development process as well as share more components across different product groups.

6

Building a Learning Organization

Improve Through Continuous Self-Critiquing, Feedback, and Sharing

To build a learning organization, Microsoft follows a strategy that we describe as *improve through continuous self-critiquing, feedback, and sharing*. We break down our discussion of this strategy into four principles:

- Systematically learn from past and present projects and products.
- Encourage feedback and improvement using quantitative metrics and benchmarks.
- View customer support as part of the product and as data for improvement.
- Promote linkages and sharing across product groups.

Organizational learning is a very broad subject that appears frequently in recent management literature. We chose to interpret this concept in very practical terms. Organizations have many opportunities to improve whatever it is that they do: They can reflect on their operations, study their products, listen to customers, and encourage different parts of the organization to share knowledge as well as the results of their separate efforts, such as in designing products and components. All firms have these opportunities, although few companies take full advantage of them. To the extent that individuals and groups in a company try to do these things and generate measurable improvements, we consider the company to be "building a learning organization."

The principles for learning that we see in Microsoft we also see in other successful companies. Good firms everywhere critique their processes and products in order to learn from past successes as well as failures. They measure and benchmark what they do. They study customers. And they try to get different parts of the organization to cooperate and share components, as well as product and process knowledge more generally. Particularly for a PC software company, however, we feel Microsoft is distinctive in the degree to which it now emphasizes these principles. We say this because we believe Microsoft is making extraordinary (though still inadequate) efforts to become more of an integrated organization.

For example, not many software development organizations routinely conduct project postmortems or audits, even though industry experts consider these to be good practices. Microsoft groups regularly conduct both postmortems and project audits. Like many software producers and firms in service industries, Microsoft is struggling to find a balance between measuring enough elements in its product-development process to manage more effectively and avoiding becoming overly bureaucratic. It does not measure as much as leading software producers from the mainframe and minicomputer world, such as IBM, Hewlett-Packard, or the Japanese computer manufacturers. Nonetheless, Microsoft is cultivating a tradition of quantitatively measuring key elements of its development process. Managers use these data to make key decisions—for example, when to move forward in a project, or when to ship a product. They are also creating benchmarks to gauge performance and promote improvement.

Microsoft probably has more customers calling by telephone and sending in electronic inquiries than any other software company in the world, if for no other reason than because it probably has the most customers. Yet we feel Microsoft takes exceptional advantage of this situation by analyzing customer contacts more thoroughly than any other company we have seen. It then channels this information quickly and directly into the product development groups. Since 1990, product groups have also placed more importance on designing components that other groups can use. This sharing has involved a major change in Microsoft's organization (including the establishment of the Office product unit), as well as in its culture and strategy as a company.

In the past, Microsoft's product groups were able to focus intensely on one product, one competitor, and one goal. For example, they concentrated on getting Windows or Windows NT out the door, or catching up with and matching Lotus in spreadsheets and WordPerfect in word processing. But even a company as wealthy and powerful as Microsoft must standardize and share features across many products to reduce costs in development, testing, and customer support. Because competing products exist, Microsoft cannot afford to make the same design mistakes repeatedly, ignore customer complaints and suggestions, or let project schedules get out of control. Learning how to become more than just a collection of independent projects with little control or coordination has probably been the most difficult transition Microsoft has had to make as an organization.

We also suspect that learning may be easier at Microsoft than at larger firms that spread out critical operations around the globe. As discussed in other chapters, Microsoft has located nearly all its product development groups at the Redmond, Washington, headquarters. Despite extensive reliance on electronic mail, Gates and other managers have also insisted that people be close enough physically to solve problems face-to-face. It is our observation that much of the learning which goes on at Microsoft does take place informally—in conversations in the innumerable corridors, as well as in individual offices, over lunch tables, in retreats, and in more casual settings.

PRINCIPLE   *Learn from past and present projects and products.*

Evaluating the performance of individual software developers and projects has always been a problem. It is difficult to determine objective measures of productivity or quality for tasks that often resemble creative writing or producing best-selling books. Giving constructive feedback and criticism to the highly talented and independent programmers that Microsoft hires is even more difficult. Microsoft people like to criticize themselves, as seen in the postmortem reports and internal memos, but groups tended to become insular during the 1970s and 1980s. Mike Maples recognized this need for a broader perspective—for groups to compare what they do to other groups within Microsoft and to other firms that may have discovered better practices for managing software development. In 1988, Maples gave this job of encouraging more learning and sharing about the process of software development to Dave Moore.

Born in 1954, Dave Moore majored in math at the University of Washington, graduated in 1976, and entered the Boeing Corporation. He worked initially on CAD/CAM systems as well as engineering standards, and he received a firsthand view of what a well-managed engineering company should look like. Moore joined Microsoft as a developer in 1981, when the company had about one hundred employees and few established modes of operations. He worked his way up to being the development lead for Multiplan, Word, Chart, Works, and other products, acquiring a reputation for shipping products successfully. In 1988, Maples asked Moore to become director of development for the applications division. Moore rose to director of development for the entire company in 1992 and served as the acting director of testing and quality assurance from 1992 to 1994, while also holding some other positions temporarily. Since 1994 he has reported to Chris Williams, the director of product development, who in turn reports to Paul Maritz.

As director of development, Moore has focused on several areas. He has encouraged groups to write postmortem reports, or at least hold meetings to discuss how projects did. He has conducted process audits to help groups analyze and solve their problems, organized formal retreats where key personnel discuss problems related to software development and quality control, and orchestrated informal meetings of people in the same functions to encourage knowledge sharing. These efforts supplement another

Microsoft custom called "eating your own dog food"—using Microsoft products and tools internally to experience firsthand how good (or how bad) they might appear to the customer. Moore also began informal efforts to benchmark Microsoft groups, an idea that the company is now pursuing more intensively.

Postmortems: Since the later 1980s, between half and two-thirds of all Microsoft projects have written postmortem reports, and most other projects have held postmortem discussion sessions. The postmortem documents are surprisingly candid in their self-criticisms, especially because they circulate to the highest levels of the company. Even Bill Gates avidly reads reports on major projects (such as Word and Excel) and new areas (such as multimedia). Gates admitted that "people are willing to be fairly critical of things that are screwed up in that process. . . . We're successful in writing software, so we can be pretty brutal about the parts we don't do well." Chris Peters concurred, noting that "the purpose of the document is to beat yourself up." Mike Maples saw the postmortems as a natural outcome of Microsoft people's love of self-analysis: "To some extent, that's part of our culture. We're always screwed up. We're always afraid of the competition, and we're always looking back. . . . One of the things is being very self-critical, and the postmortems and a whole series of things are trying to get at this, never being satisfied that what you're doing is halfway right. We're always struggling."

Groups generally take three to six months to put a postmortem document together. The documents have ranged from under 10 to more than 100 pages, and have tended to grow in length. For example, the Word 3.0 postmortem from August 1987 was 12 single-spaced pages; the Excel 4.0 postmortem from February-March 1992 totaled 41 pages; the Encarta postmortem from June 1993 was 84 pages; and the Windows NT Beta 1 critique reached 112 pages!

The documents have grown as Microsoft projects have gone beyond simply describing development and testing activities. They have added detailed sections for each function, usually written by the team leads for program management, development, testing, product management, and user education. The most common format is to discuss what worked well in the last project, what did not work well, and what the group should do to improve in the next project. The postmortem reports also contain descriptive data. These cover *people* (size of the team by functions, number of days worked), the *product* (size in lines of code, comparisons to the previous version, languages used, platform and language versions produced), *quality* (number of bugs per thousand lines of code, bug severity in four categories, types of bugs by area of the product, record of finding and fixing bugs, number of bugs carried over from the previous project versus newly introduced), *schedule* (actual versus planned dates for milestones and shipment), and *process* (such as tools used, and issues involving interdependencies on other groups or outside vendors providing product "add-ins"). The functional managers usually prepare an initial draft and then circulate this via e-mail to the team members, who send in their comments. The authors collate these and create the final draft, which then goes out to team members as well as senior executives and the directors of product development, development, and testing. The functional groups, and sometimes an entire project, will then meet to discuss the postmortem findings. Some groups (such as Excel and Windows NT) have also gotten into the habit of holding postmortem meetings after every milestone to make midcourse corrections, review feature lists, and rebalance the schedule.

The postmortem documents provide a record (though sketchy) of how Microsoft's current process for software development evolved in response to problems building Word and other products. The Word group took the lead in documenting recurring problems, beginning in 1987. The Excel group took the lead in finding solutions for relatively large projects, beginning in 1989 and 1990. Microsoft managers then began diffusing good ideas and lessons from the Excel team and other groups to projects throughout the company. They have relied on a variety of mechanisms: circulating key memos and postmortem reports, creating written documents on scheduling and project management methods (which never proved to be popular), circulating a 1990 videotaped talk by Chris Peters on the practices of the Excel group (which proved to be enormously popular), informal audits by Dave Moore, retreats to discuss quality and process issues, and a one-week course on shipping software on time, based on Peter's video. The following overview provides a flavor of the painful lessons Microsoft people learned and documented in the postmortem reports.

In the mid-1980s, Microsoft projects followed what the Word group called a "breadth-first approach." Program managers wrote a brief vision statement and functional specification outline. Developers then took a first cut at coding all the features in the new version of the product—without any attempt to test or integrate the features until they thought people were done. This approach also relied on a large integration period at the end of the project.

The breadth-first style worked with small products that had few interdependent features. Microsoft failed, however, to "scale up" this process for large, complex products, which Word and Excel, as well as Windows and the Omega (Access) database, had become. By the later 1980s, Microsoft products had too many defects within features, as well as in the interactions among features. (An example of an interaction is when someone uses the table-creation feature to make a table, and then the printing feature to print it.) Developers always had to go back and do massive amounts of coding to fix bugs and get features to work properly; the rework would then completely throw off schedules. It also became difficult and impossible in some cases to deliver reliable products. Some bugs can never be fixed very late in a project, because introducing fixes can create more bugs and lead to the state that Microsoft came to call "infinite defects."

Charles Simonyi wrote up the Macintosh Word 3 postmortem memo based on an August 13, 1987 meeting. This was an important project because of the problems that the team experienced. The Windows version of the product started in September 1984 with an estimated one-year schedule. This became hopelessly delayed, though, as the development team tried to reuse code across both the Macintosh and PC Windows platforms, as well as adapt to the changing Windows program. The Windows version finally shipped in November 1989—four years behind the original schedule. Microsoft did ship a Macintosh version in February 1987, but this contained so many bugs that Microsoft had to recall the product and send free replacements to seventy thousand users.[1] Despite the trauma that team members experienced, one can also see them rethinking their process. The Word postmortem suggested that projects move away from the breadth-first approach. Instead, it seemed wiser to divide up the product's features into milestones and proceed "depth first" by putting a small team of people on a select group of features and building these more completely, then testing them more thoroughly, before going on to other features. Simonyi commented on this:

> We had a Word 3 post-mortem review meeting on August 13, 1987. . . . Problems in Word 3 were caused by a combination of circumstances. These were: lack of early, in-depth testing (which in turn was caused in large part by the breadth-first development methodology), not fully understanding the complexity of the product, and not changing the 1.05 base enough to carry the new complexity. We plan to avoid recurrence of the circumstances by more depth-first development, organized—when possible—into "campaigns" in which 2, 3, or 4 people work together on different details of the same feature. Near the end of the campaign there will be more testing by the developers, including programmers, who were not contributing to the campaign. . . . We have some ideas how to change the program organization and coding practices to reduce the number of bugs. In many cases the ideas are applicable to other projects as well.[2]

The Word group had other bad practices, such as not reviewing developers' code before submitting it as completed. Simonyi complained: "Because of optimism about the progress and later because of the pressure of the schedule, much of the new code in Word 3 was not reviewed."[3] Nearly all companies have found code reviews to be an excellent way to detect bugs early. This post-mortem also reveals, however, that Microsoft developers were already using advanced abstraction and almost object-oriented design techniques to make code more generically useful and able to support a lot of new features. Many other aspects of Microsoft's development process and coding techniques can be seen emerging from the Word 3 project. These include emphasizing the insertion of "asserts" in the code to let other developers and testers know what assumptions the developer has made; using automated tests to find defects; and introducing "instrumented versions" of products that track every step a user makes in order to analyze bugs.

Unfortunately, the Macintosh Word 4.0 project did not do much better; the team members repeated many of the same mistakes before shipping a product in 1990. The following sampling of comments from the development postmortem, written by Chris Mason, indicates the extent of the "disaster." The team suffered from crude attempts to share code between the Macintosh and Windows versions of the program, no fixed schedule, buggy development tools, no coordination of feature designs, the tendency to fix interrelated bugs one at a time, and inadequate specifications:[4]

> The development postmortem meeting for Mac Word 4 was held on May 10 in beautiful downtown Bellevue. . . . If there were disasters in this project, they were tables and merging with Win Word. There was certainly naiveté and wasted time. We were naive to think that we could make fundamental changes in the display, PLC, and layout routines, write a lot of complex new code and have very few bugs. There was no evidence for this in the history of Word. I believe that the way we shared code with Win Word wasted their time and ours, and was ultimately a failure. . . . And, finally, Mac Word can stand as the definitive case study for how *not* to schedule a project. (p. 1)

> The scheduling on Mac Word 4 was totally inadequate. . . . We worked without a schedule. . . . This is absolute madness, and in retrospect it's no surprise that we could never give an accurate ship date. We had no idea what we were doing. (p. 5)

> The biggest problem was that we were told the development system was shippable. In fact, all components, especially the assembler and interpreter, were swarming with bugs. (p. 8)

> We tend to design features independently, without regard for their interactions with the rest of the program. . . . Bugs, especially a lot of bugs in one area, can flag interactions between features or overlooked design issues. We usually didn't take the hint in Word 4. We kept on fixing bugs one at a time. . . . We did not thoroughly understand the interactions between tables and the rest of Word. (p. 9)

> We merged Win Word code back into Mac Word three times. After the third, the two projects were sharing most of the core of the product. Win Word, on the other hand, did at least six merges. . . . Each time, the

merge severely broke their project. . . . These merges, during a time when Mac Word was radically redesigning the foundation while Win Word was trying to move ahead, were more of a problem than a solution. (p. 12)

Campaigns did not solve the problem and in fact did not even stress depth first as they were supposed to do. . . . The spec was seriously inadequate. Tables were described in only 3.5 pages. (pp. 15–16)

Nevertheless, the Macintosh Word 4.0 project reviewed more code and had a much better testing effort. The testing postmortem, written by Phil Fawcett, reflects the introduction of more systematic testing procedures, moving beyond "ad hoc testing" to more planning and analysis of specification documents. Fawcett also pleads for more automated testing tools and better project scheduling to ensure adequate time for testing:[5]

After the release of MacWord 3 it became apparent that there were serious flaws in using only ad hoc testing as a way of securing confidence in the quality of a product. To avoid blind spots and to aid in the education of testers, we decided that some testing time would be used to create feature spec documents and feature test case documents. Once these were complete, the testing effort was organized into a series of "passes" mixed with time to do completely unstructured testing. . . . The feature spec document was written early in the project and was based on preliminary information about how a feature was supposed to work. . . . We found that the most efficient use of this document was as an aid to an unstructured type of approach. (p. 2)

Of all the areas that affected efficiency of testing, lack of adequate tools had the greatest impact. We resorted to manual testing methods because of the lack of adequate automated tools. (p. 6)

Incorrect project scheduling and pressure to meet an unrealistic schedule reduced consistency throughout the testing process. The unrealistic schedule forced testing to begin ship mode in November (1988). The ship mode lasted until mid April. This means testing spent 40% of its effort in ship mode (6 months). During this exhaustive process, we noticed a loss of productivity. . . . A more realistic schedule, created from better estimates of code changes, bugs per KLOC, code complexity measures and other metrics would have given testing three more months of structured, thorough testing before beginning ship mode. (p. 7)

The Excel 3.0 and 4.0 projects, completed between 1990 and 1992, utilized the process described in Chapters 4 and 5 of this book. Excel 3.0 turned out to be high quality and a mere eleven days late. This project did not write up a postmortem document, although Chris Peters detailed the process they used in his 1990 videotaped talk. A detailed postmortem for Excel 4.0, which shipped about one month late after a short nine-month development cycle, compared the teams' experiences on the 3.0 and 4.0 projects. Because the 4.0 project skipped much of the up-front specification phase and moved directly into adding features not put in Excel 3.0, it was not a typical project. Nonetheless, the development postmortem (written by Jon De Vaan) reveals struggles within Microsoft. The challenge was to find a proper balance between not wasting time on specifications for features that will change or be cut versus writing up a document in sufficient detail to know what features should get top priority, estimate how difficult they will be to code, and schedule properly. This project also imported components from other groups and vendors, leading to a discussion of "interdependencies" that would grow more serious with future projects. It is also clear that Microsoft began adopting higher project-management and quality standards: The team analyzed why the project was late, even though it came in relatively close to the schedule compared to older Microsoft projects, and why there were so many bugs, even though complaints from customers were minimal:[6]

Development of Excel 4.0 began on July 8, 1991 and the first version (Windows, US) shipped March 27, 1992. . . . Overall the Excel 4 development process is considered a success. The product has been well received and reports from PSS indicate we have no quality problems. The shortness of the project caused us to cut corners on our development process. We believe that resulted in some schedule slippage, some poor internal and external design decisions, and late-breaking bugs. (p. 1)

The main problem we encountered with scheduling was bad estimating. The lack of up-front design resulted in less accurate estimates. . . . While Excel 4 had exactly the same Zero-Defect rules as Excel 3, the concept was not as high on each developer's priority list. Overall it is felt that Excel 4 had too many bugs. For the record, Zero-Defects for Excel 4 was:

- All changes must compile and link.
- All changes must pass the "Quick Test" on both Macintosh and Windows platforms.
- Any developer who has more than 10 bugs on the bug list has to fix them before moving on to new features. (pp. 4–5)

The Excel 4 program management postmortem, written by Mike Mathieu, described the inadequate planning before starting development and inadequate attention to the specification, as well as other problems. Mathieu noted that the vision statement "was a good reference point from which to focus the product," but "it had more in it than we could do." He described activity-based planning as "a good way to rationalize features, prioritize them, and focus the design goals," but he noted that "we did not prune the spec first, so we wasted time on features that got cut. . . . Activity teams were disorganized and changed composition frequently. . . . Working closely with developers to resolve design issues was much more fruitful than relying on spec hand-offs. It reduced turnaround time and cut through red tape." In addition, Mathieu cited the need for earlier and more usability lab testing, as well as better methods to control spec changes.[7] Marc Olson, author of the testing postmortem, also complained about the specifications ("Specs out of date, features without a spec, and incomplete specs were the three biggest problems") and dozens of other issues, such as balancing the work load among testers and speeding up the turnaround rate for bug fixes.[8]

Most projects described similar problems. For example, the new Encarta multimedia encyclopedia, which shipped in March 1993, came out of a twenty-two-month project that had about ten members. This was an important project because it had to mix text, audio, and video images. The postmortem document reflects the group's efforts to adopt the Excel development process. The project did not, however, always follow Excel's good practices; instead, it encountered the same types of problems that Microsoft projects wrote about in the 1980s. Insufficient thought and planning led to an inability to prioritize features. As a result, projects left difficult features that they could not cut until the last milestone, ultimately delaying the schedule. Half-done features (as in the old breadth-first approach) also slipped into the next milestone, giving an unrealistic view of actual progress. Scheduling was too optimistic, forcing everyone to rush and shorten time that the project should have allocated to code reviews, testing, and bug fixing. Nonetheless, Microsoft got through its first major multimedia project, and it established a base of experience for future multimedia products:

> Though the product that resulted from the Encarta effort is a competitive product that we can be proud of, the team feels we can and will do better next time. Key areas to work on will be product performance, project scheduling, and balancing workloads. With considerable schedule slips, the Encarta project was not a model project from a management perspective. In fact, it is a case study in what *not* to do in scheduling software development on a multimedia project. . . . Most problems on Encarta can be attributed to a single cause: lack of experience with MM-PUBs [multimedia publishing products] on products of this size and complexity. With Encarta under our belt, we will not have to face this hurdle again on future projects.[9]

Process Audits: One of the tasks that Maples asked Moore to perform as director of development was to conduct occasional process audits, usually of projects that were ongoing but running into some problems. In 1993, for example, Moore conducted five audits, each taking about a week of full-time effort. He usually looks at available project and quality data, talks to as many members of the project as possible, and tries to identify what they are doing well in addition to what they might do better. In general, Moore tries to find a process model that will make the group more successful, and then he either writes a report or presents detailed oral feedback to key project members. He presented his role as constructive:

> Mike [Maples] has had me go off and audit groups, too. That's always on demand, where there's a problem area, or they need help. That's where I either play a cop or a hit man. They're just policing up before I'm in there, closing down, making changes. . . . This is where I go in and audit. I basically start out with, "I'm here to help you. I inventory and disseminate

best practices. I'm here to capture the best practices that you have." And as they're describing what their best practices are, I also ask what problems they're having. If there are problem areas or practices that I believe could be improved in their group, then I'll make recommendations for improvement. I always view the audits as a constructive process where I'm there to help them. . . . I can almost say that the job I'm doing today is a full-time auditor.

Despite the pressure of the audits, Moore primarily works as an evangelist, gently trying to coax groups toward better practices by the power of logic and data from other projects. We have noted that a cultural resistance within Microsoft to mandates from executives, bureaucratic rules, or a company quality assurance (QA) staff makes it difficult to tell people what to do. Fitting with Microsoft's culture, Moore asked people to view his audits as a form of "technical exchange":

> This is probably my personal struggle. There isn't a management mandate for structure; it's just technical exchange. I don't walk into someone's office and say, "Mike has told me to carry the banner of structure, and you will comply with these standards." It's, "How are you doing this stuff? Have you tried this technique? This may solve that particular problem." That's the type of discussion. These groups pick the mode that fits the problems that they're solving. You've probably noticed there isn't a QA group going around auditing these groups. We don't have that traditional QA.

One group that Moore helped turn around developed the Visual C++ language product. Mike Maples had met with members of the project during a routine program review session. After identifying several problems, he sent Moore in for an audit. The group had thirty to forty developers, an equal number of testers, and about ten program managers, but was still using ad hoc practices. Jeff Beehler, a program manager, described changes the team made after encountering Moore: "Dave spent about two weeks interviewing key members of the product team . . . and came back with a list of recommendations . . . suggestions for development, suggestions for testing, and suggestions for program management administration. Many of those recommendations were adhered to. Sometimes we had to implement them by just brute force: 'You will implement this. We've got Dave Moore saying that this stuff is really good stuff; let's make sure it happens in this project.' As for others, the suggestions made perfect sense, and we just acted on them. Others never got implemented."

Most importantly, the group adopted the daily build process, scheduling by milestones and small tasks, and reviewing code before checking it into the build. Chris Williams applauded the results of this audit: "The Visual C++ group [was] . . . completely off the rails, and C 7 [C++ version 7] . . . was a twelve-month project that shipped thirteen months late. . . . They called Dave and said, 'Dave, help.' Dave came in and said to them, 'OK, you need to follow these kinds of processes, you need to do these kinds of things.' . . . And these guys completely reconstructed the way they do business. They're shipping stuff on time and correctly."

Retreats: In the early 1980s, Microsoft started the practice of holding at least one retreat a year for key members of the company. One purpose is to exchange information on what different divisions are doing. Another is to tackle such issues as how to compete more effectively in particular product areas (one 1983 retreat targeted Lotus and ended up defining the new Excel product) or how to improve product development and customer support processes. At some sessions, the organizer has asked attendees to read a classic work in software engineering or related areas (such as Phil Crosby on quality, or Tom DeMarco on project scheduling) and then discuss the insights from these authors and improvements that Microsoft might attempt. Senior people have reported on the readings first and led the discussions.

Perhaps the most famous retreat, immortalized within Microsoft by Chris Mason's "zero defect" memo, was the May 1989 meeting that focused on techniques and tools to reduce defects and improve quality. About thirty people attended this retreat, which Dave Moore organized as part of his new job as director of development. Moore divided the attendees into four groups and asked them to focus on zero-defect methods, tools, and other related areas. He recalled the meeting and the role of Mike Maples:

I talked with Jeff [Harbers, then Moore's boss] about how we needed to make some changes, and I just wasn't getting anywhere. I was working with my groups to make things improve. Jeff was trying things, too. But there wasn't this cohesive "We need to understand the process. We need to have concepts like zero defects moving." The fundamental change for understanding the process really would have to have come when Mike Maples came on board in September of '88. At that time, I really worked with Mike to define the structure of this retreat that set off zero defects. I'd been thinking about the concept for awhile; I'm sure other people had been thinking about the concept for awhile. But I got those folks together in a room. Charles [Simonyi] was part of that group, in fact, on zero defects. I just happened to pick Chris Mason as the guy to lead that particular group. And fortunately, that setting, that structure, the problems we had seen, allowed us to capture . . . the concepts we needed to expose to the application development teams at the time.

Microsoft has continued holding retreats every year on a variety of issues. Meetings between 1993 and 1995 focused on issues that have challenged Microsoft to operate more as an integrated company, as well as to prepare for such new technologies as on-line networks and multimedia. For example, a June 1993 retreat discussed the problem of improving synergies among the different products and business units. Another in February 1994 discussed managing "interdependencies": how to deal with the growing problems of scheduling and quality assurance when projects depended on key components developed in other projects or imported from outside the company. Chris Williams recalled that some thirty-five development managers and test managers from around the company attended this three-day retreat: "Mike [Maples] and Dave [Moore] actually hosted it and put it together. I think it was the result of a fairly widespread concern over our increasing componentization and increasing interdependence and lack of ability to manage effectively our interdependence and our process problems. So there were groups that were defined to look at managing dependencies, to look at 'if we are short in some significant tool areas, how we can go about reducing bugs exposed to testing,' those sorts of things."

Several key interdependencies now exist. For example, Visual Basic for Applications (developed in the languages area) and OLE (developed in the business systems division) are critical parts of Excel and other applications that utilize these technologies. The Office product unit must coordinate the development of Excel, Word, PowerPoint, Mail, and Access, which all need to ship together. Williams explained that Office now has less problems because it is all under Chris Peters: "One of the reasons why Office, for example, works highly effectively is because they're all in one organization. It's when it crosses these divisions that things get to be so much of a problem." A specific idea that came from the February 1994 retreat was to create a contract template between two interdependent groups. This will also serve as a sort of best-practices checklist for managing relationships between interdependent groups, spelling out who should do what in the development and testing phases, and by when.

Cross-Group Sharing: Microsoft now has so many divisions that, as in any large company, people in one area are not necessarily well informed about what people in another area are doing. Retreats help to disseminate information, but these exchanges are infrequent and at a high level. Managers such as Dave Moore have thus encouraged middle managers and other people to share what they learn more frequently and in less formal settings. One key mechanism has been regular lunch meetings for managers in the same functions. Marc Olson, test manager in the Excel group, explained how, even prior to the formation of the Office product unit, he had regular interactions with his counterparts in other groups:

> On the testing level, I speak quite frequently with the Word testing manager. We're making a lot of effort to have features that work well between Word and Excel. . . . We have testers hooked up who are working on similar features across their groups, so they share ideas and information. We share tools back and forth. . . . We meet once a month right now for lunch for two hours—the test managers from Word, Excel and Project. We talk about "what are we are facing," "how did you solve this problem," "I am thinking about this issue," "what did you guys do". . . . We meet monthly with all of the test managers within the company, within the Worldwide Product Group. . . . We do a presentation, and we all share what our groups are doing.

Chris Williams is another strong proponent of these regular but informal meetings. Managers from user education and testing seemed most enthusiastic about them. Development managers, however, did not show up in large numbers at the meetings Moore had organized, a source of frustration for Moore and Williams:

> How to get people doing a lot more of this cross-pollination is one of the more interesting problems we've got. The director of user ed has what they call a "museum meeting," where the Microsoft user ed managers get together once a week. They sit down for an hour. Each group talks about what their products are and where they're going with their product, and exposes everybody to that. And then they go into various topics: They go into HR issues, they go into technological issues, they bring in outside speakers. . . . The testers have a once-a-month meeting where the test managers get together and they come up with a year's worth of subjects to discuss. That seems to work out well for them. Dave [Moore] used to have a monthly development managers meeting in which he'd get 15 percent of them to show up.

Program managers meet regularly in what they call "blue tray" lunches, where people give talks to share experiences or information on particular projects. Microsoft records some on videotape and circulates them. Developers in particular groups also meet regularly. Excel developers, for example, meet weekly for "brown bag" lunches where people talk about different areas of the code to help new people learn the product and to familiarize experienced people with changes or areas they did not know about yet. Sometimes they circulate memos on the code details.[10]

Even without regular meetings, ideas move across Microsoft fairly quickly. It is possible, for example, to connect people from the same function through electronic mail "aliases" or group addresses. These allow, for example, Dave Moore to send a message to all development managers, or Roger Sherman to send a message to all test managers. Moore in particular uses electronic mail in this way to share good ideas, summarize findings from new books or articles, and make suggestions for readings. People also move around the company, taking good ideas with them. As Dave Maritz, formerly the testing manager for Windows and MS-DOS, noted, "We basically are very incestuous in the way that we move around between divisions here."

Eating Your Own Dog Food: Another mechanism for learning is a concept that Microsoft people refer to as "eating your own dog food." We noted in Chapter 5 that this means groups building a particular product should, as soon as possible, use that product in their own work. If the product "tastes" no better than dog food, it is too bad: The cooks, and everyone else, still have to "eat" (use) it. For example, managers insist that the team building Windows NT or Windows 95 self-host, or use that product as their operating system as soon as there is a stable version; then the team can test it for bugs themselves. The Word and Excel groups will use the new versions of these products while under development to write memos or keep track of project data.

A broader application of this idea is for Microsoft groups to use Microsoft tools and commercial products in their own work, to experience and see what customers see and provide instant feedback to other groups. For this reason, Bill Gates mandated that program managers use Visual Basic for prototyping; and Steve Ballmer mandated that Microsoft's internal management information systems (MIS) people use Windows NT when it was in an early stage of development. Similarly, Microsoft groups generally use Microsoft's commercial language compilers rather than make or buy more specialized development tools. Dave Thompson, a development manager in the NT group, commented on the role of Gates and Ballmer:

> What those guys do is try to make sure that the right natural forces are in place. Telling the MIS group to use the stuff puts in place the right natural forces to make the product great, because you have a bunch of users who are going to beat up on a bunch of providers until it's right. Another example is [when] Visual Basic was under development, and the guys that do the network administration tool development that were in my group were mandated by Bill to use Visual Basic to develop those tools. . . . They didn't like it at all. They weren't BASIC programmers; they were object-oriented C++ programmers. . . . Well, they did it anyway, and as a result, they forced a number of significant improvements

to Visual Basic. . . . Bill had accomplished his goal. He forced the VB guys to make improvements, and the VB guys, when they delivered the product, acknowledged the contributions of this development group, which gave them lots of feedback from using their stuff. So these guys will intervene to have the right natural tensions in place.

Rick Rashid has played a similar role with Windows NT. As the chief designer of Mach, a UNIX-based micro-kernel operating system that influenced NT's design, he was able to use and test NT and make comparisons to his own system. Bill Gates did not hire Rashid to oversee NT, but he relied heavily on Rashid's evaluations. In other words, Gates had another "natural force" in place to scrutinize a crucial new product and help him guide the project: "In the case of NT, we have the guy who created Mach here running our research group. . . . He was always looking over NT, pointing out any case where it wasn't able to beat Mach. And [his group] became a source of a lot of good suggestions. . . . It worked out to the benefit to NT. We didn't hire Rick to say you're the shadow NT oversight committee. . . . With Word and Excel, I've grown up with them, I know the algorithms there, I know all those developers. NT was something fairly new. So from time to time I'd ask Rick, 'What do you think of this thing?' There's a lot of people willing to provide criticism of another team's projects around here."

Another part of this idea of eating your own dog food is that developers should use computers that the average user would have—not a "super" machine with lots of RAM and hard-disk storage space. Senior vice president Brad Silverberg, as head of the Windows group, recounted his feelings on this precept (which Microsoft does not always follow):

Windows is so dependent upon fitting the needs of the installed base that it is very important the product run well on a typical 4 to 8 megabyte memory machine. Well, if you give your developers fast 486s with 16 megs, the performance that they see is completely unconnected with the performance your customer is going to see; what runs great in 16 megs might thrash like crazy in 4 meg. You can't just say, "OK, I have a test machine. I'll run it every now and then on my 4 meg machine." So what I do is, I make sure my developers have machines that are comparable to the machines I expect my customers to have. And so my developers typically have 4 or 8 meg machines. . . . It's a little bit controversial at times, because a lot of developers want the fastest machine, the coolest technology. They don't always understand, but it works. If you look at my track record, every time I've had a project where the developers did have the kind of hardware that was a generation beyond what the customers had, the product always had performance problems.

One recent case was the internal (and beta) testing for the DoubleSpace feature in MS-DOS 6.0.[11] Microsoft relied heavily on tests with 1,000 of its own employees, who generally ran Windows and new applications programs. Microsoft's 5,000 beta testers for this product had characteristics similar to the internal Microsoft users—they tended to run Windows and new Windows applications. DoubleSpace encountered some problems, though, when running on old or faulty hardware and with certain old DOS applications. It also had a tendency to clash with a memory-saving feature in MS-DOS 6.0 called SmartDrive when used with DOS (but not Windows).[12]

There were indications of these problems before Microsoft shipped the product, but they were extremely infrequent and difficult to replicate. Nonetheless, tens of millions of MS-DOS users who had not upgraded to Windows bought MS-DOS 6.0 because of the data-compression and memory-enhancement features; they also continued to use old DOS applications because their machines were too old and small to upgrade. Many of these users then encountered problems with DoubleSpace, forcing Microsoft to issue a new release of MS-DOS 6 (for which it charged customers a small fee).[13] As Ben Slivka, development manager for MS-DOS 6.0, recalled:

At the time we shipped, there were two problems I knew of. One was [that] a certain class of copy-protected applications wouldn't run, and our feeling was that there were very little of those out there anymore. [The user] had to be someone who had this old application and hadn't upgraded the application, but he was going to upgrade the operating system. It was hard for us to understand who that person was going to be. . . . Our theory there . . . is that people who bought Windows 3.1 were pretty likely to buy MS-DOS 6, and machines were shipping with Windows 3.1. The class of people who were going to buy MS-DOS 6 but didn't have Windows 3.1 seemed to be pretty small. . . . My understanding from the marketing guys is that there's a class of people who tend to upgrade, and then there's a class of people who just don't. . . . We did these random-digit dial surveys afterwards to find out who was buying it, and 80 percent or 90 percent of the people who bought MS-DOS 6 upgrades had Windows and a 386 machine. That data matched with our expectations. . . . [Also] we felt like we were shielded by Windows 3.1. . . . But, in retrospect maybe we weren't really, and we didn't think that through as carefully as we should have. . . . We had over 1,000 people at Microsoft internally running DoubleSpace. We weren't seeing any problems. Our beta testers and our beta forum in January were saying, "Ship it! Ship it! It's ready!"

Although hindsight is 20–20, we think Microsoft could have caught and fixed these problems. Company testers, as well as internal users and beta users, could have experimented with Double-Space in everyday situations on old DOS machines and with a greater variety of DOS applications. But MS-DOS 6.0 and Double-Space also provided an opportunity for learning. As we discussed in Chapter 5, for Windows 95, its next major release of an operating system, Microsoft extended the period for internal development and testing. It also increased the number of beta testing sites to 400,000. Although the product is a year and a half late, and some features still have serious problems, these and other measures reduced the likelihood of a major bug going undetected because of a rushed ship date or inadequate beta testing.

PRINCIPLE   *Encourage feedback and improvement using*
quantitative metrics and benchmarks.

Many companies have found that a key element in managing as well as improving activities such as product development is to create quantitative metrics and benchmarks. Metrics are statistical measures and data that can evaluate quality or characterize key elements of products and processes. At least partially in response to problems documented in the postmortem reports, Microsoft projects have gradually adopted a small number of metrics that they use consistently. Managers primarily refer to these metrics to make key decisions in projects, such as when to move forward in a milestone or ship. In addition, quantitative metrics and data have served as feedback to help projects share information and improve. Microsoft managers are also now trying to use metric data to create companywide benchmarks that capture best-practice development methods. These benchmarks should make it easier for all groups to contribute their good practices as well as learn from one another; the data collection process for the benchmarks extends the project postmortem documents.

We mentioned earlier that some other companies are more advanced than Microsoft in their use of quantitative metrics and data for software development. Microsoft people also acknowledge that they can do more to identify metrics and accumulate project data that capture—in a transferable way—more of the reasoning behind the decisions of experienced and successful managers. Nonetheless, metrics and data have long had a special place in Microsoft. In their absence, people may attempt to base decisions on emotional or subjective arguments, or debate endlessly whether to include a particular feature, release a product, or adopt a different practice or tool. Microsoft groups still have these arguments, but emotional reasoning and political positioning have never worked well with Bill Gates or other senior Microsoft managers. Dave Moore, for example, commented on the importance of using data to back up suggestions that people make in program reviews: "If the person isn't presenting those suggestions with technical data, it's just going to be ignored. And these people know that. Anything that's emotionally or politically backed, just ignore it; nothing's going to happen. But if it's technically backed, and it comes up in a program review that someone suggested you do something technically and you ignored it—you didn't avail yourself of all the data to make the decision—then you're going to get totally ripped and torn apart in that program review. It's going to be the major disaster of your life."

Quantitative data does seem to attract respect in Microsoft. This consensus within the company leads us to believe that Microsoft has considerable potential to improve its ability to use metrics as well as benchmarks. These should help the company manage projects more effectively in the short term as well as improve development processes and products at more fundamental levels.

Metric Categories: We have already seen in Chapters 4 and 5, as well as in the overview of the postmortem reports, examples of the kinds of metrics and data used at Microsoft. We will discuss other examples later in this chapter in our treatment of Microsoft's usability lab and customer support organization. Overall, these metrics fall into three broad categories, and they measure or track characteristics of the following:

- *Quality*—Includes bug (error) detection and fix rates per day and week; bug severity; bug resolution; bug cluster analysis; bugs found per thousand lines of source code; usability lab results; customer satisfaction; and frequency of customer problems.
- *Product*—Includes type and number of features; product size in lines of source code, bytes of memory, and bytes of executable files; change in product size from one version to the next; degree of code reuse; speed and memory usage; and code test coverage.
- *Process*—Includes feature team sizes; estimated and actual completion dates for features, milestones, and shippable products; schedule slippage; checklists for milestone completion; and effectiveness of methods for finding bugs.

Managers use this quality, product, and process metric information throughout a project. Before a project begins, they apply the metric data to help forecast resource needs (such as the number of developers and testers); they also try to forecast scheduling requirements (such as the length of integration or buffer time). During a project, managers—as well as developers and testers—use the metric data to obtain feedback on progress, stability, and performance indicators. After completing a project, they use the metric data to characterize projects, identify problem areas, evaluate the effectiveness of bug-finding techniques, explore multiple-project trends, and highlight opportunities for improvement. Debates still continue in the company, however, about the meaning or generality of some metric data that Microsoft groups and other companies have collected. It is also easy to misinterpret specific metric numbers. Accordingly, Microsoft personnel (as well as other people) need to carefully describe why and in what context they collected the metric data. We can see in Microsoft, for example, particular efforts to distinguish the characteristics of applications as opposed to systems products and projects.

Both applications and systems projects in Microsoft focus extensively on bug metrics. Systems projects, however, place more emphasis on performance metrics that characterize the execution speed and memory usage of a product. Efficient execution of the low-level functions in systems products is absolutely critical, because higher level applications products execute these functions repeatedly. Users also demand fast interactive responses from the applications. In fact, the memory usage of a systems product, such as whether it requires 4, 8, or 16 megabytes (MB) of memory, directly translates into the size of its potential market sales. For example, many older or low-priced PCs contain only 2 MB or 4 MB of memory and are unable to run systems products such as Windows NT (which can require 16 MB of memory). In contrast, applications products tend to emphasize metrics for the product ship date and the intermediate milestone dates. Applications projects usually release new products every twelve to twenty-four months and cut features if necessary to meet target dates. Systems projects often prefer to postpone the release date, if necessary, because they must deliver an indivisible set of product features that support many different user scenarios.

Example—Bug Severity Metrics: The metrics most widely used in projects throughout Microsoft deal with various errors or defects that routinely appear in software products; most people in the software industry refer to these as "bugs." Bug detection and correction activities are inherent parts of developing software at Microsoft or any other company. Because Microsoft developers write a lot of code, and create daily incremental builds of products, they produce as well as fix a lot of bugs. Hence it is not surprising that so many metrics focus on bugs. As discussed in Chapter 5, bug data reflect the overall quality of a product and the degree and rate of improvement in product quality during development and testing. Microsoft projects also use metrics that characterize the types of problems that occur and identify areas for improvement, as well as assess progress and evaluate the readiness of a product for release. Ultimately, the number of bugs on a project is a function of many things: the skill of the people, the number of people (especially new hires), changes in the specification, the amount of new and changed code, difficulty of understanding the code, thoroughness of testing, compatibility with other products, and other factors.

Projects categorize bugs using a variety of schemes to identify their severity, how and when they were detected, when they were resolved, and how they affected features in the product. Most groups rely on a four-level severity classification scheme that resembles others in the software industry:

- *Severity 1:* The bug causes the product to halt ("crash") or be inoperable.
- *Severity 2:* The bug causes a feature to be inoperable and an alternative ("work-around") solution is not possible.
- *Severity 3:* The bug causes a feature to be inoperable and a work-around solution is possible.
- *Severity 4:* The bug is cosmetic or minor.

Table 6.1 summarizes the percentage of bugs detected across severity levels during the development of various products. These are bugs detected in a product's "official" daily build, as well as in testing releases such as beta tests. (Microsoft detects and corrects these bugs prior to the final public release of a product.)

For this particular set of projects, the bug data suggest a downward trend in the percentage of level 1 bugs in products released from year to year. For example, MacWord 4.0 came out in April 1989 and had 31.5 percent level 1 bugs.[14] Works for Windows 2.0 appeared in September 1991 and had 21.2 percent level 1 bugs.[15] Money 2.0 was released in August 1992 and had 10.2 percent level 1 bugs.[16] Improvement in software development methods provides one possible explanation for this trend.

Managers also like to see the percentage of higher severity bugs decrease from one product version to the next version. For example, the percentages of higher-severity bugs—levels 1, 2, and 3—decreased

Table 6.1　Distribution of Bug Severity Levels

Release Date	Product	Severity Level (%)			
		1	2	3	4
4/89	MacWord 4.0	31.5	19.1	38.1	11.3
	MacWord 5.0	28.7	14.2	34.5	22.6
9/91	Works for Windows 2.0	21.2	25.8	39.0	14.0
3/92	Excel 4.0	17.3	24.1	42.7	15.9
3/92	Project for Windows 3.0	17.0	34.0	40.0	9.0
8/92	Money 2.0	10.2	21.6	47.5	20.7

Note: Rows add up to approximately 100 percent, representing all bugs for a particular product. Source: "MacWord 4.0 Development Postmortem"; "MacWord Cumulative Bug Rates"; "Works for Windows 2.0 Development Postmortem Report"; "WinWorks 2.0 Testing Postmortem"; Jon De Vaan, "Microsoft Excel 4.0 Post-Mortem,"6/8/92; Glenn Slayden, "Microsoft Project for Windows Version 3.0 Development Postmortem," 3/16/92; "WinProj 3.0 Post Project Analysis," 4/2/92; and "Money 2.0 Test Summary Report" (all Microsoft internal documents).

slightly between MacWord 4.0 and MacWord 5.0. If this trend continued for this particular product, it would suggest that developers were adding or changing features in a less error-prone manner.

Limitations of Current Metrics: Microsoft's current metrics are simply a minimal (or perhaps a subminimal) set. They need to include much deeper process and product metrics that help anticipate and understand problems before they occur; projects then would have more lead time to prevent problems, or at least prepare to react to them. Companies such as Motorola, Hewlett-Packard, NEC, and Hitachi have successfully applied metrics to accomplish these deeper goals. Mike Maples argued, however, that Microsoft people find and fix more bugs than they formally count: "The only reservation I have about KLOC [the thousand-lines-of-code metric] is that we're not as rigorous as some people in tracking it. In errors per KLOC, we don't record all the errors that developers find in design reviews and the errors that the developer finds as he's writing his code. Now, as a concept, we want to keep moving more and more of the error-finding earlier and earlier in the project. Zero defects and a lot of things keep moving errors early in the project, but the way we do our counting would make it look like there are fewer bugs found."

Furthermore, even though Microsoft collects and uses a variety of metric data, its projects still rely on many subjective rules of thumb that the company has not yet quantified into metrics. Dave Moore tried to capture this subjective knowledge using metrics and collections of historical data, but he encountered resistance from developers and managers who argued that their projects or products were unique or different. Chris Williams commented on this frustration:

> One of the problems we've got is that we have a great deal of this seat-of-the-pants information that is very, very poorly transmitted from one [person] to another. You look at the kinds of things that Chris [Peters] and some of these people who have shipped a lot of software know. They just know it in their gut. . . . It's very difficult for them to get it into a form that can be transmitted. So we end up with a videotape of Chris talking about it. Well, that's not good enough. Chris, come on, what was the thing that kicked you over into thinking this wasn't going to ship? It's a *metric*. It's an "I looked at the [bug] open/close chart, and it just looked wrong to me." Why did it look wrong? . . . It's just that there are people who give seat-of-the-pants [data], but they don't refer to them as metrics.

Metric-Based Process Improvement: In 1994, Mike Maples created a new organizational structure to bring together people focusing on process improvement and training within the functional groups. He tapped Chris Williams, who had been somewhat outspoken with regard to the need to be more systematic in software development, to become director of product development and head of the new structure. Williams, a thirty-eight-year-old computer science graduate from Bowling Green University, had been working for Fox Software as a development manager when Microsoft acquired this company. He worked in compiler development for Microsoft before taking on the new post.

Under the reorganization, all of the functional directors now report to Williams. These include the directors of testing, development, program management, user education, and internal tools. Also reporting to Williams are the manager of training (who heads a group of fourteen Microsoft people plus some outside contractors) and the manager of usability testing (who heads a group of thirty to thirty-five people). (The total number of people reporting to Williams is around one hundred, including Middle East product development, which has special language needs.) Williams viewed the reorganization as a deliberate effort to improve knowledge transfer, self-examination, and learning across the different groups. These goals have taken on a new importance in Microsoft because product units are now trying to share more components. Projects now need to predict schedules and produce quality products for each other, as well as for outside customers. They can no longer focus solely on creating the best possible product for their own needs, or for their individual set of customers:

> I think the big thing that Dave [Moore], other people, and I have recognized is that our development process has been so focused on creating an outstanding product . . . that, in some cases, we've driven toward that at the expense of following a procedure that allows us to control the process. Some groups have obviously done more of it than others, but it's been largely inconsistent. We don't do a good job of leveraging between the groups, and sharing the lessons learned between them. So my focus is headed towards trying to leverage as much as possible the knowledge that people have gained from one group to another, as well as to get people to do more self-examination of how they do things, so they get better at them. We're surrounded by incredibly bright people who, if given the priority of figuring out the best possible procedures to do something, will be very good at it. But in the past, their priority has been always to create the best possible product at the right time in the marketplace. And we're now starting to learn, as we get more "componentized" and more interdependent, that having some common practices and procedures is important.

Process-Focused (Not Product-Focused) Postmortems: As part of this initiative for process improvement, Chris Williams, Roger

Sherman, Dave Moore, and others are now working to improve metrics both for technical developers and project managers. In particular, they see the need for more process metrics that explain *why* something went wrong during a project, as opposed to just what went wrong. In addition, projects sometimes do not use the same terms or do not define them consistently, a situation that Williams and other managers plan to change. (For example, Microsoft does not really have a uniform definition for the pivotal milestone term "code complete.") Williams and his team also intend to modify and extend the project postmortem process to incorporate more metric data, including both the gathering of new data and the sharing of relevant existing data. Finally, they hope to use the metric data to define and communicate companywide benchmarks that capture best-practice development methods.

Williams is especially anxious to take the postmortem process to the next level. Groups have done a fine job of chronicling their problems in these reports, but the postmortems often fall short on analyzing why problems occur and what solutions are possible. Furthermore, individual groups do not have a consistent process in place to ensure that they do not repeat the same mistakes in future projects, nor is there a systematic way for projects to learn from one another. Williams observed, for example, that almost every postmortem in every group cites problems with schedules getting out of control because team members keep adding features:

> Consistently, you go back through them and you will always find a significant "I'm out of control because I haven't shut the faucet off on the features." It's sad that we learn that lesson over and over. I think in some measure that's the way things are. I think in another measure it's because we do a lousy job of estimating, therefore we do a lousy job of costing the additional feature when we get around to it. . . .
>
> One of the things that Dave [Moore] did . . . very well was to get people to take a look at their postmortem process and how they did things. People have done a very good job at the time of a postmortem of examining how they did things and what could have gone better. The only problem we've had is that they haven't made it into a cycle of reevaluating, establishing some new priorities, and moving ahead. . . . They say we're going to change it, but nobody says we're going to change it by how

much, and nobody stops to look six months later—did you change it by that much? . . . Postmortem is a phase that everyone has built into their brains already. Everybody understands what that means, and everybody counts on spending some time doing that. We just want to . . . focus a little bit less on what happened and focus more on how it happened. How did you get out of control? Not "So and so never gave me the bug list when I needed it," but "What was missing in order to make sure you got a bug list when you needed it?" . . . The problem with the postmortem is it's . . . not done in an orderly fashion where you work your way through the development process from the beginning to the end. And that's what we were hoping to control. . . . Largely what's captured now on a postmortem is pissing and moaning.

Dave Moore agreed with this assessment of the postmortems: "The whole thing about postmortems is that it's good to have them, but . . . people . . . complain about the same problem over and over again. A lot of whining—that sort of thing. A lot of times that's all it is: Get it off your chest. Okay, fine, it's off your chest; go try and make some improvement. That applies to some of the things that are in the postmortems. There's other stuff in the postmortems we definitely should have been fixing. There should have been accountability for making improvement in the process for the next release."

Best-Practice Benchmarking: The best-practice benchmarking idea combines the concept of a postmortem with a process audit. It should also take less time than writing up a postmortem report, and it should create an easily shared list of good practices. To do this, Williams, Sherman, and Moore have been devising best-practice benchmarking questions. (For example: "Did development deliver a detailed testing release document or a similar document with the release?" "Did you estimate the number of bugs to be found in Milestone X?" "Did you review your feature list?") These may serve as a basis for process audits and provide a framework for conducting a partial benchmark analysis during a project—after Milestone 2, for example. This would provide some early in-process or "leading" indicators if a project is in trouble or not. The full benchmarking process will examine internal practices for each function, compare practices in different groups, and compare Microsoft performance with external process benchmarks and performance standards; these might include the Software Engineering Institute and the International Standards Organization, or industry customer satisfaction data. Williams explained the goals:

> We're working to develop a system of process assessment that will be very much tuned to our development process. This is substantially different than your standard consultant relationship with his vendor or with his supplier. We're calling it our Best Practices Benchmark Program. We are developing a set of development practices, all the way through the entire process, . . . that people should be paying attention to. . . . We want to use a postmortem as an opportunity to benchmark yourself. How did you do things against the best wisdom we've gathered to date? We presume this will evolve into a standard. Our goal is to lay out some fairly concrete metrics at that time. . . . We're probably going to end up with something in the neighborhood of 250 [guidelines].

Williams will not force groups to do the benchmarking, but he is starting with projects that have expressed an interest. If this benchmarking effort succeeds, Williams will have the metrics that he wants for groups to manage projects more effectively as well as learn from each other more systematically. Like Dave Moore before him, however, Williams expects to encounter resistance, especially since his new team is attempting a much broader initiative to influence how projects organize and manage themselves:

> We're very interested in not making this be a radical departure, but being an encouragement for self-examination. . . . The last thing I want . . . is someone to come into it as if they were going to a dental exam. So what we want to do is first work with groups that are interested and have already expressed an interest. Then I plan to go selling to groups after that. And I presume that at that point some groups will have found this of interest and discussed it with other groups, and there will be some groundswell of value here seen. . . . My gut feel is that 75 to 80 percent of the groups will decide that this is of value and want to do this. Over a period of eighteen months or two years, we'll have gotten there. . . .
>
> I think that this program will be an abject failure without some ability to correlate metrics to it. I'm a big fan of "You can't control what you

can't measure." I don't necessarily think we need to be wildly anal and be tracking all kinds of things, but I think we don't do a very good job of tracking a bunch of things in a consistent fashion—like, for example, bugs per developer week . . . One of the things that I'm pushing for right now is that we do a lousy job of examining estimated versus actual, particularly with elapsed time. So, for example, a developer will say, "I think that'll take me three weeks." And four and a half weeks into it, we'll go, "Are you done yet?" And he'll go, "Almost." Then he finishes, and we go, "Whew!" We never stop to say, "Okay, that took you four and a half weeks. Why? What was wrong? What kinds of things did you run into?"

Roger Sherman, who became director of testing in 1993, is especially concerned with writing process documents that capture good practices. Only a few groups did this during 1988 and 1989 following a Maples request after he first came to Microsoft (see Chapter 1). Sherman joined Microsoft in 1988 after studying computer science and music at Oberlin College. He worked at Boeing and then entered Microsoft as a tester in consumer software; his group wrote a document on their development and testing processes in 1988, but did not update the material. Sherman is also now looking to define common terms and metrics so that Microsoft groups can learn from different projects more consistently and define a standard process that they can all work together to improve:

> What I'm doing is writing a document, an updated version of all of these, with commonly defined terms. Then I plan to take that to the development community at Microsoft and say, "I'd like for us to agree that this should be the standard way in which we develop products." Now there are a couple of things to say that are fairly important. One is, what I mostly would like to get is a standardized set of terminology so that when we pull metrics out of multiple products we can do valid comparisons. I think this is a strategic advantage that Microsoft has. We've got so many development projects going on that we can learn a lot faster about what works and what doesn't work because of the multiple instances of these projects. But if one group defines what "code complete" is in a completely different way than another group, then all your statistics . . . are bad. The second thing is I'd like to have . . . a standard off-the-shelf process. I don't want it to be a cohesive process; I would like people to experiment with it. When they do something that's different, I

would like them to register what they're doing with us so that we track it as a difference. And if it works better, spread the word about that, or change the standard to accommodate it. I would like to see this become a best-practices document . . . that is constantly updated and incorporates the best practices that we know and does not become a bureaucratic, burdensome thing.

PRINCIPLE   *View customer support as part of the product and as data for improvement.*

In addition to trying to learn more from internal sources—company projects—Microsoft has recently made extraordinary efforts to learn from external sources: its tens of millions of customers. Customers can be an invaluable source of information, and they now have many opportunities to provide feedback directly into Microsoft's product development groups (see Figure 6.1). For example, program managers analyze activity-based planning data as well as information from customer "Wish Lines" and monthly *Offline Plus* reports that analyze customer calls. Program managers and developers test prototypes in Microsoft's usability labs during projects; projects also release an alpha version of their product for internal use and feedback. An external beta release to selected customers follows for real-life testing. Developers then rely on this feedback to make additional refinements before releasing a final product to manufacturing and the marketplace.

Even Microsoft's product support services (PSS) division uses the usability labs to conduct what it calls "supportability testing." This examines how difficult new features are to support, as well as experiments with different ways of diagnosing problems. After shipping a new product, Microsoft puts developers and testers on PSS phone lines and in "situation-room teleconferences" with PSS personnel from Microsoft's various support centers. These practices provide an opportunity for developers and testers to hear directly about what makes customers complain. PSS also conducts surveys of customer satisfaction with Microsoft products, customer support, and the company overall. In addition, it cooperates with marketing groups to research how customers use products

Figure 6.1 Customer Input During Product Development

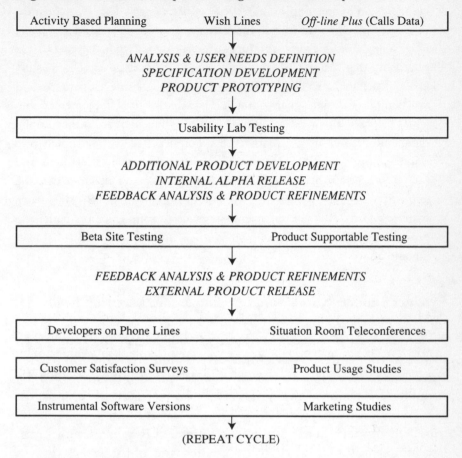

made by Microsoft and its competitors. Microsoft also releases "instrumented versions" of its products that track every keystroke and mouse click to create an electronic record of how users actually use products. The cycle then repeats.

It is clear from this sequence of activities—which Microsoft did not follow systematically before 1990—that customer support and customer feedback have become tightly integrated with improving products and the development process. The benefits are twofold: reduce support costs, and increase sales by creating more satisfied customers. An application for a quality award that Microsoft submitted in 1993 describes this philosophy for customer support:

Microsoft's support philosophy emphasizes that every customer support contact is an opportunity to improve product design—and, consequently, to reward customers with products that are more usable and less likely to require attention from a product support organization. As practiced at Microsoft, this customer-driven approach to product design changes the goals of the software development cycle. Previously, developers focused on "computer design" goals—they felt satisfied if they implemented elegant designs without extra coding. Now, they feel satisfied if they implement features that users can understand on first use. . . . The first step in implementing usability at Microsoft is to learn what tasks users face, and how they use software to accomplish them. This data helps to decide the appropriate feature set for new or enhanced software. PSS staff work with product developers at every stage of this information gathering process, using data from customer contacts and assisting in special testing and analysis.[17]

Product Support Strategy and Organization: Microsoft has had a public image as being relatively unresponsive to customers. It has released products that are hard to use (such as MS-DOS compared to Apple's Macintosh operating system), and slow and clumsy for some sets of users (such as Macintosh Word 6.0). It has survived a reputation for not paying much attention to customer support (at least compared to WordPerfect, known for unlimited and usually excellent support on a toll-free line). Richard Barth, a senior product manager for Windows NT, recalled the old days: "It was a laugh if you thought about what you put up with as a customer for support three to five years ago. You could call us only during certain hours; you might or might not get somebody who knew what the hell they were doing. We had some very, very talented people, but that was not a priority for anybody in the industry."

In Microsoft, this began changing with the introduction of Windows 3.0 in 1990, and the changes intensified with Windows 3.1 in 1992. The new Windows operating system and the new Windows applications were selling in the tens of millions, and thousands of customers were beginning to call Microsoft every day with questions. In addition, Microsoft was in the process of shifting from selling software primarily to computer hardware manufacturers to selling mainly to individual customers through retail stores. Individual customers who purchased software were much more likely to demand support from the software maker. Market research also indicated that PC customers, like mainframe and minicomputer customers before them, were increasingly viewing support from the software provider as part of the software product. To keep these millions of new customers, Microsoft had to change.

One alternative was to follow the path of WordPerfect (which is now owned by Novell) and build a huge organization to answer telephone lines more quickly and effectively. Another alternative was to try to capture information from telephone calls more systematically, channel this information and other customer data into the development organization, and make products much easier to use—thereby reducing the need for customers to call. A third alternative was to become more efficient in handling the rising number of calls, such as by automating as much of the support process as possible, and by charging different fees to discourage calls, make calling periods more predictable, and help finance the support operations.

As it turned out, Microsoft would do all these things. Bill Gates led the way: He concluded during one of his "think weeks" (which resulted in a memo sent to Microsoft executives and leaked to the press) that Microsoft could no longer afford to neglect customers and had to improve its support policies and organization. He also promised the public that his company would provide better support for its new Windows products. Accordingly, Microsoft significantly expanded the number of people it has answering phones. This rose from a couple dozen in the mid-1980s to more than two thousand in the United States alone (almost one out of five of Microsoft's U.S. employees); another thousand support personnel work overseas in thirty-six countries. Microsoft organizes the phone technicians by product groups. All told, they support approximately two hundred products. Trish May, an MBA from the University of Wisconsin and former director of marketing for product support services, recalled the transition that Microsoft has undergone:

> I'd say the turning point was about two and a half years ago. . . . It was in two places. One was [when] Bill publicly stated in a forum that sup-

port is a very important part of our business, and we will ensure that when you call on Microsoft Windows—and this was at [the] Windows 3 launch—you will be assured of getting high-quality support. The other . . . was the internal memo that eventually made its way to the press that Bill wrote about [in] his "Bill Think Week" piece. One of the comments was that he wanted to invest in product support and that it was an important part of the business, and that it was going to continue to be an important part of the business. . . . We have research that shows that it's an integral part. And so approximately two and a half years ago, we significantly increased the amount of investment and brought in a management organization to focus on how we really enhance this.

May acknowledged that there were two pillars to the new strategy: One was to make products easier to use, and the other was to build up the support organization. The latter included initiatives to automate as much as possible and make customers more self-sufficient by providing more information to them, such as through CD-ROM disks. May said that Microsoft studied WordPerfect but did not want to duplicate its costly and free support organization:

The strategy has two parts to it. One is . . . to reduce the amount of calls that we'll have in the end by designing a user interface and product to address questions in advance, and having support and documentation that will reduce the number of questions. But the other strategy is a very significant investment to ensure that the quality of the service that we deliver is high. And so I would say it's an equal degree of emphasis. We've looked at the way WordPerfect administers support, for example, and we're learning from them. But we also look at how you most efficiently and effectively deliver high-quality support. What are the attributes that drive satisfaction? So, with an input-output model, let's look at where can you get the most efficient spike in customer satisfaction by affecting what attributes, and really fine-tuning that model. Our goal is, for every dollar spent, how do you move that dial most effectively? . . .

When you look at what we call our one-to-one incidents versus our one-to-many, which is electronic services, two years ago, I believe over 80 percent of the incidents we had were handled by people over the phone. Today, only 50 percent of our incidents are handled by people. The other 50 percent are handled electronically through forums, our FastTip service, our bulletin boards, and other electronic medium, which expands our reach more cost-effectively. So we've significantly invested in how we deliver the service and what is a cost-effective way to reach more people.

Calls Data and Handling: As Bill Gates noted in his list of company strengths in product development (see Chapter 1), the enormous number of calls to Microsoft provides an extraordinary opportunity to analyze customer needs and frustrations. Microsoft receives approximately sixty thousand inquiry "incidents" *per day*—forty thousand electronic queries by computer and touch-tone telephone, and twenty thousand phone calls handled personally by support engineers. The telephone calls average about 1 for every 3 product units or "boxes" sold, a significant improvement over the one call for every 1.5 to 2 boxes that Microsoft experienced several years ago. Each telephone call into PSS averages about twelve minutes in length: Support engineers spend five to seven minutes diagnosing the problem, two to three minutes discussing a solution, and one to two minutes closing the conversation. The average delay for answering calls was about four minutes in 1991; this dropped to between one and two minutes during 1992 and 1993, despite a doubling of the number of calls. Microsoft answers about 80 percent of the calls in less than one minute.[18] Detailed analyses of call patterns provide much useful information on how to improve products to reduce the number of calls. The data also suggest how to price services to discourage calls or, at least, make call demand more predictable.

Telephone Calls Analysis. People who call PSS are in the minority of customers. Microsoft data indicates that 70 percent of software users never call, and 15 percent of customers generate 70 percent of the call volume. Most people who call only do so once or twice per product and usually within the first ninety days after a purchase, when calls are free. Historical data indicates that 40 to 60 percent of calls in the first ninety days relate to setting up or installing the software; other common questions concern printing, usage of new or changed features, the operating environment, and interoperability with other products.[19] Most users first resort to asking a neighbor for help if they have a problem. Then they will go to the product's help files, the manual, or the retailer that sold them their computer or the software. Because calling Microsoft's customer support lines is a last resort for most customers, understanding the needs of this select group of users is important to reduce the number of calls. Studying these people has encouraged Microsoft to make certain features easier to use, as well as to offer better help files and manuals. Microsoft also decided to provide more information and training to computer retailers, software consulting firms, and experienced users who tend to help people around them.

Microsoft also knows which type of products generate the most calls and over what periods of time. In 1993, for example, 70 percent of all calls came for the five products that were among the highest volume sellers: 31 percent for Windows, 15 percent for Word, 12 percent for Excel, 8 percent for FoxPro, and 4 percent for MS-DOS. Microsoft also carefully tracks how long the average call is for each product and the directly correlated figure of how much the average call for each product costs. The overall average cost per call is around $12 for Microsoft (below the industry average of more than $15).[20] But costs, call patterns, and call lengths varied widely by product; for example, the average call on Word for the Macintosh cost Microsoft merely $7 in 1993, compared to $12 on Word for Windows. This difference appears to reflect that the Macintosh product was still a bit easier to use. Windows users also tend to call more often, perhaps due to large numbers who have been switching from DOS programs.

Microsoft used to ask each division to contribute equally to financing the product support organization. Since July 1991, however, Microsoft has been charging support costs to the individual product units. This means that if a group makes a product that is difficult to use and has many features that become "call generators," the product unit has to pay for all of those support costs. "Activities-based costing" is the term that Microsoft has given the collection of procedures that it uses to determine the exact cost of each call and how to charge the individual product units. Mike Maples, driven by Gates's newfound concern with PSS but also by his more general efforts to cut costs, explained how he became involved in redirecting PSS:

Two and a half years ago I started looking at the head count. We had ignored them at that time. All of a sudden I realized there was more head count over there than we had in developers, and I said, "This is a bad trend." So the first thing we did is, we started directly accounting all of the product support costs to the products. Now every product gets a monthly report of how many calls, what percentage of their revenue, what are the problems that they're having. It's been enlarged to be worldwide. The reason I started on this is that when I first came, nobody paid any attention to the cost of the product: You know, $20 out of $500 revenue, who cares about the product cost. So we put a task force together, and we came up with some simple guidelines. We were able to reduce 8 or 10 percent off the cost of goods—8 or 10 percent off of 20 percent. Big, big changes. All that just comes right to the bottom line in terms of profit.

And so it became obvious that the thing to do when you have a problem is let everybody worry about it, and so that's what we started doing with PSS; we started reporting to everybody what happens. Then we had some really simple guidelines, like, why not, on every release of your product, have half as many calls per unit or half as much time per unit as you had before as an objective? And then you start thinking, well, how do you solve that problem? Well, it's obvious. You have to work on the highest-volume problems. So, if printing envelopes is a high-volume problem, then put some folks on worrying about making that better.

Maples set a target of limiting total support costs to 8 percent of product revenues (compared to about 16 percent for WordPerfect, according to Microsoft estimates). Again, there were wide differences among products: About 7 percent of Excel and Word revenues went to product support, and 6 percent of revenues for consumer products. This compared to 20 percent of Windows revenues and 25 percent of Windows NT revenues. Microsoft quickly found out that corporate client-server products such as Windows NT and LAN Manager are more expensive to support, because they generate more and longer calls than more common PC software and require more sophisticated support engineers. A successful move into these new product domains, therefore, has required a significant parallel investment in the support organization.

The pricing structure, as well as an analysis of the correlation between the type of product and the type of calls received, are essential to control and forecast demand for phone support on new and existing products. Some products generate most calls in the first few weeks or months, while others generate calls over longer periods. Microsoft and other PC software companies generally give customers free support at least for the first three months after purchasing a product, but customers have to pay for the phone call (except for WordPerfect). The industry trend, including at Novell's WordPerfect division for its new products, has been to move away from unlimited free support to fee-based support. To deal with products that it expects to generate calls for many months if not years, Microsoft has also instituted pricing policies comparable to what other firms have done in other industries. For basic products such as Word and Excel, customers can receive free support during working hours via a toll call. For these and most other Microsoft products, after ninety days, customers pay $2 per minute on a 900 number for twenty-four hour support. Customers who want support twenty-four hours a day (such as for corporate products) also have a choice of payment schemes: $2 per minute, $25 a call, $195 a year, or $20,000 a year for premium support services. With this pricing schedule, on average, 50 percent of calls for a new product over its lifetime (including all versions) come in the first six months.

Support Technology. Microsoft's use of computers and communications technology to make customer support less costly as well as to analyze incoming information more effectively takes three forms: the computer system or "workbench" used by the support engineers, the telephone system, and the automated information services available to customers.

The "PSS Workbench" includes a set of integrated tools, created by Microsoft's internal information technology group, running on a high-powered PC. These tools track issues raised by customers (call volumes, lengths, wait times, calls per product, calls per customer type, and calls per problem type), and they store customer-specific information on system configurations and issues. They also create specific to-do lists for individual engineers to follow up on, track individual work loads, produce reports based on the Workbench data, facilitate ordering of no-charge items for customers (such as replacement disks), and provide access to the Microsoft Knowledge Base, which is an electronic database or library of technical support information.[21] Support engineers can search through the database using regular search words and phrases; they can also add to the database by writing articles to answer previously unasked questions. Microsoft distributes part of this knowledge base to customers on CD-ROMs and over on-line networks, including CompuServe and Genie.

The phone system includes a feature called "Wrap-Up." This allows technicians to "punch in" digits on the telephone in order to record some minimal information on each call that Microsoft receives. Mark Seidenverg, a PSS product development consultant and veteran of nine years in Microsoft, praised the technology as the "Cadillac" of phone systems, which includes a software "bridge" to the PSS workstations. The objective of the workstation and phone systems is to analyze customer calls quickly and create lists of prioritized problems for the product development organization. Seidenverg described the process and benefits of logging information from a customer phone call:

> Every customer contact is an opportunity to improve our products. . . . We get some amount of information about every call. Right now there's a standard template for each product . . . [with] some standard categories that it starts out with. We want to see overall some big area stuff, like how many calls are on setup, how many are on printing, how many are on general usage, how many are on the operating environment, how many are on interoperability. . . . Then, below that, we track number of features or issues, basically, what was the call about. This is done through the Wrap-Up mechanisms on the telephone today. You have a paper list, and then you plug some data into the telephone that represents what the issue is about. It's summary information. You can take a product code, which is three digits, and then add on the UCC code, which is that level that I just told you about. It's just another digit. And then we have problem code digits that come after that. So if it's a specific problem with setup, we can know how many calls we got on that.
>
> This all goes back to the older days of support: Your support guys and you would go tell somebody about a problem and they'd go, "How many calls did you get on it?" You'd go, "Oh, we don't know." And they'd say,

"Well, if I can only fix ten things, what are the ten most important things for me to fix?" And you'd go, "Well, I don't know." This allows us to prioritize this stuff.

Most important in the area of automated support—which eliminates the need for people to answer phones—is FastTips. This round-the-clock service available over touch-tone phones provides technical information on key areas of Microsoft products and answers to common questions. Another automated support system, MS Down-load, is an electronic bulletin board where Microsoft puts out new drivers (software that runs peripheral devices like printers, video screens, or pointing devices), product fixes (patches), and product notes; users access this system over modems. PSS also runs the Microsoft Information Network. This includes the Microsoft Developer Network, which provides technical information to developers on CD-ROM disks updated four times a year. It also includes the Microsoft TechNet, another CD-ROM database updated monthly that provides detailed product information and training information, as well as parts of the PSS Knowledge Base tool, the library of technical support information used by PSS support personnel.[22]

Feedback for Product Improvement: A key challenge for Microsoft is to organize and analyze the massive amounts of information it receives daily from customers from various sources. It must then channel this information in a useful and parsimonious form to the development groups. Handled correctly, this information can help development groups set priorities in fixing bugs, make products easier to use, and provide new features that customers really want. Another problem is that statistical summaries convey limited amounts of information.

To exploit customer feedback, Microsoft recently established a Product Improvement Group and introduced other mechanisms to analyze and channel customer information to the product groups. So many feature ideas and improvements have come from customer input that it is impossible to list them here; key examples include product setup, the design philosophy behind drivers for printing and video displays in Windows, and standardization of tool bars and features across products. Managers also ask developers to spend more time making products easier to use and even have them answer telephone calls whenever Microsoft introduces a new product. These measures complement other types of user research and product usability testing.

Product Improvement Initiatives. In 1991, Microsoft organized a Product Improvement Group of about half a dozen senior PSS technicians. Each specializes in different products and acts as a consultant to the development organizations for those products. Mark Seidenverg, an Excel specialist, discussed the idea of such a group with Pete Higgins, Jeff Raikes, and Mike Maples and then launched it, calling it "Microsoft's secret weapon. We are called the Product Improvement Group and we are product development consultants. . . . Our mission is to help Microsoft better meet its customers' needs, improve our products through customer feedback and suggestions. Our strategy to accomplish that is to develop methods, systems, procedures that will capture that information, quantify it, and deliver it in an easily testable format, meaningfully. It really means developing really great ways of boiling down a lot of anecdotal information into something statistically valid."

The Product Improvement Group established two invaluable mechanisms for analyzing customer data: the monthly report called *Off-line Plus*, and a separate customer suggestion database. The report is organized primarily by the activities defined in the product, and it analyzes all the key information gathered from customer calls to Microsoft for the preceding month, broken down by product. Particularly important is a list of "the 'top ten' reasons why customers contact PSS worldwide for each product."[23] Microsoft distributes *Off-line Plus* on paper and through electronic mail to individuals in the product groups as well as to managers. The main source of input for the suggestion database is the Microsoft Wish Lines, a phone number system that customers can call to make suggestions for new functions or features. (Customers can also write in by letter.) PSS staff transcribe the suggestions into a database available throughout the company. Issues of *Off-line Plus* include the top fifteen suggestions for each product.

Problems and suggestions identified in *Off-line Plus* get high visibility; Gates and other senior executives are avid readers. As a result, product groups generally respond within three or four hours to problems identified in the report and let PSS know what they intend to do about them. As Seidenverg observed, "The communication loop works so that somebody from each product group comments back on each of our issues saying, basically, 'Here is the problem.' And they say what they're going to do about it or when they're going to do something about it. Sometimes they've already done things about those problems." Usually, a person from the testing group takes responsibility for logging the problems identified by PSS into their product group database and making sure that developers work on the problems that still exist. Program managers are concerned both with what features need fixing in the next version of the product and with customer suggestions for new features or feature changes. Individual products may get hundreds of suggestions from customers in any given month, so the prioritization that Seidenverg's group does is important:

> Now all of those suggestions, too—and it varies for Excel between two and six hundred a month—go into a database. And we not only review them monthly, but they are accumulated in a database. Then during the planning process all of those get reassigned back out to program managers, who go through them yet again. We don't want those things to get lost. We really feel like it is a competitive advantage. . . . Your program managers own a set of features. They will say what are the calls you get on those features. . . . Then our job is to tell them in a really qualified and quantified way what needs to be fixed or, if there's a trade-off to be made, which is the best way to go on the trade-off, because everything just isn't that clean.

The Product Improvement Group also holds intensive sessions with people in marketing, program management, development, testing, and user education from each product group. These sessions analyze in more depth why people call PSS for a particular product, and what type of changes in features or in documentation might help reduce calls. Seidenverg referred to this as "premorteming" a new product:

We spent eight hours with about eighty people from the Excel business unit over a two-day period reviewing everything that anybody calls about on any kind of regular basis. We do those surveys a few times a year. We do them for "pre-morteming" a product and "post-morteming." . . . As we go through the process, we'll collect a lot of information about how people are using our products and what problems they are having and what things they would like to see. And we will give them this huge fifty- to sixty-page document and a database. . . . Then we start with the vision statement and the spec. Then, as we go through the spec, when we re- view the specifications, they'll say if they are doing this because of PSS stuff. And they'll ask us, does this solve the problem you told us about, are customers going to understand this implementation, how should it be documented—those kinds of things. So we get through the specifica- tion review side and alpha code review. . . . Then we go through a docu- mentation review where there's a person, an engineer, one of our group, that sits in on every piece of documentation creation to represent the customers—what do they need to know, what are the key concepts they need to understand.

Reallocation of Developers' Time. **Data from PSS have helped Mi- crosoft shift the time that developers spend. Mike Maples recalled that when he joined Microsoft, developers mostly worked on new features. They paid little attention to making existing features eas- ier to use or better in some other respect:** "What we'd like to do is have developers spend about a third of their time on improving what already exists, about a third of their time on new features, and about a third of their time on *compatibility*, or consistency with the rest of the world. That could mean running Lotus spread- sheets or fitting into somebody's network, or whatever, and/or just being consistent or compatible with your past stuff. Before that, we would probably have thought that we would spend 80 percent or 90 percent of our time on new features, instead of on features that make things simpler or better. . . . PSS really helps us a lot fig- uring out what are those areas."

Maples and other managers have also insisted that developers spend some time over in PSS to help staff the phone lines after shipping a new product. Administrative assistants in the groups take on the job of this scheduling. Some developers manage to avoid this duty when schedules are tight; in general, however, developers seem to feel that spending time in PSS is an important use of their time. It is useful both for developers to train and assist PSS staff, as well as to gain firsthand experience with users frustrated enough to call Microsoft directly. Brad Silverberg recalled when he started this practice in the systems group after his team introduced Windows 3.0 in 1990:

> Whenever we ship a product, for the next week, or two weeks, or three weeks, whatever is necessary, the development team is assigned to tech support. . . . They have these big peaks, and they can't handle the demand, so [developers] go over there and train them. . . . That was probably the first thing that I did when I came to Microsoft. Windows 3.0 had just launched, and it was a big success, and they were overwhelmed. So I sent my entire development team to product support for two weeks to help do the support. And it really does sensitize them to the customer. That's another philosophy of mine, which is to really get the developers, everybody, to take the end-user point of view. To remember that they're our boss, that the only reason we're successful is that they like our products.

Maples was a strong supporter of this policy in the applications groups, where particular problems such as "mail merge" (a feature in Word that allows a user to merge a list of addresses with a common data source, such as a form letter) have become infamous. Sending developers over to PSS both helps to sensitize the developers and give a signal to PSS people that their jobs are important, too. Maples described one of his visits:

> We try to get every developer to go sit for a day a quarter with PSS and just listen on the phones, and to encourage that I go over and do that. I was walking around in the Word group one time, and they had this couch behind these guys. . . . I said, "Well, what's that?" And they said, "That's the mail-merge couch. Whenever we get a mail-merge call we know it's a thirty-minute call, so a guy takes it and just walks over and lays on the couch, and talks the user through it." An interesting problem to fix! But putting people over there makes the PSS guys feel a lot better. It's kind of the old Hawthorne effect. . . . Just as importantly, they will hear and see the things that trigger that there is some area that needs to be improved.

In addition, PSS has established the practice of holding "situa-tion-room teleconferences" twice a week or so after the launch of each new major product. These bring together an entire develop-ment team and link them with support technicians at Microsoft's different support locations, providing another close look at what types of problems customers are having. Microsoft also circulates minutes from the teleconferences to let other groups know what happens in these sessions. As with other process innovations, the Excel group started this practice.

User Research and Usability Testing: Apart from phone calls and other PSS contacts, Microsoft now utilizes a variety of mecha-nisms to study users in different contexts. These studies include re-search on user activities and products in the field, as well as testing product features under development—in other words, the usability lab analyses.

PSS Studies. Microsoft spends half a million dollars per year on market research just on product support services and customer sat-isfaction. One major element is the annual End-User Customer Sat-isfaction Benchmark survey, done by an outside research firm for Microsoft, which tries to measure customer satisfaction by identify-ing what is necessary to get and keep a customer. This survey cov-ers more than a thousand users, divided roughly in half between Microsoft and non-Microsoft users. The questions to Microsoft users analyze satisfaction with Microsoft products, with Microsoft as a company, and with Microsoft product support. Customers who are very satisfied in all three areas and who would definitely buy and definitely recommend Microsoft products rate as "secure" cus-tomers (users unlikely to switch to another company). The survey also compares satisfaction levels between Microsoft and key com-petitors and their products and support services. The data indicate a very tight relationship between product design and customer sat-isfaction with support and the company overall. For this reason, products designed for the Macintosh, which has an easier interface to use, tend to rate higher in customer satisfaction than Windows products, even though the products are practically identical. Trish May described this finding:

There's some intercorrelation between [the customer satisfaction rating] and what products, and how the product is designed. For example, we've done some cross-tabulations that show that if someone is very satisfied with the product, they're going to be very satisfied with the service. If you have an interactive user interface, then you're generally going to be more satisfied with the service. And there's sort of this halo interactive effect. Generally speaking, we have the same engineers answering a question on Mac Excel and on Windows Excel. So you sort of hold constant the person. The Macintosh interface is a little bit easier, or was in the past, and so we have higher satisfaction scores on some of our Mac Excel support questions than we do on Windows Excel in the early stages of the Windows development.

The other major PSS survey is of customer satisfaction among callers to Microsoft. PSS people analyze these data monthly, looking at trends and asking a small percentage of the callers to participate in a twenty-minute telephone survey. Data from these surveys suggest that Microsoft's efforts have worked: After relatively low satisfaction rates in the past, a recent tabulation indicated that 78 percent of customers were very satisfied with PSS, 64 percent would definitely repurchase, 61 percent would definitely recommend the product, and 54 percent were very satisfied with the product, resulting in a "Microsoft product secure" rate of 41 percent.[24] Table 6.2 provides an example of a satisfaction analysis done on 163 customer calls during one week in June 1993.

Product usage studies. Microsoft relies on several mechanisms to understand user habits and needs by studying products in general use. In refining Word in the early 1990s, for example, Microsoft identified two hundred WordPerfect users and studied them for a year by doing monthly interviews. Microsoft also does occasional "segmentation studies" in the United States, taking randomly selected phone numbers from different areas of the country and identifying eight hundred or so users willing to answer twenty-minute questionnaires (about fifty questions). These provide general information on prototypical users of particular kinds of products. Microsoft also researches its user registration base by product, recognizing that these people may not be typical users. In addition, noted product manager Christine Wittress, marketing

Table 6.2   Customer Satisfaction Data by Product, June 1993

	Very Satisfied	Somewhat Satisfied	Total Satisfied
Total (weighted)	*74.1%*	*16.1%*	*90.2%*
Word for Macintosh	83.3	12.5	95.8
Excel for Windows	85.0	10.0	95.0
Windows 3.1	84.2	10.5	94.7
Fox for Windows	72.7	18.2	90.9
MS-DOS	61.1	27.8	88.9
Word for Windows	65.2	21.7	87.0
Windows for Workgroups	65.2	17.4	82.6
Access	68.0	8.0	76.0

Source: Microsoft Corporation, Product Support Services, "ITAA Award Application," June 1993, p.13.

groups do detailed case studies of particular users (especially large corporate users) to gather information on customer needs and provide data for marketing publicity.

Chris Peters recalled some of the key insights from the product usage studies: 20 percent of spreadsheet usage is simple list keeping, despite the power of the program; 40 percent of all documents are simple letters; 30 percent of all documents are memos; and only 5 percent of all documents are newsletters. Peters offered his conclusions: "Basically, what it really found out is that usage of these products in real life is far simpler than anyone had ever imagined—which makes sense, because we're now selling these products to millions and millions of people in Safeway stores. . . . This research is actually one of the few things that is very confidential. . . . We saw this as a significant competitive advantage, that we actually understood what pool we were selling to and no one else did."

Another important source of information has been Microsoft's instrumented product versions. These copies of the product have a separate file that records every mouse click and keystroke of a user, as well as how long it takes to perform each action. They are essential for studying how people actually use a product and what options they choose to accomplish particular tasks. Microsoft gives these special versions to companies that agree to serve as test sites, then studies the data as it comes in. Microsoft has done these studies for every new release of Excel and Word since the later 1980s, sending them out a few months after the first shipments; groups use the data to improve or redesign the next version of the product. (The instrumented version of Word was important to identify the mail-merge feature, as well as various shortcuts for formatting documents.)

Other sources of user feedback are beta testers, who report back to Microsoft via the on-line CompuServe network. Beta testers primarily offer data on what bugs to fix before the final product release, but they also provide ideas for the next product version. As discussed in Chapter 5, users selected as beta testers sign a nondisclosure agreement, then get the software as well as bug forms to fill out and return electronically.

Usability lab testing. We described in Chapter 5 how Microsoft's usability lab provides another invaluable source of feedback on new products. Other software producers, ranging from IBM to Intuit, have had usability labs for many years to study how users react to potential new products and features. We believe Microsoft is distinctive, however, in the degree to which it has integrated this form of testing into its regular software development process. This is important because, unlike other sources of feedback (such as PSS data or beta test reports), product groups can gather this vital information *during* the development process, not before or after.

The idea to institute regular usability lab testing began around the time Microsoft was developing Excel 3.0 in 1989 and 1990. Some developers were already testing product prototypes with prototypical users. They did not do this regularly, however, and Microsoft had no laboratory facility to analyze and collect data. Mike Maples recalled the origins of the lab:

> The usability lab is a group that started with a small number of folks. . . . They're a service organization, trying to help each product. To some extent there was a real breakthrough there. If you went back five years ago, when we started the usability group, the usability group would tell the

development group, "Six out of ten couldn't do this." And the developers' reaction would be, "Where'd you find six dumb people?" Then we started getting the developers into the usability lab, watching and participating. Then we did the instrumented versions. And then we got this idea of, as they were developing features, getting six, eight, or ten usability people and having the developers just walk around and talk to the users about what was working and what wasn't. And it's become a religious thing with the developers—"Have you usability tested that? What did you find out?" I think . . . they realized that they don't think like their users think.

Chris Peters, in 1989 and 1990 the development manager for Excel, had similar recollections of the lab's origin and growth in popularity. He emphasized that even Microsoft's best developers need more than their own common sense to make features easy to use. Moreover, Microsoft's "smart" developers did not realize their limitations until they saw users struggling with features in the usability lab. Since then, use of the lab has become routine:

I don't know exactly the day, but it started happening around the Excel 3.0 time. We had some lucky accident where some of the developers were watching the usability test. When you actually see one live, twenty ideas just immediately come to mind. First of all, you immediately empathize with the person. The usual nonsense answer—"Well, they can just look in the manual if they don't know how to use it," or "My idea is brilliant; you just found ten stupid people, that's why it doesn't work in the usability lab"—that kind of stuff just goes out the door as soon as you see one live. . . .

It was just a very clear way of getting your stuff better. It was very obvious that you could make it better. . . . People often thought that they could design based on common sense, or being smart. But the way humans interact with software is way too complicated. Our best designers, and I think this is true for anybody, can get it about 60 percent right. And then the second time through, first time through the lab, they can usually boost it to 80 percent. By the third time through, they can usually get to 90 percent.

Getting something "60 percent right" refers to the simple metric that Microsoft adopted to measure results in the lab: the number of people who, without referring to a manual, do a task correctly the first time, or the percentage of the task (such as the percentage of total steps) that people get correct the first time they try it. For example, a developer may ask a set of users to type in some text and then search for every instance of a word (for example, *programme*) and automatically replace all cases with another spelling (for example, *program*). This task involves several steps within the "search and replace" feature.

As Peters observed, developers put most features through the lab more than once in order to improve their usability. Some features, however, get low priority in the waiting line and do not go through the lab at all. One example is the feature to debug a macro on Excel. Very few people actually use this, and Microsoft expects those who do to be sophisticated; therefore, developers are likely to skip testing this kind of feature in the lab. Conversely, a feature such as search and replace in Word has a high priority, because nearly everybody uses this. In some cases of high-priority features, developers might send a feature through the lab half a dozen times because they still get scores of only 50 percent or so. At this point, unless they have another good idea on how to fix the problem, they will redesign the feature or its user interface, or perhaps even cut it.

The usability lab is available for all groups, although the applications groups take advantage of this most often. Peters explained why: "The groups that have the religion use it more than groups that don't have the religion. . . . Word and Excel, then most of the [other] applications, have the religion. . . . Systems and languages are probably still further behind, because they usually have more sophisticated users in general, so they get less of the problem in the first place." Systems developers tend to test for usability only interface features or functions that average users access, rather than functions that operate behind the scenes or that only other software developers are likely to access.

Even PSS has gotten into the act. It employs the usability lab to test the effectiveness of different approaches to supporting new products and features. Mark Seidenverg described this: "We actually usability-test supportability. We've gone into the lab and said, 'Given a customer has this problem, we're going to give this customer the manual and a telephone. We're going to set up a problem for them, and then they're going to call a technician who's in another part of the lab. And we're going to film them both and see them try to solve this problem."

People whom Microsoft taps to test products in the usability lab can be anybody, such as people in user groups or from "off the street." If developers want to check compatibility with a competing product, such as WordPerfect, they find a user of this product. ("They get a free coffee mug for coming in," Peters noted.) Peters explained that "we started branching out and doing this non-formal user kind of testing, because the concept is a person who has never seen a feature before, when given a task, should do something. So now it's not uncommon for a developer to call in another developer who's next door and say, 'Sit down. Do this.'" Microsoft people also have discovered that it does not take a large group of users to test a feature. Peters commented on this finding: "It's based on kind of a funny assumption, but it seems to be quite true that a small number of people will still all do the same thing. You'd think that with a user base of ten individuals, you wouldn't get much data, but it turns out that if something is really wrong, you'll get a zero for ten. And if you fix it, you'll get a seven out of ten. . . . People tend to mess up in similar ways."

Peters listed his favorite "lessons learned" from observing users in the usability lab. One is that common sense on the part of the developer does not always lead to a product that is easy to understand and use. He gave the example of tools options, called "tools preferences" on the Macintosh. Microsoft decided to put this in one place on Word 2.0 for Windows and adopt the Macintosh term. The objective of the usability lab testing was to see whether people could understand a "multi-panel dialog" menu if they had never seen one before: "Only one out of ten people brought up the dialog, because they didn't understand the word *preferences*. They scanned past it. The task was to turn off the horizontal scroll bar." After the team changed the term to *options* instead of *preferences*, five or six out of ten people got it right. The team also found that simply adding some explanatory text to the dialog box—such as explicitly saying "To see more options, click on the list at the left"— greatly helped people find their way through the menus. This addition of text also did not slow down the operating speed. Now, noted Peters, "in more modern dialogs, at least in Microsoft products, they usually contain more informative text. That was based on this—if you've run out of ideas on how to boost the usability score, usually adding text to the dialog will help." After adding text, Peters' group got the usability score up to six or seven out of ten. Then they put colorful icons on the left to draw further attention to the function, and the score improved to eight or nine out of ten. "So there's an example where something went from one out of ten to eight out of ten, just based on dumb little changes. And I would maintain that none of those were commonsense changes."

A second lesson Peters learned is that manuals are largely unnecessary, because most people do not use them: "The greater concept, which was the breakthrough, is that the manual doesn't have to exist. Because that was the cop-out we always used in the past." Only 30 percent of users read the manual first when they do not understand a feature. Most users with a problem will initially consult a neighbor; if that does not work, they usually call product support. Only as a last resort will most customers consult the manual.

Peters admitted that people in other companies, and to some extent in Microsoft as well, have complained that usability testing every feature during development can be too slow and expensive. Without some controls on this type of testing, it is possible for overzealous developers to spend years refining their features and never ship anything. He explained the cost objections:

> I've told this to lots of different companies, and they say that that sounds very expensive, we can't afford to do that. And I say you can always afford to at least, first of all, admit that no one's going to open the manual, or that people will at least attempt a feature without a manual. And that a person who's unfamiliar with the design should see it, and you should pay attention to how they fail, even if it is just the programmer next door. So I think even a ten-person or a five-person team working on something at MIT could benefit, if they had that greater concept of "Can this person do this task without a manual," and then watch them and pay attention.

To reduce costs, Microsoft projects generally collect features that can be run together and test them at one time, and they try not to run features through the lab more than twice. Groups such as Excel and Word also try to limit their lab work to two half-day sessions per week, with each session testing about three features.

The lab staff then sends reports to the developers and program managers. The program managers assigned to the feature, rather than the lab staff, also take responsibility for scheduling the testing. Maples tried to contain the cost of the lab as well, limiting the staff to around thirty-five people and the facilities to a half dozen or so actual rooms. (Each room can have only one or two usability testers at a time.) Microsoft has also maintained only one centralized lab, although Maples admitted there were pressures to create multiple facilities for the different design groups. He commented on this struggle to run an economical usability lab:

> There's virtually no guideline, and the usability lab is 200 percent or 300 percent oversubscribed because it's become such an important part of the product that everybody wants to do it to everything. The usability lab would like to have 100 people and 50 labs. But anytime you have a free service, it's pretty hard to tell what the trade-offs are. . . . What we're in the process of doing is breaking the design group up, and we'll probably do the same thing with usability. As soon as it gets big enough that we can make multiple groups and put it closer to the customers, and make the trade-off of what they do a smarter trade-off, we'll do that. The other reason it's centralized is that it started off as two people, and you do have the problem of the facilities.

The lab has had concrete benefits in making products easier to use and easier to support, as PSS data indicates. In fact, Peters credited the usability lab with halving the number of customer calls per "box" sold: "No one's ever happy to call product support. So it's a fine example [of] where there's a total win-win situation. If you can make it so they don't need the call, you win. And they don't want to call in the first place, so they win." Peters also claimed that the lab has helped prevent program managers and developers from adding too many unnecessary and complex features. This "feature creep" is a concern among many users frustrated with the growing size of PC software products and the amount of memory and storage space they require: "We think that, with usability testing, we can actually add more features and make a product easier and easier to use. So we no longer think that feature creep actually applies if you do things right. That implies that there's a trade-off between power and ease of use. So much so had that gotten indoctrinated in the industry that people were starting to do things like executive word processors—i.e., we can't make this thing easier to use, so we'll just start deleting features. But I think the right way actually is to use usability testing, so you can have power and ease of use. I don't think they are opposites."

PRINCIPLE   *Promote linkages and sharing across product groups.*

A final issue in building a learning organization is for different product groups to learn how to share components and work together as an integrated company. Microsoft's increasing emphasis on integrated feature-rich products, such as Office and Windows 95, now demands a systematic approach to designing interfaces, sharing components, and improving consistency in project scheduling and product quality. Microsoft and other software producers can no longer afford to keep large independent product groups and let them "reinvent the wheel" as they please at the expense of profits and customer complaints about inconsistencies or incompatibilities across the same company's product portfolio. At one point, for example, Microsoft managers determined they had fourteen different collections of text-processing code in their products; they also had several versions of code that did math calculations, graphing and charting, help functions, and other tasks.

Microsoft now has a variety of linkages and communication ties across product groups to facilitate components sharing and feature standardization across their products. Beyond just explicit reuse of designs and code, projects are working to define component-based architectures. They are also building individual components that different products can utilize through mechanisms such as dynamic link libraries (DLL) or Object Linking and Embedding (OLE). This "component-based architecture" approach contrasts with Microsoft's earlier approach of building primarily stand-alone applications. Applications products, especially Office, need to reuse shared components (such as a toolbar, drawing tool, or window frame) in order to provide a consistent user interface to customers. This reuse also decreases the effort required to add new capabilities to individual applications. At the same time, standardizing and sharing components reduce effort needed in customer service to support similar functions done somewhat differently in different products.

Interoperability Group: Learning how to share has not been easy. Microsoft has actually taken several years to achieve systematic sharing of components across its different product units, and it can still do more. Bill Gates has had to play a major role by mandating that new product versions incorporate the OLE technology and pursue sharing in other ways as well. One of Microsoft's first steps in this direction was to create an interoperability committee, and then an interoperability group, several years ago. The latter included OLE, the interoperability design group, the original Office group (the group that integrated Office and shipped it as a product), the usability testing group, and the visual interface design group. In 1993 the interoperability group evolved into the current Office product unit.

The interoperability group worked to persuade the separate applications groups to adopt common user interfaces (such as standardized menus and tool bars) and then identified common functions across the major products. According to Dave Moore, the interoperability group, which had twenty-six people in 1993, was designed to be a "third party" to work with the Excel and Word groups. If there was a disagreement or a deadlock between those two groups on how to design a common feature, the interoperability group was there to make the decision: "It's the third leg of the stool. You've got to make decisions. And so, if Excel and Word can't decide, you have a third party. Any function that is common between the two products—file open, file close, copy, paste, anything you see in one that has the same function in the other—they're working to make sure that the function is presented in the exact same way. If there's a dialog that opens, the dialog is exactly the same. The controls for the dialog operate exactly the same way."

Interoperability personnel emphasize consistency from the end-user perspective, not consistency in the sense of code reuse. The interoperability group did not review people's code to ensure commonality but rather focused on the specification, making sure that developers designed the commonality into the feature. Developers can code the feature in different ways, but it must appear the same to the user in both programs. Without the presence of a group whose focus is making features look and behave the same, the user interfaces produced by major product groups simply diverge as they focus solely on making best-of-class products. The interoperability group led the identification of a common (or "core") set of features across products, as Chris Graham, former director of applications interoperability, summarized:

> We created the position of apps interoperability because we felt that . . . suites of applications are becoming very, very important in the market. And the only way we're going to get our products to work well together is by putting good people on it and devoting a significant effort. The entropy of separate product groups focusing on making the best products in their category just causes things to diverge. It's easier to make decisions if you just want to be the best spreadsheet or the best word processor, but it's much harder to work with the other group to reach a consensus on doing something the same way. So we created the interoperability group to get OLE into the applications and to develop what we call the core feature set that we would get into not just Word and Excel but other applications. This is just a very simplistic view of what we mean by core features; they're worksheet features, word processing, database, and so on. They're a set of features that are common to all applications and are frequently enough used by users that they encounter them in all applications and expect them to work the same.

An important reason for the success of these efforts in interoperability and sharing has been the tireless efforts of key managers such as Chris Graham. Born in 1949 in Ireland and raised in Vancouver, Canada, Graham studied applied science and engineering at the University of British Columbia, then worked as a software developer, consultant, and manager at various firms before joining Microsoft in 1989. He initially worked in a four-person group that explored ways to standardize the architectures across Microsoft's major applications products. This group made little progress, and within four months Graham switched to the Excel group as a program manager. There he headed a feature team that tried to redefine the architecture of Excel as well as achieve compatibility with

Lotus 1-2-3. Within three months he took over as the group program manager for Excel. He then became director of applications interoperability, overseeing OLE development, interoperability design, visual interface design, and coordination for the Office product. After the fall 1993 reorganization, Graham briefly worked as head of the interoperability design group within the new Office product unit, reporting to Chris Peters. He later took a leave of absence before moving on to another assignment, although other people have continued this effort to promote the design and use of common features.

Core Set of Common Features: In 1993 the interoperability group identified about thirty-five major features that were common—but not shared—among products. Microsoft then created a process whereby particular product groups that had the expertise (such as the Word business unit with text-processing code, or the Excel business unit with math calculations code) took the lead in building a particular feature and encapsulating it using OLE. Other groups adopted the OLE interfaces so they could incorporate those features as "objects" into their programs. This became an ongoing process of redesigning and sharing, as now seen primarily in the Office suite of applications. Microsoft wanted users to perceive that its products looked and behaved similarly. Chris Graham elaborated: "We want to make the Microsoft products look like a family of products, and so we want people to immediately perceive that within the first ten minutes of using a group of products. We want people to feel that they're the same, so the features need to be consistent that people see first or use most frequently. The products should act like they're part of the family. They should work together well."

The core set of common features includes tool bars, copy-cut-paste features, fonts, dialog boxes for printing, and various menus. Microsoft research indicates that roughly 85 percent of users' actions require about thirty-five product features; the common feature set defines these features and specifies their user interface appearance, as well as the behavior of the buttons, menus, dialog boxes, and other items. The marginal returns of making consistent the hundreds of remaining features diminish rapidly, as Graham recalled: "For this round we were fortunate in that of the hundreds of features, about 85 percent of what users do are only about thirty-five features. All the rest are things that users don't do very much, so you wouldn't gain much by making them consistent. So by concentrating on thirty-five features, although that's maybe only 10 percent of the total features, it's 85 percent to 90 percent of what users experience. So there's a lot of bang for the buck. As you go to less frequently used features, there's a rapidly diminishing return."

Within the set of thirty-five features, most users would say that 25 to 50 percent of them already look and behave pretty consistently in existing products such as Word, Excel, and PowerPoint. Interoperability people, however, note that at least 50 percent of the common features have significant differences across the products. Jim Conner, program manager for applications interoperability, commented: "In about at least 25 percent of the cases and maybe as many as 50 percent of the cases, the degree of consistency is pretty good. I think most naive users who look at these different implementations would say, 'Oh yeah, that's pretty much the same.' In at least 50 percent of the cases, there are significant differences. Some of those are justified by functional differences among the products—they really needed an extra button, because they do different things. But I would say that . . . at least 25 percent of the visual elements or functional elements of those features are randomly different."

Gathering Data on Common Features: Microsoft people gathered extensive data on what features to include in the common set. First they considered and evaluated more than three hundred features from their major products, such as Excel, Word, PowerPoint, Publisher, Project, and Windows. Excel, Word, PowerPoint, and Project alone have a total of over six hundred features, so Microsoft initially considered only a likely subset of all existing features. Second, they used instrumented versions of Excel and Word to gather detailed usage and frequency data for features. They then generated estimates for the other products. Graham noted that they tabulated the command usage frequency based on discussions with users and instrumentation data: "We considered maybe three hundred features. . . . We did a lot of research to determine what are the most leveraged set of features. I realize that it's very hard to get a consensus on designs across a lot of groups, so we need to develop a process where we pick the most important things and make sure we do those really well. So we talk to a lot of users. We used instrumented versions of the products . . . so we know how frequently users do various actions."

Finally, the team supplemented this information with insights from activity-based planning (see the detailed discussion of this technique in Chapter 4). The activity studies showed, for example, that users transferred data between products quite frequently, and this highlighted the importance of common cut-copy-paste operations as well as preserving fonts and other formatting across products. Users also want to build compound documents that include text, data, and graphics. As Graham explained:

> It turns out that, not surprisingly, the most important integration activity was copying and pasting or cutting and pasting between applications. So that was one we concentrated on. Another one was building compound documents. . . . We used activity-based planning as a . . . way of determining the features we do. What are the common activities that users experience when working with a family of products? Transferring data between products is a common activity. Then you have to break it down into what types of transfers are common, which directions is the data transferred, what problems are users experiencing, what's their real intent rather than what they're doing today? So you think about the user's activity. Then you break it down into what are the things which you can do to make the most difference. So for each of the features, we did a writeup of the activities that users go through more globally rather than just concentrating on "Get this feature the same."

Office Integrated Product Suite: Microsoft introduced the Office product suite as a shrink-wrapped collection of the major applications products: Excel, Word, PowerPoint, Access, and Mail. As we discussed in Chapter 3, Microsoft has priced Office very aggressively, and it has sold tremendously well, with approximately 15 million copies now in use.[25] Chris Graham exclaimed: "They buy Office. More than 50 percent of our sales of Word and Excel are as part of Office now. We would like to see that go as high as we can push it." Initially, the applications products packaged in Office had no additional integration or cooperation among themselves, beyond what they had as stand-alone products. The only value-added of Office was the convenience of buying them all at once and, of course, the heavily discounted price.

The interoperability people wanted to increase dramatically the degree of sharing and integration in the Office suite. Their common feature-set research enabled them to affect the architecture of Office, so that it now has better user interface consistency and a component-based architecture approach. Office 4.0 shipped in October 1993 and provided users, for example, with a consistent appearance across the different applications. Most of the top-level menu items are identical across Word, Excel, and PowerPoint, as Bill Gates observed:

> We've been very rigid across the product groups in imposing a standard. So we can see at the very top level in all of these products that eight of the nine top-level menu items are absolutely identical. The only thing that's different is that in the word processor you have the table command, in PowerPoint you have draw, in Excel you have data, so that seventh menu item is specific to the application. If you go down the level below this, you'll find that all the commands in File and Edit and Window—anything that's shared between these applications, even the dialog box you get—will work in exactly the same way. That's just an enabling step. That's to make it comfortable for people to think of this as a single application, as opposed to several different applications.[26]

The Office product unit now has twenty-four dedicated developers. They build most of the shared components themselves, although Microsoft contracts with external companies to build some specialized components. The Office project also has a single coordinated schedule for building all its applications (Excel, Word, PowerPoint, and so on) and shared components. The matrix feature team structure ensures that the shared components meet the needs of the individual applications. A matrix feature team for a particular set of features includes Office developers as well as representatives from the relevant applications, as Graham illustrated: "This is another tool that we use to manage the interoperability process. . . .

We created feature teams like matrix feature teams where there were representatives from each group on a particular feature area. And so here we have Excel, Word, PowerPoint, Mail, Project and so on. These are the representatives on the feature teams."

Office managers and developers have to spend extra time and effort to coordinate these features with the individual applications. But the charter of the Office group is to provide infrastructure for them, as Jon De Vaan acknowledged: "We're in this situation where we're just getting bootstrapped with building a set of shared code that everyone uses. There's a lot of pain in that. One of the particular pains is that the Office people have to work really hard to understand how things work today in the client applications. We have to go through a process of validating our designs with them. That causes a bunch of overhead, relative to what it was like when we were a single product developer. . . . The job of the Office development group is to provide more infrastructure for those [applications]." (Projects outside Office, such as Publisher and Works, are also increasing their use of components from the Office group.)

The Excel and Word teams initially resisted the Office concept, because it would not necessarily help make Excel a better spreadsheet application or Word a better text-processing application. But Microsoft's use of the Office approach has given customers a better integrated application set. Consumers voted with their dollars by buying Office instead of the individual applications, so the Excel and Word teams compromised. Excel and Word developers also realize that a major technical advantage of the Office approach is less memory usage by the individual applications; this either frees more memory for other more specialized purposes or improves user response time. Decreased memory usage provides another competitive advantage, according to Graham: "If you take half of Word, half of Excel, half of PowerPoint, and take those away, that's a big reduction in the working set [memory size] for an Office user. And it would be a big incentive for someone to buy Office as compared to stand-alone applications from Borland, WordPerfect, and Lotus, where they don't share code."

Interdependencies Among Products and Components: The component-based approach has led to significantly increased interproduct dependencies, which can work against achieving goals such as creating excellent individual products, improving on-time delivery, or maintaining the daily build philosophy. Projects previously developed single products where they implemented and controlled their own code. Now projects depend on groups outside their own team to produce components they critically need. Projects try to track the progress of their needed components very closely by monitoring as many of the component provider's internal milestones as possible. John Fine, group program manager for Excel, told us that, "One trick that works really well is you make sure to write down and track many milestones—events that must occur. If I'm a component user, I want to track for my component provider many milestones that occur at short durations of time. That gives me a tool to check on the progress of my component provider." Component providers and component users also need to communicate frequently to make sure that they both have a clear, current understanding of the component's features, interfaces, and schedule. Fine continued:

> The fundamental problem is lack of . . . communication. The component provider will make assumptions over the days and weeks of the project that the component user doesn't know about, or vice versa. Then they discover that later, and therefore they each did work that ends up having to get thrown away or it's inefficient. So any kind of critical path scheduling doesn't help. What helps is over and over again, at short intervals of time, for both of those groups to ask the other group—verify for themselves that all of the things that the other group is doing, they're really doing, and the things they think they're not doing, they're really not doing.

A project that provides a component to no more than two users usually has a very tight, effective working relationship. Component providers who have one or two users can stay in constant communication with them, and they can more accurately estimate the component availability date because the specification for the component tends to change more predictability. The developers for Visual Basic for Applications (VBA), for example, first provide the VBA component to Excel and then consider other users. Dave Moore emphasized this: "What really works best is only two clients. There you can service all their needs, you know exactly what they want, you're always providing what they want—a very nice relationship. The applications group in the past typically had only one client, so it was very easy to fix the ship date, fix the number of resources, fix the feature set, fix the performance. . . . In some cases there were two [clients]. Maybe you're looking at your strict end users—home users—and here's corporate users. It's very easy to specify what they wanted."

Systems projects always provide components in the sense that an operating system constitutes a very large component that users need to run applications. This component "provider-user" perspective results in another major difference between applications and systems products. Systems products have many more component users than do applications, and component providers with large numbers of users tend to have more difficulty predicting their ship dates, as Moore described:

> The systems group is providing a component. They're providing all these services. What you find with a component provider who has probably more than ten clients is they need to service the requirements of those ten clients, and they have to get it right. They can't necessarily service an individual client. . . . They have to work extremely hard to satisfy all the needs of those clients. That's extremely difficult. There's a major difference in building that kind of product as opposed to a component provider who's working for three to nine clients. . . . Systems are always providing for ten or more clients. What are the needs of a spreadsheet developer? What are the needs of a word processor developer? What are the needs of a desktop publishing developer? What are the needs for all these diverse sets of applications working in this environment? There were requirements coming from multiple vendors who are also working on spreadsheets. . . . A spreadsheet developer of Excel at Microsoft has different requirements than a spreadsheet developer at Lotus. So those diverse sets of requirements really drove their product definition much differently than what was done in the applications arena.

Sharing and Interoperability Mechanisms: Microsoft developers interconnect the Office components (or any other shared components) and applications using a variety of interoperability mechanisms, such as Object Linking and Embedding (OLE) and dynamic link libraries. Developers call these "interoperability" mechanisms because they enable two or more applications to cooperate by sharing components and data or synchronizing operations.

We noted in Chapter 3 that OLE is a specific Microsoft product that enables object sharing and interoperability. (This product unit has fifteen developers, fifteen testers, three program managers, and three user education personnel; the developers use C++.) OLE enables one application to request a service (such as "draw this graph" or "format this text") from another application; it can then embed the results of the request into the output that the original application displays. Users can build compound documents including text, data, and graphics using OLE. Chris Graham recalled a humorous incident where someone demonstrating Excel requested a text-editing service from Word using OLE, and it fooled Bill Gates (but only for a minute):

> OLE is a huge investment we've made in integration. An example is: Bill Gates was walking through the Excel hallways. To boost the morale of the development teams, he will tour the development hallways sometimes and talk to each development feature team lead. The team lead will show his features, and Bill will comment on them. And when he was looking at OLE, they switched to OLE in-place editing using Word. And for the first minute or two, Bill didn't realize that. He thought Excel looked kind of funny. And all of a sudden he realized that Word was doing the in-place editing. So the integration of working using components in compound documents will be very high, and we think that's a scenario that matters to users.

OLE affects not only applications products but systems products and custom-built applications as well. For example, two of the OLE 2.0 architects spent 50 percent of their time talking to developers for systems products. OLE team members also consulted ISVs who want to use Office as the basic building block for their products; OLE provides a flexible mechanism for them to write specialized components or "servers" that encapsulate their products and enable close integration with the Office applications.

Dynamic link libraries (DLLs) provide another general sharing technique, but they are not a specific product. A DLL is an "add-in" piece of software that the operating system can load into memory automatically while an application is running. Various application programs can then share this as a "service." Different applications can share DLL services such as spell-checking, special device drivers, foreign language interfaces, and many other components that do not need to be loaded in memory and accessed continually. A major advantage of DLLs is that they reduce the maximum amount of memory consumed by an application at any given time.

Reuse: Microsoft reuses a significant amount of code (over 50 percent) within a series of versions for a particular product, such as from version 1.0 to 2.0 and across the PC and Macintosh platforms. Reusing code decreases costs and reduces effort because a developer can simply implement a feature once, rather than once for each version or platform. Excel 4.0, for example, had 69.4 per-

Table 6.3   Product Code Reuse Metrics for Excel 4.0

Source Code Type	Code Shared Across Windows And Macintosh	Macintosh-Specific Code	Windows-Specific Code	Total by Source Code Type	Percent Shared	Percent of Total Code
C code	528,287	56,522	59,710	644,519	82.0%	75.7%
Assembler code	0	47,793	44,579	92,372	0%	10.8%
Include, token, etc., files	62,839	27,152	24,586	114,577	54.8%	13.5%
Total by Platform Type	591,126	131,467	128,875	851,468	69.4%	100.0%
% of Total Code (851,468)	69.4%	15.4%	15.1%	100.0%		

Source: Jon De Vaan, "Microsoft Excel 4.0 Post-Mortem," 6/8/92.

cent code shared across the Windows and Macintosh platforms, 15.4 percent Macintosh-specific code, and 15.1 percent Windows-specific code (see Table 6.3).

Microsoft also applies many approaches for reusing code across separate products, such as sharing components (VBA for example), sharing a common API, or "stealing what you can" opportunistically. In the component reuse approach, developers provide stand-alone utilities such as drawing or graphing functions that products can share via OLE or DLLs. The Microsoft Foundation Classes (MFC) provide a set of reusable C++ functions and are one example of the common API approach, as Dave Moore explained: "People use these foundation classes as the basis for their coding. The theory is . . . that there will be a set of routines from every application that has a greater chance of being shareable, since they have a common structure of memory use and function management from a standard library. But we haven't mandated that people use these object-oriented techniques. . . . The foundation class is a component library that's shipped with our Visual C++ tool set." Common APIs such as MFC may dramatically reduce the number of API calls necessary to system and user interface services by as much as a five-to-one ratio, according to Chris Graham.

Projects also opportunistically copy code from other products and then adapt it to their needs. Of the approximately 4 million source lines of code in Windows NT, for example, developers reused about 35 percent from previous systems such as Windows 3.1, DOS 4.0, and OS/2 as well as from the languages group. Lou Perazzoli elaborated on the steal-what-you-can reuse approach on Windows NT:

> Windows [3.1] has the same [debugging utilities]. In fact, we ripped off a lot of their code. So don't think we invented everything from scratch. That is not NT—we [took] code from the Windows group when appropriate. . . . Windows is split into this function called User and GDI [Graphics Device Interface], where User manages the square windows and GDI does the drawing stuff. We took all their User code, because it was in C, and ported that. . . . All the applications were ported over, like the file manager and the shell. The command interpreter was . . . written for a product called DOS 4, which then evolved to OS/2. So we took that com-

mand interpreter and ported it to NT. . . . The languages guys gave us C run-times [libraries]. We didn't care where they came from.

In general, Microsoft has extensive opportunities to reuse existing code because developers have written tremendous quantities of code for a multitude of products. The small-team, self-sufficient Microsoft culture provides one possible explanation why developers have not reused code more often. The fast pace of change in the consumer software industry provides another explanation, although this can also be an excuse not to make more of an effort to share. Microsoft groups are now learning how to share more of what they build; nevertheless, even Gates acknowledged that projects still do not reuse as much code as they could:

> We use these small development teams—they love to be very self-sufficient, so they don't go and share code across other teams as much as they could. Now we have more code than most places have, so we share more code than I think anybody else you'll find in the world. We also fail to share more code than anybody else you'll find in the world. I can give you some great successes. . . . There's only one piece of charting code in the whole company. But there's a lot of pieces of text-processing code. I can explain how we got there, and why it's not as stupid as it might seem. But if we'd been super clever about architecting the requirements and the framework, we could have avoided a lot of inefficiency there.

7
Attack the Future!

In our descriptions of Microsoft's strategies and their specific principles, we have detailed a number of company strengths. We will review them here briefly while highlighting capabilities that are useful for other companies to learn from, and that should help Microsoft perform well in the future. We also discuss what we feel are Microsoft's key weaknesses—both actual and potential—and the lessons these provide for other firms. We then conclude this book with a discussion of Microsoft's strategic challenges, and how we think Microsoft will implement its most fundamental strategy—*attack the future*—based on how products, markets, and technologies seem to be evolving.

Underlying our thoughts in this final chapter are several assumptions about the future. First, we believe that PC software will become even more sophisticated in terms of functionality, and thus more difficult for companies like Microsoft to build. New products will bring together numerous features previously found in separate applications programs, operating systems, and network communications products. Second, at the same time we believe that future PC software, from the user's perspective, will become even simpler and more reliable. It will enable millions (and perhaps billions) of novice home consumers to use computers for a variety of daily tasks with increasing frequency. Third, we believe that high-technology markets such as PC software change quickly enough so that we cannot reliably predict whether Microsoft will still be the world's most powerful software company a decade from now. Nor can we say for certain that Microsoft will successfully leverage its current market positions and extend its dominance to new and very different markets, such as on-line services or multimedia publishing. All we know is that we would not bet against Microsoft; we are sure that it will compete aggressively in these and other new markets. It also brings a host of existing products, customers, standards, technical capabilities, and organizational resources that will make it one of the world's most powerful companies for many years to come.

KEY STRENGTHS

Microsoft is one of those rare companies where leadership, strategy, people, culture, and opportunity come together to create an extraordinarily effective organization. This should be apparent whether a reader likes or dislikes Microsoft products or how the company behaves.

The Company: The seven strategies and sets of principles that we have enumerated in this book reflect fundamental strengths that enable Microsoft to function so effectively. We summarize them below.

First, we must point to Microsoft's *exceptional chief executive and senior management team*. Bill Gates is an extraordinary leader, and he has assembled an effective "brain trust" to support him. Microsoft managers know their technology and markets, and how to make money with this knowledge, as well as or better than any top management team in any company. They have also created an organization superbly tailored to competing in a rapidly evolving and expanding set of markets.

Second, Microsoft has thousands of *carefully screened and talented employees*, known for their intelligence, technical skills, and business savvy, as well as their aggressive, entrepreneurial spirit, and willingness to work countless hours on behalf of the company. They come from a wide and growing variety of backgrounds, which creates diversity within the organization. These people also have the talent to take on extensive responsibilities, including defining their job skills, hiring and training new people, and creating linkages across different parts of the company.

Third, Microsoft exhibits *highly effective and coherent competitive strategies and organizational goals*. It is clear to Microsoft employees that the company leaders do not value technology for technology's sake, or believe in adhering to rules or procedures over shipping products. Bill Gates and other Microsoft managers value making money: They are interested in "bang for the buck" and mass markets, and they believe that delivering value to customers will make the most money. Gates and other managers also seem to know when to enter new or evolving markets and when to shift their focus. They replace obsolete technologies before the competition does this for them. They clearly understand how to cultivate a huge installed base of products and customers. They set standards that maintain sales and profits as well as generate new markets, and they take advantage of being the standards provider. They can also see that the true mass market of the future centers around the novice home consumer.

Fourth, Microsoft has *a flexible, incremental approach to product development and organizational evolution*. Microsoft's system of product development enables teams and individuals to alter specifications and designs during a project and build products by incrementally evolving features targeting specific customer activities. Moreover, Microsoft's organization exhibits the same type of flexibility and incrementalism we see in its products and projects. We have seen the company shift relatively easily from one market and customer set to another. Managers move people around, add groups, and reorganize continuously as technologies and markets change. And Microsoft people manage the evolution of products, projects, and the overall organization with a remarkable minimum of politics and bureaucracy.

Fifth, Microsoft clearly has *processes for product development and other operations that combine efficiency with the ability to work in parallel*. Company profits are high, despite the fact that Microsoft prices products relatively low. At least part of the reason is that Microsoft takes advantage of scale and scope economies in many areas: It has accumulated vast knowledge in developing and testing software products, and it now shares many components and tools across different projects. It produces huge numbers of new products and moves them into wholesale and retail sales channels with astounding ease. The company funds growing amounts of research and development from corporate revenues. Different groups rely on the same centralized usability lab, and there is centralized training and tools development for customer support. The thousands of calls that Microsoft receives daily provide an invaluable source of feedback from customers. Other areas subject to scale economies include operations such as product packaging, distribution, and advertising. At the same time, Microsoft's processes for product development and other operations promote efficiency and flexibility by organizing many tasks in parallel, with overlapping responsibilities and skills, and work assigned to small multifunctional teams.

Sixth, Microsoft people have *an orientation toward self-critiquing, learning, and improving.* Product groups study past projects, looking for what went right and what went wrong, and what to do the next time around. Unlike in past years, Microsoft also pays close attention to customer questions, complaints, and suggestions, analyzing this information as if it were a gold mine and channeling this feedback quickly into the product development organization. Microsoft is increasingly using quantitative measures or metrics to understand products, projects, and customer reactions. And the various product groups are finding new ways to share technology and components to reduce redundancies, present a more coherent set of products to customers, and become even more integrated and efficient as a company.

Seventh, Microsoft people have demonstrated a *relentless pursuit of future markets.* They have not yet become complacent, as Richard Barth observed: "Steve Ballmer is pretty aggressive about reminding us that we put our pants on one leg at a time, and that there are other people who are at least as hungry as we are coming after us." We also think that "attack the future"—a strategy we will elaborate on later in this chapter—is an accurate characterization of Microsoft's behavior since 1975. Bill Gates and Paul

Allen displayed this attitude first by going after what then was a practically nonexistent mass market for PC programming languages. Since then, Microsoft has gone after other waves of new or evolving mass markets, and created some markets as well. Gates and his staff continue to look several years into the future as they evaluate new ideas such as multimedia publishing, interactive television, and other products and services for the information highway and the novice consumer.

Product Development: Microsoft, like any company, is really a human system. It works because of how well Microsoft people bring together various technical skills and the market knowledge necessary to compete and then put their ideas into practice. It is difficult to say that any one element is more important than another. In this book, however, we have spent considerable time talking about the strategies and principles by which Microsoft develops new products. Our reasoning is that product development is central to everything Microsoft does. The company's survival and prosperity have always depended on new products, from Altair BASIC to MS-DOS, Word, Excel, Windows, Office, Windows NT, Windows 95, the Microsoft Network, and beyond.

For example, Microsoft's revenues would have collapsed in the 1990s if it had not been able to deliver new versions of Word and Excel, then integrate both within the Office suite. These products now account for about half of revenues and profits. Simply to sustain its sales of operating systems, Microsoft has had to move beyond MS-DOS to Windows; it has now successfully built two versions of Windows NT, and early indications are that it will have a commercially successful new product in Windows 95. Microsoft must also continuously add useful features to convince its millions of existing customers to buy new versions of products that are already adequate for most people. To grow in the future, Microsoft plans to create a huge variety of consumer products that incorporate advanced multimedia and network communications technologies. Clearly, a critical question Microsoft faces is whether the company can continue to evolve its development capabilities and build ever larger and more intricate software products and software-based information services. As we have suggested, Microsoft must also greatly simplify many of these products in order to market them successfully to the world's billions of novice home consumers.

We have argued that Microsoft has already demonstrated impressive capabilities in product development, and that the company deserves credit for continually refining these capabilities. Overall, we feel that Microsoft's product development organization is really the heart and future of the company and should continue to do well because of the strengths it exhibits.

First, the product development organization *effectively supports Microsoft's competitive strategy*, which is to design products for the mass market and then improve these products incrementally by enhancing existing features or adding new ones. Microsoft also tries to establish industry standards and then take advantage of these new standards with new products. Product units support this objective by turning out continual streams of compatible new products and new versions, for which millions of customers pay additional money each time they upgrade.

Second, the product development organization works well because its processes and objectives are *highly consistent with Microsoft's culture and goals*. Program managers and developers have large amounts of freedom to evolve features by experimenting with designs and user reactions. The emphasis is on individual specialists making decisions but sharing responsibilities and working in small teams, with a minimum of bureaucratic control. Older firms in the software industry may describe this as a "hacker" culture, due to the lack of firmer controls over what people and projects do. But the synch-and-stabilize techniques we have described—daily builds, milestone integration periods, buddy testers, and private releases—allow individuals and small teams to work relatively independently, as well as together.

Third, like the company organization overall, Microsoft's culture promotes a process for product development that *combines efficiency (and structure) with flexibility*. Divisions easily expand their product portfolios. Individuals have the freedom to make many changes in the products they develop and to alter or tailor their processes and tools. Throughout the company, however, there is a reasonably well-defined process for software development and other key activities.

Flexibility is especially important in software development because it is difficult to predict at the beginning of many projects how products will ultimately turn out, or how users will respond to product features. In the packaged (as opposed to custom) software business, companies also face a problem somewhat akin to writing best-selling books and then sequels that please a dedicated audience. A single highly structured development process is not always useful, because there is no specific formula for producing a best-seller: however good the process is, the ideas, the people who do the actual writing, the market timing, and advertising and customer support have more to do with ultimate success. Nonetheless, what firms can do is create product development processes that provide just enough structure for teams to experiment with designs and still successfully bring together the evolving pieces of the product they are creating. This requires subtle but effective coordination and communication.

Fourth, Microsoft's approach to product development contains several mechanisms for *incorporating feedback and learning*—especially from customers—directly into the development process. We can see these in the analysis of user activities for product planning and the use of customer support data to prioritize features as well as generate feature ideas. We can also see these in the extensive reliance of program managers and developers on prototyping features in the usability lab, in how testers try to replicate the functional usage of a product, the huge beta tests at customer sites before the release of major new products such as Windows NT and Windows 95, and how developers and testers staff customer-support phone lines after they introduce new products.

Fifth, Microsoft's synch-and-stabilize approach has enabled the company to *scale up the loosely structured small-team* style of its early years and build sophisticated software systems relatively cheaply and quickly. There are some limits to Microsoft's techniques, which we discuss later. Still, although several Microsoft products and projects are now quite large, the employee groups devoted to them continue to work very much like nimble small teams. We believe that, with some modifications, Microsoft can continue to scale up its operations and build the complex software systems of the future.

WHAT SYNCH-AND-STABILIZE ACHIEVES

The principles behind the synch-and-stabilize philosophy achieve a difficult aim: They add a semblance of order to the fast-moving, often chaotic world of PC software development. There is no magic here. Rather, there are specific tools and techniques, a few rigid rules, and highly skilled people willing to follow these rules. Microsoft's entire development process helps individual developers frequently synchronize their work with other members of a team, and stabilize their product in increments as components evolve. As we have suggested throughout this book, several elements distinguish synch-and-stabilize from older sequential and more rigid styles of product development (Table 7.1).

First, Microsoft, similar to what is becoming more common in software and other industries, does not follow a sequential "waterfall" process. It does not treat product development and testing as separate phases done one after the other, albeit with iterations back and forth if things do not proceed exactly according to plan. Rather, Microsoft teams *do development and testing in parallel*. The process is similar to how individuals might "hack away" at designing, coding, and testing as they go. It also resembles incremental development and concurrent engineering practices in other industries that overlap many activities and phases.

Second, Microsoft does not try to "freeze" a complete functional specification and detailed design before starting to build a product's components. Rather, Microsoft *allows specifications to evolve*—adding or cutting features, experimenting with design details—as projects proceed. The complete specification thus is more an output of a project than an input to the development process. Microsoft also has vision statements but no real detailed design or documentation phase; the code is the detailed design and the documentation. This is, again, reminiscent of a hacker approach, but we think Microsoft has particularly effective mechanisms to keep changes more or less under control.

Table 7.1   Synch and Stabilize versus Sequential Development

Synch and Stabilize	Sequential Development
Product development and testing done in parallel	Separate phases done in sequence
Vision statement and evolving specification	Complete "frozen" specification and detailed design before building the product
Features prioritized and built in 3 or 4 milestone subprojects	Trying to build all pieces of a product simultaneously
Frequent synchronizations (daily builds) and intermediate stabilizations (milestones)	One late and large integration and system test phase at the project's end
"Fixed" release and ship dates and multiple release cycles	Aiming for feature and product "perfection" in each project cycle
Customer feedback continuous in the development process	Feedback primarily after development as inputs for future projects
Product and process design so that large teams work like small teams	Working primarily as a large group of individuals in separate functional departments

Third, Microsoft does not try to build all the pieces of a product simultaneously, such as by breaking down a detailed design and assigning all the modules or features to different people and teams. Rather, Microsoft *breaks up a design into features, prioritizes them, and then builds clusters of features* in three or four milestones. Teams usually work on the most important features in the first milestone, the second-most important features in the second milestone, and so on. For products where features are not so closely coupled, a project team will drop features from the last milestone if it falls too far behind in the schedule.

Fourth, Microsoft does not try to bring together all the pieces of a product for the first time in one late and large integration and system test phase at the end of a project. This would occur if a project builds all pieces in parallel and has no way to synchronize or test them together during the development process. Rather, Microsoft uses the concept of frequent builds to *synchronize the work of many individuals and teams* on a daily or weekly basis; it also uses the concept of milestone subprojects to *stabilize subsets of features* in three or four increments. These practices resemble "concurrent engineering" and "incremental builds" used in some other firms. Nonetheless, we think Microsoft stands out for how well it has refined and institutionalized this style of product development.

Fifth, Microsoft does not necessarily try to complete and perfect every feature proposed at the beginning of a project. Rather, and particularly with applications products, Microsoft will set time and personnel limits, then establish goals for reducing the most severe bugs. Teams will wait until the next "release" of the product to add features they could not complete in the previous project, or to fix minor bugs that they did not detect or could not fix. In this way, Microsoft *avoids the common dilemma of working and reworking a product in an endless cycle* of changes, additions, and bug fixes. Other software firms have multiple release cycles, as do companies in industries that put out annual or frequent "model changes." Microsoft, though, has pushed this style of development and marketing further. It has even brought the idea of annual model changes to software—hence the names Windows 95 and Office 95. (Of course, this strategy of annual models will backfire if Microsoft groups cannot predict schedules accurately. Adding the year to product names, however, creates additional pressure to finish within a given year.)

Sixth, Microsoft does not wait until after it has finished and marketed a product to collect and utilize customer feedback. Rather, Microsoft *incorporates customer feedback continuously throughout the development process*. This begins with analyses of users in the product planning phases, and continues with the testing of prototypes in a usability lab and the delivery of pre-release versions to beta test sites. Furthermore, Microsoft sends to its development groups detailed weekly reports on customer inquiries made to the product support organization. This information affects future product designs as well as features currently under development.

Seventh, Microsoft does not allow developers to write software as if no one else existed in the company. Nor does Microsoft build software with huge teams divided into designers, developers, and testers working sequentially in separate departments, "handing off" work to the next phase amid lots of rigid procedures and required documentation. Rather, Microsoft develops software in multifunctional teams, organizing its efforts so as to *make large teams work like small teams*. Mike Maples at least in part referred to this when he told us that "we spend more of our time figuring out how to act small, be small, and think small, than we do act big and think big."

MAKING LARGE TEAMS WORK LIKE SMALL TEAMS

The strategies and principles behind Microsoft's synch-and-stabilize approach also suggest valuable lessons for how to organize large teams—a common problem in many companies and industries. Part of the difficulty is in technical and management education. University science and engineering departments and management schools generally do not teach students how to work in or control large teams. University engineering projects are nearly always small in scale; people learn how to work alone or within a small group. The reality in many firms, however, is that large teams are necessary to build complex products in relatively short amounts of time. This is true even though small teams of highly skilled people are probably the best way to design almost any type of product, whether it be a computer software program, an automobile, or an airplane. We think that Microsoft and other "young" companies (especially those from relatively new industries like PC software) have a lot to teach the world about managing teams and innovation. Table 7.2 and the sections that follow return to the strategies and principles that we have already discussed, but pull out the key elements that Microsoft uses to scale up its style of small-team development.

Project Size and Scope Limits: We have discussed how Microsoft tries to place limits on the size and scope of its projects as one way to keep projects small. This happens in several ways, which we discuss below.

Table 7.2   Making Large Teams Work Like Small Teams

- Project size and scope limits (clear and limited product vision; personnel and time limits)

- Divisible product architectures (modularization by features, subsystems, and objects)

- Divisible project architectures (feature teams and clusters, milestone sub-projects)

- Small-team structure and management (many small multi-functional groups, with high autonomy and responsibility)

- A few rigid rules to "force" coordination and synchronization (daily builds, "don't break the build" bug rules, milestone stabilizations)

- Good communications within and across functions and teams (shared responsibilities, one site, common language, non-bureaucratic culture)

- Product-process flexibility to accommodate the unknown (evolving specs, buffer time, evolving process)

Clear and limited product vision. Microsoft projects try to set clear boundaries on what each project will attempt to accomplish. Program managers, working with developers and product managers, and data from customer support, do this through a concise vision statement that sets an achievable goal for the project. Chris Peters emphasized this point in his 1990 video: "You have to have a clear goal.... This is what helps a whole group of people, a group of a hundred people, move in a common direction and helps decide what to do and what not to do. It's just as important to decide what a product that you're working on is not going to be as it is deciding what it will be."[1] Microsoft finds this clarity of goals easier to achieve with second, third, or later versions of a product compared to totally new products.

It is also usually possible for projects to prioritize features according to "bang for the buck." If a feature "looks cool" but will take six people the entire development schedule to do, and only a few customers are likely to use it, they will cut it.

Personnel limits. We have noted that the product unit structure creates a de facto ceiling of how many people will work together on any one project. Microsoft is really a collection of small development centers, usually with no more than three or four hundred people each. Each represents a multifunctional product development team composed of specification, development, testing, user education, and product planning specialists. Their size is relatively large compared to the days when Microsoft measured total employment in the dozens and projects had four or five people, but small compared to the thousand or more developers often used by competing software firms. Microsoft also focuses nearly all its people on shipping products, rather than on building up components or technologies for "inventory" or documenting processes and products. This focus on shipping products has both positive and negative elements: for example, a lack of process and product documentation can force teams to reinvent solutions to common problems. It also gives people more time, though, to focus on getting the product at hand to market.

Time limits. Projects now set stricter boundaries on how much time people can spend on a given effort. Usually this is between twelve and twenty-four months for a new version of an existing product. These times are often longer for totally new products (such as Windows NT 3.0 or Microsoft Exchange), or major new versions of operating systems (such as Windows 95). We have discussed why operating systems are more difficult than applications to build in a predictable time frame. (They require extensive testing to cover all possible user scenarios and present fewer opportunities to cut features or functions if the project runs behind schedule.) Nonetheless, setting time limits—at least internally— helps people focus their creativity on getting a working version of the product together, even if it is not "perfect" or ready for commercial release to the marketplace. Projects will have time to make refinements later.

Because projects prioritize features and create a working product as they go along, applications projects can often stop when they run out of time and still ship a marketable product. In contrast to the past, when some Microsoft projects were years late, many applications products in second or later versions now ship within a month or two of the originally estimated ship dates. Microsoft's record is far from perfect, however, with totally new products or major operating system changes. Complications also arise with interdependent components coming from other projects, such as those contained in recent versions of Office.

Divisible Product Architectures: Perhaps more important than overall limitations on project resources, product architecture plays a crucial role in breaking down large teams into small teams. Modularization is common and necessary in the software industry and in many other engineering fields, and most companies design products by features, functions, or subsystems. Microsoft in the past has not always paid a lot of attention to defining a high-level architecture that is separate from the source code in its products. This is changing, however, as Microsoft's development groups (including those for OLE, Office, and Cairo, among others) are increasingly thinking in terms of divisible product architectures and shared components. Microsoft teams also effectively coordinate and synchronize the development of their components through the daily and weekly build process, as well as the milestone stabilizations.

Modularization by Features and Functions. We have talked about how Microsoft breaks down applications products into features; operating systems contain features as well as parts better described as functional components or subsystems. Since many of these components interact, projects must test them together at some point; however, teams can design many features or functional components independently. This makes it possible to break up one relatively large project into a set of small projects.

Modularization by Subsystems and Objects. Microsoft is increasingly organizing features and functions as dynamic link library (DLL) subsystems or Object Linking and Embedding (OLE) components that more than one product can use. These subsystems and objects require extensive coordination in the initial planning and design stages to define their technical details and interfaces. Designing products from shared subsystems and objects, and designing code to be shared, involves many adjustments during the development process. In general, however, these components again make it possible to subdivide projects into teams that work relatively independently, at least during the development stage.

Divisible Project Architectures: We have discussed how Microsoft divides projects in a way that mirrors the structure of its products. This practice helps teams create products with logical and efficient designs, and it results in project organizations with logical and efficient groupings of people.

Feature and component teams. Projects contain several feature teams or component teams. Each concentrates on building one or more of the features or functions that make up the design of the product. The team structure thus mirrors the product structure, and keeping the number of teams and their size small usually results in a more tightly integrated product.

Feature (and Component) Clusters. Microsoft prioritizes features and then divides them into clusters based on how important or technically interdependent they are. Projects build one cluster at a time, with small teams creating the highest-priority features or functional components in parallel.

Milestone Subprojects. The feature and component teams go through a full cycle of development (design and coding), testing, and stabilization for each cluster of components before moving on to the next milestone. The result is that managers do not have to control projects that, for example, consist of building a large number of features in parallel during eighteen or twenty-four months. Rather, from the perspective of day-to-day project management, the targets are to build only a few features within a three-month period.

The milestone approach may appear to take more calendar time than developing all components simultaneously, then just integrating and testing them once at the end of the project. Even in conventional firms, though, software components tend to change a lot during a project and are difficult to specify exactly in advance. Changes or differences from the original specification then make a product difficult to integrate and test later on, unless there are strict controls over what individuals and teams build. The milestone approach lets teams of almost any size act like small teams and change designs or flush out details of their components. They have this freedom because they can stabilize major parts of the product several times during a project—before so many changes creep into the product that integration and stabilization become nearly impossible.

Small-Team Structure and Management: With the principle of subdividing a product into features (and even features into subfeatures), projects can break down product assignments into pieces that a handful of people who are responsible for their own fates can usually build in just a few weeks or months.

Small Multifunctional Groups. We have discussed how the core group for each team is generally one program manager and three to eight developers, including a feature team lead. The extended team includes a parallel feature testing team roughly equal in number to the developers.

Autonomy and Responsibility. Chris Peters noted that "large teams work when you've pushed the organization, or pushed the responsibility, very, very low. They work well and they are very, very competitive. But having the responsibility pushed very low is absolutely critical to having them work."[2] The alternative would be to give more responsibility and authority to managers (such as team leads) to closely direct the work of team members. Instead, Microsoft gives each team, and each individual, considerable autonomy and responsibility. This follows the basic principle of hiring smart people who can work and learn on their own. Autonomy and responsibility allow each team to work relatively independently; for example, individuals and feature teams are responsible for setting and maintaining their own schedules. In addition, they have relatively few rules required for changes—individuals and feature teams "own" their features. Projects also tailor development processes and tools.

A Few Rigid Rules to Force Coordination and Synchronization: While Microsoft teams have considerable autonomy, projects rely on rigid discipline at a few key points to make sure that teams coordinate their work.

Daily Builds. Nearly all projects do daily builds of their products. Developers are free to come in to work whenever they please, as well as to contribute to the product build as frequently or rarely as they like. When developers check in their work, however, they have to check it in by a particular time (usually either 2:00 or 5:00 P.M.), after which the project creates a new build. Inspired by people like former tank commander Dave Maritz, product groups adhere to the build rules as if Microsoft were the Israeli military! The daily build process forces individual developers and teams to synchronize their work as frequently as possible. The longer developers wait to check in their code, the more likely they are to encounter conflicts with other features that cause the build to fail.

Don't Break the Build. Teams detect problems in the code before creating a new build through continuous testing, both automated and manual, with "buddy" testers assigned to each developer. Once they decide to check in, however, a key rule for developers is not to violate the architectural interfaces or interdependencies between features and functional subsystems, or make any other errors, that cause the build to fail. Developers responsible for bugs that break the build must fix them immediately; these "guilty" people also may have to take responsibility for putting together the next day's build or pay an embarrassing fine. Dave Thompson expressed the seriousness of this rule: "We're absolutely rigid about [the idea that] you better not break stuff, and you have to code things robustly."

Milestone Stabilizations. Within certain architectural constraints and practical project limits, individuals and teams are free to change component designs or alter the feature set in the new product. Groups almost always end up changing their final shipping date. During the project, however, managers do not consider it acceptable for people to miss their intermediate milestone deadlines.

Communications Within and Across Technical Specialties and Teams: Several elements contribute to good communications within and across the technical specialties and the feature teams within projects.

Shared Responsibilities and Tasks. We have discussed how despite some functional specialization and divisions of labor, Microsoft blurs the divisions so that people share tasks and responsibilities. Program managers and product managers together write up product vision statements; program managers and developers together define the product features; developers and testers both test code; and program managers, developers, and testers all help answer customer support phone lines after the release of new products.

One-Site Development. All major development efforts take place at Microsoft headquarters, except for some acquisitions. This makes it possible for team members to communicate and solve problems quickly in face-to-face meetings. (Bill Gates insists on this, despite his affinity for electronic mail.)

A Common Language. Projects rely on a common development language (primarily C). Applications projects also use Microsoft's internal "Hungarian" coding name conventions. Many developers believe Hungarian makes it easier for them to understand each other's code, even without separate design documents. This practice facilitates code sharing and problem solving.

Open Culture. The culture of Microsoft is still not too far away from the loosely organized world of hacker programmers. Its people abhor political "turf battles" as well as bureaucratic rules and procedures, unnecessary documents, or overly formalized modes of communication. As a result, individuals and teams act quickly on issues they feel are important.

Product-Process Flexibility to Accommodate the Unknown: It is often essential for a company to have products and processes flexible enough to accommodate unforeseen changes or initiatives taken by individuals and teams. This is particularly true in a work environment where managers give individuals and teams significant responsibility to act independently and in an industry where the technology and market needs change quickly.

Evolving Specifications. We have described how product managers and program managers create a vision statement and a prioritized feature list at the beginning of a project. Some groups (such as Excel) write lengthy functional descriptions of all or most features. Nevertheless, teams do not feel locked into these descriptions; the specification and details of the features can evolve along with the project. The final feature list may change and grow 20 to 30 percent, depending on how work proceeds, what competitors do, or what type of feedback the project members get during development.

Buffer Time. Microsoft projects include a portion of the schedule as buffer time: about 20 percent in application projects, and as much as 50 percent in systems projects and totally new projects. The buffer is useful to accommodate unforeseen changes due to un-planned changes in features, unusually difficult bugs, or other un-foreseen problems (which always seem to occur). Managers schedule this time in between each of the milestone periods and be-fore final release. Mike Maples explained that projects need to "fig-ure out the set of deltas that always happen" to upset the schedule. Many delays result from what he called "things that happen that you don't know you don't know. It turns out that to a great extent a team has the same optimism or lack of understanding from project to pro-ject to project. Once you figure out what the factor is, the routine is almost a constant. They will always underestimate by X percent."

Evolving Process. Microsoft managers do not lock the organization into particular practices or tools if superior alternatives exist. If someone has a better idea how to do something and can demon-strate this, teams might alter their process during or after a project. Chris Peters commented on this ability to evolve: "I think we know what the current best practices are, and as they change, we change."

KEY WEAKNESSES

Like any company, Microsoft has many actual and potential weak-nesses that managers in this and other companies would do well to understand and remedy. The potential weaknesses are so many because, carried too far, every strategy and principle that we have described in this book can itself become a liability over time.

Organizing and Managing the Company: When we review the principles behind how Microsoft people organize and manage the company, four concerns come to mind:

- Even a smart CEO has limited knowledge, attention, and longevity.
- Promoting mostly technical people can create a shortage of good middle managers.
- An emphasis on "bang for the buck" can discourage truly creative people.
- Increasing interdependencies among product units can reduce their market focus.

The first possible liability is Microsoft's *dependence on Bill Gates* as the company leader. It is an understatement to say that Microsoft has done well by this "weakness" so far. Not only have his instincts been excellent, but Gates has also brought an impressive number of technical experts and executives to Microsoft. He has not made the mistake of many company founders in trying to retain too much control over an organization that becomes too large and diverse for one person to handle. Still, he retains control over strategic decisions as well as key elements of product strategy, and he mediates between product groups. It remains to be seen whether any one person can deeply understand the broad range of technologies and new businesses that Microsoft is now into as a company.

Gates launched Microsoft by seeing the future ahead of his peers, or at least acting with more conviction and deftness. His company then skillfully rode what amounted to an exploding balloon of mass-market waves for PC software, from simple programming languages to operating systems to desktop applications and beyond. In Microsoft's new businesses, however, Gates has many more complex scenarios to consider; there are many more (and some very large) competitors compared to when Microsoft was establishing its position in the 1970s and early 1980s. Gates is no doubt right that consumer software and the information highway will be huge areas of future growth. But it is not clear that Gates and his senior management team understand how to exploit these new technologies and business opportunities better than anyone else. This is not to say that we would bet against Gates and Microsoft, especially since early maneuvers in these new areas, such as the Microsoft Network, appear to be very cleverly conceived. The extent of Gates's advantage beyond desktop software, though, remains an open question.

A related concern is Gates himself—his attention span as well as his longevity and potential succession. He remains the undisputed leader of Microsoft, and it has often required the full force of his personality to get different Microsoft groups to cooperate. Gates has stated that he expects to head Microsoft at least for the next ten years, and then to take on a lesser role in the company.[3] Whenever he leaves the post of CEO, he will probably not stray too far and will certainly remain on the board of directors, just as Paul Allen has. Nonetheless, there will be a huge vacuum at the top that will be difficult to fill. The recent rise of young executives such as Nathan Myhrvold, Pete Higgins, Paul Maritz, and Chris Peters indicates that Microsoft can produce talented general managers, but there is no one obvious person likely to carry on wherever Gates leaves off.

A more immediate danger is that Gates has already spread himself and Microsoft too thin, with too many businesses and personal investments to follow all of them with his usual intensity. At least one veteran Microsoft observer has even asked whether the Intuit acquisition attempt suggests that Gates is "going soft."[4] Gates and Microsoft once had the will to take on every player in PC software, doing whatever was necessary to win: They challenged Digital Research, the maker of CP/M, with DOS. They overtook Lotus and 1-2-3 with Multiplan and then Excel. They topped WordPerfect with Word. They defied Apple and the distinctiveness of the Macintosh by building Windows. They challenged Novell's NetWare, various versions of UNIX, and IBM's OS/2 with Windows NT. They are heading for a direct conflict with on-line network providers by marketing the Microsoft Network along with Windows 95. In contrast, as discussed earlier, Microsoft launched Money to challenge Intuit's Quicken, then tried to spend over $2 billion to acquire the company—greatly upsetting competitors and antitrust regulators by this decision. After opposition from the U.S. Department of Justice, Microsoft managers decided that this acquisition was not worth the trouble and the money. But we wonder why Gates did not insist earlier that his people make more of an effort to turn Money into a successful product.

Second, below Gates and his team of senior managers, Microsoft has *weaknesses in its middle management* corps. We have discussed how Microsoft tends to promote developers into management positions, based primarily on their technical skills and accomplishments rather than their managerial skills. Microsoft also grew so quickly in the late 1980s and early 1990s that very young developers took on extraordinarily great responsibilities, such as managing multimillion-dollar and even billion-dollar businesses. Some developers have met the challenge of general management with great aplomb, but they may be exceptions. This is a serious problem because, in almost any company, middle managers make the organization work.

Microsoft's primary strategy to deal with this issue is threefold: (1) Grow a bit slower, giving people more time to accumulate experience at their current levels of responsibility; (2) continue to hire experienced managers from other companies when needs and opportunities arise; and (3) pay more attention to cultivating middle managers. Microsoft is holding more meetings, retreats, workshops, and training sessions for managers to discuss common issues, exchange experiences and information, and receive more formal management education. Microsoft has also appointed functional directors to facilitate learning across the product groups. Thus it is our impression that Microsoft's top executives are sufficiently aware of this serious weakness. It also seems that these measures, along with slower growth, will do much to alleviate deficiencies in middle management.

A third potential weakness is the *"bang for the buck" type of personalities* that Microsoft has hired over the years. Recruiting "smart" people in Gates' sense—quick-witted young men and women who combine an acute business sense with technical understanding and the ability to learn—has clearly served the company well. But Microsoft employees have generally focused their creativity on developing product features that will sell to large audiences. Most features consist of incremental innovations, and many products have followed the lead of other companies. The consumer and research divisions are diversifying Microsoft's capabilities and stock of people, but Microsoft will probably need more inventive employees in its basic lines of business to keep these areas fresh and moving forward.

Fourth are the *interdependencies associated with Microsoft's efforts to promote more sharing* across its product groups. Strategically and technically, the arguments for doing more sharing and more integrating are compelling. The problem is that Microsoft's underlying organization by products is firmly entrenched in the company culture and, more importantly, presents its own set of advantages. In the past, separate business units have been able to focus their attention on one competitor and one product, and they have had all the resources they needed to build and deliver their own products. This is no longer the case. Furthermore, managing two or three interdependent projects simultaneously is far more complex than managing one project at a time, which Microsoft is still in the process of mastering. More interdependencies will likely result in more product delays and product compromises, at least until Microsoft gets all its key groups marching in step together. Many products are only as good—and only as timely—as their weakest component.

Managing People and Skills: Microsoft's principles for managing people and skills suggest four areas of concern:

- Too much overlapping of responsibilities can lead to confusion and wasted effort.
- Learning by doing and mentoring can be inadequate for many complex products.
- A dislike for "bureaucracy" can result in too much reinvention as well as trial and error.
- Retention of key employees becomes critical when knowledge is mostly tacit and unwritten.

First is the *degree of overlapping among the technical specialties* that Microsoft has sanctioned. These tracks are essential for cultivating expertise in such highly specialized areas as software development and testing. They have been more difficult to define, however, for groups such as program management, which overlaps considerably with both product management and software development. The danger of formalizing the tracks too much is that this might promote an unhealthy compartmentalization of people and skills, which would not help Microsoft's shortage of people with broad enough skills to be effective middle managers and team leaders. The danger of too much overlapping of tasks and responsibilities, though, is that this can lead to confusion and wasted efforts, or efforts that cross purposes. This appears to occur in Microsoft when program managers and developers cannot agree on feature priorities, and neither the program management lead nor the development lead has clear authority to make a decision. Work then proceeds on more features than are really necessary for the product to succeed in the marketplace, or on features that projects later discard. Gates and other Microsoft managers seem to prefer the lesser of two evils: some confusion and redundancies due to overlapping tasks and responsibilities, rather than an overly compartmentalized organization. Gates and other senior technical people are also available to resolve conflicts, although instances where they mandate solutions to independent-minded employees and managers are rare.

A second weakness is *Microsoft's approach to orienting and educating new employees*. The company has avoided excessively formalizing this process, ending a lengthy "college" it once ran for new developers. In theory, training on the job, with guidance from more experienced people serving as mentors, is a superb way to train new people. It allows experienced employees to communicate knowledge that is difficult to codify. In practice, though, this approach is time-consuming and depends on having enough experienced people capable of being good mentors. The system seemed to break down during Microsoft's most rapid periods of growth and within busy projects with tight deadlines. If Microsoft's growth slows, especially in the hiring of developers, the severity of this problem should lessen. Nevertheless, Microsoft and other companies that follow this approach need to provide some guidance to mentors and schedule in time for people to mentor.

A third weakness is that there is probably *more reinvention, as well as trial and error, than there need be* in Microsoft. Company people dislike formal or written rules and procedures. This attitude is good to the extent that it minimizes bureaucracy and has helped Microsoft to change its organization or adopt new and better practices as they come along, but there needs to be a balance. The postmortem documents, for example, indicate that projects too often repeat common mistakes and do not learn as much from other projects as they might. Nor do product units have processes in place to follow up on suggestions consistently. Similarly, products are now large and complicated, and functional jobs—writing specifications and manuals, developing and testing code—have become correspondingly complicated. Yet much of what people learn is still communicated orally, from person to person and from one group to another.

Fourth, *retaining employees is critical because so much knowledge is tacit* and communicated orally rather than written down. Retention rates appear high after a person stays in Microsoft for several years. Testers tire of testing, though, and developers and program managers grow weary of changing specifications and code under extremely tight deadlines that they themselves feel pressured to set. The career tracks, opportunities for promotion, or interesting technical challenges help people stay motivated, but many people "burn out" and leave or take extended vacations. Microsoft's testing and daily build processes in particular rely very heavily on extremely bright people to find and fix obscure defects quickly. Developers and testers already have impressive automated tests and checklists that capture some process and product knowledge; they could capture more knowledge, however, by more consistently documenting a product's design and implementation structure. The trade-off here, of course, is the time needed to keep documents up to date versus the current ease of changing the product. In any case, vulnerability to tacit knowledge and employee turnover will increase as products become even more varied functionally and difficult to build.

Competing with Products and Standards: There are several strategic issues that we discuss in the next section as challenges to Microsoft. Here we would like to highlight four potential weaknesses in Microsoft's product portfolio and competitive strategy:

- It is difficult to move from incremental innovation to truly radical innovation or invention.
- It is difficult but necessary to balance being technology-driven with being consumer- and content-driven.
- Content-driven products are cumbersome to internationalize.
- A company can lose focus by diversifying into many markets, even closely related ones.

One problem we see is that Microsoft has *relied primarily on incremental innovations* to compete. Occasionally it bunches these innovations together, combines them with some new technologies, and introduces new products that make old ones obsolete. Windows 3.1, Windows NT, and Windows 95 all appear to be radical innovations compared to any version of MS-DOS. Yet the underlying technologies, as well as the style of development and product introduction, still represent mostly incremental innovation. Though it should be enormously successful as a product, even Windows 95 is similar to the ten-year-old Macintosh operating system. It also builds extensively on Windows 3.1, with MS-DOS code still present within the system and some features borrowed from Windows NT. In the last few years, Microsoft has created new divisions for advanced consumer products, an on-line network, and research; it has also established dozens of partnerships and made numerous acquisitions. We believe that all these initiatives significantly expand Microsoft's capabilities. The company remains vulnerable, however, to competition from more specialized firms that are better at inventing new technologies or introducing innovative products for new markets. These companies have included Intuit, with Quicken in personal finance software; Novell, with NetWare for office networking; and Lotus, with Notes for office groupware.

A second weakness is that Microsoft may need to *become even more consumer-driven and content-driven* than it is now. It has non-programmers in high-ranking positions, thousands of marketing and sales people, and hundreds of program managers and product planners who try to act as advocates for customers. In addition, the advanced consumer systems and consumer systems divisions are helping Microsoft shift more resources and attention to the largest mass-market—the novice home user. But although Bill

Gates and other senior people have access to enormous amounts of data on customers, they still see much of the world in terms of software that Microsoft can sell. Applications development teams, in turn, tend to see the world in terms of features and products they can build.

This is not all bad. The ability to create software technologies and specific features and products enables Microsoft to enter a variety of new markets with at least something to offer. At the same time, however, other factors will probably drive future sales of home-consumer products and information-highway services: content, low prices, ease of use, and ease of access. Microsoft and Gates personally are constantly acquiring entertainment, education, and information content; the company is learning how to make products easier to use; and it often lowers prices, as seen in Office. These are all the right things to do, strategically. Still, Microsoft has little background in content or novice consumer products. Microsoft also faces stiff potential challenges from large, powerful competitors, ranging from telecommunications companies and video-game software producers to book publishers and movie production houses. (Video-game hardware and software producers are another source of competition, although they may actually expand the market for Microsoft software.) Given the density of customer information now flowing into Microsoft, and the variety of people now in the company, we believe that major parts of Microsoft will make the transition successfully. The transition will be bumpy, however, and other companies may compete in these new markets more successfully than Microsoft does.

Third, we believe that the *marginal effort required to create foreign-language versions of products will increase substantially* as products become more content-driven rather than feature-driven. Because 70 percent or so of Microsoft's retail revenues come from overseas, this is a critical issue. The movies, educational materials, financial data, news, and other types of content that new products offer tend to be country-specific, and may need to change for each new international product version. In current Microsoft products, developers can produce a new international version simply by replacing one electronic file that contains English labels (for dialog box buttons, menu item selections, and the like) with their foreign-language equivalents. This technique is intractable, though, with multimedia products or information databases. To deal with this problem effectively, Microsoft will probably have to give significantly more financial and technical responsibility to overseas subsidiaries to develop and customize products for local markets. This would further complicate decision making as well as the management of product development.

Fourth is the problem of *overdiversification and declining market focus*. Microsoft already has some 200 products and dozens more under development, ranging from games for children to video-server systems for telephone and cable TV companies. This is such a broad expanse of products and markets that, surely, Microsoft cannot pay equal attention to all these diverse customers. There is a real danger that Microsoft will lose its focus and ability to build its core products—desktop operating systems and applications. The philosophy of "bang for the buck" helps people concentrate on the largest, most profitable markets. This, however, is not a customer-centered or technology-centered focus; it is about money. Already we can see Microsoft having problems keeping up with Macintosh applications, one of its strongest markets. Windows products now have priority, and Microsoft bases Macintosh versions on core code designed primarily for Windows. With forethought and planning, this approach can work well, as in the case of Excel; done clumsily, it can alienate customers, as in the case of Macintosh Word 6.0. We expect Microsoft to improve Word and other Macintosh applications out of sheer pride, if nothing else. This incident, however, may be indicative of problems Microsoft has paying attention to small (but important) markets.

Defining Products and Development Processes: We see four areas of concern—all of which are common to many firms, not only in the software field—in the principles by which Microsoft defines products and organizes their development:

- Feature-driven development leads to feature proliferation and underemphasizes the importance of product architectures.
- Product concepts and features should address user behavior as well as user activities.

- Allowing specifications and features to change too much hinders effective development and project management.
- Increasing interdependencies among product units complicate project management.

One problem is that Microsoft's feature-driven approach tends to result in products that contain more features (or more new features, in the case of product upgrades) than users really need. This is less true for systems products, although even Windows 95 has an abundance of new functions that have taken far longer than initially planned to develop, test, and debug.[5] At the same time, a preoccupation with features encourages projects to *underemphasize the importance of the underlying product architecture*. Without a good architecture to define how components interact, it can become extraordinarily difficult and time-consuming to develop, rework, test, and debug all the different features that teams add or change. Like features, architectures need periodic updating to make it easier for teams to extend the capabilities of a product.

Some Microsoft groups have realized that they must take time to refine product architectures and have instituted a de facto "milestone zero" where they can do this work. Other groups rotate, with one team working on major features and architectural changes while a parallel team works in shorter projects on minor features. Even so, intense pressure to add new features and get products completed quickly still takes time away from refining and evolving product architectures. Furthermore, Microsoft relies primarily on developers to compartmentalize functionality into components while they are writing code, rather than having a distinct high-level design phase in which to do this. Feature proliferation also causes products to grow unnecessarily in terms of memory and disk space requirements, and projects often change half of the code from one product version to the next, introducing defects and increasing testing requirements. If projects placed more emphasis on refining the existing architecture and feature designs early in each project, they would probably change and rework less code. Testing and debugging features would be easier, and the long-term product architecture would have a more coherent structure from the viewpoint of both developers and users.

A second weakness is Microsoft's *preoccupation with user activities, rather than with user behavior*. Activity-based planning provides an effective technique to analyze how people write documents, define budgets, and engage in other "creation-oriented" activities, and then to map these to features. This is a far better approach to defining products than having engineers dream up product concepts and features that do not match what people actually do. But because this focus on activities did not uncover the need for computer-supported collaborative work, Microsoft did not introduce a groupware product like Lotus Notes until it saw the product in the marketplace. Moreover, to move more deeply into the market of the home consumer, Microsoft and other firms need to study consumer-oriented behavior in depth—to understand, for example, what types of products and services people want in fields such as entertainment, education, communication, and information or news retrieval. Then they need to introduce whole products (as well as individual features) that map to behavioral patterns, which are more difficult to measure than specific activities such as writing a document. The contextual inquiry technique that Microsoft has used occasionally helps somewhat in analyzing user behavior, although it may be too vague and time-consuming to utilize regularly.

Third is the issue of *too much evolution and change in specifications*. The specification document is the key mechanism for determining personnel needs and schedules. The ability to allow this to evolve and still keep projects under control is a great strength of Microsoft's development process. There are practical limits, however, and some projects go beyond these limits. As people complained about in the postmortem reports, specifications can be too sparse or change too much during a project. In these cases, project managers as well as individual developers and testers have trouble estimating how much time and how many people they need to build, test, and deliver the product. (Similarly, if product architectures are poorly defined or become outdated, then projects will underestimate potential feature interactions, the resulting number of bugs, and the amount of testing and rework that may become necessary.) We do not mean to suggest that this balance is easy to achieve. Because managers want specifications to evolve somewhat, project members may simply have to live with a high degree of schedule uncertainty, rework, and testing. They can also try to do more up-front design work, prototyping, and usability lab testing as part of the planning phase rather than as part of development, or they can schedule in more buffer time for very new or extensively changing products.

A fourth weakness relates to *how interdependencies among projects complicate project management*. Managing one software project at a time is difficult enough, particularly when specifications and features change a lot during development. When one project depends on other projects to deliver essential components, then the complexity of manpower estimation and scheduling grows dramatically. It also becomes more difficult to catch problems through frequent-build synchronizations and milestone stabilizations unless every interdependent group stays close to its schedule and delivers components for the frequent builds to other groups. Microsoft already has trouble living by deadlines, especially in systems products. It is possible to build in more buffer time to handle uncertainties; however, this leads to longer development times. There is also the possibility that many people will sit idly by waiting for one late group to finish its component. Interdependencies may become further complicated if more groups work away from Microsoft headquarters as a result of acquisitions or overseas customization.

There are, however, solutions to these problems. Products need to have very clear architectures and interfaces among the components. Interdependent groups need to follow a disciplined development process (in other words, they cannot change critical parts of the specifications on their own) and record thoroughly in specification documents all feature dependencies on underlying components. Then they must carefully coordinate and continually review the progress of all interdependent projects. At least for some components and projects, Microsoft is already adopting these types of practices.

Developing and Shipping Products: We can identify three main weaknesses (that we have not yet touched upon under other topics) that relate to Microsoft's principles for developing and shipping products:

- Prevent errors by "building in" quality rather than "testing in" quality, using techniques such as design reviews.
- Testing should emphasize typical user scenarios as well as defect detection.
- Effective quality and project control require quantitative metrics and reliable historical data.

First, it is now a truism in management and engineering circles to say that *building in quality is better than testing in quality*. This is easier said than done in software. No matter how carefully a company conceives and constructs a software product, there are always potential errors or problems that only testing seems to uncover. The challenge should be to prevent errors or catch them early in a project, before they become embedded in code that becomes intertwined with other code. Microsoft, however, primarily relies on its testing process (automated quick tests, private release testing by testers, automated tests on the daily builds, tests of the milestone builds, and so forth) to catch errors. Projects also allow features to change and evolve, a policy that creates lots of errors due to poorly understood feature interactions even if everyone codes individual features correctly.

Microsoft also conducts relatively few formal or intensive reviews of specifications, designs, or code. Newcomers usually have their code reviewed by a mentor or team lead, and developers often ask one other person to check over their code. Critical features or shared components usually undergo specification reviews. But Microsoft could probably avoid some rework and testing not only by paying more attention to how features interact, but also by reviewing specifications and code more intensively. Of course, if specifications and code change significantly during a project—which they do in Microsoft—then some of the time spent doing reviews will be wasted.

There is no easy solution to this problem. Nonetheless, numerous organizations (such as IBM, TRW, and the Jet Propulsion Laboratory) have published studies that document the effectiveness of design and code reviews, including intensive code reviews called inspections. They have found these useful in detecting and fixing problems before developers incorporate them into the product. Reviews also help refine product architectures and feature designs on a continual basis, and they educate junior developers about design and implementation techniques as well as product details.

Second is the *scope of user testing* that Microsoft (and other software companies) still need to do. For Windows 95, as previously discussed, Microsoft launched an unprecedented beta test that involved up to 400,000 customer sites examining pre-release versions of the product. This type of information comes too late to make major changes in a product. It is useful, however, to detect problems that typical users might encounter with different combinations of hardware and applications programs. Microsoft's in-house testers could never hope to replicate these diverse "user scenarios" in a reasonable amount of time and at an acceptable cost; the massive Windows 95 beta testing effort is an exception in the company (and the industry). In the past, Microsoft has run into problems with products such as MS-DOS 6.0 and Macintosh Word 6.0 that earlier and more extensive testing with customers and in different user scenarios might have detected. Part of the problem is within Microsoft, which has sometimes relied too heavily on its own nontypical employees for feedback on products before commercial release. Companies that want to move into the true mass market of novice consumers need to test all of their products in a manner that resembles more closely how the average person will use those products.

A third weakness is the *limited quantitative metrics and historical data* that Microsoft possesses to facilitate scheduling, personnel estimations, quality analysis, and the product-shipping decision. Hitachi of Japan has project data going back to the late 1960s; IBM, NEC, Toshiba, and Fujitsu have databases going back to the early 1970s.[6] Microsoft has been in business since 1975, and its many projects collect large amounts of data, but it has yet to establish a rich set of common metrics and central databases to which all projects contribute. Over time, we expect metrics and historical data to become even more important for Microsoft. This will occur as more projects depend on other projects for components, and as customers demand higher levels of reliability (no Pentium-type bugs, for example) and more predictability in delivery dates.

Learning as an Organization: Microsoft has made significant progress in its efforts to learn from past experiences in product development and to share more process knowledge and components across different product groups. Here as well, however, Microsoft people themselves feel the company can do more. We highlight three concerns:

- Postmortems chronicle problems but do not engage in deep analyses or implement solutions.
- Loosely organized companies may have trouble sharing knowledge across groups.
- Both too few or too many metrics and controls create problems.

First, the project postmortems suggest that Microsoft people are good at criticizing themselves and identifying problems, and reasonably good at suggesting solutions. They are not as good at doing *deep analyses of underlying problems or implementing solutions* to ensure that groups do not easily repeat the same mistakes. Part of the problem has been Microsoft's traditional disdain for bureaucracy; there are relatively few formal training programs or written process documents to guide people, and there is no centralized quality assurance group. Microsoft is building up its training efforts and functional directors involved in product development and testing. But the best solution is to get senior project people to take this type of fundamental problem solving more seriously. We have seen movement, but not a full-scale cultural change as yet.

Second, Microsoft has *limited formal mechanisms for sharing process knowledge* across groups. Again, this is part of the nonbureaucratic company culture, and it has positive and negative consequences. Sharing seems to occur best among narrow technical specialties such as testing, where trading tools and techniques is clearly useful. Developers and program managers have been more reluctant to codify processes and share their know-how. Some of the problem here is the nature of design work in general and software development in particular: It is partially art, partially science, and partially engineering. The functional directors try to encourage learning, and often they find themselves serving as little more than well-paid organizers of occasional lunches and retreats. They are writing guidelines and updating process documents, such as how to do project management, daily builds, or testing. These may, however, prove to be less valuable than the lunches and even counterproductive if people react to them negatively. We conclude that Microsoft is still struggling to find a balance between informality and formality in promoting the sharing of knowledge.

Third is a problem of balance with metrics and controls. Microsoft projects follow a small number of quantitative product and process measures. They could use more, but a company can go too far. For example, there was a proposal to replace postmortems with a 250-item questionnaire and audits done by the functional directors. This probably would have introduced a level of bureaucracy that few groups would have tolerated, and could have destroyed the tradition Microsoft has successfully created of evaluating past projects seriously—and even humorously—in the postmortems. We conclude that Microsoft is still struggling to find a *balance between what and what not to measure and control*. At the same time, improving project management and decision making surely requires more comprehensive metrics and controls than Microsoft currently uses.

STRATEGIC CHALLENGES

Apart from weaknesses internal to the company, there are several strategic challenges that Microsoft faces:

- It is rare for the same firm to dominate multiple generations of a technology.
- New mass markets may require new skills and different competitive scenarios.
- Partner companies may demand a larger piece of the financial pie.
- Antitrust measures may restrain successful practices if a company becomes too powerful.
- Competitors can form alliances to counter the power of a dominant company.
- Other companies can create and link components, too.

First, history is against Microsoft. Companies with 70–80 percent market shares (which Microsoft has for PC operating systems and the Office applications suite) usually have only one way to go, and that is down. For a variety of reasons, few firms that dominate one generation of a product continue to dominate the next generation, depending on how radical the change is.[7] Dominant companies often become so complacent, arrogant, or attached to their existing investments that they become vulnerable to major shifts in customer needs or technologies, or to threats from more nimble competitors. In particular, market positions based on de facto technical standards seem unlikely to endure in a fast-moving industry for more than a few years.

The computer industry is full of companies—IBM, DEC, Wang—who failed to sustain their market advantages. We can also see this phenomenon in the histories of well-known companies such as Ford, General Motors, Xerox, and Kodak, which once had near-monopolies. Recognition of this need to move forward explains why Microsoft so aggressively backed graphical user interfaces in the 1980s. It also explains why Microsoft invests so heavily in new product versions as well as basic research, and has expanded into new businesses and formed partnerships with different types of companies. Microsoft is already unusual; it has moved from character-based to graphical computing and remained the market leader in operating systems as well as increased its position in applications. But any company is vulnerable to radical change. Next year, some competitor could hypothetically introduce an operating system that is compatible with every program written in the past, requires little memory, and responds to everyday language commands. This would make Windows 95 and Windows NT, as well as some of Microsoft's applications products, obsolete.

We do not know when or if the PC software industry will experience such a radical shift in technology. We do not think it will be soon; most technological change is incremental, and the future of PC software may well consist of bundles of incremental changes in technology and product usage—a type of competition in which Microsoft excels. For this reason, we believe Microsoft's lofty market position is likely to remain for at least a decade. It will probably take this long for the current generation of PC users simply to re-place their machines and software.

Second is the longer-term issue of whether Microsoft can ac-quire or cultivate the technology and other skills needed to com-pete in truly new arenas. There are several still-evolving mass markets of great interest to Microsoft: networked operating sys-tems, multimedia publications and applications, home consumer products, workplace products, interactive TV, and information highway services. These may take a decade or more to reach their full potential. Microsoft is investing in and entering all of these new markets at a rapid pace. The company seems technically well positioned in some segments, such as with Windows NT or the Mi-crosoft Network, yet it seems unlikely to dominate so many new areas. Novell dominates corporate networking, Intuit dominates personal finance, and Lotus dominates office groupware. A variety of companies, such as CompuServe (owned by H&R Block), Prodigy (owned by IBM and Sears Roebuck), America Online, and MCI Communications are far more experienced in on-line ser-vices. Other companies, such as Oracle and Hewlett-Packard, have advanced capabilities in video-server technology. Many companies around the world are more skilled in telecommunications. And video-game companies such as Nintendo and Sega have the ability to produce incredibly powerful and cheap home computers as well as entertainment software for truly novice consumers—children. These and many other firms all want a piece of Bill Gates' vision of the future.

Of course, to be successful in its investments, Microsoft does not have to reach an 80 or 90 percent share of these vast new markets, or even a 40 or 50 percent share, although critics may hold Gates up to this high standard. In balance, therefore, Microsoft has everything to gain by exploring new, rapidly growing markets. This is true even if it comes in no better than second, third, or fourth in most of them, and even if it remains primarily a provider of PC operating systems and a few basic applications, with an on-line network thrown in as a side business. Conversely, no company is better positioned than Microsoft to offer customers a bundle of products and services that integrate functions from operating systems, applications, and network communications programs. With this type of integration possible, Microsoft's position as the provider of the PC software infrastructure may become more rather than less valuable over time, and be easily leveraged across these different arenas.

A third challenge may come from current Microsoft partners who want a bigger piece of the financial pie. For example, home banking and other on-line consumer services will clearly be part of the infrastructure package that Microsoft will offer. Even if it does not own much of the content, Microsoft will be able to charge for each transaction, rather than just selling individual products. But Compaq and other high-volume PC hardware manufacturers may resist paying Microsoft to bundle software products that generate additional revenues primarily for Microsoft. Hardware companies may demand part of the royalties or actually start charging to bundle certain types of programs, such as those that generate fees from connections to the Internet or on-line services. This would be a radical reversal of long-standing practices for licensing software. Other partner companies for the information highway (such as cable TV companies, telephone companies, banks, content providers, and the like) may all want more money if the electronic network market keeps growing in size and value. There should be enough money to go around, but software producers like Microsoft may not get as much as some people now believe.

A fourth issue is that of antitrust concerns and whether Microsoft will continue to alter its behavior given that government antitrust officials and judges are closely watching. Competitors are also anxious to bring complaints to government authorities. Novell did this in Europe, leading to the 1994 consent agreement discussed earlier. Several companies also funded a report that helped the U.S. Department of Justice oppose Microsoft's attempt to acquire Intuit.[8] Other companies are combining forces to make sure Microsoft does not exploit its own on-line network.[9] Many large and small companies, including Apple, frequently file suits claiming that Microsoft has stolen or illegally copied their technology. (A recent Apple suit, for example, stopped Microsoft from distributing certain parts of its Video for Windows developer kit. The complaint alleged that Microsoft illegally used elements of Apple's Quicktime for Windows multimedia technology.[10])

These threats and constant vigilance, we think, will make it more difficult for Microsoft to continue orchestrating the evolution of the industries in which it competes. It will be more difficult for Microsoft to bundle products and acquire more companies, and future confrontations with the U.S. Department of Justice and federal courts may force more changes in how Microsoft operates. Even the July 1994 consent agreement (which Microsoft agreed to follow, even though a U.S. federal judge did not initially ratify it) will make it financially easier for hardware vendors to offer alternatives to Windows, such as OS/2 or Apple's operating system for the Macintosh.[11] And Microsoft clearly has vulnerabilities: It has failed to sell successfully some products (such as LAN Manager and Money) that are outside its traditional areas of expertise.

The 1994 agreement is limited, however. Microsoft remains free to form alliances with customers, offer volume discounts, bundle and discount products, preempt the competition with future product announcements and acquire more companies. It will be difficult to stop Microsoft from designing applications products to its advantage, offering new tools and languages to support its products, or utilizing the knowledge its programmers have of Windows. Furthermore, Microsoft can still use the banner of Windows compatibility to boost sales of its applications products, operating systems, and even hardware devices (such as a new "natural" keyboard, introduced in 1994). If there is a new consent agreement in the future, it will surely place more restrictions on Microsoft, but how many and to what effect are not yet clear. Any settlement should balance the need to foster competition, which generally benefits consumers (except when there is market confusion over standards, as in the case of VHS versus Beta in video recorders), with the danger of placing too many restrictions on perhaps the most internationally competitive company in the United States.

A fifth concern is that competitors may continue to gang up on Microsoft and eventually succeed in reducing its influence. Examples of this are the agreement between former archrivals Apple and IBM to develop a common PowerPC, and Apple's decision to reverse a decade-old policy and license the Macintosh software to other firms in order to create its own clone market. Many other competitors appear eager to pool resources to take on the most powerful firm in their industry. IBM has acquired Lotus and the hot Notes product. Novell, WordPerfect, and Borland's spreadsheet division merged to counter Microsoft Office. Lotus and AT&T have formed a partnership to bundle Notes with AT&T network software. Aldus and Adobe merged in printing fonts. Apple, IBM, WordPerfect, Novell, and Lotus have proposed an alternative to OLE. Apple, AT&T, IBM, and Siemens are creating a standard to allow telephones and computers to connect to each other, duplicating some of the capabilities of Microsoft At Work and Windows 95. Other alliances include various efforts to make workstations as well as video-game machines more competitive with desktop PCs. In the information-highway arena, there exist many powerful competitors and partnerships that do not include Microsoft.

Sixth is Microsoft's vulnerability to component-level competition. Building products from components that multiple projects can share is efficient technically and allows a company like Microsoft to offer customers a lot of functionality at a low price. If the sharing mechanisms are available in the marketplace, though, other companies can build components that compete with Microsoft's components. This is technically feasible within the Windows architecture, which enables different products and components to work together. The increasing diffusion of OLE makes this even easier to achieve. Microsoft's strategy is to integrate products into packages or suites, then discount the price. This dissuades customers from buying different products and doing this sort of component substitution, such as buying both Excel and WordPerfect and using these together rather than just buying Microsoft Office (or Novell's Perfect Office or Lotus's Smartsuite) for half the price. It is certainly possible, however, for competitors to create highly innovative products (such as for groupware functions or networking), then link these into Microsoft products and sell them instead of Microsoft's alternatives. This opportunity arises whenever Microsoft does not offer components that are comparable in price and functionality to those of its competitors.

ATTACKING THE FUTURE

Microsoft has always faced technical and marketing hurdles as it follows perhaps its most basic strategy: Attack the future! We have described a bit about what the company is doing in research and new product development, but what product and user scenarios is Microsoft likely to pursue beyond what it has already announced? What technical skills does it need? We now address these issues—relying on our own observations and speculation, and not on proprietary or confidential information from Microsoft.

Given everything that the company is doing in its systems, applications, consumer, and research groups, we believe that Microsoft is laying a foundation to offer the consumer an unprecedented level of integration and access for all its products and services. This integration and product access can build on the MS-DOS/Windows user base and the Windows family technology. It can also extend offerings already existing or under development as part of Microsoft Office and the Microsoft Home product line, as well as products like the integrated Bob application and the new Microsoft Network. More specifically, we believe Microsoft has the capability to do the following:

- Shift its target market from people who create things to people who consume things
- Develop increasing numbers of products that include both up-front purchase prices and per-activity or per-transaction fees
- Package almost all products into a few simple unified offerings that appear in new versions nearly every year
- Blur the distinctions among the functions provided by formerly separate applications, operating systems, and network products
- Remove many of the differences among underlying computer hardware platforms, televisions, and cable TV systems

Consumer Market Emphasis: Microsoft seems to be shifting its market emphasis to people who consume things as opposed to people who create things. Products like Office primarily support people engaged in creation activities: people who write letters, reports, memos, and books; people who produce and analyze budgets and data in various forms; people who make presentations, slide shows, diagrams, and the like. The current Office product supports these creation-oriented activities extremely well, and that is one reason why this product has 70 percent of the application suite market. Most people in the world, however, spend more time consuming things than they spend creating things. What do people consume? They consume entertainment, information, educational materials, communication, and financial data, among other things.

Microsoft people also appear to believe that this consumer market for software "in the home" will increase dramatically in the years to come. Accordingly, the company will likely push broad, integrated products that meet these consumer-oriented needs. Microsoft Bob, which packages together basic programs for the home, is a step in this direction. A more advanced version of this might itself be called "Microsoft Home," as an analogue to Microsoft Office. (Names that Microsoft considered for the Bob product actually included "Home Foundation" and "Essential Home," so our suggestion is not outlandish.[12]) A more advanced product would contain more sophisticated personal, family, and household features in a variety of categories, such as the following:

Communication

- Electronic mail and electronic bulletin boards
- "Groupware" for exchanging messages, sharing ideas, and keeping track of family information and ties

Entertainment

- Popular entertainment programs, such as movies or games
- Sports scores and game analyses

Financial

- Financial, tax, and budget planning software
- Stock market quotes, electronic banking, and bill paying

Education

- Popular educational book titles, including those for children and adults

- Access to public libraries, databases, and government publications

Information

- Internet access software (such as through the Microsoft Network)
- Access to electronic versions of newspapers, magazines, and books

Travel

- Airline and train schedules and reservation services
- Hotel information and reservation services

Over the next decade, it is likely that a home computer will become an indispensable household item—an appliance or tool that a person uses several times every day. The household computer will deliver a world of knowledge and sensational experiences to every user. Of course, Microsoft will continue to expand the individual desktop and office market that has been instrumental in the company's success. Most new market volume, however, will probably come from as-yet-untapped home consumers. The potential installed base of such a Microsoft Home or advanced Bob product includes all households in the developed world.

These consumer-oriented software products embody many content issues. The value added by the software depends on the content it delivers, such as works of art, videos, news, or stock market data. Microsoft will either have to generate more of this content itself (very difficult in many cases) or continue to acquire or license it from other sources. An underlying technical problem is that much of the content inherently reflects country-specific culture or interests. We have noted that Microsoft and other companies cannot offer these products in foreign markets simply by changing the native language on the dialog boxes or user interface screens. (For example, French consumers probably do not want an electronic version of the U.S. Farmer's Almanac; they want electronic versions of materials relevant to France.) In addition, many of these products will combine video with text and sound. These multimedia products are more difficult to design than conventional software products. Microsoft already has some experience from developing the Encarta encyclopedia and other multimedia products, but it needs to expand this experience base to different product groups throughout the company.

Products with Both Purchase Prices and Per-Activity Fees: In the future, we believe that the pricing for many home-consumer software products will include both an up-front purchase price and a per-activity or per-transaction fee. When people buy a software product today, they pay a purchase price (for example, $100) and then own a license to use the software. In most cases, the customers can use that software an unlimited number of times for as many years as they desire. We expect, however, that much of the software in a Microsoft Home–type product will also require small fees (such as 25 cents) that users will pay each time they use particular features or services that are part of an on-line network. These fees will occur because many of the consumer software products require access to or usage of some external service or product that is not part of the original product; examples include accessing a movie owned by a Hollywood studio, retrieving checking account information from a local bank, or referencing an electronic newspaper from a publisher in New York. These external dependencies contrast with today's products that provide predominantly stand-alone functions, such as creating a document or changing a spreadsheet.

The possible financial rewards for charging per-transaction or per-activity fees are enormous. As a simple case, let's say that sometime during the next few years 100 million people worldwide are using a new version of Windows or Windows NT. (This number is not unrealistic. Windows has about 70 million users today and MS-DOS about 140 million, and Windows 95 should eventually come bundled on 30 million or so computers each year.) If just one out of ten of these people logs onto the Microsoft Network, then Microsoft will have 10 million users of its network. Each person might select on average two services per day—such as paying a bill and checking the stock market prices, or checking the sports scores and viewing a movie. If the fee to Microsoft for each transaction is 25 cents, then the company would receive $5 million in revenue per day. That is $1.8 billion per year, about the same size as Microsoft Office revenues in 1994. If twice as many users sign up and use four services a day on average, then daily revenues quadruple and would come to over \$7 billion per year, or over 50 percent more than Microsoft's 1994 level of sales! If fees increase to 50 cents per transaction, we have \$14 billion in revenues if usage levels remain the same. What is attractive about this market is the potential for multiplicative revenue increases (the number of users times the number of fee-based transactions times the price).

Of course, Microsoft will have costs associated with these revenues. It must buy content or pay royalties to the various studios, banks, publishers, artists, and other organizations that provide these products and services. It will have to pay fees to carriers such as telephone companies or cable TV providers. It may have to pay hardware companies that bundle this type of software on new PCs. Microsoft must also fund the development of software to surround these services, and have people available to answer customer questions. Nonetheless, the potential for large profits is many times what Microsoft can earn for charging a customer once for purchasing a specific software product.

In terms of technical hurdles, many of these per-transaction products require real-time software functions, meaning that the computer software and hardware must consistently complete a specific function within a fixed time interval. For example, if consumers want to view a movie, pay a bill, make a purchase, or get a stock-price quote, they expect up-to-date results in a matter of seconds. Developing real-time software is common for telecommunications companies or defense-industry producers. It is not common for a PC software firm, although networked, multitasking operating systems like Windows NT and Windows 95 have some real-time functions or similar capabilities, as do some sophisticated applications (such as multimedia or relational database management products).

Successful development of advanced real-time software requires a deep mathematical understanding of the types of requests users make. It also requires the ability to model those functions mathematically and then simulate them on a computer early in the product development cycle, as part of the requirements analysis and specification process. Companies must also do considerable work on product architectures and component interfaces to make sure the system works without any glitches. Microsoft does not normally do mathematical analysis, computer simulations, and extensive architectural design work in its applications projects. The research division has hired some people with these skills, but Microsoft and other PC software makers will need more of these people in various parts of the organization if they want to create lots of real-time transaction features.

Products Packaged into a Few Unified Offerings: The trend in Microsoft and other PC software companies is to bundle together multiple products into a smaller number of unified or integrated product offerings. We can see this in Office and Bob as well as in Windows and MS-DOS, which now contain screen savers, communications functions, task organizer software, data compression software, and the like. We expect Microsoft to continue bundling many separate products into Windows, Office, and future versions of Bob or our hypothetical Microsoft Home, with varying degrees of integration. This means that most customers will not buy Excel, Word, or Complete Baseball in isolation anymore; they will probably buy Windows, Office, or Bob (Home). Each of these major unified products may also have annual "model changes" analogous to the yearly release of new automobiles, with new features or improved ease of use. Revenues will be substantial if most people buy the latest product version every year (or at least every other year), and prices might be low enough to make this happen. Ordinary consumers do not want to have to be software experts to evaluate what products to buy. And Microsoft wants to make the purchasing decision really simple: If the year is 1997 and the software is for use in an office, then customers should buy Office 97 (and Windows 97, if they don't have this already). If the year is 1997 and the software is for use in a home, then they should buy Home 97 (or Bob 97).

Annual, unified product versions will cause a web of interproduct dependencies internally at Microsoft and result in the development of "product fragments," or components integrated using a skeleton-type of architectural framework. Small teams (no more than ten to fifteen developers) should be able to create most of these product fragments in short six-month or so development cycles. Larger, more sophisticated features and architectural changes will require multiyear development cycles. If this is the case, then major new features in the software would appear only every other year, or even less frequently for Windows. We expect that many parallel, multiyear projects will stagger their results so that the annual product offerings contain enough new features to attract buyers each year. Daily builds will become more difficult to carry out in this scenario, as Microsoft has already found out with Office and Windows 95. Microsoft will probably also need a dedicated build team, even for applications projects, to coordinate across the product fragments and the multiyear projects. We would expect projects to use a combination of daily builds for individual or closely coupled components, as well as weekly builds for multiple components and whole systems.

Blurring of Applications, Operating Systems, and Networks: We have noted that there is a trend in Microsoft to blur the distinctions among functions provided by previously separate layers of software products. The logic behind this "integration" is simple and elegant. As we discussed in Chapter 3 (see Table 3.1), there are three primary layers: applications that run on top of operating systems; operating systems that sit on top of the hardware; and network communications programs that connect individual users to other users or to on-line networks.

A user should not care which type of software or how many software programs an activity or a particular feature requires. Microsoft should also want these distinctions to be invisible to its customers. Moreover, it should want to use basic products like the operating system or mass-market applications like Office or Bob to extend its market reach into new areas such as networking and information highway services. Microsoft is strong in operating systems and in stand-alone applications, but it is a relative newcomer to the network market. The new frontier for software, however, consists of networking products and services. These include software that links users within one office or company as well as software that connects users to the global Internet and other outside on-line networks. If Microsoft continues to blur the distinctions among traditional software layers, then its customers will be able to communicate with other users and access on-line products and services in one or two painless steps, directly from within the operating system or an application program. Of course, Novell, AT&T, DEC, and other network-software providers would like to keep traditional layers of software distinct so that they can sell networking programs as totally separate products. And CompuServe, Prodigy, America Online, and other companies would like to retain these distinctions as well so that they can continue to sell their online network services as separate from the operating system and applications provider.

The logical extreme of the unified product packaging strategy of Office, Bob, and Windows could lead to the creation of a single product: a "Microsoft 2000." This might include all the software products that most users would ever want to buy. While this level of bundling and integration may seem farfetched, it is technically feasible. It also provides a simple packaging and marketing scheme. Hypothetically, someone at Microsoft could try to bundle a single "mega-glob" of software with every PC made on earth. Antitrust concerns will probably prevent Microsoft from adopting this strategy too overtly. Still, the future direction is unmistakable: Microsoft (and other companies) will continue to integrate functions and features now found in separate applications, operating systems, and network products. We also think that Microsoft is in an excellent position to build various "hooks" into its operating systems and applications products to enhance the performance of various products that customers can buy later. The hooks will let customers create their own integration of software, should they so desire. As long as the sharing mechanisms remain open (such as DLL or OLE standards), customers will be able to incorporate components from other companies as well.

To make this strategy work to Microsoft's advantage, the company will need to become more expert in networking and electronic communications technology. Consumer-oriented products and services require the capability to send and receive tremendous amounts of data continuously and reliably. Future networking products must overcome current technical and logistical limits in the capacity and reliability of existing networks, which mostly run on a mix of telephone lines, cable, and optical fiber. Microsoft has also aggressively pursued partnerships with cable TV companies, which have a network infrastructure with more capacity than current telephone lines. Another longer-term alternative is to link up with cellular telephone companies that have access to satellite networks. One potential example of this is Bill Gates' partnership with Craig McCaw, founder of McCaw Cellular Communications, in the Teledesic venture. The plan is to link hundreds of satellites around the globe into a massive digital communications network, with PCs or other hand-held computers as the basic communications device.

Blurring of Computers, TVs, and Cable Systems: Beyond making the distinctions among operating systems, applications, and networks less obvious, we expect that Microsoft will try to remove many of the remaining differences among underlying computer hardware platforms, televisions, and cable TV access. In the future, when users want entertainment or news, they should be able to turn to their computers and not need a television set or cable TV access. Broadcast television and cable television will still exist, but consumers will view them on their computers. (This is already possible with an attachment to a PC that costs several hundred dollars.) Television networks, movie studios, and cable companies will continue to produce programming content, but they will no longer provide or control the computer-based delivery or viewing mechanisms.

At least some home computers in the next few years will have large, high-precision color monitors that reproduce pictures, video, graphics, music, voice, data, and text with pristine accuracy. These monitors will be flat-panel displays (similar to the displays on today's notebook computers), but they may measure as much as two feet by three feet, and be only a few inches deep. Many vendors will produce the underlying computer chips that drive the display monitors. Differences in the chips apparent to consumers will simply be price and performance, not the architectural incompatibilities and "look-and-feel" subtleties that exist today between machines like a Windows PC and the Macintosh. Computers could run future versions of Microsoft Bob as the application and Windows as the operating system and network.

Users will not know or care, but elsewhere on the network, outside of their home, "back-end" or server computers might be running a future variant of Windows NT. The servers will provide storage, retrieval, and connectivity functions for the multitude of on-line products and services available. In order to deliver on this integrated computer-TV-cable vision, Microsoft will have to delve deeper into the multifaceted problems of multimedia and real-time systems as well as high-capacity data-storage devices and displays, all of which need to run reliably over a network of computers. These products cannot simply display static text or data; they must provide realistic experiences, mimicking the sights and sounds of everyday life.

Microsoft has already demonstrated these types of products and technical capabilities in prototype form or in shipped products. It has yet to put them together and make them so reliable, cheap, and simple that any computer novice can use and pay for them, but we have not described anything that is not feasible today.

One important question is whether Microsoft can build more than just prototypes of the complex software components underlying these new products and services. The software needed to make the Microsoft Network into a new tool for tens of millions of people must integrate multimedia content, real-time transactions, and network communications functions. It must have no major flaws; it must also be very easy to use and inexpensive. Microsoft will be competing with large-scale telecommunications producers that have their own sets of customers, and experienced network and on-line service providers and other companies that have more technical expertise in networks and real-time software. And the software technology is only one dimension; Microsoft must continue to gain access to different types of content. It must also understand the behavior of the novice home consumer, and feed this understanding back to marketing as well as product planning and development.

We think Microsoft will do well over the next decade, because the company has many strengths that it can use to "attack" the future. Microsoft will continue to develop a flurry of new products and on-line services, and most will be competitive and improve over time. The company is acquiring new people, skills, and partners at a rapid pace. To do as well in the future as it has in the past, however, will not be easy. Microsoft will have to lead in creating the next generation of PC software technology, or it will fall victim to change and time (a more common fate for dominant firms).

We really have no idea if Microsoft will still be around twenty or thirty years from now. It has a long way to go before it reaches the longevity of Ford, General Motors, or IBM, all founded in the early twentieth century. Other global giants, such as AT&T, NEC, Toshiba, and Siemens, date back more than a hundred years. Nonetheless, Microsoft has already made a huge mark on history after merely two decades of existence. Competitors, government regulators, and not a few customers fear Microsoft will abuse its considerable influence. We think that a combination of antitrust regulations and market forces—competition and user vigilance— will probably keep Microsoft in check and allow the company to continue building better and cheaper products. As the usage of PCs becomes ubiquitous in the home as well as in the office, the world's most powerful software company may someday become the world's single most powerful company in any industry. This will be much to the chagrin of competitors. But it will clearly be to the credit of Bill Gates, his senior management team, and the thousands of Microsoft people who make the company work so well.

Microsoft Chronology (Selected Events)

1975   Paul Allen and Bill Gates introduce BASIC for MITS Computer's Altair PC.

Allen and Gates form Microsoft, locating in Albuquerque, New Mexico.

MITS releases Microsoft BASIC for 4K and 8K computers.

1976   Gates publishes an "Open Letter to Hobbyists" in the Altair user newsletter, complaining of illegal copies of BASIC.

Microsoft introduces an improved version of BASIC.

1977   Microsoft releases a version of FORTRAN for microcomputers.

Microsoft sells its BASIC license to Radio Shack and Apple.

Microsoft introduces BASIC in Japan.

1978   Microsoft introduces a version of COBOL.

Microsoft begins an operating agreement with ASCII Corporation in Japan.

1979   Microsoft moves to Bellevue, Washington.

[VisiCalc and WordStar introduced.]

[WordPerfect founded.]

Microsoft introduces Macro Assembler.

1980   Microsoft licenses UNIX and begins work on a PC version, XENIX.

Steve Ballmer joins Microsoft from Stanford Business School.

Microsoft signs a contract with IBM to help develop the PC.

IBM asks Microsoft to develop versions of BASIC, FORTRAN, COBOL, and Pascal for its new PC.

Microsoft releases SoftCard for the Apple II, allowing it to run CP/M programs.

Microsoft buys the rights to 86-DOS from Seattle Computer, then signs a contract with IBM to provide the IBM PC operating system.

1981   Microsoft establishes a U.S. sales network and formally incorporates.

[Xerox introduces the graphical Star workstation, which later influences Apple's Lisa and Macintosh, as well as Microsoft's Windows.]

Microsoft releases DOS 1.0 with the IBM PC.

Microsoft and Apple begin collaborating to develop applications software for the new Macintosh.

1982   Microsoft releases FORTRAN for the PC.

Microsoft establishes a European subsidiary in England.

Microsoft introduces GW-BASIC for advanced graphics support, COBOL for MS-DOS, and Multiplan for Apple II and CP/M machines.

[WordPerfect 1.0 introduced.]

[Lotus Corporation founded.]

1983   *InfoWorld* magazine chooses Multiplan as the software program of the year.

[Lotus Corporation releases the Lotus 1-2-3 spreadsheet.]

[Apple introduces Lisa, with GUI and mouse.]

Microsoft releases MS-DOS 2.0 for the IBM PC XT.

Microsoft introduces Word (with a mouse); new 16-bit languages for MS-DOS, including Pascal, C, and a BASIC compiler; and XENIX 3.0 operating system.

Microsoft announces Windows (November).

1984   [Apple introduces the Macintosh.]

Microsoft introduces Multiplan, BASIC, and Word 1.0 for the Macintosh.

Microsoft introduces Project (a project planning and management applications package) and Chart (a graphics program) for the PC and Macintosh.

Microsoft introduces MS-DOS 3.0 for the IBM PC AT and 3.1 for networks.

NEC asks Microsoft to develop a Japanese-language version of MS-DOS for what becomes the best-selling Japanese PC.

1985   [IBM releases the Topview graphical environment, predecessor to Presentation Manager and the graphical OS/2 interface.]

Microsoft introduces Word 2.0 for the PC (with a spelling checker).

Microsoft and IBM begin collaborating on a next-generation operating system (OS/2).

Microsoft releases the Excel spreadsheet for the Macintosh.

Microsoft releases Windows 1.03.

1986   Microsoft is listed on the New York Stock Exchange.

[Compaq introduces a 386-based PC-compatible, beating IBM to the 80386 market.]

Microsoft announces Works and Word 3.0 for the Macintosh.

1987   Microsoft acquires Forethought, publisher of the PowerPoint graphics program for the Macintosh.

Microsoft introduces Windows 2.0, Windows 386, PC Excel, Word 4.0 for the PC, and Word 3.0 for the Macintosh.

Microsoft and IBM release OS/2 1.0.

1988   [Apple files a lawsuit against Microsoft for Windows 2.03 and Hewlett-Packard for New Wave.]

Microsoft introduces PC Works and OS/2 LAN Manager for networked PCs.

1989   Microsoft introduces Quick Pascal, SQL Server, and Macintosh Excel 2.2.

Microsoft acquires Bauer, a producer of printer driver software.

Microsoft releases Excel for IBM's Presentation Manager.

1990   Microsoft introduces Windows 3.0, Office, and Word for Windows 1.0.

1991   Microsoft introduces MS-DOS 5.0, which takes advantage of more system memory, allows the running of multiple programs simultaneously (though only running one at a time), and provides limited task-switching capabilities.

1992   Microsoft introduces the highly successful Windows 3.1 upgrade.

1993   Microsoft introduces Windows NT as well as Office 4.0 (an integrated applications suite containing Word 6.0, Excel 5.0, and PowerPoint 4.0, plus Mail and Access) and MS-DOS 6.0 with DoubleSpace.

1994   Microsoft loses patent infringement suit by Stac Electronics; it recalls MS-DOS 6.0 and 6.2 with DoubleSpace and issues a replacement version.

Microsoft introduces Chicago (Windows 95) in beta release and Windows NT 3.5.

Microsoft signs a consent agreement with the U.S. Department of Justice and the European Union relating to their inquiries into potential antitrust violations.

Microsoft announces an agreement to purchase Intuit, maker of Quicken personal finance software.

Windows NT 3.5 and Office 4.0 win *PC Magazine*'s annual

awards for technical excellence in the systems software and applications categories.

1995   Microsoft and the U.S. Department of Justice successfully appeal a federal judge's decision not to ratify the 1994 consent agreement.

The U.S. Department of Justice files suit to stop Microsoft's acquisition of Intuit; Microsoft withdraws its offer.

Microsoft introduces Windows 95, Office 95, and the on-line Microsoft Network.

Main Microsoft Desktop and Business Applications

Product	Description
Office	Microsoft's top-selling application product. Consists of Word, Excel, PowerPoint, and Mail, with Access in the Professional version. Initially offered in 1990 as a discounted bundle. Now with a standard user interface and technically integrated, using Object Linking and Embedding (OLE) and other approaches to share features and data objects. Accounts for half of Microsoft sales, and more than half of Word and Excel sales. The leading application "suite" in the market, with 70 percent market share and weak competition from application suites by Lotus and Novell. Winner of 1994 *PC Magazine* annual award for technical excellence in application software.
Excel	Microsoft's flagship spreadsheet product. Excel 1.0 for the Macintosh, introduced in 1985, helped establish the Mac; a 1988 PC version helped establish Windows. About 80 to 85 percent of Windows and Macintosh versions of Excel is shared code. Competes with Lotus 1-2-3 for best-selling

Product   *Description*

spreadsheet. Has accounted for as much as $1 billion per year of Microsoft's sales. Named the best spreadsheet product of 1994 by *PC Magazine*.

Word

Microsoft's flagship word processor. First introduced in 1983 for the PC, but not a market success until version 3.0 in 1986. About 80 to 85 percent of Windows and Macintosh versions of Word is shared code. Head-to-head competitor of WordPerfect for best-selling word processor. Has accounted for as much as $1 billion per year of Microsoft's sales. Named the best word-processing product of 1994 by *PC Magazine*.

PowerPoint

Graphical presentation program originally developed by Forethought, Inc., a company Microsoft purchased in 1987 for $12 million. Available in both Macintosh and PC Windows versions, and as part of Office. Competes with Harvard Graphics.

Access

Entry-level database management program for individual users. Originally purchased by Microsoft. Also sold as part of the Office Professional suite. Named the best database product of 1994 by *PC Magazine*.

Mail

Basic electronic mail program. Origins in two acquired products: MacMail and PCMail. Also part of the Office suite. Runs on Windows, Macintosh, MS-DOS, and OS/2 systems. Competes with Lotus's cc:Mail.

Schedule+

Appointment scheduling and list-management program introduced in 1992. Works with Microsoft Mail.

Works

Popular integrated applications package for novice users, introduced in 1987. Contains a word processor based on Word, a spreadsheet based on Multiplan and Excel, and a database management feature. Frequently bundled with new PC hardware by original equipment manufacturers (OEMs).

Project

Popular project management program for critical-path analysis, scheduling, budgeting, and cost analysis. Runs on Windows and Macintosh machines. Introduced in 1984.

Product	Description
FoxPro	Advanced database product, primarily for software developers. Bought by Microsoft when it acquired Fox. New version 2.5 for Windows extremely well received. Competes with Borland's dBase.
Money	Personal finance and home-banking program introduced in 1991. Third version improved but has sold only 1 million copies, compared to 7 million for Intuit's Quicken.
Microsoft At Work	Set of hardware and software standards and technologies to link digital office equipment such as fax machines, printers, copiers, and telephones through Windows PCs. Included within Windows 95. Supported by more than seventy equipment makers.
Publisher	Basic desktop publishing program introduced in 1988.

Appendix 3

Microsoft Operating Systems

Product	Description
MS-DOS	Powerful and fast 16-bit character-based individual operating system for Intel 8088 or 8086 and then more powerful microprocessors. Version 1.0 introduced with the IBM PC in 1981. Competed with CP/M, but now the standard for Intel-compatible PCs. Memory limit of 640K for direct access. Version 6.22 introduced in 1994. Out of 170 million PCs worldwide, approximately 140 million use MS-DOS.
Windows	Graphical 16-bit layer that operates on top of MS-DOS. Runs on Intel 80386 or higher microprocessors. Does simple (in other words, cooperative) multitasking. Version 1.0 (1985) and 2.0 (1987) were commercial failures. Version 3.0 (1990) overcame 640-K boundary of MS-DOS and laid foundation for the extraordinary success of 3.1 (1992). 32-bit application programming interfaces (APIs) extension, called Win32s, added in 1991. Version 3.1 supports OLE 1.0 and 2.0 and is installed on about 70 million PCs worldwide, plus 90% of new PCs prior to introduction of Windows 95.

461

Product	*Description*
Windows for Workgroups	Peer-to-peer (rather than individual or client-to-server) networking Windows product, introduced as version 3.1 in April 1993. Not a commercial success because of limited features. Version 3.11 (October 1993) was better received, and includes Microsoft At Work. Networking features incorporated into Windows 95.
Windows NT 3.0	32-bit, multithreaded, preemptive multitasking, multi processor (Intel-based and RISC machines) networking operating system for high-end or corporate users. Introduced in July 1993 as version 3.0. Full set of security features and protection against program crashes for 32-bit applications. Requires 12 to 16 megabytes of RAM and a powerful 486 or better microprocessor. Comes in individual and server versions. Sold 300,000 copies in first year, only one-third of expected volume.
Windows NT 3.5	Upgrade of the original NT, shipped in September 1994; code-named Daytona. Runs with less hardware and memory, using the NT 3.0 interface. Improved speed and graphics facilities; improved ability to run 16-bit Windows applications by using separate address spaces. Winner of the 1994 *PC Magazine* annual award for technical excellence in system software and named as the best operating system product of the year. Brought NT sales to 1 million by December 1994.
Windows 95	Code-named Chicago; also referred to as Windows 4.0. Mass-market 32-bit multitasking and multithreaded successor to Windows 3.1. Shipdate of August 1995 and in beta test since June 1994. Features include support for "plug and play"; 32-bit processing; a new user interface, with a TaskBar and elimination of separate File Manager and Program Manager; 255-character file names; system protection from application crashes; modest hardware requirements (4 to 8 MB memory); built-in fax, electronic mail, and networking capabilities; and simplified connection to the Microsoft Network. Microsoft expects to sell at least 30 million copies in the first year.

Product	Description
Cairo	Version 4 of NT, under development. Object-oriented for high-end or corporate users who want advanced networking capabilities. Customizable interface and new file system utilizing "distributed OLE" that can track linked files and objects across a distributed network. No announced shipping date, but expected in 1996 or 1997.

Applications Division Employee Survey[1]

Key: D = % that disagree or strongly disagree; A = % that agree or strongly agree

D	A	Question Summary
		PERCEPTIONS OF MICROSOFT
3	88	"one of the best places to work in the high-tech industry"
10	63	"a company that takes risks"
6	79	"a visionary company"
10	65	"aggressive in R&D"
6	74	"aggressive in marketing efforts"
83	5	"product mix is too varied"
39	25	"pace . . . [is] too frenetic."
53	18	"expectations for employee performance . . . [are] too high"

465

D	*A*	*Question Summary*

COMMUNICATION

| 17 | 58 | "feelings and thoughts will be seriously considered and passed on to higher levels" |
| 8 | 75 | "management . . . practices an open-door policy" |

TRAINING AND PROMOTIONS

44	21	"new employees receive adequate training"
10	71	"I have opportunities to learn/develop new skills"
27	39	"there are a lot of politics involved in getting promotions and recognition"
15	57	"women are given the same opportunities . . . as men having similar qualifications"
9	59	"minorities are given the same opportunities as nonminorities"

SENIOR MANAGEMENT

8	67	"capably handling the development of effective business strategies"
10	58	"handles internal business effectively."
8	46	"works well as a team"

DIVISION STRUCTURE

56	18	"excessive rules, administrative details, and red tape"
50	19	"high level of rivalry, tension, and conflict among business units" within applications division
26	29	"high degree of cooperation among business units"
28	33	"pleased with the level of cooperation" with systems division

D	A	Question Summary
8	68	"pleased with the level of cooperation" with product support division

WORK GROUP AND WORKING CONDITIONS

D	A	
64	21	"there are . . . persons . . . who do not carry their share of the work load"
9	76	"people . . . help each other out during peak work-load periods"
9	74	"my immediate work group works well as a team"
32	43	"conflict . . . between quality of performance and quantity of work"
11	71	"my work is interesting and varied"
38	32	"I feel pressured to work many more hours/days than I am comfortable with"
2	93	"The buildings and campus . . . provide . . . a comfortable environment."
8	79	"can expect guidance . . . within a reasonable amount of time."
5	83	"have the freedom to take independent action"
15	58	"immediate manager . . . plans and schedules work realistically"

SALARY/COMPENSATION

D	A	
41	30	"salary is equitable"
13	64	"total compensation package (salary plus benefits) is equitable"

Selected Chronology of Microsoft Agreements for the Information Highway[1]

1993

Microsoft signs an agreement with Pacific Gas & Electric to use the Tele-Communications, Inc., cable TV system to link the utility and its customers, and to deploy Microsoft software to track energy consumption and handle billing.

Microsoft agrees to write software for TV set-top boxes jointly being developed by Intel and General Instrument.

Microsoft enters into an agreement with Rogers Communications, the largest cable company in Canada, for a variety of interactive video and other experiments.

1994

Microsoft announces an agreement with the Sega video-game company to provide operating system software for the latter's new game machine. This will allow the machine to handle text or control a cable TV box using a 32-bit chip made by Hitachi.

Microsoft purchases a leading supplier of tools for Hollywood special effects for $130 million in stock. The company, called Softimage, Inc., is based in Montreal; its tools were used in *Jurassic Park* and other films.

Microsoft announces an agreement with Mobile Telecommunications Technologies Corporation (Mtel) to jointly develop a nationwide wireless network for sending and receiving data from a variety of devices, including laptop computers. Mtel is the largest paging company in the United States, with 350,000 pager units in place at the end of 1993. The new joint venture is called Nationwide Wireless Network. Mtel invested $100 million in the venture, Microsoft $30 million, and Bill Gates and Paul Allen another $10 million each. The new network should be operating by the end of 1995.

Microsoft announces a $5 million investment in Metricom, Inc., for data communications technology for hand-held communications devices.

Microsoft announces a deal with Tele-Communications, Inc. (TCI), the U.S.'s largest cable operator, to test interactive TV and video-on-demand services between employees of the two companies at their homes in the Seattle and Denver areas. Microsoft is supplying the operating system software, and TCI the digital network.

Microsoft signs a joint agreement with Deutsche Bundepost Telekom in Germany that includes support for a new standard, CAPI (common application programming interface). This allows PC hardware and software developers to use a common set of interfaces for ISDN (integrated services digital network) applications and peripheral devices.

Microsoft joins with Nippon Telephone and Telegraph (NTT) of Japan to provide multimedia access through Microsoft At Work via the NTT telephone network. Microsoft will provide the operating system software and NTT the communications technology. Users will receive CD-ROM disks but need a "key" to open them on their PCs. NTT will send the key over phone lines for a nominal fee.

Nationwide Wireless Network, a company backed by Gates and Microsoft, purchases an $80 million license for a nationwide paging network that can send and receive spoken and written messages.

Microsoft acquires Altamira Software Corporation, a digital graphics specialist.

Microsoft forms an alliance with Hewlett-Packard, U.S. West, Telstra

(Australia), Deutsche Telekom, NTT, Olivetti, Anderson, and Alcatel to develop set-top boxes and software for interactive TV.

Microsoft forms an agreement with Visa International to develop software for electronic shopping and payments with credit cards.

Microsoft forms an alliance with Southwestern Bell for interactive video trials. Southwestern Bell also plans to license Microsoft's new operating system software, still under development, that will support video on demand and home shopping.

AT&T and Sprint in the United States, British Telecommunications in the United Kingdom, and Unitel Telecommunications in Canada agree to help Microsoft carry its Microsoft Network on-line service to thirty-five countries for access through telephone lines.

Tele-Communications, Inc., becomes a 20 percent partner in the Microsoft Network with an investment of $125 million, and agrees to provide access to the network for its 14 million cable TV customers as well as to provide programming.

1995

Microsoft announces an agreement with UUNet Technologies, which will build and maintain for Microsoft a high-speed information service (twice the speed of competing services) with direct links to the Internet provided through the Microsoft Network. Microsoft also purchased a minority stake in the company.

Microsoft licenses NCSA Mosaic and Spyglass Enhanced Mosaic to include in future versions of Windows. These programs allow users to search for and manipulate information on parts of the World Wide Web of databases on the Internet.

Microsoft announces an agreement with Sony Corporation of Japan to develop video-on-demand systems for the home (TV set-top boxes) and for central computer delivery over cable or telephone networks.

Fifty companies in the PC industry, including Hewlett-Packard, Dell, Lotus, and Borland, reach an agreement with Microsoft to sell and service their products over the Microsoft Network.

Microsoft becomes a minority partner in DreamWorks SKG, the new Hollywood studio formed by Steven Spielberg, Jeffrey Katzenberg, and David

Geffen. The two companies also formed a joint-venture software company called DreamWorks Interactive, which will develop adventure games, interactive stories, and other multimedia software for home consumers.

Forty-five companies from a variety of industries, including Home Shopping Network, QVC, Ziff-Davis Publishing, and American Greetings Corp., agree to offer their products and services on the Microsoft Network.

Microsoft forms an alliance with General Electric's NBC television network to create and market multimedia products as well as interactive television programs for the Microsoft Network.

INTERVIEWS

Name	Date(s)	Recent Position and Product Group
Anil Bhansali	8/5/93	Software Design Engineer, Excel
Richard Barth	8/4/93	Senior Product Manager, Windows NT
Jeff Beehler	8/2/93	Program Manager, Visual Basic
Chuck Yoong Chan	8/4/93	Software Design Engineer, Windows NT
Jim Conner	8/2/93	Program Manager, Applications Interoperability (Office)
Mike Conte	4/13/93, 9/29/94	Senior Program Manager, Office
Bob Davidson	8/3/93	Development Manager, Advanced Development Tools
Jon De Vaan	4/15/93, 9/29/94	Development Manager, Office
Moshe Dunie	4/13/93	Director, Windows NT
John Fine	8/4/93, 8/5/93, 9/28/94	Group Program Manager, Excel

Name	*Date(s)*	*Recent Position and Product Group*
Ed Fries	4/14/93	Development Manager, Word
Bill Gates	8/3/93	Chairman and Chief Executive Officer
Chris Graham	8/3/93	Director of Applications Interoperability
Jonathan Manheim	9/27/94	Test Manager, Windows 95
Mike Maples	4/16/93	Former Executive Vice President
Dave Maritz	4/15/93	Former Test Manager, MS-DOS and Windows
Trish May	8/5/93	Director, Product Support Services Marketing
Dave Moore	3/17/93, 4/12/93, 4/14/93, 4/16/93, 8/2/93, 9/29/94	Director of Development
Max Morris	4/28/95	Program Manager, Windows 95
Marc Olson	4/13/93	Test Manager, Excel
Sanjay Parthasarathy	8/4/93	Group Product Manager, Advanced Consumer Systems
Lou Perazzoli	4/15/93	Software Engineering Manager, Windows NT
Chris Peters	4/12/93, 9/27/94	Vice President, Office
Rick Rashid	4/12/93, 9/27/94	Vice President, Research
Mark Seidenverg	4/15/93	Product Development Consultant, Product Support Services
Roger Sherman	9/28/94	Director of Testing
Steven Sinofsky	8/3/93	Group Program Manager, Office
Jeanne Sheldon	4/14/93	Test Manager, Word

Name	*Date(s)*	*Recent Position and Product Group*
Brad Silverberg	8/4/93	Senior Vice President, Personal Operating Systems
Charles Simonyi	4/14/93	Chief Architect, Microsoft Research
Ben Slivka	8/4/93, 9/29/94	Development Manager, MS-DOS
Dave Thompson	4/15/93	Development Manager, Windows NT
Marc Walker	8/2/93	Software Design Engineer, Word
Brad Weed	8/2/93	Lead Designer, Visual Interface Design Group
David Weise	8/3/93	Software Design Engineer, Windows 95
David Whitney	8/3/93	Software Design Engineer, Workgroup Applications
Chris Williams	9/27/94	Director of Product Development
Christine Wittress	8/3/93	Product Manager, Systems Line Marketing

NOTES

PREFACE

1. See Stanley A. Smith and Michael A. Cusumano, "Beyond the Software Factory: A Comparison of 'Classic' and 'PC' Software Developers" (MIT Sloan School Working Paper #3607-93/BPS, September 1993), and Stanley A. Smith, "Software Development in Established and New Entrant Companies: Case Studies of Leading Software Producers" (unpublished master's thesis, MIT Management of Technology Program, June 1993).

INTRODUCTION

1. These market numbers are based on a variety of sources and are our estimates of the size of the PC market (including MS-DOS/Windows and Macintosh machines) as of fall 1995.
2. Two cases, for example, are Geoffrey Gill, "Microsoft Corporation: Office Business Unit" (Harvard Business School, Case #9-691-033, 4/25/91), and Philip M. Rosenzweig, "Bill Gates and the Management of Microsoft" (Harvard Business School, Case #9-392-019, 10/9/92). For general books, see Daniel Ichbiah and Susan Knepper, *The Making of Microsoft: How Bill Gates and His Team Created the World's Most Successful Software Company* (Rocklin, CA, Prima Publishing, 1991); James Wallace and Jim Erickson, *Hard Drive: Bill Gates and the Making of the Microsoft Empire* (New York, John Wiley & Sons, 1992); and Stephen Manes and Paul Andrews, *Gates: How Microsoft's Mogul Reinvented an Industry—and Made Himself the Richest Man in America* (New York, Doubleday, 1993).
3. "Playboy Interview: Bill Gates," *Playboy*, July 1994, p. 63.

4. Edward B. Roberts, *Entrepreneurs in High Technology: Lessons from MIT and Beyond* (New York, Oxford University Press, 1991).

5. See the account of People Express in Peter Senge, *The Fifth Discipline: The Art and Practice of the Learning Organization* (New York, Doubleday, 1990).

6. See Michael A. Cusumano, *The Japanese Automobile Industry: Technology and Management at Nissan and Toyota* (Cambridge, MA, Harvard University Press, 1985).

7. See, for example, John Markoff, "The Wrath over Microsoft's Word," *New York Times*, 1/20/95, p. D1.

8. See examples in Steven C. Wheelright and Kim B. Clark, *Revolutionizing Product Development* (New York, Free Press, 1992).

9. See Victor R. Basili and Albert J. Turner, "Iterative Enhancement: A Practical Technique for Software Development," *IEEE Transactions on Software Engineering*, Vol. SE-1, No. 4 (December 1975); Barry W. Boehm, "A Spiral Model of Software Development and Enhancement," *IEEE Computer*, May 1988; and Mikio Aoyama, "Concurrent-Development Process Model," *IEEE Software*, July 1993.

10. See Steven Levy, *Hackers: Heroes of the Computer Revolution* (New York, Anchor/Doubleday, 1984).

11. See Michael A. Cusumano, *Japan's Software Factories: A Challenge to U.S. Management* (New York, Oxford University Press, 1991).

CHAPTER 1

1. Biographical details are based primarily on Stephen Manes and Paul Andrews, *Gates: How Microsoft's Mogul Reinvented an Industry and Made Himself the Richest Man in America* (New York, Doubleday, 1993), with the quotes found on pp. 15–19. Other sources include Daniel Ichbiah, *The Making of Microsoft* (Rocklin, CA, Prima Publishing, 1993); James Wallace and Jim Ericson, *Hard Drive: Bill Gates and the Making of the Microsoft Empire* (New York, John Wiley & Sons, 1992); and Robert Cringely, *Accidental Empires* (New York, Harper Business, 1993).

2. Charles H. Ferguson and Charles R. Morris, *Computer Wars: The Fall of IBM and the Future of Global Technology* (New York, Times Books, 1993), p. 67.

3. John Seabrook, "E-Mail from Bill," *The New Yorker*, 1/10/94, p. 59.

4. Ichbiah, pp. 182–183.

5. Manes and Andrews, pp. 205, 231, 317, 366; Ferguson and Morris, p. 70.

6. Manes and Andrews, pp. 248–249.

7. Manes and Andrews, p. 329.

8. Chris Mason, "Zero-defect code," Microsoft memo, 6/20/89; and Geoffrey Gill, "Microsoft Corporation" (Harvard Business School, Case #9-691-033, 1990).

9. Manes and Andrews, pp. 370–371.

10. Manes and Andrews, p. 316.

11. Manes and Andrews, p. 398

12. Manes and Andrews, pp. 373, 398–399.

13. "The Research Behind Microsoft's Revolutionary Technology: Interview with Nathan Myhrvold," *IEEE Software*, May 1993, pp. 98–99.

14. This discussion is based on Richard Brandt and Amy Cortese, "Bill Gates's Vision," *Business Week*, 6/27/94, pp. 57–62; Myhrvold interview in *IEEE Software*; interview with Sanjay Parthasarathy, Group Product Manager, Business Development, Advanced Consumer Technology, 8/4/93; and interviews with Rick Rashid, Vice President for Research, 4/12/93 and 9/27/94.

15. Myhrvold interview in *IEEE Software*, p. 99.

16. Alan Deutschman, "The Next Big Info Tech Battle," *Fortune*, November 29, 1993, p. 42.

17. "Playboy Interview: Bill Gates," *Playboy*, July 1994, p. 60.

18. The biographical details listed in this section are taken from Microsoft Corporation, Form 10K (Washington, D.C., U.S. Securities and Exchange Commission, June 1994). The ages are as of September 1995.

19. For a discussion of hiring practices for software developers in Japan as well as in some U.S. companies, see Michael A. Cusumano, *Japan's Software Factories: A Challenge to U.S. Management* (New York, Oxford University Press, 1991).

CHAPTER 2

1. See Geoffrey Gill, "Microsoft Corporation: Office Business Unit" (Harvard Business School, Case #9-691-033, 4/25/91), p. 6.

2. For a description of the role of project managers, see Kim B. Clark and Takahiro Fujimoto, *Product Development Performance* (Boston, Harvard Business School Press, 1991); and Steven C. Wheelright and Kim B. Clark, *Revolutionizing Product Development* (New York, Free Press, 1992). For a description of multi-project managers, see Kentaro Nobeoka and Michael A. Cusumano, "Multi-Project Management, Inter-Project Interdependency, and Organizational Coordination in New Product Development" (MIT Sloan School Working Paper #3732-94/BPS, October 1994).

3. Bruce Ryan, "Microsoft Program Management," internal training document, 3/19/93, p. 3.
4. Gill, p. 5.
5. Gill, p. 5.
6. Ryan, p. 8.
7. See the discussion of Simonyi in Robert X. Cringely, *Accidental Empires* (New York, Harper Business, 1992), pp. 104–117.
8. Microsoft Corporation, "Development: An Overview," undated training document.
9. "Development: An Overview."
10. Microsoft Corporation, "Testing at Microsoft," undated training document.
11. See Michael A. Cusumano, "Objectives and Context of Software Measurement, Analysis, and Control," in D. Rombach et al., eds., *Experimental Software Engineering Issues: Critical Assessment and Future Directions* (Berlin, Springer-Verlag, 1993).
12. See Stanley A. Smith and Michael A. Cusumano, "Beyond the Software Factory: A Comparison of 'Classic' and 'PC' Software Developers" (MIT Sloan School Working Paper #3607-93/BPS, September 1993).
13. Ryan, p. 2.
14. Microsoft Corporation, Product Support Services, "ITAA [Information Technology Association of America] Award Application," June 1993.
15. Microsoft Corporation, "User Education," undated training document.
16. Michael Meyer, "Culture Club—Microsoft," *Newsweek*, 11 July 1994, p. 42.
17. Stephen Manes and Paul Andrews, *Gates: How Microsoft's Mogul Reinvented an Industry and Made Himself the Richest Man in America* (New York, Doubleday, 1993), p. 396.
18. Manes and Andrews, pp. 145, 176, 379, and Microsoft annual reports.
19. "ITAA Award Application."
20. Interview with Mark Seidenverg, Product Development Consultant, PSS Strategic Services, 4/15/93.
21. "ITAA Award Application," p. 21.
22. Microsoft Corporation, "Proxy Statement for Annual Meeting of Shareholders," 27 September 1994, pp. 3–4.

CHAPTER 3

1. For a discussion of the VCR story, see Michael A. Cusumano, Yiorgos Mylonadis, and Richard S. Rosenbloom, "Strategic Maneuvering and Mass-Market Dynamics: The Triumph of VHS Over Beta," *Business History Review*, Spring 1992; and Richard S. Rosenbloom and Michael A. Cusumano, "Technological Pioneering and Competitive Advantage: The Birth

of the VCR Industry," *California Management Review*, Vol. 29, No. 4, 1987 (Summer).

2. See Rebecca M. Henderson and Kim B. Clark, "The Reconfiguration of Existing Product Technologies and the Failure of Established Firms," *Administrative Science Quarterly*, Vol. 35, 1990.

3. Kathy Rebello et al., "Is Microsoft Too Powerful?" *Business Week*, March 1, 1993, p. 87; and John Markoff, "Microsoft's Barely Limited Future," *New York Times*, 7/18/94, pp. D1, D4.

4. Laurie Flynn, "From Novell, a Customer-Designed WordPerfect Suite," *New York Times*, 9/11/94, p. F8; Brenton R. Schlender and David Kirkpatrick, "Information Technology Quarterly Report," *Fortune*, 3/20/95, p. 86.

5. The best accounts of Microsoft's early history are Stephen Manes and Paul Andrews, *Gates: How Microsoft's Mogul Reinvented an Industry and Made Himself the Richest Man in America* (New York, Doubleday, 1993); and Daniel Ichbiah, *The Making of Microsoft* (Rocklin, CA, Prima Publishing, 1993). See also James Wallace and Jim Erickson, *Hard Drive: Bill Gates and the Making of the Microsoft Empire* (New York, John Wiley & Sons, 1992).

6. Manes and Andrews, pp. 156–175.

7. Manes and Andrews, p. 433.

8. Ichbiah, pp. 101–103, 108–110.

9. Ichbiah, pp. 112–113, 118.

10. Manes and Andrews, p. 258.

11. Ichbiah, pp. 148–149, 153–156, 201.

12. Ichbiah, pp. 108–110.

13. Manes and Andrews, p. 138.

14. Ichbiah, p. 128.

15. Manes and Andrews, pp. 166–168; Robert X. Cringeley, *Accidental Empires* (New York, Harper Business, 1992), pp. 104–117.

16. Ichbiah, pp. 122–129, 137; Manes and Andrews, p. 239.

17. Bill Gates, talk at Boston Computer Society to launch Office 4.0, 10/18/93.

18. Manes and Andrews, p. 188.

19. Gates talk at Boston Computer Society.

20. Manes and Andrews, p. 438.

21. John Markoff, "Microsoft is Winning in Trademark Case," *New York Times*, 8/29/94, p. D1.

22. Manes and Andrews, pp. 382–383. For a full account of the NT story, see G. Pascal Zachary, *Show-Stopper: The Breakneck Race to Create Windows NT and the Next Generation at Microsoft* (New York, Free Press, 1994).

23. Joseph Panettieri, "Bill Gates' Enterprise Embrace," *Information Week*, 12/5/94, pp. 12–15.

24. Richard Brandt and Amy Cortese, "Bill Gates's Vision," *Business Week*, June 27, 1994, p. 61; Dale Lewallen, Scot Finnie, and Ed Bott, "Windows NT," *PC/Computing*, July 1993, pp. 119–152; G. Pascal Zachary, "Agony and Ecstasy of 200 Code Writers Beget Windows NT," *Wall Street Journal*, 5/26/93, p. 1.

25. Manes and Andrews, p. 398.

26. Currid & Company, *Software: What's Hot and What's Not* (Rocklin, CA, Prima Publishing, 1994).

27. Michael J. Miller, "The 11th Annual Awards for Technical Excellence," *PC Magazine*, 12/20/94, p. 115; and Robin Raskin, "The Best of 1994," *PC Magazine*, January 10, 1995, pp. 111–155.

28. Ichbiah, pp. 251–255; Manes and Andrews, p. 268.

29. See a series of articles in the *New York Times* from 2/24/94, p. D1; 3/6/94, p. F7; 5/16/94, p. D6; and 6/11/94, p. 37.

30. See Tom Halfhill, "How Safe is Data Compression?" *Byte*, February 1994, pp. 56–74, especially p. 72; P. Watt, "How Happy Are You . . . Really?" *PC Magazine*, July 1993, p. 311; J. Prosise, "DOS 6.0: The Ultimate Software Bundle?" *PC Magazine*, April 13, 1993, pp. 124–139; J. Bertolucci, "IBM DOS One-Ups DOS 6," *PC World*, August 1993, p. 64.

31. Ichbiah, pp. 193, 206.

32. Watt; "Products of the Year," *PC Computing*, December 1992, pp. 135, 192; "The *Window User* Best Awards," *Window User*, April 1993, pp. 135, 192; C. Stinson, "The New Spreadsheets: Diversity Blossoms Amid the Rows and Columns," *PC Magazine*, November 10, 1992, p. 111; J. Walkenbach, "Excel for Windows 4.0 Sets New Standard," *InfoWorld*, April 27, 1992, p. 74.

33. Ichbiah, pp. 130–131.

34. Ichbiah, pp. 134–136.

35. Watt; C. Abes, "Sixth Annual World-Class Awards," *MacWorld*, August 1992, p. 120; D. Tynan, "Touch of World Class," *PC World*, December 1992, p. 115; "Products of the Year," *PC Computing*, December 1992, pp. 135, 192; K. Carlson, "War of the Words," *PC Computing*, August 1993, p. 124; W. Harrel, "Word Processor or Desktop Publisher?" *PC World*, June 1993, p. 181; J. Heid, "Reviews: Microsoft Word 5.0," *MacWorld*, April 1992, p. 175; B. Livingston, "Word for Windows Bugs and Hidden Features," *InfoWorld*, 3/22/93, p. 24; D. McClelland, "Beyond Words," *MacWorld*, September 1992, p. 248.

36. See, for example, John Markoff, "The Wrath Over Microsoft Word," *New York Times*, 1/20/95, p. D1.

37. These comments are based on our usage of Excel, Word, and PowerPoint, as well as review articles cited earlier, and Microsoft's product documentation.

38. Manes and Andrews, p. 346; Ichbiah, pp. 189–191.

39. Manes and Andrews, pp. 346–348, 396–398.

40. Watt; S. Johnston, "Microsoft Beefs Up Windows 3.0 Support: Jammed Phone Lines Prompt Expansion," *InfoWorld*, 7/2/90, p. 14; J. Pepper, "Microsoft Windows 3.1: More Reliable, More Powerful" *PC Sources*, June 1992, pp. 371–372; D. Tynan, "Touch of World Class," *PC World*, December 1992, pp. 135, 190; S. Canter, "Will the New Standard Please Stand Up?" *PC Magazine*, 11/10/92, p. 250.

41. D. Strom, "Five Metrics to Rate the Level of Service for Network OSes," *InfoWorld*, 3/29/93, p. 63; Len Feldman, *Windows NT: The Next Generation* (Carmel, Indiana, SAMS Publishing, 1993); D. Coursey, "NT Isn't Worth the Wait," *Computerworld*, 6/14/93, pp. 45, 47; S. Johnston, "Programs Will Need New Drivers for Windows NT," *InfoWorld*, 8/3/92, p. 6; J. Udell, "Windows, windows everywhere?" *Byte*, June 1993, p. 73; A. Cortese, "NT Beta 2 Earns Kudos," *PC Week*, 3/29/93, p. 8.

42. Adam Meyerson, "Chicago Preview: Windows for 1995," *PC Computing*, July 1994, p. 64.

43. Internal documents that we received include "Cairo: An Introduction to the Next Generation," Microsoft confidential report, 6/24/93; and "Application Model in the Cairo Paradigm Shift," 8/6/93, Microsoft internal memo from Steve Madigan to Bill Gates and others.

44. A detailed preliminary description of Cairo can be found in John Rymer, Michael Guttman, and Jason Matthews, "Microsoft OLE 2.0 and the Road to Cairo," *Distributed Computing Monitor*, Vol. 9, No. 1, January 1994. See also Norvin Leach and Mary Jo Foley, "Distributed OLE to Debut Next Month," *PC Week*, 12/19/94, p. 1.

45. These comments on Windows 3.1 and Windows 95 are based primarily on Ed Bott, "Inside Windows 4.0," *PC Computing*, March 1994, pp. 124–139; Adam Meyerson, "Chicago Preview: Windows for 1995," *PC Computing*, July 1994, pp. 58–69; and "WinPad on Windows 95?" *Information Week*, 12/5/94, p. 102.

46. Interview with Jonathan Manheim, Windows 95 (Chicago) Test Manager, 9/27/94; and Peter Coffee, "Win 95 Raises New Questions," *PC Week*, 4/10/95, pp. 1, 89.

47. Robert Hess, "Microsoft's Not Alone: Apple Delays Copeland OS Release," *PC Week*, 12/26/94–1/2/95, p. 106.

48. Manes and Andrews, p. 202. Also quoted in Andrew Schulman, *Unauthorized Windows 95* (San Mateo, CA, IDG Books, 1994), p. 13.

49. Steve Ballmer, Microsoft Executive Vice President, keynote talk at colloquium on "Colliding Worlds: The Convergence of Computers, Telecommunications and Consumer Electronics," Harvard Business School, 10/5/94.

50. Stratford Sherman, "The New Computer Revolution," *Fortune*, 6/14/93, p. 74.

51. Ballmer talk at Harvard Business School.

52. Manes and Andrews, pp. 77, 82; Ichbiah, pp. 19–26.

53. Manes and Andrews, pp. 91–92, 297.

54. Manes and Andrews, pp. 162, 193.

55. "Playboy Interview: Bill Gates," *Playboy*, July 1994, p. 64.

56. Manes and Andrews, pp. 192–193.

57. See Stuart Taylor, Jr., "What to Do with the Microsoft Monster," *American Lawyer*, November 1993; and Schulman, pp. 6–7.

58. Manes and Andrews, p. 346.

59. *Informationweek*, 3/7/94, p. 13; Mary Jo Foley et al., "Win 95 OEMs Grin and Bear It," *PC Week*, 11/28/94, p. 1; Amy Cortese and Richard Brandt, "No Slack for Microsoft's Rivals," *Business Week*, 12/19/94, p. 35.

60. Ichbiah, pp. 176–178.

61. Bott, "Inside Windows 4.0," p. 136.

62. Peter H. Lewis, "Friendlier Software by IBM," *New York Times*, 9/8/94, p. D1.

63. Manes and Andrews, p. 210.

64. Manes and Andrews, pp. 126, 131, 207, 228–229, 250; and Tom Cottrell, "Fragmented Standards and the Development of Japan's Microcomputer Software Industry," *Research Policy*, Vol. 23, No. 2, March 1994, pp. 143–174.

65. Ichbiah, pp. 114–119, 134–136.

66. "Microsoft Shares Fall After Judge Rejects Pact," *Asian Wall Street Journal*, 2/16/95, p. 1.

67. "Microsoft Antitrust Deal Rejected," *Japan Times*, 2/16/95, p. 13; "U.S. Government Appeals Ruling in Microsoft Case," *Japan Times*, 2/18/95, p. 11.

68. "PC Seller Dumps Microsoft System," *Japan Times*, 3/10/95, p. 11; Douglas Lavin, "Vobis Drops Microsoft's MS-DOS in Favor of IBM Operating System," *Asian Wall Street Journal*, 3/10–11/95, p. 15.

69. "Microsoft, Vobis End Fee Dispute," *Japan Times*, 3/17/95, p. 11.

70. Washington Post, 7/17/94, p. A7; Edmund L. Andrews, "Microsoft's Antitrust Accord Loosens Its Grip on Software," *New York Times*, 7/17/94, pp. 1, 8.

71. See Andy Cortese and Kelly Holland, "Bill Gates is Rattling the Teller's Window," *Business Week*, 10/31/94, p. 50; Elizabeth Corcoran, "Microsoft to Buy Maker of Quicken Software," *Washington Post*, 10/14/94, p. C1; Lawrence M. Fisher, "Microsoft May Make Quicken the Home Banking Standard," *New York Times*, 10/16/94, p. F9; and G. Christian Hill, Don Clark, and Viveca Novak, "Microsoft's Dropped Bid for Intuit Hands U.S. a Victory," *Asian Wall Street Journal*, 5/23/95, p. 6.

72. Michael Schrage, "Japan Gives in to US' New Digital HDTV Standard," *Boston Globe*, 2/27/94, p. 84.

73. Ferguson and Morris, p. 59.

74. Don Clark, "Microsoft Will Keep Making Products for Apple's Macintosh, Gates Pledges," *Wall Street Journal*, 3/22/95, p. B6.

75. Ferguson and Morris, p. 153. See, for example, Andrew Schulman, David Maxey, and Matt Pietrek, *Undocumented Windows: A Programmers Guide to Reserve Microsoft Windows API Functions* (Reading, MA, Addison-Wesley, 1992).

76. Gates talk at Boston Computer Society.

77. Gates talk at Boston Computer Society.

78. Rymer, Guttman, and Matthews contains an excellent discussion of OLE and its evolution.

79. See, for example, the 917-page *OLE 2 Programmer's Reference Volume 1* by Microsoft Corporation (Redmond, WA, 1994), available in nearly any bookstore with a computer section.

80. See Leach and Foley.

81. Rymer, Guttman, and Matthews; Laurie Flynn, "Preparing for the Battle in Mix-and-Match Software," *New York Times*, 5/22/94, p. F10.

82. "Microsoft to back off on Win 95 terms," *PC Week*, 2/6/95, p. 3.

83. Lawrence M. Fisher, "On the Road to Chicago, Little Time for Leisure," *New York Times*, 9/4/94, p F8; Don Clark, "Microsoft Said to Pick Label 'Windows 95,'" *Wall Street Journal*, 9/8/94, p. B4; Sullivan, p. 217.

84. Microsoft, "Microsoft Unveils Software Architecture for the Workplace," News Release, 6/9/94, pp. 1–3.

85. Richard Brandt, "The Battle of the Network Stars Boots Up," *Business Week*, 4/25/94, pp. 128–130; *Boston Globe*, 2/24/94, p. 61; David Kirkpatrick, "Why Microsoft Can't Stop Lotus Notes," *Fortune*, 12/12/94, pp. 141–157; Paula Rooney, "Exchange Beta 1 Gains Initial Plaudits," *PC Week*, 2/27/95, p. 8.

86. Panettieri, pp. 13–15.

87. Manes and Andrews, pp. 407–410.

88. Laurie Flynn, "Now, Microsoft Wants to Gather Information," *New York Times*, 7/27/94, p. D1.

89. See Stephen Manes, "Bob: Your New Best Friend's Personality Quirks," *New York Times*, 1/17/95, p. C8; William Casy, "The Two Faces of Microsoft Bob," *Washington Post*, Washington Business Section, p. 15, 1/30/95; and Don Clark, "How a Woman's Passion and Persistence Made 'Bob,'" *Wall Street Journal*, 1/10/95, p. B1; Richard Brandt, "Microsoft: He-e-e-re's Bob!" *Business Week*, 1/9/95, p. 42; Laurie Flynn, "Microsoft Prepares 'Bob,' A Guide for PC Novices," *New York Times*, 1/5/95, p. D3.

90. Tim Bajarin, "Microsoft's Ambitious Windows Strategy," *Boston Computer Currents*, April 1994, p. 13.
91. Interview with Rick Rashid, Vice President, Research, 9/27/94; "Microsoft Joins Sony in Deal," *New York Times*, 1/24/95, p. D2.
92. Ballmer talk at Harvard Business School.
93. Ballmer talk at Harvard Business School.
94. Richard Brandt, "Microsoft Hits the Gas," *Business Week*, 3/21/94, pp. 34–35.
95. This discussion of the Microsoft Network is based on Richard Brandt and Amy Cortese, "Bill Gates's Vision," *Business Week*, 6/27/94, pp. 57–62; Mitchell Martin, "Microsoft Plugs an Interactive Tomorrow," *International Herald Tribune*, 11/15/94, p. 9, 13; Laurie Flynn, "Getting On-Line—the Microsoft Way," *New York Times*, 11/20/94, p. F10; Richard Brandt and Amy Cortese, "Microsoft Wants to Move into Your Family Room," *Business Week*, 11/28/94, pp. 92–93; Jared Sandberg, "Microsoft to Unveil Its On-Line Service, Marvel, at Comdex," *Wall Street Journal*, 11/8/94, p. A3; Peter Lewis, "Microsoft Expected to Disclose Plans for an On-Line Network," *Wall Street Journal*, 11/14/94, p. D3; Don Clark, "Microsoft Launches Its On-Line Network," *Wall Street Journal*, 11/15/94, p. B6; Lawrence M. Fisher, "Microsoft and Visa in Software Deal," *New York Times*, 11/9/94, p. D2; Paul Farhi, "TCI Joins Microsoft in Venture," *Washington Post*, 12/22/94, p. B9.
96. Ballmer talk at Harvard Business School.

CHAPTER 4

1. Interview with Dave Moore, Director of Development, 3/17/93; and Microsoft Corporation, Office Business Unit, "Scheduling Methodology and Milestones Definition," unpublished internal document, 9/1/89.
2. See Winston W. Royce, "Managing the Development of Large Software Systems," *Proceedings of IEEE Wescon*, August 1970.
3. See Barry W. Boehm, "A Spiral Model of Software Development and Enhancement," *IEEE Computer*, May 1988.
4. See also "Scheduling Methodology and Milestones Definition."
5. Chris Peters, "Shipping Software," Tech Talk Seminar Video, 1990.
6. Peters video.
7. Peters video.
8. Fine interview, 8/4–5/93, and John Fine, "How to Write a Great Spec," Microsoft blue tray (lunch) presentation, 2/93.
9. "How to Write a Great Spec."
10. "How to Write a Great Spec."

11. "How to Write a Great Spec."
12. Peters video.
13. Jon De Vaan, "Microsoft Excel 4.0 Post-Mortem," 6/8/92.
14. G. Pascal Zachary, *Show-Stopper* (New York, Free Press, 1994).
15. Peters video.
16. Adrian King, *Inside Windows 95* (Redmond, WA, Microsoft Press, 1994); Steve Fox, "Windows 4.0," *PC WORLD* (August 1994), pp. 128–135.
17. Ben Slivka and Mike Dryfoos, "MS-DOS 6 Development Post-Mortem," 9/93.
18. Bruce Ryan, Program Manager, Worldwide Products Division, "Microsoft Program Management," 3/19/93.
19. See the discussion of Hitachi and other Japanese companies in Michael A. Cusumano, *Japan's Software Factories: A Challenge to U.S. Management* (New York, Oxford University Press, 1991).
20. "MS-DOS 6 Development Post-Mortem."

CHAPTER 5

1. Chris Peters, "Shipping Software," Tech Talk Seminar Video, 1990.
2. Stanley A. Smith and Michael A. Cusumano, "Beyond the Software Factory: A Comparison of 'Classic' and 'PC' Software Developers" (MIT Sloan School Working Paper #3607-93/BPS, September 1993).
3. Frederick Brooks, "No Silver Bullet: Essence and Accidents of Software Engineering," *Computer*, Vol. 20, No. 4, April 1987, pp. 10–19.
4. Jon De Vaan, "Microsoft Excel 4.0 Post-Mortem," 6/8/92.
5. John Markoff, "The Wrath Over Microsoft Word," *New York Times*, 1/20/95, p. D1.
6. Charles Simonyi and Martin Heller, "The Hungarian Revolution," *BYTE*, August 1991, pp. 131–138; and Doug Klunder, "Naming Conventions (Hungarian)," Microsoft internal document, 1/18/88.
7. Klunder, "Naming Conventions (Hungarian)."
8. Klunder, "Naming Conventions (Hungarian)."
9. Simonyi and Heller.
10. "Microsoft Excel 4.0 Post-Mortem."
11. Eamonn Sullivan, "NT Versions of Word, Excel Add Little," *PC Week*, 11/14/94, p. 217; and electronic mail correspondence with Chris Peters, 12/5/94.
12. Barry Shaw, "Works for Windows 2.0 Development Postmortem Report," 1/13/92; and Mike Blaylock and Clay Gautier, "WinWorks 2.0 Testing Postmortem," 11/4/91.
13. David Anderson, Moshe Dunie, Ken Gregg, Jonathan Manheim, S. So-

masegar, and Jim Thomas, "NT Test PDK 1 & PDK 2 Critique," 4/92, pp. 4–5.

14. Bill Gates, talk at Boston Computer Society to launch Office 4.0, 10/18/93.

15. Gates talk at Boston Computer Society.

16. David Anderson, Richard Dill, Moshe Dunie, Kenneth Gregg, Jonathan Manheim, S. Somasegar, Richard Turner, and Arden White, "Windows NT Test PDC & Beta 1 Critique," 1993, p. 3.

17. "Windows NT Test PDC & Beta 1 Critique," pp. 2, 13.

18. "Windows NT Test PDC & Beta 1 Critique," pp. 1, 17–18. The bugs listed for Windows NT include those bugs found during development prior to 12/19/92; the Beta 1 release shipped 10/92.

19. "Windows NT Test PDC & Beta 1 Critique," pp. 17–18.

20. "Microsoft Excel 4.0 Post-Mortem."

21. WesC, "Am I Done Yet?," Microsoft internal document.

22. Excel 5.0 Test Plan, 4/13/93, and "Testing at Microsoft," Microsoft internal presentation.

23. Phil Fawcett, "Mac Word 4.0 Postmortem Report," 5/25/89.

24. Scott Leatham, "Money 2.0 Test Summary Report," 9/15/92.

25. "Works for Windows 2.0 Development Postmortem Report" and "Win-Works 2.0 Testing Postmortem."

CHAPTER 6

1. Stephen Manes and Paul Andrews, *Gates: How Microsoft's Mogul Reinvented an Industry—and Made Himself the Richest Man in America* (New York, Doubleday, 1993), p. 39.

2. Charles Simonyi, untitled Microsoft memo, 13 August 1987, p. 1.

3. Ibid., p. 7.

4. Chris Mason, "Mac Word 4.0 Development Postmortem," 5/19/89.

5. Phil Fawcett, "Mac Word 4.0 Post Mortem Report," 5/25/89.

6. Jon De Vaan, "Microsoft Excel 4.0 Post-Mortem," 6/8/92.

7. Mike Mathieu, "Excel 4 Post-Mortem," 2/12/92, pp. 1–3.

8. Marc Olsen, "Excel 4.0 Post Mortem for Marc's team," 6/92.

9. Craig Bartholomew, "Encarta '93 Post-Mortem Analysis," 5/18/93, p. 5.

10. Interview with Anil Bhansali, Software Design Engineer, Excel, 8/5/93.

11. This discussion of DoubleSpace and MS-DOS 6 is based primarily on interviews with Ben Slivka, Microsoft MS-DOS Development Manager, 8/4/93 and 9/29/94, as well as on a telephone interview with a Microsoft customer support engineer for MS-DOS, January 10, 1994, and Tom

Halfhill, "How Safe is Data Compression?" *Byte*, February 1994, pp. 56–74, especially p. 72.

12. Two bugs resulted when DoubleSpace attempted to utilize the high memory space allocated to special drivers, or had occasional conflicts with special memory caching techniques. Also, because DoubleSpace copied and then compressed data to another "virtual" drive on the computer, copy protection schemes tended to interpret this as a user illegally copying the program files to *another machine*. On some user's machines, these problems resulted in lost files. Other problems, such as shutting machines off before files were fully stored, could result in cross-linked files that corrupted a user's hard disk, although this was more a difficulty or feature of MS-DOS rather than DoubleSpace per se.

13. Microsoft recalled copies of MS-DOS 6.0 and 6.2 with the DoubleSpace feature because of a patent infringement with Stac Electronics' product, not because of quality problems. Microsoft fixed the two major bugs in 6.0 that could destroy files for a new release (version 6.2) shipped in November 1993, and added some tools to help users diagnose and fix any problems that might occur. Microsoft then shipped 6.21 in April 1994 with no data compression, and 6.22 in June 1994 with another data compression system that did not violate the Stac patents.

14. "Mac Word 4.0 Development Postmortem."

15. Barry Shaw, "Works for Windows 2.0 Development Postmortem Report," 1/13/92; and Mike Blaylock and Clay Gautier, "WinWorks 2.0 Testing Postmortem," 11/4/91.

16. Scott Leatham, "Money 2.0 Test Summary Report," 9/15/92.

17. Microsoft Corporation, Product Support Services, "ITAA [Information Technology Association of America] Award Application," June 1993, p. 15.

18. These data come from Microsoft Corporation, "Case Study: The New Microsoft Support Network," undated and unpublished document, especially p. 18; ITAA application, p. 16. Also, interview with Mark Seidenverg, Product Development Consultant, PSS Strategic Services, 4/15/93; Peters interview, 4/12/93; and interview with Trish May, Director, Product Support Services Marketing, 8/5/93.

19. "Case Study: The New Microsoft Support Network."

20. For industry data, see Peter Lewis, "Free Technical Support: An Endangered Species of Service," *New York Times*, 10/10/93, p. F10.

21. ITAA application, pp. 17–18.

22. ITAA application, Introduction.

23. ITAA application, p. 16.

24. ITAA application, p. 31.

25. Interview with Mike Conte, Senior Program Manager, Office, 9/29/94.
26. Bill Gates, talk at Boston Computer Society to launch Office 4.0, 10/18/93.
27. "Microsoft Excel 4.0 Post-Mortem."

CHAPTER 7

1. Chris Peters, "Shipping Software," Tech Talk Seminar Video, 1990.
2. Peters video.
3. "Playboy Interview: Bill Gates," *Playboy*, July 1994, p. 63.
4. G. Pascal Zachary, "Intuit Gambit May Signal that Gates is Going Soft," *Seattle Times*, 12/9/94.
5. Mary Jo Foley, "Stakes are High for Win 95 Team," *PC Week*, 2/20/95, p. 116.
6. See Michael A. Cusumano, *Japan's Software Factories: A Challenge to U.S. Management* (New York, Oxford University Press, 1991).
7. Rebecca M. Henderson and Kim B. Clark, "The Reconfiguration of Existing Product Technologies and the Failure of Established Firms," *Administrative Science Quarterly*, Vol. 35, 1990.
8. See Gary Reback et al., "White Paper: Technological, Economic and Legal Perspectives Regarding Microsoft's Business Strategy in Light of the Proposed Acquisition of Intuit, Inc." (Unpublished manuscript, Wilson, Sonsini, Goodrich & Rosati, 11/14/94). Also see Don Clark, "Microsoft Plan to Buy Intuit Faces Scrutiny of Antitrust Concerns," *Wall Street Journal*, 11/22/94, p. B6.
9. Jared Sandberg, "Microsoft On-Line Rivals Assail Its Planned Service," *Asian Wall Street Journal*, 3/2/95, p. 9.
10. Apple Computer, Inc., Electronic Press Release, 3/2/95.
11. Laurie Flynn, "I.B.M. Plans to License Macintosh," *New York Times*, 11/18/94, p. D5.
12. Don Clark, "How a Woman's Passion and Persistence Made 'Bob,'" *Wall Street Journal*, 1/10/95, p. B1.

APPENDIX 4

1. Source: "Microsoft Applications Division 1991 Survey Results," Business Unit/Job Function Summary, April 1991, prepared by Manus Services Corporation.

APPENDIX 5

1. Sources for this table include references in Chapter 3, especially Richard Brandt, "Microsoft Hits the Gas," *Business Week*, 3/21/94, pp. 34–35; Richard Brandt and Amy Cortese, "Bill Gates's Vision," *Business Week*, June 27, 1994, pp. 59–62; John Hyatt, "Microsoft and TCI in Pact," *Boston Globe*, 3/4/94, p. 71; John Markoff, "Oracle Hopes to Steal a March on Microsoft," *New York Times*, 2/15/94, p. D4; Kathryn Jones, "Mtel to Join Microsoft in Data Deal," *New York Times*, 3/25/94, p. C3; *Information-week*, 4/11/94, p. 22; Andrew Pollack, "Microsoft and N.T.T. in Delivery Venture," *New York Times*, 3/24/94, p. C4; John Markoff, "Microsoft Or-ganizes Its Interactive TV Team," *New York Times*, 11/2/94, p. D6; Mitchell Martin, "Microsoft Plugs an Interactive Tomorrow," *Interna-tional Herald Tribune*, 11/15/94, p. 13; Peter H. Lewis, "Microsoft's Next Move is On Line," *New York Times*, 1/13/95, p. D1; "Microsoft Joins Sony in Deal," *New York Times*, 1/24/95, p. D2; Ralph King, "Microsoft Signs Up On-Line Vendors," *Wall Street Journal*, 2/8/95, p. B6; Thomas R. King and Don Clark, "Gates Invests a Byte of Money for Cache of Hollywood Stars," *Wall Street Journal*, 3/23/95, p. A3; Don Clark, "Microsoft Re-cruits 43 On-Line Partners," *Asian Wall Street Journal*, 5/12–13/95, p. 10; "Microsoft, NBC network form alliance," *Japan Times*, 5/18/95, p. 13.

ACKNOWLEDGMENTS

We have many people and institutions to thank for this book. First, we thank people at Microsoft for their cooperation, beginning with Dave Moore. He was our first contact in the company. He immediately became intrigued by the idea of writing a book on how Microsoft develops software products; he got us access to people and company materials, and he facilitated our contacts for the two years that it took to complete the project. We thank Bill Gates and Mike Maples, and no doubt other people unknown to us, for supporting Dave's position that Microsoft should allow us to write this book.

We would also like to thank everyone who met us for one or more interviews, in alphabetical order: Richard Barth, Jeff Beehler, Anil Bhansali, Chuck Yoong Chan, Jim Conner, Mike Conte, Bob Davidson, Jon De Vaan, Moshe Dunie, John Fine, Ed Fries, Bill Gates, Chris Graham, Jonathan Manheim, Mike Maples, Dave Maritz, Trish May, Dave Moore, Max Morris, Marc Olson, Sanjay Parthasarathy, Lou Perazzoli, Chris Peters, Rick Rashid, Mark Seidenverg, Jeanne Sheldon, Roger Sherman, Brad Silverberg, Charles Simonyi, Steven Sinofsky, Ben Slivka, Dave Thompson, Marc Walker, Brad Weed, David Weise, David Whitney, Chris Williams, and Christine Wittress. Steve Ballmer also allowed us to quote from a colloquium talk he gave in October 1994.

We owe special thanks to Microsoft people who took the time to give us detailed feedback on the manuscript as it evolved. Dave Moore patiently read and made suggestions on two chapter drafts. He also made sure to circulate copies within the company and get

493

other people's comments to us. Steven Sinofsky spent many hours critiquing what we wrote; he inspired important changes and improvements. Roger Sherman gave us several comments that corrected and sharpened our accounts of Microsoft's history and strategy. Ben Slivka and Mitch Mathews commented on sensitive discussions and, with Dave Moore and Steven Sinofsky, helped us be fair. Jon De Vaan, Mike Maples, Chris Peters, and Chris Williams provided factual corrections and editorial suggestions. Of course, despite this extensive feedback from Microsoft people, only we are responsible for the book's content and arguments, as well as any errors that remain.

We thank our editor at the Free Press, Bob Wallace, and his assistant, Catherine Wayland. Bob supported the project with great enthusiasm from the very beginning, providing early feedback that led to major improvements in the manuscript. He helped us craft the subtitle, channeled (with Catherine's help) various materials on Microsoft to us, and rallied the troops at the Free Press and Simon & Schuster to produce and market the book.

Both authors thank Lisa Breede of MIT and her crew (Kathleen McMahon and Lauren Howard) for transcribing the interviews so professionally. Michelle Fiorenza of MIT commented on the jacket designs. We want to acknowledge as well Carol Franco of Harvard Business School Press and Herb Addison of Oxford University Press. Their avid interest in the book proposal and initial suggestions inspired us to create a more readable product. We regret that we could choose only one publisher.

Michael Cusumano's personal thanks begin with Stanley Smith, now of IBM Austin. His master's thesis for the MIT Management of Technology program in 1992–1993 included a case study of Microsoft and a visit to the company in March 1993 with Cusumano. This visit inspired the book proposal. Nancy Staudenmayer of MIT provided research assistance on Microsoft's postmortems as well as extraordinarily useful comments on the first draft of the manuscript, including key suggestions for restructuring. She also prepared the index. Cusumano received other invaluable comments from people who read the 600-page manuscript out of both interest and friendship. He thanks Neil Wasserman of Unisys, Mel Horwitch of Theseus, Michael

Scott Morton of MIT, and Victor Basili of the University of Maryland, all of whose suggestions greatly enhanced the structure and arguments of the book.

Yaichi Aoshima, Chris Tucci, Rebecca Henderson, and Ed Roberts of MIT also read parts of the manuscript and made helpful suggestions. In addition, several MBA and Management of Technology students at MIT wrote master's theses under Cusumano during 1993–1994 that provided useful background information on PC software and the information highway; special thanks go to Ian Curry, David Daimond, Anders Fornander, J. Mathew Gardiner, Veronica Lee, Greg Tobin, Jennifer Toomey, Alan Trefzger, and Tim Wood (who also worked at Microsoft as a summer intern). William Welch of Washington, D.C., provided research assistance on Microsoft products during the summer of 1993.

Cusumano would like to thank participants in various seminars for challenging and insightful comments that helped refine arguments in the book. Presentations at the MIT Sloan School included seminars for the Operations Management Group, the Strategy and International Management Group, the International Center for Research on the Management of Technology, and Theseus students visiting from France. Other presentations include talks on Microsoft at the Harvard Business School, the Institute for Advanced Computer Studies and Department of Computer Science at the University of Maryland, the Department of Computer Science at Carnegie-Mellon University, the School of Business at Georgetown University, the EPOCH Foundation in Taiwan, and the Valparaiso School of Business in Chile, as well as Hitotsubashi University, Tokyo University, Kobe University, the Nara Institute of Science and Technology, and several other public and company forums in Japan. Special thanks to Larry Druffel, Bill Peterson, and Joe Besselman of the Software Engineering Institute and Carnegie-Mellon University for their important feedback.

The International Center for Research on the Management of Technology at the MIT Sloan School funded several months of Cusumano's time on this project, as well as some research assistance. He expresses his special thanks to the center's sponsors for their generous support. Discretionary funds from the MIT Leaders for Manufacturing program covered additional time and expenses.

The Institute for Advanced Computer Studies at the University of Maryland provided office space for part of a sabbatical year during 1994–1995 used to write up major portions of the manuscript. The University of Tokyo economics faculty provided office space for the last few months of work on the book. Thanks also to Nobuko Ichikawa of the World Bank. She patiently allowed her husband to intrude on her e-mail account during the summer of 1993 and seven sabbatical months spent in Washington, D.C., during 1994–1995.

Richard Selby extends his personal thanks to many people who contributed to this book directly or indirectly. Victor Basili of the University of Maryland and Barry Boehm of the University of Southern California defined numerous seminal ideas in software engineering that provide a foundation for many concepts in this book. Koji Torii of the Nara Institute of Science and Technology in Japan, and Dieter Rombach of the University of Kaiserslautern, Germany, provided many insights and opportunities to study state-of-the-art software development methods in Asia and Europe. Harlan Mills and F. Terry Baker, both formerly of IBM, originated several approaches for large-scale software development that deepened our understanding of effective techniques.

Members of the Arcadia software environment project—especially Richard Taylor of the University of California at Irvine and Leon Osterweil of the University of Massachusetts—established pivotal ideas for advances in software engineering that provide points of reference for this work. Will Tracz and Lou Coglianese, both of Loral (formerly of IBM), demonstrated the benefits of architecture-based software development that we describe. Members of the STARS software technology project—especially Hans Polzer, Teri Payton, Tom Shields, James Baldo, and Ed Guy of Unisys, Hal Hart and Rick Hefner of TRW, Dick Drake of Loral (formerly of IBM), and Major Clint Heintzelman of Peterson Air Force Base—validated approaches for technology integration from which this book benefits.

Selby thanks several other persons with whom he has had ongoing insightful discussions of best-practice software development methods (in alphabetical order): Bill Agresti of Mitre, Bob Balzer of the University of Southern California, Randy Corke of Digital Equipment Corporation, Bill Curtis of TeraQuest Metrics (formerly of MCC and SEI), Greg Daich of the Air Force Software Technology Support Center, Larry Druffel of the Software Engineering Institute/Carnegie-Mellon University, Stu Feldman of Bellcore, Peter Freeman of Georgia Tech, John Gannon of the University of Maryland, Amrit Goel of Syracuse University, Dennis Hebert of Digital Equipment Corporation, John King of the University of California at Irvine, Barbara Liskov of MIT, Frank McGarry of Computer Sciences Corporation (formerly of NASA), Lloyd Mosemann of the Office of the Secretary of the Air Force, Jerry Page of Computer Sciences Corporation, Avinash Patil of Digital Equipment Corporation, Walker Royce of Rational (formerly of TRW), Tim Standish of the University of California at Irvine, Tony Wasserman of IDE, and Marv Zelkowitz of the University of Maryland.

A number of Selby's students in the Ph.D. program in information and computer science at the University of California at Irvine helped with the book by conducting various projects related to Microsoft and best-practice development (in alphabetical order): Jeffrey Blevins, Eli Charne, Deborah Dubrow, Roy Fielding, David Hilbert, Michael Kantor, Peyman Oreizy, Ron Reimer, Jason Robbins, John Self, Jonathan Shaw, Andrew Tipple, and Doris Tonne. Andrew Tipple and Deborah Dubrow also drew several figures and tables, and Peyman Oreizy also provided his perspective from being a summer intern at Microsoft.

Selby's software research from 1987 through the present has been funded by the Advanced Research Projects Agency (ARPA) (and administered through the National Science Foundation or Rome Laboratories). He is very grateful for this support. ARPA managers who played critical roles in establishing and continuing this funding as well as sharing technical visions are (in alphabetical order): Duane Adams, Barry Boehm, John Foreman, John Salasin, Bill Scherlis (now at Carnegie-Mellon University), Steve Squires, and Ed Thompson. Selby also thanks the MIT Sloan School of Management and Laboratory for Computer Science for hosting him in 1993, when this book project started, and Osaka University for hosting him on sabbatical during 1992.

Selby would also like to express special thanks to his family who was extremely flexible and provided patient support during the book-writing period: Kimberly, Paige, and Colfax Selby; Richard and Nancy Selby, Sr.; Peter and Tracy Pavlick; Ross and Barbara Ofria; Anna Caliri; and Brian and Laura Ofria. Paige and Colfax encouraged Selby to explain concepts so that even five- and four-year olds might grasp them, and throughout the whole process, his wife, Kimberly, gave endless support and enthusiasm.

Both authors also thank Microsoft for inviting them to attend and contribute to a behind-the-scenes executive retreat. Selby presented a critique of the company's software development methods to Microsoft's top fifty management and technical executives; he thanks Bill Gates, Mike Maples, Paul Maritz, and Chris Williams for endorsing his contribution.

Some readers may be curious about what hardware and software we used to write this book. Cusumano started with an AT&T 386 desktop computer (4 megabytes of RAM and an 80 megabyte hard drive) and a Texas Instruments 386 laptop (6 megabytes of RAM and a 40 megabyte hard drive); as a word processor, he ran Word-Perfect 5.1 for DOS (with MS-DOS 5.0, followed by MS-DOS 6.0 and 6.2). He then switched to an NEC Versa 486 laptop (20 megabytes of RAM and a 340 megabyte hard drive). He also adopted Word 6.0 from Microsoft Office 4.2 as a word processor, which he ran on Windows 3.1 and MS-DOS 6.21. Selby used Word 5.0, Excel 3.0, and MacDraw II 1.1 on a Macintosh PowerBook 170 with version 7.0 operating system (4 megabytes of RAM and a 40 megabyte hard drive), Publisher 2.0 on a Compaq desktop computer, as well as various editors and tools on a Sun Microsystems SparcStation II workstation with SunOS 4.1.3 operating system (16 megabytes of RAM and a 424 megabyte hard drive).

INDEX

499

ABOUT THE AUTHORS

Michael A. Cusumano teaches the strategic management of technology at Massachusetts Institute of Technology. He has acted as consultant to a range of major companies and institutions in the United States and abroad, including AT&T, Ford, IBM, Texas Instruments, and the World Bank. The author of two previous books, *The Japanese Automobile Industry* and *Japan's Software Factories*, he has also written articles on competitive strategy and technology management in the automobile and computer industries. He lives in Cambridge, Massachusetts.

Richard W. Selby teaches information and computer science at the University of California, Irvine. He has consulted worldwide for numerous companies and organizations, including Alcatel, AT&T, Digital, IBM, Litton, Loral, Raytheon, SAIC, TRW, and Unisys. He founded Amadeus Software Research, Inc., which develops and distributes a market-leading software measurement tool. He has published over sixty technical and management articles on software systems and development. He lives in Irvine, California.